Crafting Country

Tom Austen Brown Studies in Australasian Archaeology
Peter Hiscock, Series Editor

The Tom Austen Brown Studies in Australasian Archaeology series publishes new research on the archaeology of Australia and the adjacent regions. It aims to develop our understanding of Australasia's human past, with particular focus on the archaeology of Aboriginal and Torres Strait Islander peoples during both prehistoric and contact periods.

Animal Bones in Australian Archaeology:
a Field Guide to Common Native and Introduced Species
Melanie Fillios and Natalie Blake

Between the Murray and the Sea:
Aboriginal Archaeology in Southeastern Australia
David Frankel

Crafting Country:
Aboriginal Archaeology in the Eastern Chichester Range,
North-West Australia
Caroline Bird and James W. Rhoads

Crafting Country

Aboriginal Archaeology in the
Eastern Chichester Range,
North-West Australia

Caroline Bird and
James W. Rhoads

SYDNEY
UNIVERSITY
PRESS

First published by Sydney University Press

© Caroline Bird and James W. Rhoads 2020
© Sydney University Press 2020

REPRODUCTION AND COMMUNICATION FOR OTHER PURPOSES
Except as permitted under the Act, no part of this edition may be reproduced, stored in a retrieval system, or communicated in any form or by any means without prior written permission. All requests for reproduction or communication should be made to Sydney University Press at the address below:

Sydney University Press
Fisher Library F03
University of Sydney NSW 2006
Australia
sup.info@sydney.edu.au
sydneyuniversitypress.com.au

 A catalogue record for this book is available from the National Library of Australia.

ISBN 9781743326169 paperback
ISBN 9781743326176 epub
ISBN 9781743326855 mobi

Cover photo of Fortescue Marsh taken at 14 Mile Pool by Kirsten Bradley (2012)
Cover design by Miguel Yamin
Layout and typesetting by Duncan Blachford, Typography Studio

CONTENTS

List of Figures	vii
List of Tables	xiii
Acknowledgements	xix
Foreword	xxi
Preface	xxiii
Welcome to Country	xxvii
1. Background: compliance archaeology and research in the Pilbara	1
2. Research framework	21
3. Natural environment and cultural contexts	55
4. Surface artefact scatters	93
5. Rockshelters	169
6. Site and landscape	229
7. Crafting country	283
References	291
Index	315
Appendices	https://sydneyuniversitypress.com.au/products/111632

LIST OF FIGURES

Figure 1.1: North West Australia, showing bioregions, based on Interim Biogeographic Regionalisation of Australia (IBRA).   3

Figure 1.2: The inland Pilbara.   17

Figure 1.3: Cloudbreak–Christmas Creek project area.   17

Figure 2.1: Sites in the Pilbara region with dates older than 30,000 years.   23

Figure 2.2: Selected inland Pilbara rock shelter sites.   24

Figure 2.3: Inland Pilbara radiocarbon determinations.   30

Figure 3.1: Samphire flats bordering the Fortescue Marsh.   57

Figure 3.2: General view of the outwash plains.   58

Figure 3.3: The foothills of the Chichester Range.   58

Figure 3.4: Geology of the Fortescue Marsh area.   59

Figure 3.5: Quarried outcrops and exfoliating nodules.   60

Figure 3.6: Stone raw materials found as cobbles in creeks and on the outwash plains.   61

Figure 3.7: Hydrology of the study area, showing yinta and unnamed water points along the northern margin of the Fortescue Marsh.   62

Figure 3.8: Sandy Creek in flood.   64

Figure 3.9: Vegetation communities.   66

Figure 3.10: Mulga woodlands (*Acacia* spp.).   70

Figure 3.11: Hummock grassland, comprising spinifex (*Triodia* spp.) and scattered trees and shrubs.   71

Figure 3.12: Creek channels with eucalypt open forest.   71

Figure 3.13: Language map of the Pilbara region.   79

Figure 4.1: Log10 percentile distribution of area for surface artefact scatters.   96

Figure 4.2: Map showing general distribution of surface artefact scatters and isolated artefacts.   98

Figure 4.3: Observed (O) and expected (E) distribution of surface artefact scatters and isolated artefacts in relation to vegetation formations.   100

Figure 4.4: Christmas Creek survey area, showing location of group sample areas.   104

Figure 4.5: Results of Principal Components Analysis on group samples.   109

Figure 4.6: Ratio of basalt to BIF for each landscape sample group.   116

Figure 4.7: Distribution of basalt and BIF isolated artefacts.   116

Figure 4.8: Group samples: linear regression between sample size and number of raw materials.   118

Figure 4.9: Results of SHE analysis of raw material diversity for group samples and individual sites.   119

Figure 4.10: Cortex type by raw material (upper) and by group (lower). 123

Figure 4.11: Cortex type by group for each raw material. 125

Figure 4.12: Cortex ratios for basalt, BIF, chalcedony and chert group samples in relation to landform. 137

Figure 4.13: Mean volume (mm^3) of cores by raw material and landform. 145

Figure 4.14: Mean volume (mm^3) of cores by amount of cortex for each raw material. 145

Figure 4.15: Mean volume (mm^3) of single and multiplatform cores for each raw material by amount of cortex. 146

Figure 4.16: Proportion of different types of cortex, in relation to raw material and landform. 147

Figure 4.17: Mean length (mm) of complete flakes for individual sample groups. 150

Figure 4.18: Mean length (mm) of complete flakes by cortex group. 151

Figure 4.19: Relationship between flake size and flake to core ratio for sample groups. 157

Figure 4.20: Linear regression: sample size and occurrence of individual artefact types. 163

Figure 4.21: Comparison between artefacts recorded as part of surface artefact scatters and as isolated artefacts for each sample group with respect to raw material. 165

Figure 4.22: Comparison between artefacts recorded as part of surface artefact scatters and as isolated artefacts for each sample group with respect to major artefact class. 167

Figure 4.23: Comparison between mean sizes of complete flakes and cores of main raw materials, recorded as isolated artefacts or in sites.   167

Figure 5.1: Rock shelters and stone features in the study area.   171

Figure 5.2: Comparison between excavated and unexcavated shelters with respect to estimated floor area.   172

Figure 5.3: Aspect of excavated and unexcavated shelters.   173

Figure 5.4: Examples of artefacts stored in shelters.   178

Figure 5.5: Examples of stone features.   179

Figure 5.6: The site complex associated with CB09-249.   182

Figure 5.7: CB08-103 and its setting.   183

Figure 5.8: Plan of the CB08-103 site complex.   184

Figure 5.9: Distribution of archaeological remains in the vicinity of CB08-103, with 500-metre buffer shown.   185

Figure 5.10: Estimated overall artefact discard rates (N/100 years, corrected for area excavated) for all shelters.   196

Figure 5.11: Distribution of calibrated radiocarbon dates in space and time.   200

Figure 5.12: Summary of changes in the distribution of occupied rockshelters through time in the study area.   201

Figure 5.13: Results of Principal Components Analysis for shelter assemblages.   209

Figure 5.14: Representation of different raw materials in flaked stone assemblages.   211

Figure 5.15: Excavated assemblages. 216

Figure 5.16: Relation between log10 sample size and log10 number of raw material types for individual rockshelter assemblages. 217

Figure 5.17: Size of flakes and percentage of cortical flakes for rock shelter assemblages. 218

Figure 6.1: Group 1A: Site distribution. 235

Figure 6.2: Group 1A: distribution of recorded surface artefacts and grinding material. 239

Figure 6.3: CB08-511: site plan. 241

Figure 6.4: Group 1A: summary raw material composition for each site. 241

Figure 6.5: Group 1A: stone features. 243

Figure 6.6: The Group 1A taskscape. 248

Figure 6.7: Archaeological features along Kakutungutanta Creek. 249

Figure 6.8: Kakutungutanta Creek: vegetation. 250

Figure 6.9: Group 3B: cortex type by raw material. 254

Figure 6.10: Group 3B: the taskscape along Kakutungutanta Creek. 255

Figure 6.11: Group 8S: distribution of surface artefact scatters and isolated artefacts. 257

Figure 6.12: Group 8S: distribution of artefacts in relation to vegetation. 258

Figure 6.13: Group 8S: raw material assemblage composition for individual artefact scatters. 259

Figure 6.14: CB08-114: raw material assemblage composition for individual sample squares. 260

Figure 6.15: Group 8S: cortex type by raw material. 261

Figure 6.16: The Group 8S taskscape. 268

Figure 6.17: Group 9S (CB06-68): distribution of artefacts. 271

Figure 6.18: CB06-68: detailed site plan. 272

Figure 6.19: Distribution of surface artefact scatters and isolated artefacts in relation to vegetation in the vicinity of CB06-68 (Group 9S). 273

Figure 6.20: Group 9S: distribution of artefacts. 274

Figure 6.21: The Marandu Creek taskscape. 275

Figure 6.22: The Christmas Creek study area: local connections. 277

Figure 6.23: The Christmas Creek study area: long-distance connections within Nyiyaparli country and beyond. 278

Figure 6.24: Baler shell (*Melo amphora*) from a surface artefact scatter in Nyiyaparli country. 279

LIST OF TABLES

Table 2.1: Inland Pilbara land-use model, as developed by Archae-aus (Edwards et al. 2012, 37; after Veth 1993).   39

Table 2.2: Summary of reduction sequence model as used by Archae-aus (Edwards et al. 2012, 37).   40

Table 2.3: Site types occurring within the Christmas Creek study area.   54

Table 3.1: Christmas Creek and environs vegetation communities (FMG 2010, 40–2, Figure 7).   67

Table 3.2: Plant species occurring in the study area and their documented uses for food and material culture in the Pilbara and adjacent areas.   84

Table 3.3: The distribution of ethnographically documented plant resources in different vegetation communities in the Christmas Creek study area.   88

Table 4.1: Distribution of surface artefact scatters in relation to major landforms.   97

Table 4.2: Distribution of surface artefact scatters and isolated artefacts in relation to vegetation formations.   99

Table 4.3: Summary data for group samples.   107

Table 4.4: Results of Principal Components Analysis on group samples.   108

Table 4.5: Raw material composition: all recorded flaked stone artefacts from group samples. 110

Table 4.6: Raw material composition: MNF. 112

Table 4.7: Raw material composition: volume. 114

Table 4.8: Amount of cortex by group. 121

Table 4.9: Cortex type by raw material. 122

Table 4.10: Mean volume and surface area for all cores with 80% cortex or more. 127

Table 4.11: Banded iron formation: cortex and volume ratios. 129

Table 4.12: Basalt: cortex and volume ratios. 131

Table 4.13: Chalcedony: cortex and volume ratios. 133

Table 4.14: Chert: cortex and volume ratios. 134

Table 4.15: Dolerite: cortex and volume ratios. 135

Table 4.16: Observed (O) number of cores and expected (E) number of cores based on total volume of raw material. 136

Table 4.17: Core type by raw material. 139

Table 4.18: Ratio of multiplatform to single platform cores (mp:sp) by raw material and landform. 140

Table 4.19: Dimensions of single and multiplatform cores: summary statistics for five main raw materials. 142

Table 4.20: Volume (mm^3) of cores, by type, raw material and landform. 143

Table 4.21: Cores: percentage of cortex. 144

Table 4.22: Dimensions of complete flakes: summary statistics. 149

Table 4.23: Mean length (mm) and standard deviation of complete flakes by cortex group. 152

Table 4.24: Mean length (mm) and standard deviation of complete cortical flakes by cortex type. 153

Table 4.25: Percentage of platform types for each raw material. 153

Table 4.26: Percentage of complete flakes and proximal flake fragments with overhang removal. 154

Table 4.27: Flake:core ratios for individual sample groups by raw material. 156

Table 4.28: Percentage of retouched artefacts for each sample group. 158

Table 4.29: Retouched artefact types for each raw material. 159

Table 4.30: Summary data for each sample group used in the regression analysis. 161

Table 4.31: Results of the regression analysis. 162

Table 4.32: Raw material composition: comparison between artefacts recorded as part of sites and all isolated artefacts. 164

Table 4.33: Percentage of retouched artefacts recorded from sites and as isolated artefacts for each sample group. 166

Table 4.34: Percentage of major artefact classes recorded from sites and as isolated artefacts for each sample group. 166

Table 5.1: Summary dimensions of rockshelters recorded in the Christmas Creek study area. 173

Table 5.2: Summary of surface artefacts recorded at excavated rockshelters. 175

Table 5.3: Summary of surface artefacts recorded at unexcavated rockshelters. 176

Table 5.4: Radiocarbon date list. 188

Table 5.5: Summary of artefact assemblages likely to be from contexts older than about 4000 years. 204

Table 5.6: Summary of rockshelter assemblages in terms of mobility indicators. 206

Table 5.7: Results of Principal Components Analysis on rockshelter assemblages. 208

Table 5.8: Summary assemblage composition from all rockshelter test pits. 212

Table 5.9: Raw material composition for the 6 mm sieve fraction in individual rockshelter assemblages, compared with composition of associated surface assemblages. 214

Table 5.10: Length (mm) of complete flakes for each raw material with sample size >20. 219

Table 5.11: Retouched artefact types by period and raw material. 223

Table 6.1: Group 1A: recorded artefact sites. AS: artefact scatter. RA: reduction area. 236

Table 6.2: Group 1A: raw material composition of individual artefact sites. 240

Table 6.3: Group 1A: cortex and volume ratios for individual artefact sites. 244

Table 6.4: Group 3B: raw material composition.   253

Table 6.5: Group 8S: cortex and volume ratios for individual artefact sites.   262

ACKNOWLEDGEMENTS

First and foremost, we acknowledge the Nyiyaparli people and Karlka Nyiyaparli Aboriginal Corporation, who have consistently supported research into the archaeology of their country and the lives of their ancestors. We particularly thank the members of the Nyiyaparli Heritage Subcommittee: Billy Cadigan, Raymond Drage, Victor Parker, David Stock, Leonard (Michael) Stream, Brian Tucker and the late Gordon Yuline. Karlka staff Henk Rhee and John Cross were always supportive.

This project is based on compliance fieldwork and site recording by Archae-aus Pty Ltd associated with Fortescue Metals Group's Cloudbreak–Christmas Creek project. Fortescue Metals Group (FMG) provided funding to support this additional research, and supplied detailed base mapping and satellite imagery, as well as logistic support for the fieldwork program. The contributions and support of the following individuals at FMG are particularly acknowledged: Deirdre Willmott, Alexa Morcombe, Lisa Maher, Roberta Molson, Joanne Forster, Leonard (Michael) Stream, Rob Turner, Grant Preller and Cheng Yen Loo.

Many Archae-aus staff contributed to the success of this project through field surveys, data collection, excavations, post-excavation analysis and report writing. Stuart Rapley managed the overall Cloudbreak–Christmas

Creek field program. Stuart Rapley, Adam Dias and Kate Edwards directed the excavations. Reports were co-ordinated and edited by Monica Jimenez-Lozano and Lucy Sinclair. The overall research program, of which this study was a key component, was conceived and proposed to FMG by Fiona Hook and Peter Veth.

Alexandra Rouillard kindly supplied the photographs of Nyiyaparli country on pp. xxvi and xxvii. All other photographs are by Archae-aus staff. We particularly thank Stuart Rapley for his assistance with locating photos. All drawings are by Caroline Bird, unless otherwise acknowledged. The maps were drawn in QGIS and use base mapping by Geoscience Australia, unless otherwise acknowledged.

Pauline Grierson, Alexandra Rouillard, Greg Skrzypek and Adrienne Markey all provided information on aspects of the natural environment and hydrology of the Fortescue Marsh area. We thank them for their interest in the project.

Previous drafts were critically read by David Frankel, Peter Hiscock, Fiona Hook, Peter Veth, Eddie McDonald and Sander van der Kaars. We greatly appreciate the thought and effort they put into their feedback and the final manuscript has benefited from their comments.

Finally, we thank Fiona Hook, Managing Director of Archae-aus, for her unfailing encouragement and support. This project would not have happened without her vision, enthusiasm and commitment.

FOREWORD

CRAFTING COUNTRY IS AN impressive illustration of one way that high-value research can be accomplished in contemporary Australian archaeology. The volume is not strictly an output from consultancies carried out during investigations preparing for development, but it reveals how research can utilise those impact evaluations to test models and develop understandings of the prehistoric past in Australia. The book examines the Pilbara, an environmentally diverse region which has had more intensive archaeological investigation that almost any other part of the Australian continent. In many ways the analysis crafted by Bird and Rhoads exploits conventional qualities of archaeological research in Australia, such as the study of a single region using comparisons between different environments as the basis for understanding adaptive strategies. And yet this regional study offers several features that make it a compelling investigation of human life in prehistoric Australia. One is a coherent and powerful framework for thinking about both technology and its spatial distribution. Their integration of Ingold's concept of *taskscape* with established principles of how lithic technology and forager mobility interact provide them with a platform for interpreting assemblage variation. When combined with quantitative analysis of the substantial dataset that has been compiled from the extensive survey and excavation in the Pilbara in the face of mining development, the result is a detailed and rigorous exploration of the likely patterns of landscape use in this stark and dramatic arid/semi-arid region. This book will provide important guidance for forthcoming research on human use of Australian niches, in both academic and public archaeology.

One noteworthy element of the analyses presented here is the way Bird and Rhoads accomplished their synthesis through a complex interweaving of techniques and conceptual frameworks. They have drawn on demonstrably effective interpretative approaches for different research questions to create ways to examine human interactions within these evolving niches. This process has also embraced frameworks beyond academia, such as reshaping archaeological categories and interpretations to be conformable to concepts of settlement and sites advocated by Aboriginal peoples, an explicit act to facilitate convergence between scientific and traditional views. That convergence of views will no doubt be explored in further projects, but it is one instance of the novel combinations of methods and theory employed to great effect in this study. Bird and Rhoads have crafted a substantial and valuable understanding of human existence in this country, and their book will inform future investigations into ancient human–landscape interactions.

Peter Hiscock
Tom Austen Brown Professor of Australian Archaeology,
University of Sydney

PREFACE

Fortescue is very pleased to see this monograph come to fruition because it showcases the contribution mining makes to academic knowledge of Aboriginal heritage. The Nyiyaparli People welcomed Fortescue onto their country and the heritage surveys required for our mine and rail projects in the Pilbara provided a chance for the Elders to teach their young people about Country. The Nyiyaparli Elders willingly shared their knowledge of country and have capitalised on the long-term jobs and business opportunities that mining continues to create for Nyiyaparli People.

Accordingly, this monograph is based on data collected over more than a decade of archaeological survey and research undertaken to facilitate mine and rail projects in the Chichester Ranges. Fortescue is proud to have supported this work showcasing Nyiyaparli connection to country and how Nyiyaparli People used to their country for their economic and social welfare – how Nyiyaparli crafted country over millennia.

It is works such as this that highlight what can be achieved when we work together to understand the country and its stories while creating economic opportunities for its people.

We thank Sydney University Press for supporting the publication of this work, the authors Drs Caroline Bird and Jim Rhoads for their diligent and deep research and the archaeologists and anthropologists who have spent many years surveying and researching the archaeological and ethnographic landscape on Nyiyaparli Country. We particularly acknowledge Archae-aus which has worked with Nyiyaparli People and Fortescue in the Chichester Ranges for over a decade, and who were instrumental in conceiving and making this monograph a reality.

But most importantly we reflect at these moments on the contribution of the Nyiyaparli People past and present. Of course, it is the Nyiyaparli ancestors who left this most remarkable record for us to witness. And it is the generosity and the giving of knowledge and time from the Nyiyaparli Elders and senior knowledge holders involved in heritage surveys and studies that has made this monograph possible. Finally, we acknowledge those Nyiyaparli Elders who gave their knowledge and time to this project in so many ways, but who are no longer with us to see the publication of this work.

Tom Weaver
Group Manager,
Government & Community
Fortescue Metals Group

14 Mile Pool at Fortescue Marsh

Mile Pool at Fortescue Marsh

> *'Pakanma nyaniwali yurluyu wirtyata.'*
> —Come here and see country.
> David Stock
> Nyiyaparli Elder

CHAPTER 1

BACKGROUND: COMPLIANCE ARCHAEOLOGY AND RESEARCH IN THE PILBARA

A LONGSTANDING UNEASY RELATIONSHIP between research and consultant archaeologists is a feature of Australian archaeology. The development of heritage protection legislation and associated government regulation means that, in practice, most archaeological work now takes place within a commercial context and in response to land and resource development (Colley 2002; Ulm et al. 2013). This situation is not unique to Australia, although the details of how archaeology is funded and regulated distinctly differ elsewhere in the world (Carver 2011). Australian consultants are generally not paid to do research or publish their results, although much field archaeology is now conducted in a commercial consulting environment. Incorporating this vast store of information – often referred to as 'grey literature' – into Australia's corpus of archaeological knowledge and research frameworks remains extremely challenging. There is, in addition, still a status divide between academic and commercial archaeologists. Moreover, consultant archaeology is often regarded as constrained, at best, in its capacity to contribute to broader archaeological questions (Carver 2011, 68; Colley 2002, 45–50). This project is unusual in that it develops a comprehensive research program based on a body of data collected by consultant archaeologists in the course of compliance archaeology in the Pilbara region of north-western Australia. It demonstrates how the results of consulting archaeology can be transformed from constraint to opportunity.

Here we report on data collected in the course of archaeological field surveys and excavation associated with the development of Fortescue Metals Group's Christmas Creek and Cloudbreak mines, in the eastern Chichester Range, north-western Australia. The Nyiyaparli are the Traditional Owners of this country. FMG began development here in 2004 and, since 2006, archaeological consulting firm Archae-aus has surveyed more than 430 km² for FMG, in co-operation with the Traditional Owners, and identified and recorded about 2000 sites. These include 45 rockshelters, 19 of which proved on excavation to have cultural deposits.

In 2013, FMG funded a research study to analyse and publish the results of the excavations and surveys, as part of a wider cultural, community and research program on the heritage of the Cloudbreak and Christmas Creek area. The Nyiyaparli community also supported the investigation in order to find out more about the lives of their ancestors and to make the results available to the general public. As well as this monograph, the results of the program to date have included a community publication (Nyiyaparli Community, Bird and McDonald 2015) and four journal articles (Bird, Hook and Rhoads 2016; Bird and Rhoads 2015; Bird, Rhoads and Hook 2019; Dias and Rapley 2014) as well as several conference presentations.

THE PILBARA REGION AND ITS ARCHAEOLOGICAL RECORD

The Pilbara biogeographic region covers a vast area of about 179,000 km², bounded on the west by the Indian Ocean, by the Great and Little Sandy deserts to the east and north-east, and by the Gascoyne and Carnarvon regions to the south (McKenzie, van Leeuwen and Pinder 2009) (Figure 1.1). It is environmentally diverse, ranging from broad coastal plains to inland ranges drained by large river systems to sandy deserts. The region is semi-arid to arid with considerable variation in rainfall on a yearly basis, both locally and regionally. The Pilbara is rich in mineral resources,

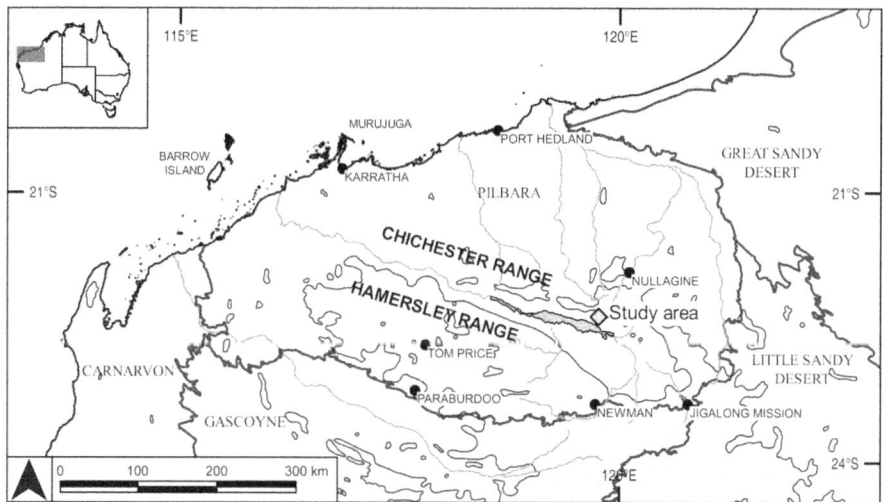

FIGURE 1.1: North West Australia, showing bioregions, based on Interim Biogeographic Regionalisation of Australia (IBRA) (after Thackway and Cresswell 1995), land above 500 metres, and location of study area.

particularly iron ore and offshore oil and gas. The region, though remote and sparsely populated, is thus of great economic importance to Australia.

Despite Western Australia making up a third of the continental land mass of Australia, the total number of professional archaeologists working here over the last 35 years is relatively small. Little fieldwork was conducted in most of the state prior to the 1980s, and the Pilbara region, like other remote areas, was largely unknown. The accelerating exploitation of the Pilbara's mineral resources since the late 1970s fostered intensive archaeological investigation in the region, primarily where large-scale mining operations and associated infrastructure development were established. The scale of development in the Pilbara region led to an explosion in the amount of archaeological survey, recording and excavation, primarily by archaeological consultancy firms. Large areas have been intensively surveyed and thousands of sites recorded. As a result, a number of early dates confirm that occupation in the region can be traced back more than 40,000 years and highlight the significance of Pilbara archaeology to broader archaeological research questions, including the timing and nature of the peopling of the ancient continent of Sahul, the occupation of the arid zone and responses to climatic change. Unfortunately, unpublished consulting reports comprising the primary documentation for this work are often difficult to access. Moreover, few, if any, attempts have been made to publish significant results or synthesise this large corpus of scattered and now largely irreproducible information (Morse 2009, 1). Research beyond that accompanying primary documentation or salvage has been haphazard and publication of significant results is more often preliminary than comprehensive. Furthermore, it is only relatively recently that academic archaeologists have systematically explored the region's research potential. The last decade, for example, has seen the establishment of major research programs focused on Murujuga (e.g. McDonald 2015; McDonald and Berry 2017; McDonald, Reynen, Ditchfield et al. 2018) and Barrow Island (e.g. Veth, Ditchfield and Hook 2014; Veth et al. 2017; Ward et al. 2017).

The research themes of the 1980s in the then archaeologically unexplored Pilbara region were primarily concerned with the most basic issues of distribution of archaeological remains in space and time. The proliferation of archaeological information as a consequence of regional development has continued to focus on the antiquity of Aboriginal occupation and resulted in most published information directed toward this question. Preliminary reports on rockshelters, mostly from the Hamersley Range excavated as a result of resource development (Brown 1987; Edwards and Murphy 2003; Hughes, Quartermaine and Harris 2011; Law, Cropper and Petchey 2010; Marwick 2002; Maynard 1980; Morse, Cameron and Reynen 2014; Slack, Fillios and Fullagar 2009; Veitch, Hook and Bradshaw 2005), still comprise most of the published archaeological information from the inland Pilbara. More comprehensive publications are now beginning to appear, although there is still a marked focus on questions of antiquity and Pleistocene occupation (e.g. Cropper and Law 2018a; Marsh et al. 2018; Reynen et al. 2018; Slack, Law and Gliganic 2018). Published analyses of surface sites in the Pilbara are particularly scarce (e.g. Hook 2009; Ryan and Morse 2009), despite the fact that surface artefact scatters dominate the regional archaeological record and documentation of these sites is the subject of the overwhelming majority of consulting reports. There are also scattered publications on particular site types such as stone arrangements and other types of structures (Bindon and Lofgren 1982; Hook and Di Lello 2010; Wallis and Matthews

2016), grinding patches (Fullagar and Wallis 2012) and, in coastal areas, shell middens (Clune 2002; Clune and Harrison 2009; Lorblanchet and Jones 1979; Veth and O'Brien 1986). The Pilbara is also a major rock art province (McDonald and Veth 2008b; 2013; Wright 1968) and includes the highly significant concentration of petroglyphs on Murujuga (the Dampier Archipelago) (e.g. Bednarik 2006; Bird and Hallam 2006; McDonald 2015; McDonald and Veth 2009; Mulvaney 2009; 2015; Vinnicombe 2002).

The limited publication of archaeological results from the Pilbara is a direct consequence of the development context within which most excavation and survey occurs. This is seen in all areas of Australia – and indeed is a global issue. In the Pilbara, however, compliance archaeology arguably plays a particularly dominant role. The primary aim of most of these investigations is assessment and, sometimes, salvage. The construction and dissemination of knowledge is not part of the remit of developers and it is still rare for them to fund more comprehensive research. Post-excavation analysis is therefore commonly restricted in scope. Moreover, there is neither a central repository for archaeological data nor any legislative requirement to lodge salvaged archaeological data with either the Department of Aboriginal Affairs or the Western Australian Museum. The results of site surveys, recordings and excavations are often held by archaeological consulting companies or retained by their clients under commercial-in-confidence arrangements or through enforceable contracts that place restrictions on, access to, and dissemination of, primary data. Traditional owners also, occasionally, place restrictions on the publication of results. Commercial pressures inhibit consultants themselves from engaging in post-fieldwork analyses, because they have neither the time nor funding to undertake research. It is only in the last ten years or so that academic archaeologists have stepped in to fill this research vacuum (e.g. McDonald 2015; McDonald and Veth 2013a; Veth et al. 2007), and, until recently, few postgraduate students have chosen to investigate aspects of Pilbara archaeology (e.g. Berry 2018; Clune 2002; Ditchfield 2017; Mulvaney 2010). The research potential of data collected by consultants remains largely untapped (Morse 2009).

Our understanding of the archaeology of the Pilbara region as a whole is thus characterised by patchy and disparate evidence collected under strict constraints and with limited analysis, and poorly integrated into our understanding of the deep time history of occupation of Australia. The last attempt at a regional synthesis in the Pilbara (Brown 1987) is now 30 years old and focused on the Hamersley Range. Consequently, consultants work within a generalised regional research agenda concerned mainly with issues of antiquity of occupation, and site location and distribution.

This has had three fundamental consequences that, in turn, influence how consultants record and assess archaeological sites. First, antiquity has assumed great importance when assessing sites. Old dates can, of course, be linked to the continental research agenda concerning the timing and nature of the initial colonisation of Australia and their significance is thus easy to assess. Sites with evidence of very ancient use can attract interest, as well as additional funding for further investigation (e.g. Cropper and Law 2018a; Law, Cropper and Petchey 2010; Marsh et al. 2018; Morse, Cameron and Reynen 2014; Reynen et al. 2018; Slack, Fillios and Fullagar 2009; Slack et al. 2018). By contrast, rockshelters with recent dates are very likely to be assessed as lacking sufficient significance to require further investigation (Bird, Hook and Rhoads 2016). Paradoxically, therefore, there is perhaps more detailed information available about earlier periods in the inland Pilbara than for more recent adaptations. This, in turn, tends to reinforce a research agenda within which rockshelters with evidence for old dates can be evaluated. Second, preoccupation with chronology and antiquity means that the surface sites that dominate the Pilbara archaeological record receive little analytical consideration and their significance is likely to be underestimated. This is despite a widespread belief that rockshelter use in the region was probably ephemeral and marginal (Ryan and Morse 2009). Third, important research questions about how Aboriginal peoples lived in the inland Pilbara over perhaps 50,000 years and how they adapted to major environmental change tend to be addressed within the context of responses to the Last Glacial Maximum. Adaptation to the post-glacial world remains largely unaddressed in the inland Pilbara, despite presenting fundamental and long-held concerns for archaeological research at continental, regional and local scales.

The priority afforded to questions of antiquity means that much attention is focused on rockshelters with cultural deposits. These are likely to be assessed by test excavation. However, because of time and resource constraints, these are normally limited in scope and it is unusual for test pits to be extended or for additional excavation to be recommended (Bird, Hook and Rhoads 2016). Limiting the extent of excavations is problematic for several reasons. First, as elsewhere, archaeological remains in Pilbara rockshelters demonstrate considerable horizontal variation. It is not unusual for multiple test pits in larger sites to present quite different results (e.g. Morse, Cameron and Reynen 2014; and see this volume, Chapter 5 and Appendix 5). This variability is poorly understood. It may relate to intra-site spatial patterning of past use by Aboriginal peoples, or alternatively be attributable to site formation processes. Second, the density of cultural material is typically low in Pilbara rockshelters and the preservation of organic remains is exceptionally poor, so the quantity of cultural remains recovered is often small. As a consequence, the archaeological evidence collected from test pits may give a misleading view of the nature of local and regional activity, land use and settlement patterning. Moreover, small sample sizes means that the data are difficult to analyse and interpret, and uncommon cultural items are rarely found (Hiscock 2001; Langley, Clarkson and Ulm 2011). Third, recovery techniques also affect the nature and amount of archaeological remains found. Choosing sieve sizes, using wet or dry sieving, decisions on whether to sort sieve residues in the field or in a laboratory environment, and electing to use trained or untrained personnel all affect recovery rates for small artefacts, bones and rare items, such as exotic raw materials, beads or bone tools (Bird et al. 2014; Graesch 2009; Johnson 1980; Langley, Clarkson and Ulm 2011). Similarly, charcoal is often poorly preserved in Pilbara rockshelters, so there is limited scope for radiocarbon dating. Alternative dating techniques are expensive and subject to long delays. Technical requirements of data collection for sophisticated dating techniques such as Optically Stimulated Luminescence (OSL) are difficult to justify to commercial clients when conducting preliminary site testing. It is arguable, therefore, that many test pits do not provide adequate information for determining archaeological significance, especially when the grounds for assessment are poorly set out (see discussion below).

The surface scatters that dominate the archaeological record in the Pilbara, as they do in the rest of Australia, range from isolated artefacts or small discrete scatters to extensive and sometimes dense accumulations of stone artefacts. Notwithstanding the ubiquity and richness of surface artefact scatters, these cultural remains are particularly complex to research and archaeologists have generally struggled to develop an effective analytical framework to make sense of the surface archaeological record (e.g. Ebert 1992; Holdaway et al. 1998; Holdaway and Fanning 2014; Lewarch and O'Brien 1981; Rossignol and Wandsnider 1992).

Surface aggregations of stone artefacts usually result from multiple episodes of lithic artefact production, reduction, deposition and re-use. Assigning relative or absolute ages to surface artefact scatters is particularly difficult as they lack stratigraphy and datable material is normally absent. In Australia, this problem is exacerbated because there are few well-dated examples of distinctive artefact types that can be used as chronological markers. This impediment means that the integration of archaeological data from excavated sites with that from surface occurrences is deemed too difficult because of the very different timescales that come into play. Nevertheless, it is important to recognise that the archaeological remains from rockshelters and caves are also often time-averaged palimpsests with low resolution (Bailey and Galanidou 2009; Stern 2008). This is particularly relevant to the Pilbara, where stratigraphic resolution in shelters is generally low, sample size is small and charcoal is often poorly preserved. Furthermore, because test excavation commonly occurs in the context of compliance archaeology, many rockshelters in the Pilbara have an inadequate number of radiocarbon determinations from which to assess the site's history or significance. Thus, in these circumstances it may be appropriate to regard the entire excavated assemblage as a single analytical unit, commensurate with time-averaged surface scatters. In essence, many rockshelters may in fact differ little analytically from surface artefact scatters, except that rockshelters are spatially constrained and may include datable material offering some temporal limits for the accumulation of cultural material.

Establishing a long timescale of occupation for the Pilbara and the effects of the Last Glacial Maximum on human occupation dominate the regional research agenda. The relationships between people and a changing environment in the post-glacial world have generally received less attention. The impact of changing sea levels on the now-inundated North West Shelf and in coastal areas is an exception (Clune and Harrison 2009; Manne and Veth 2015; McDonald 2015; McDonald and Berry 2017; Veth, Ditchfield and Hook 2014; Veth et al. 2007; Veth, Ward et al. 2017), but little is known about corresponding changes in the inland Pilbara. The Holocene is widely thought to be a time of significant social change and technological innovation in Australia. However, evidence of these changes within a sound chronological framework is largely absent in the inland Pilbara. Most sites in the region cannot be easily linked to questions of antiquity or change through time. Either they relate to more recent periods or, because of limitations of dating and resolution in surface sites, they are more relevant to considering spatial questions relating to long-term patterns of land use.

CONSULTANCY AS CONSTRAINT

Consulting archaeology in the Pilbara undeniably operates under significant constraints that militate against developing a sound understanding of the region's archaeology. The paramount consideration in structuring most survey strategy and site recording, unsurprisingly, is the need for developers to address the requirements of the *Aboriginal Heritage Act 1972* (WA). Western Australia's Aboriginal heritage legislation dates to the first wave of attempts at protecting Aboriginal sites (Ward 1983) and the prominence it gave to Aboriginal viewpoints and the protection of sites of spiritual significance was unusual at that time (Wright 1979, 381). Unlike comparable legislation in most other Australian states, however, it has not been significantly amended or replaced by a new legal and regulatory framework more in keeping with current best practice in heritage conservation and management. There is wide agreement that the legislation should be modernised, but so far there is no consensus on how this might be achieved.[1]

The *Aboriginal Heritage Act 1972* (WA) defines the places and objects to which it applies and requires the establishment of a register of sites. It also sets out a process (section 18) whereby, following advice from the Aboriginal Cultural Material Committee, the minister can consent to uses of land that would otherwise breach section 17 by damaging Aboriginal sites. The 'section 18' process is thus incorporated within the state system of development approvals. Over the years, there have been numerous regulatory changes in how the Act has been interpreted and administered. The Department of Aboriginal Affairs (DAA) was the most recent agency responsible for administering the Act, until April 2017 when its heritage and land functions were absorbed into the newly created Department of Lands, Planning and Heritage.[2] Following the passage of the *Native Title Act 1994* (Cth), a substantial amount of archaeological investigation associated with development is now also carried out in relation to native title under various agreements with specific requirements (McGrath 2016; Stevens 2016).

From the late 1970s, the scale of resource extraction in the Pilbara has meant that the requirements of industry dominate the formulation of standard approaches to archaeological investigations. This has a number of practical implications with respect to how data are collected, analysed, interpreted, archived and published. Critical issues include standards of recording and data collection, site definition and significance assessment.

STANDARDS OF RECORDING AND DATA COLLECTION

The *Aboriginal Heritage Act 1972* (WA) neither sets out nor supports the application of archaeological recording standards. For example, primary data recording is contingent on meeting inconsistent and variable government

---

1 The incoming Western Australian state government initiated a comprehensive review of the *Aboriginal Heritage Act 1972* (WA) in 2018. It is likely that new legislation will be introduced, but at the time of writing it is unclear to what extent and how the issues of concern discussed here will be addressed.

2 Since the DAA was the agency responsible during this project, we continue to refer to it by this name.

administrative procedures. The requirements and guidelines issued by the different instrumentalities responsible for Aboriginal heritage are difficult to police. The procedures and standards employed by different consultants also vary. Large development companies may even enforce their own requirements for the conduct of archaeological investigation based on their interpretation of the threshold required to meet the current administrative procedures.

Consultants typically work under severe time constraints which limit the information that can be recorded. Indeed, 'site avoidance' surveys are specifically designed to identify areas free of sites that, thereby, can be 'cleared' for development. Where site recording cannot be avoided, standard recording forms are used to submit information to the DAA. However, these have varied considerably over time in the detail required, generally focusing on the most basic, or minimum, information needed to assess sites for the register. In addition, the criteria used to assess Aboriginal sites under the Act are open to different interpretations, and these too have changed over time. Since this project began in 2013, for example, the DAA's interpretation of significance has seriously narrowed. The result is that many, if not most, Aboriginal archaeological sites in Western Australia are now deemed to be below the threshold for which there is an obligation to report them. Many previously reported sites, particularly surface artefact scatters, are also increasingly being deregistered (Dortch and Sapienza 2016). In no sense does the documentation held as part of the register constitute a comprehensive record of sites even in areas that have been surveyed. Detailed recording and/or salvage may only occur where site destruction in whole or in part is unavoidable (Morse 2009). As a consequence, the quality and quantity of information recorded about sites varies considerably.

SITE DEFINITION

The current framework for recording sites in Western Australia is defined by the requirements for lodging sites on the register. This is a site-based approach, comparable to that used by other state and national systems for administering heritage in Australia. It focuses on defining and delimiting discrete 'sites' as foci of human activity. While this is administratively convenient, archaeologists have long recognised that archaeological 'sites' are constructs that commonly define local concentrations or exposures of artefacts and features in what may be actually a continuous distribution (Dunnell and Dancey 1983; Ebert 1992, 8; Foley 1981a, b). Furthermore, this practice of delimiting discrete 'sites' for management purposes disconnects them from their landscapes and severs their relationships with other sites (Tilley and Cameron-Daum 2017). This is particularly problematic when considering the archaeology of mobile hunter-gatherer groups and, in the Australian context, clearly conflicts with Aboriginal concepts of country and the use of land (Byrne 1996, 102). Aboriginal understanding of heritage and country relates to and derives from a complete cultural landscape, while the heritage protection regime exemplified by the Western Australian *Aboriginal Heritage Act 1972* (WA) seeks to 'identify and manage the competing values of places within such a landscape' (McGrath and Lee 2016, 4).

The requirement to demarcate site boundaries also means that the archaeological record is typically subdivided into small discrete units. As noted above, under the DAA's current interpretation of the legislation, many archaeological sites, particularly small surface scatters, often do not meet the reporting standard to qualify as relevant, significant or worthwhile. In any case, their generic character means that they can be individually assessed as having low significance. Connections between sites and their cultural and environmental context receive less weight than features of the cultural record and attributes. As a result, there now seems to be considerable pressure placed on consultants to pre-empt the assessment process within the DAA and make the decision in the field not to record 'sites' that will not meet the DAA threshold. This, of course, facilitates destruction of sites by developers and the irretrievable loss of archaeological information.

The focus on the site as the unit of recording and analysis has other implications for interpretation of data and assessment of significance. It encourages the notion that sites represent discrete manifestations of past human activity, which are equivalent to ethnographically observed 'campsites' or other types of 'activity locations'. These interpretations are attractive because they are easily communicated to clients. As a result, archaeologists commonly interpret the regional archaeological record as if the occurrences of artefacts in the landscape are directly equivalent to ethnographically observed camps or other loci of activity, even though the temporal and spatial scales of archaeological and ethnographic data do not match (Allen et al. 2008).

The general, and longstanding, practice in Pilbara compliance projects of separating ethnographic and archaeological surveys exacerbates this problem (Clarke 1983; McDonald and Coldrick, in press). Moreover, this practice militates against integrating Aboriginal and archaeological understandings of sites and landscapes. Archaeology, of course, has a long tradition of considering spatial aspects of human culture and the interaction between people and place at different scales, although the term 'landscape archaeology' has only become common since the 1980s (David and Thomas 2008). The idea of cultural landscapes has increasingly gained currency in the practice of global heritage management, in recognition of the complex intertwining of people and the environment, with cultural landscapes recognised by the World Heritage Committee in 1992 (Head 2000, 91). Heritage and land management agencies struggle with these concepts, although alternatives to a site-based approach have been proposed and applied with varying success in a range of research and heritage management contexts in Australia (e.g. Barton 2003; Bird and Rhoads 2011; Brown 2012; Harrison 2004; Holdaway and Fanning 2014; New South Wales Dept of Environment, Climate Change and Water 2010; Ridges 2006). However, in the context of compliance archaeology, landscape approaches are often assumed to be impractical. This is because time and resource constraints, legislative requirements and the general absence of an appropriate analytical framework, together, are major inhibiting factors. By contrast, approaches based on delimiting discrete 'sites' have direct application to compliance with legislation. Consultants in the Pilbara therefore commonly focus on identifying and defining 'sites' that can then be assessed under the Act. This perspective has the propensity in turn to reify and reinforce the idea of the site as essential, discrete and static.

SIGNIFICANCE ASSESSMENT

Like standards of recording, legislated requirements for significance assessment and the mitigation of development impacts on the archaeological record lack clarity in Western Australia. The criteria for assessment of significance set down in sections 5 and 39(2) of the *Aboriginal Heritage Act 1972* (WA) include general reference to 'historical, anthropological, archaeological or ethnographical interest' (section 5). The nature of this interest is not specified in further detail. In Western Australia, the Aboriginal Cultural Material Committee is presumed to have among its members the appropriate expertise (sections 28–29) to address significance assessment. Amendments to the legislation have changed little as regards the relative significance of Aboriginal heritage sites. The lack of clear legislative guidance, changing administrative interpretations and the pressures of development, together with our relatively limited understanding of Aboriginal archaeology across the vast extent of Western Australia, means significance assessment is difficult and inconsistent. The outcomes for Aboriginal heritage are correspondingly ill-founded, inconsistent and contingent on local or project-specific factors. Consequently, common practice involves detailed field recording, collection and storage of artefacts, but not comprehensive analysis or additional research into the data recovered. For companies whose interest is limited to furthering their development projects, such research may be seen as an 'extra' and unnecessary cost to acquitting their obligations under the Aboriginal Heritage Act.

The recording, documentation and assessment of Aboriginal archaeological sites thus occur primarily in response to potential threat. However, the DAA does not publish meaningful, strategic level guidance for heritage conservation. Focusing on sites, as well as the methods used to define, record and assess them, underplays the significance of archaeological remains, particularly those from more recent periods. The absence of a regional research framework and the difficulty of making comparisons at a local or regional level seriously hamper consultants when they assess significance and make recommendations.

CONSULTANCY AS OPPORTUNITY

Consulting archaeology can, on the other hand, be viewed as an opportunity. The last few decades of development in the Pilbara have produced large amounts of primary data, the potential of which is largely untapped and unknown. While it is important to remember that 'archaeological consulting is not research and is rarely carried out with research questions in mind' (Morse 2009, 1), the primary data derived from consulting can certainly be applied to carefully chosen research questions. The scale and extent of survey in the region, beyond what is usually possible in an academic research project, provide large quantities of data that might be used to address both regional research questions and a range of methodological questions that could in turn be applied to the improvement of archaeological consulting practice in the Pilbara.

It is clear the Pilbara is an exceptionally diverse region and this is likely to be reflected in its archaeology. Intensively surveyed and salvaged areas, like the Cloudbreak–Christmas Creek area, which is the subject of this study, offer opportunities to investigate regional diversity and to test the validity of regional interpretations. They also offer the chance to explore the archaeological record at different scales and interpret individual archaeological occurrences within an integrated landscape framework. Such a framework is more congruent with an archaeology of mobile foraging peoples (Holdaway and Fanning 2014). It is also more in keeping with Aboriginal concepts of country (Byrne 1996; McGrath and Lee 2016). This has practical implications for the practice of archaeology in the Pilbara region, where archaeological sites have heritage significance for contemporary Aboriginal communities as well as archaeological significance. The FMG's provision of research funds for additional data analysis and publication of archaeological material recorded from the Cloudbreak–Christmas Creek development thus presents a rare opportunity to bring together compliance fieldwork and research. This in turn allows a range of methodological issues to be investigated and a synthesis developed at the local scale.

PROJECT OBJECTIVES

The research opportunity provided by primary data collected within the constraints of consulting archaeology then forms the context for this study.

Our overarching aim is to highlight the research value of data collected in the course of compliance archaeology fieldwork in the inland Pilbara. In this study, we take advantage of the comprehensive survey of the Cloudbreak–Christmas Creek mining development to explore patterning in archaeological remains in time and space beyond the site scale, incorporating a landscape perspective. This dataset offers an ideal opportunity to explore the research potential of information collected during compliance fieldwork. This enables us to move beyond site-based significance assessments to develop an integrated interpretation of archaeological remains within a landscape both experienced and shaped by Nyiyaparli people and their ancestors. The potential of this data is generally unrealised in Australia, particularly for the writing of regional syntheses, although there are exceptions (e.g. Attenbrow 2007; Brown 1987; 2008; White 2011).

Our focus is on the area of FMG's Cloudbreak–Christmas Creek project in the inland Pilbara at the eastern end of the Chichester Range. This is, in fact, the first major archaeological investigation conducted in the Chichester Range (Figure 1.2). To the south, the project area borders the Fortescue Marsh. Christmas Creek, in the east of the project area, was developed first and went into production in 2008. The archaeological data for that area is more comprehensively recorded and reporting is largely complete. All excavated rockshelters are located there. At the time of writing, Cloudbreak was still under development and reporting for that part of the project area was not yet complete. This volume therefore primarily presents an analysis of archaeological remains from the Christmas Creek study area (Figure 1.3). In addition, some data is also available from areas immediately to the south, mostly collected during surveys for access tracks and other peripheral infrastructure. These archaeological finds provide a body of comparative data from the northern shore of the Fortescue Marsh and thus a more complete context for the archaeology of the eastern Chichester Range.

The data presented in this study have several advantages.

BACKGROUND | 17

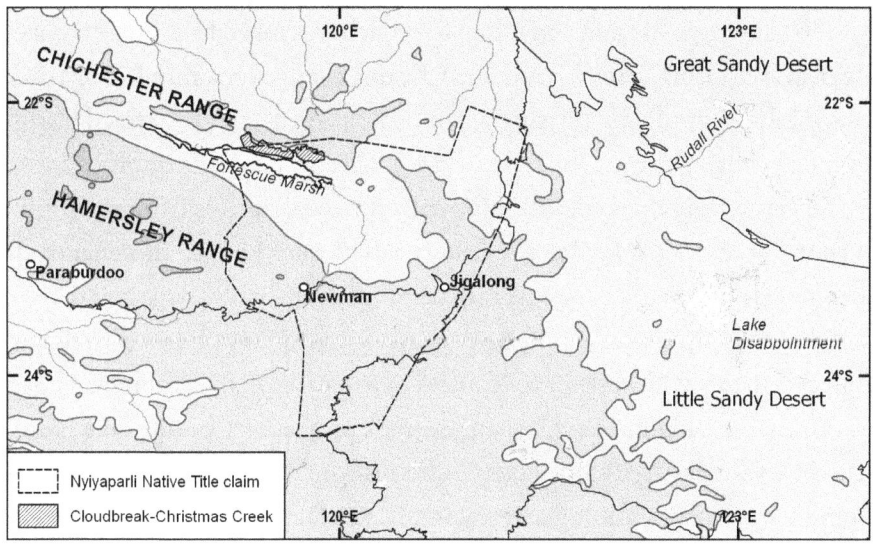

FIGURE 1.2: The inland Pilbara.

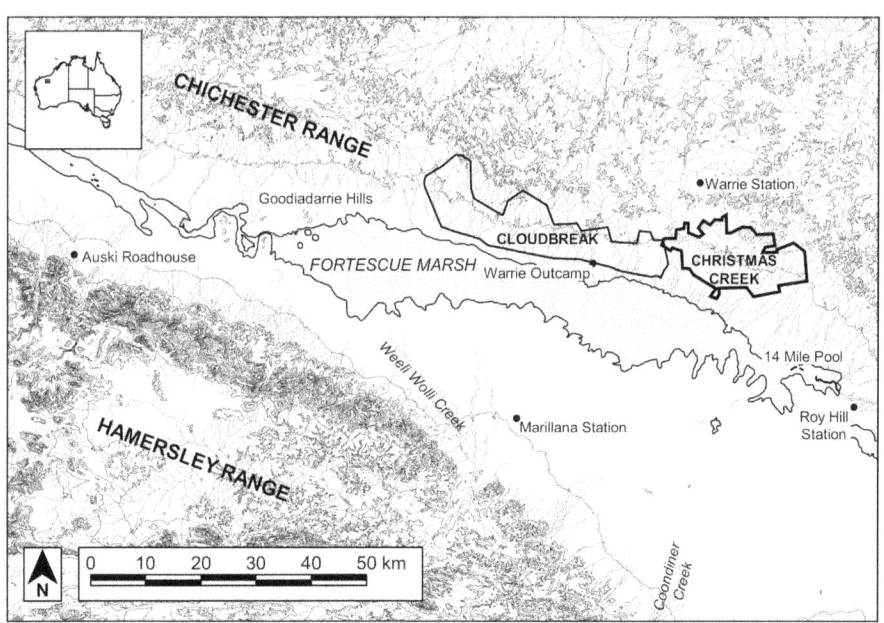

FIGURE 1.3: Cloudbreak–Christmas Creek project area.

First, a systematic and consistent approach was taken by a single archaeological consulting firm (Archae-aus) for one client over a number of years. This minimises problems arising when comparing datasets collected by different consulting firms, which may have different standards or procedures.

Second, the archaeological information we use derives from a comprehensive survey of 430 km² in the eastern Chichester Range. This effectively constitutes complete survey coverage of an area sufficiently large and diverse to support an investigation of the patterning of different types of archaeological remains with respect to features of the natural environment.

Third, the Cloudbreak–Christmas Creek project area borders the Fortescue Marsh (Martuyitha). Because of concern over the possible impacts from the increasing mining activity in the surrounding areas, a number of environmental research projects relating to the Marsh have been recently conducted or are in progress (e.g. O'Donnell et al. 2015; Rouillard et al. 2015; Rouillard, Greenwood et al. 2016; Rouillard, Skrzypek et al. 2016; Skrzypek, Dogramaci and Grierson 2013; Skrzypek et al. 2016). These studies offer high quality information about past environments that enhances the interpretation of the archaeological data.

Fourth, during the site assessment process, test excavations were conducted in several rockshelters with diverse characteristics. Several contained cultural materials and provide a chronological framework for our study. All occurred in the Christmas Creek section of the project. Our analysis thus focuses mainly on this area (Figure 1.3).

Chapters 1 to 3 provide a context for the study. We discuss issues about the problems and opportunities offered by compliance archaeology in the Pilbara, and the regional and methodological research context. We also present data on the specific cultural and environmental context for the Cloudbreak–Christmas Creek project area, setting it within current understandings of the Pilbara region. Chapters 4 to 6 present an analysis of data collected in the course of field survey and excavation in the Christmas Creek study area. Chapter 7 provides a synthesis and discusses our findings in relation to issues outlined in Chapters 1 and 2. We also explore implications for how compliance archaeology in the Pilbara region might more effectively contribute to archaeological research questions and communicate the significance of findings to clients, government and the wider community. Finally, five appendices present more detailed information about methods and contextual information, as well as a summary of primary data from the rockshelter excavations.

CHAPTER 2

RESEARCH FRAMEWORK

RESEARCH THEMES IN THE inland Pilbara echo more general issues in Australian archaeology and especially those for the arid zone. Major questions include the timing and nature of initial human occupation, patterning of the evidence for human occupation in time and space, responses to changing environmental regimes of the Late Pleistocene and Holocene, development of new technologies during the Holocene, and recent social change. It is now well-established that people had reached Australia by about 60,000 or 70,000 years ago. Reliable dates of more than 40,000 years from several sites across the continent demonstrate the first colonists must have arrived earlier. How much earlier has been controversial (Allen and O'Connell 2014; Cane 2013; Hiscock 2008, 20–44), although recent research at the Arnhem Land site of Madjedbebe (formerly Malakunanja II) suggests a new minimum date of 59–71,000 years ago for first colonisation (Clarkson et al. 2017). A similar age is likely for the Pilbara with the oldest evidence from the region indicating the first use of Barrow Island between 51,100 and 46,200 years ago (Veth et al. 2017). In the Australian arid zone generally, increased research over the last ten years has seen significant advances in understanding of all these issues. It is now clear, for example, that occupation of the arid zone, including the Pilbara, dates back more than 40,000 years (Hamm et al. 2016; Hiscock and Wallis 2005; McDonald, Reynen, Petchey et al. 2018; Smith 2013, 78; Veth et al. 2009), and that the habitation of at least some sites and areas continued through the hyper-aridity of the Last Glacial Maximum (Williams et al. 2013), although responses undoubtedly varied regionally. The late Holocene probably saw the establishment of the patterns of occupation observed ethnographically (Smith 2013, 210).

INLAND PILBARA ARCHAEOLOGICAL SEQUENCE

BEFORE 30,000 YEARS AGO

The climate became drier and cooler from about 45,000 years ago, with falling sea levels and the failure of the southern monsoons. Dune fields developed across some areas of the exposed continental shelf by about 30,000 years ago (Hesse, Magee and van der Kaars 2004). The open eucalypt forests and woodland plant communities that had existed over much of the period since 100,000 years ago were replaced first by mixed eucalypt shrubland and then by herbaceous vegetation with a scattering of low trees (e.g. *Callitris* spp.) and shrubs (see Appendix 2 for a more detailed review).

Apart from Barrow Island (Veth et al. 2017), firm evidence for occupation before 30,000 years ago comes from several inland Pilbara sites in the Hamersley and Chichester Ranges and the Abydos Plain (Allen and O'Connell 2014, Table 2; Cropper and Law 2018a; Dias and Rapley 2014; Law, Cropper and Petchey 2010; Marsh et al. 2018; Morse, Cameron and Reynen 2014; Reynen et al. 2018; Slack, Fillios and Fullagar 2009; Slack, Law and Gliganic 2016; Smith 2013, Table 4.1; Veitch, Hook and Bradshaw 2005) (Figure 2.1). Cultural remains from most of these sites are sparse and difficult to interpret. The use of rockshelters in the ranges was episodic and ephemeral, and the main focus of activity was more likely to have been along the major river systems and intermittent wetlands, such as the Fortescue Marsh. These environments would have provided significant well-watered access routes for early populations, although direct evidence is still lacking.

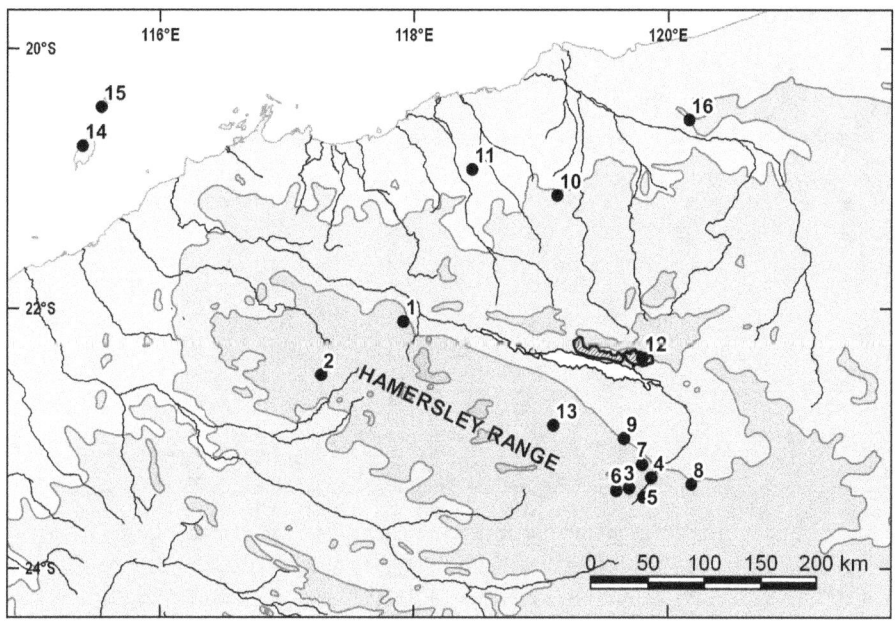

FIGURE 2.1: Sites in the Pilbara region with dates older than 30,000 years. (1) YIN09-002. (2) Juukan-1. (3) Newman (P0187) Orebody XXIX rockshelter. (4) Newman (P2055.2) rockshelter. (5) RH12-01. (6) PAD10-17, RS10-01. (7) OB24 2004/13. (8) PIL_364. (9) COO13-43, COO13-45. (10) Yurlu Kankala. (11) Kariyarra Rockshelter. (12) Kakutungutanta/ CB10-93. (13) Hope Downs 1, including Djadjiling, Jundaru, HS-A1, Hope 1-41, HD07-3A-PAD13. (14) Boodie Cave. (15) Noala Cave. (16) Watura Jurnti.

30,000–12,000 YEARS AGO

Sea levels continued to fall until about 20,000 years ago at the height of the Last Glacial Maximum. Coastal vegetation patterns were similar to those today and grasslands covered much of the exposed continental shelf. Summer monsoons reappeared with the rise of sea levels following the Last Glacial Maximum and open vegetation communities became established on the coast. From about 15–13,000 years ago, mangrove communities reappeared and began to dominate the waterways of the continental shelf. Eucalypt woodlands appeared on higher ground.

Increasing aridity and a corresponding decrease in the availability of resources starting about 30,000 years ago would have required reorganisation of regional settlement patterns. This would have involved changes in residential mobility and reconfiguration of land use to focus on reliable

24 | CRAFTING COUNTRY

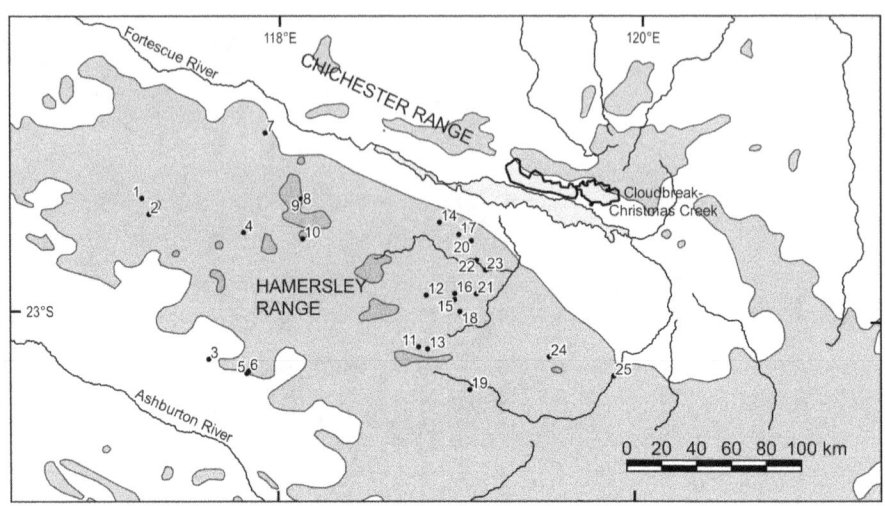

FIGURE 2.2: Selected inland Pilbara rock shelter sites. Shaded area is land above 500 metres. (1) Mt Brockman BM99-10. (2) Juukan-1 & 2. (3) ERP-04, 15, 22, 26. (4) TP00-04. (5) CME-A-18, 13. (6) Yirra. (7) YIN09-002. (8) Manganese Gorge 8. (9) Power Corridor 5. (10) Manganese Gorge 2. (11) RR3 & 8. (12) Bastion (P05315), Whispering Trees (P05316), Coffee Table (P04623) & Phantom (P04627) Shelters. (13) DFSH3 to 6. (14) Milly's Cave. (15) MACC-FS13, MACC-FS14, MACC-FS17. (16) PIL_5841. (17) Cleft Rock Shelter. (18) Hope Downs sites. (19) Newman Orebody XXIX. (20) Yandi P06107. (21) Djadjiling. (22) Marillana A & B, Y97-28. (23) Y02-12. (24) Whaleback Creek. (25) Newman Rock shelter & P00959.

water sources in areas that would have acted as refuges. The inland Pilbara is likely to have been one such area and archaeological evidence provides increasing support for occupation throughout the Last Glacial Maximum, although individual site histories attest to changes in land use.

Several rockshelters have evidence dating to this period (Figure 2.2). As noted above, published information about many of these sites is limited and, therefore, difficult to interpret reliably. Some sites (such as Watura Jurnti, Yurlu Kankala, Yirra, Juukan 2 and the Hope Downs sites of Jundaru, Djadjiling and HD073A-PAD13) do suggest some shelters continued to be used through the harshest period (24–18,000 years ago), although perhaps at a lower intensity (Cropper and Law 2018b; Law, Cropper and Petchey 2010; Marsh et al. 2018; Morse, Cameron and Reynen 2014; Reynen et al. 2018; Slack, Fillios and Fullagar 2009; Veitch, Hook and Bradshaw 2005). The evidence from other sites (such as Newman Rockshelter and Newman

Orebody XXIX, Manganese Gorge 2 and J24 at Mesa J) is less clear cut. The low numbers of artefacts and available dates make it difficult to suggest continuity of occupation and it is possible none of them were visited during the Last Glacial Maximum (Comtesse 2003; Edwards and Murphy 2003; Hughes and Quartermaine 1992; Hughes, Quartermaine and Harris 2011; Marwick 2002; 2009; Maynard 1980; Slack, Law and Gliganic 2018; Veth 1993).

In the case of Milly's Cave, the highest densities of artefacts have been reported to occur in the stratigraphic unit associated with the Last Glacial Maximum. However, there is some doubt as to whether all the material is artefactual.[1] A feature of many Pilbara rockshelters formed within the banded iron formation is the presence of numerous small thermally fractured roof fall fragments and considerable care is required to distinguish artefacts from non-artefactual material (Brown 1987, 24; Marsh et al. 2018, 142). The reported percentage of angular pieces is very high throughout the sequence at Milly's Cave (55–68%), with complete flakes making up less than 10% (Marwick 2002, 28). This contrasts markedly with percentages of complete flakes reported for other Pleistocene sites in the region (e.g. Brown 1987; Slack, Fillios and Fullagar 2009).

Conditions slowly improved following the intensely arid period 24–18,000 years ago. Sites first used after 18,000 years ago include Kunpaja, Cleft Rockshelter and Marillana A (Marwick 2002; Morse, Cameron and Reynen 2014). Nevertheless, these sites simply counterbalance sites with evidence of earlier occupation that fall out of use, or were only intermittently used, until the Holocene. These include Milly's Cave and Mesa J J24. This might suggest that the response to improving conditions was reorganisation of land use. However, the number of sites is still very small and limited analysis means that the overall trajectory of human occupation remains poorly understood.

The sparse archaeological remains, small artefact assemblages and low temporal resolution typical of Pilbara rockshelter deposits raise a number of interpretive issues with regard to identifying continuity in occupation at

---

1 Fiona Hook, personal communication, 2013.

individual sites, as well as extrapolating regional patterns of continuity and change through the Pleistocene (Frankel 1988; Smith 2013, 130–31). The limited number of dates from most sites, coupled with low chronological resolution, means that these issues are particularly difficult to address, while the problems of small samples and incomplete publication also constrain interpretation. Discard rates are difficult to calculate in these sites, but they do seem to be generally low (Smith 2013, Table 5.5). Where more detailed information is available, the use of inland Pilbara rockshelters through the Pleistocene appears episodic and intermittent. Individual histories of shelter use seem likely to be contingent on local factors rather than reflecting large-scale regional trends. The evidence from Watura Jurnti, for example, indicates a complex pattern of cycles of use and abandonment (Marsh et al. 2018). Caution is, of course, required when extrapolating regional patterns from individual sites.

FROM 12,000 YEARS AGO

From about 12,000 years ago, climate and environment improved greatly, with Australian ecosystems generally stabilising during the mid-Holocene. Sea levels rose to their current levels by approximately 6500 years ago. Rainfall peaked about 7000 years ago and then declined with drier conditions established about 4000 years ago. This broadly coincides with intensification of the El Niño/La Niña Southern Oscillation (ENSO), although the actual impact of ENSO on the inland Pilbara remains uncertain (O'Donnell et al. 2015). Vegetation patterns across the region were quite complex, changing over the early phases of this period. Generally, there was a progression toward the semi-arid vegetation communities that are characteristic of the region today.

Substantial changes are recognised in the archaeological record elsewhere in Australia during the Holocene. This period is marked by the introduction of new stone tool types, plant processing and landscape modification technologies, changes in rock art and economic modes of production. Holocene Australia is generally characterised by cultural dynamism and an expanding population, together with an increasing trend towards regionalisation. Accounting for these changes in Aboriginal lifeways has long preoccupied Australian archaeologists (Hiscock 2008, 106, 182–86; Lourandos 1997, 296–323; Mulvaney and Kamminga 1999, 257–72). The current consensus sees most changes as unique Australian cultural developments, rather than an introduced 'package' of cultural traits arriving from South-East Asia (Hiscock 2008, 152; Mulvaney and Kamminga 1999, 257–58). The identification, documentation and explanation of these changes does, however, remain a significant focus of archaeological research, with particular emphasis on disentangling the interaction of environmental and social factors in the diversification of technology, art and modes of production.

In the inland Pilbara, documentation and analysis of Holocene changes and long-term links with the adjacent Western Desert are hampered by lack of evidence. The regional focus on antiquity means that while some publication and further investigation of Pleistocene sites does occur in the context of compliance archaeology, more recent sites are almost completely neglected and normally remain unpublished. Information about sites with more recent archaeological deposits may be reported as an adjunct to the presence of older material, but few publications deal with sites containing only Holocene cultural remains. Investigations in the Packsaddle area of the Hamersley Range are a notable exception (Brown 1987; Hook and Di Lello 2010; Wallis and Matthews 2016). Since few excavated sites have been adequately published, the potential for detailed identification and interpretation of trends in site numbers and distribution, rates of sedimentation and artefact discard, and the timing of the appearance of new artefact types is severely constrained.

The use of regional and continental scale analysis of distributions of radiocarbon dates as proxies for timing and intensity of human activity has a long history in Australia (e.g. Attenbrow and Hiscock 2015; Bird and Frankel 1991; Holdaway and Porch 1995; Marwick 2009; Smith and Ross 2008; Smith and Sharp 1993; Williams 2012; 2013; Williams, Ulm et al. 2015; Williams, Veth et al. 2015). Recently, the analysis of large radiocarbon datasets with a particular focus on demographic change has become common (Johnson and Brook 2011; Smith et al. 2008; Williams 2013; Williams et al. 2010; 2013; Williams, Veth et al. 2015). Interpreting these analyses presents a number of problems. Critics raise questions relating to sources of bias, including better preservation of more recent evidence and the choice of dating samples in relation to research aims, as well as whether these data can be legitimately interpreted in demographic terms (Attenbrow and Hiscock 2015; Bird and Frankel 1991; Contreras and Meadows 2014). A consideration of the dating evidence from the general arid zone has been interpreted to suggest expansion of population about 8000 years ago and again at about 2000 years ago (Smith et al. 2008, 395; Williams, Veth et al. 2015). Occupation of new areas, more intensive use of existing sites and increased reliance on seed grinding, which characterises the archaeological record in Central Australia and the Western Desert in the last 2000 years, provides some support for suggesting that population expansion may be a contributor to the pattern observed in the time-series data (Smith and Ross 2008; Smith 2013, 178, 199–200). This has, in turn, been linked with the hypothesised spread of Pama-Nyungan languages in the early Holocene and the expansion of the Wati languages into Central Australia in the late Holocene (McConvell 1996; McDonald and Veth 2013a; Smith 2013, 333–35; Williams, Veth et al. 2015). The Pilbara has been suggested as a likely source area for the expansion of Wati languages into the Western Desert on the grounds of similarities in material culture and shared information networks evidenced by common mythological narratives and art (McDonald and Veth 2013a; Veth 2000). There is, however, at present little clear support for these speculations in the archaeological record.

In the inland Pilbara, like the broader arid zone, the distribution of radiocarbon determinations shows a marked proliferation of younger dates, particularly those falling within the last 1000 years (Williams, Veth et al. 2015). It is difficult to compile a comprehensive dataset of radiocarbon determinations for the region as so many dates occur only in grey literature. However, Figure 2.3 plots a subset of inland Pilbara radiocarbon determinations from the AustArch database (Williams, Ulm et al. 2014) and indicates that nearly half of all determinations are younger than 2000 years. The compliance context of most excavations means that many sites have relatively few radiocarbon determinations. Commonly, obtaining basal dates is a priority in these circumstances, although it is often difficult to obtain adequate samples of datable material from secure contexts, especially from older deposits. Of the 78 sites with radiocarbon determinations included in

Figure 2.3, only 14 (19%) have more than three dates while 22 (28%) have only one. The median number of dates per site is two. The site with the most determinations (12) is Djadjiling (Law, Cropper and Petchey 2010).

Recent publication of additional suites of radiocarbon determinations from the Hope Downs area (Cropper and Law 2018b) and the eastern Hamersley Plateau (Slack, Law and Gliganic 2018) do not materially change this observed pattern, although both projects have expanded the number of Pleistocene sites. For example, of the 42 Hope Downs radiocarbon dates now available (including Djadjiling), 36% are younger than 2000 years. The number of dates per site ranges from 1 to 12 and the median number of dates per site is 2.5 (Cropper and Law 2018b, 436–37). The new suite of eastern Hamersley Plateau dates does include a higher proportion of older dates with more than half (60%) older than 10,000 years ago. The median number of dates per site in the 22 sites included in the eastern Hamersley Plateau project is three, with a range of one to six. Six of these new dates come from new excavations at the previously recorded Newman Rockshelter and four from new excavations at Newman Orebody XXIX. However, the increased number of older dates in this particular sample is arguably a consequence of the project research design. More than 100 rockshelters were excavated, 22 of which yielded Pleistocene age deposits. Reporting of the remaining sites without Pleistocene deposits would presumably produce a more balanced result with a preponderance of Holocene dates (Slack, Law and Gliganic 2018).

The lack of contextual information for most dates from the region, as a consequence of limited publication, means that it is difficult to assess their significance. Associated cultural material is commonly sparse – exacerbated by small sample size from a few small test pits. Bias in choice of samples for dating cannot be controlled effectively since this is constrained by the availability of datable material. The lack of preservation of charcoal in older deposits is a problem, and probably contributes to the skewed distribution and proliferation of younger dates. Furthermore, the aim of dating test pits within the compliance context is usually to assess significance rather than to understand the chronology of shelter use. Thus, basal dates are commonly targeted, if sufficient charcoal is available. The limited number of dates per site means that it is difficult to understand individual

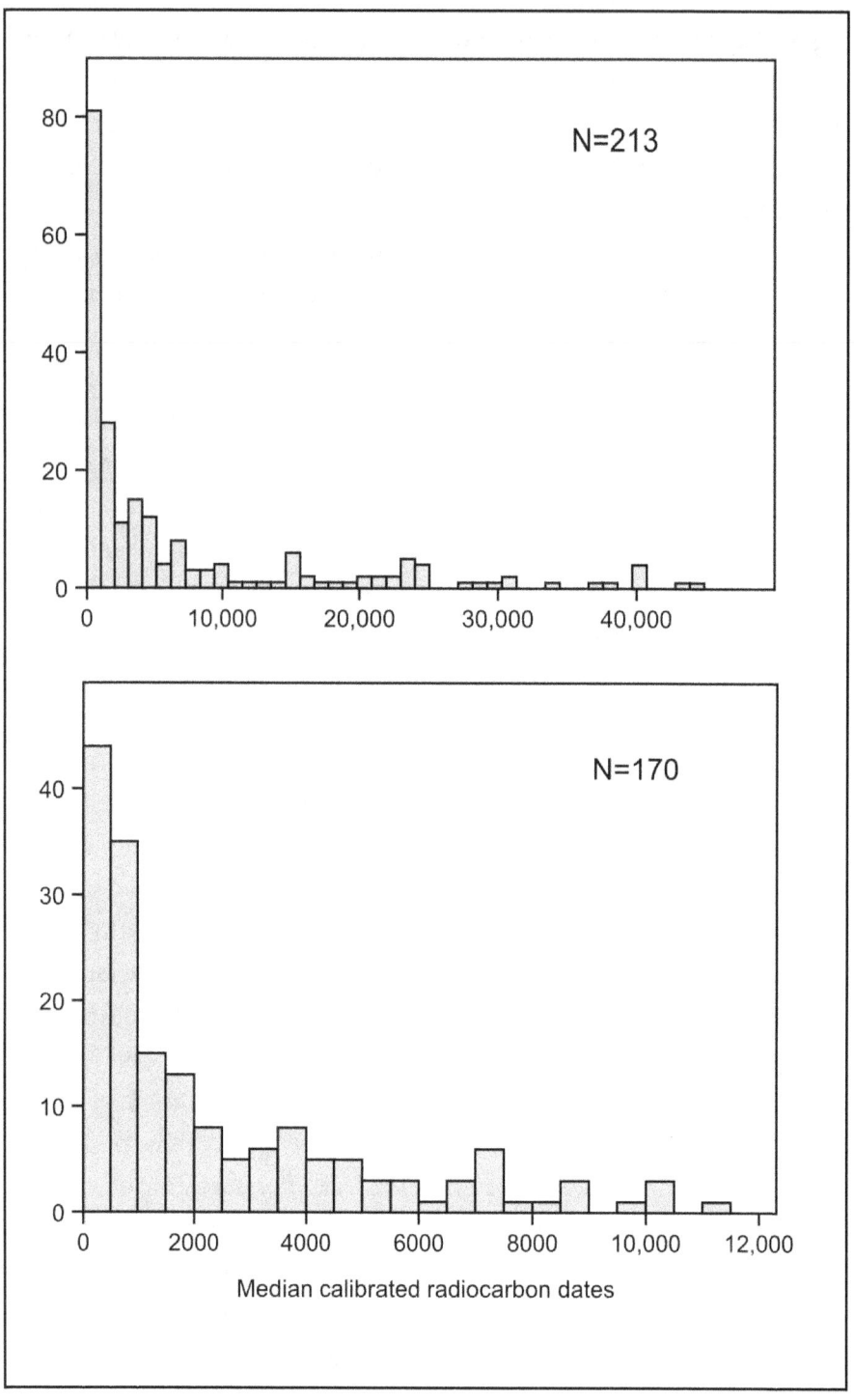

FIGURE 2.3: Inland Pilbara radiocarbon determinations.
Source: AustArch database (Williams, Ulm et al. 2014).

site occupation histories and their relationship to regional trends. It is noteworthy that nearly all the sites with more than five dates also have Pleistocene deposits. This reflects the greater significance assigned to older sites, and consequently greater research interest, but also serves to inflate the number of Pleistocene determinations. Nevertheless, dates from the last few thousand years still predominate. It is likely that the distribution of radiocarbon determinations for the Pilbara primarily reflects sampling bias and poor preservation of charcoal, rather than demographic change.

Evidence for the critical early Holocene period in the inland Pilbara is particularly scarce. A number of sites used during the Pleistocene also have cultural material dating to the early Holocene, but others do not seem to have been used again until the late Holocene. Several sites in the Hamersley Range first show evidence of occupation in the early Holocene, including Bastion Shelter (P5315) (Brown 1987, 42), DFSH4 (Dias, Hook and Veitch 2006), Manganese Gorge 8 (Veth 1995) as well as PAD 3, HN-A7 and HS-A2 at Hope Downs (Cropper and Law 2018, 439). More striking is the increase in the number of rockshelter sites first occupied in the last 1000 years. It is likely that better preservation of younger sites may partially account for this pattern, but this evidence does offer some support for the view (McDonald and Veth 2013a; Veth 2006) that the last 1000–1500 years was a period of change, perhaps as a result of increasing population and altered group boundaries. There is, however, little support for an early Holocene demographic pulse as suggested for the arid zone generally (Smith et al. 2008; Williams, Veth et al. 2015).

Unfortunately, the lack of detailed information available for most excavated sites means that it is difficult to generalise about their occupation histories. The limited number of dates available from most sites means that temporal resolution is very poor. Depth-age curves are difficult to construct under these circumstances and it is difficult to infer artefact discard rates. It is likely that most sites were used sporadically and episodically, with pulses of occupation of unknown length. Such a pattern of intermittent use is particularly well documented for Watura Jurnti (Marsh et al. 2018). This of course makes inferring regional trends in frequency of use problematic, whether from individual sequences or from regional datasets of radiocarbon determinations. Sedimentation rates at several sites do appear to increase in the mid to late Holocene. This might be interpreted as an increase in site use, but it is also possible that some compression of older deposits accounts for this through the loss of organic material. Sites with long-term evidence of occupation often show apparent increases in discard rate after about 4000 cal BP. This increase is often discussed in terms of technological change, changes in mobility and/or duration of site occupation (Marwick 2002; Veth, McDonald and White 2008; Veth 2005b). However, the inadequacies of the dataset for the inland Pilbara mean that attempts to interpret the distribution of radiocarbon determinations in terms of demographic or behavioural change (e.g. Williams, Veth et al. 2015) should be treated with caution. The chronological relationship between the archaeological records of much of the Pilbara and the Western Desert remains largely speculative (e.g. McDonald and Veth 2013a).

Stone arrangements provide evidence of possible changes in ceremonial organisation during the last 1000 years. While these sites are difficult to date, recent work suggests that the arrangements in the Packsaddle area date to the late Holocene (Hook and Di Lello 2010). McDonald and Veth (2013a, 75) suggest that stone arrangements replaced engravings as a marker of social identity and a component of the ceremonial repertoire in the Pilbara region in the last millennium. However, given the lack of research on both art and stone arrangements in the inland Pilbara and the difficulties of dating both these classes of archaeological data, this suggestion is purely speculative.

The timing of the introduction of new artefact types during the Holocene is a key issue in Australian archaeology. If the inland Pilbara uplands hosted groups throughout the Last Glacial Maximum, then this refugium was probably important in the re-establishment of permanent territories in lowland areas and then sand ridge deserts to the west (McDonald and Veth 2013a). Historical linguistic models also suggest that the Wati language in the Western Desert might originate in the Gascoyne/Pilbara borderlands (Smith 2005; Veth 2000). This in turn implies cultural links between the archaeological records of the Pilbara and the Western Desert at some time and that at least some of the elements of technology postulated as critical to occupying arid environments should appear first in the Pilbara region.

Seed-grinding technology, particularly wet milling, has been proposed as an enabler for groups to adapt to arid environments, when returning to or establishing their homelands throughout the Western Desert (Smith 1986; Veth 1993; 2006). The late Holocene proliferation of elements of the so-called Australian Small Tool Tradition, including backed artefacts and tulas, has been identified as a factor in the colonisation of new and risky environments (Hiscock 1994; Veth, Hiscock and Williams 2011). Macroblades are also a feature of the most recent period in central and northern Australia (Allen 1997; Smith 2013). However, issues such as these shared cultural inventories in the Pilbara and Western Desert and the nature of Holocene change remain largely speculative because of the limited data from the Pilbara. As the following discussion demonstrates, the key artefact types are rare at excavated sites, and the lack of adequate dating and limited publication militate against addressing these issues, although the recent analysis of relatively large assemblages from some of the sites at Hope Downs has provided new information on some of these issues (Cropper and Law 2018a).

Backed artefacts appear in the mid-Holocene in this region. The earliest securely dated backed artefacts come from Hope Downs where four backed artefacts were recovered from a feature at PAD3 dated to 4686 cal BP. Another backed artefact was also recovered below this feature (Cropper and Law 2018b, 444). Also at Hope Downs, the lowermost backed artefacts at Jundaru occurred below a feature dated at 3899 cal BP, while at HS-A2 the deepest backed artefact is bracketed by dates of 6583 cal BP and 2279 cal BP. At Y02-12 at Yandicoogina the oldest backed artefact is bracketed by median calibrated dates of 4031 cal BP and 4342 cal BP (Dias and Hook 2012). Seven backed artefacts were recovered from this excavation. Five backed artefacts were found in the upper levels of Newman Rockshelter, the oldest of which came from a hearth directly dated to 4047 cal BP (Brown 1987, 27). All other age estimates come as a result of interpolating depth-age curves. A backed artefact from Marillana A is bracketed by median calibrated dates of 3961 to 10,444 cal BP, while one from Newman Orebody XXIX is dated to between 3185 and 6039 cal BP (Comtesse 2003). Backing is claimed to occur at Juukan 2 in spit 5 estimated by interpolation at about 8000 cal BP, but no detailed information is available about the artefacts from this site

(Slack, Fillios and Fullagar 2009). All other dated backed artefacts in the inland Pilbara, including those reported in this volume, occur in contexts that are less than 4000 years old.

Hafted tulas are a distinctive item in the desert tool kit, produced using a specialised knapping technique. They are mostly used for working hardwoods, although they are employed for a range of other tasks. They show a characteristic wear pattern during use and are commonly discarded as distinctive 'slugs'. Tulas occur throughout the arid zone and are characteristic of late Holocene occupation of the region. The origins and history of this technology are unclear as dated tulas are rare. The situation is complicated by problems of definition since other hafted woodworking tools with worn-down slug forms are also found and commonly referred to as 'adzes', with 'non-tula adzes' and 'burrens' also widely used terms (Holdaway and Stern 2004, 251–59). Current evidence suggests that tulas first appear in the archaeological record about 3800 years ago and are widely dispersed throughout the arid zone (Smith 2013, 187; Veth, Hiscock and Williams 2011). In the Pilbara, excavated tulas are rare and published information about them is scarce, although all occur in the most recent levels of sites. The adze slug from Newman Rockshelter is not directly dated, but is reported to be younger than about 4000 cal BP (Brown 1987, 29). At the Hope Downs sites, tulas and burrens only occur in deposits dating to the last 1000 years (Cropper and Law 2018, 444).

Macroblades and their quarries are documented for the inland Pilbara but they rarely occur in dated contexts (Hook 2009). They have received little attention and their relationship to *leilira* – large blades that feature in ethnographically documented long-distance exchange systems in Central Australia – is unclear. Hook (2009, 28) lists six sites where blades have been reported, with estimated ages from 10,000 BP to recent. She notes that inspection of the specimens from Newman Orebody XXIX held at the Western Australian Museum, attributed to the early Holocene, showed that they were actually parallel-sided flakes without the dorsal ridges characteristic of true blades. Given that few of the other reported blades from excavated sites have been published or illustrated, their status must remain questionable. At Djadjiling, a heat-shattered retouched blade associated with a hearth was dated to 2858 cal BP (Law and Cropper 2018, 259). Two other blades occur in deposits younger than 3000 cal BP at the same site (Law, Cropper and Petchey 2010). Blade technology is otherwise rare at the Hope Downs sites (Cropper and Law 2018b, 443). A macroblade is also reported from Y02-12, a rockshelter in the Yandicoogina area, bracketed by radiocarbon determinations of 3957 cal BP and 4270 cal BP (Dias and Hook 2012).

Ground stone artefacts are generally rare in excavated sites. Most are undiagnostic fragments and therefore do not shed light on the question of the origin of specialised wet-milling technology. Dolerite fragments with evidence for use as grindstones are reported from throughout the sequence at both Mesa J J23 and J24, and some of those from J24 are inferred to be Pleistocene in age (Hughes, Quartermaine and Harris 2011). HD07-3A-PAD13 at Hope Downs has yielded several ground stone fragments of Pleistocene age, including a polished river cobble from the oldest occupation deposits dating between 47,100 and 33,900 years ago. At Jundaru, grindstones appear in the sequence from just before 7686 cal BP (Cropper and Law 2018, 442). A muller and an amorphous millstone fragment from Y02-12 are associated with a date of 7016 cal BP (Dias and Hook 2012).

DISCUSSION

This outline of the regional archaeological sequence in the inland Pilbara highlights that, despite the quantity of archaeological investigation conducted as a consequence of the resources boom since the 1980s, our understanding of the occupational history of the Pilbara region remains sketchy and largely speculative. What we do know is that occupation in the Pilbara extends back more than 40,000 years. The proliferation of early dates since the 1990s has attracted attention and highlighted the relevance of Pilbara compliance archaeology to debates about the colonisation of the continent, the timing and nature of occupation of the arid zone, and whether the region served as a refuge area for human populations during the Last Glacial Maximum. In some cases, this has attracted additional funding for research on specific sites. Nevertheless, limited publication and analysis mean the dates and associated archaeological deposits remain difficult to interpret. What is clear is that cultural material in most Pilbara rockshelters is generally sparse and the small samples greatly constrain the characterisation and comparative analysis of these early assemblages. Temporal resolution is also poor at most sites. Moreover, it is particularly difficult to identify whether site occupation sequences are continuous or have significant gaps. Indeed, the limited published information available tends to suggest that individual sites in the region with long sequences have distinctive occupation trajectories, perhaps resulting from contingent local factors. It is thus impossible to go further than to register the presence of people at many inland Pilbara sites.

The situation for more recent occupation sites is, if anything, worse, largely because the main criterion for assigning significance is antiquity and such sites have attracted little interest. There are many more excavated sites with only Holocene cultural material, particularly dating to the last millennium, but most remain undescribed. Detailed information, other than the dated evidence of stone artefacts and therefore the presence of people, is scarce. Sites with evidence of Pleistocene occupation are more likely to be reported in detail because they link the Pilbara archaeological record to overarching continental themes of colonisation and adaptation to changing environments, particularly through the Last Glacial Maximum. Since most test excavations yield recent dates, these sites cannot be related to these general research themes and further investigation is rarely recommended (Bird, Hook and Rhoads 2016). The results of most test excavations thus remain unpublished within grey literature. Of course, surface artefact scatters are entirely neglected in this overview of inland Pilbara archaeology, even though they form the lion's share of site identification and recording in compliance archaeology in the region and are arguably more 'typical' or 'representative' of past human occupation (Ryan and Morse 2009).

THEORETICAL FRAMEWORK

As Ryan and Morse (2009, 11) note, Veth's (1987; 1993; 1996; 2005b) pioneering archaeological research in the Rudall River area has been 'an important point of reference for any interpretation of archaeological sites in the arid zone of Australia and has implications for the interpretation of surface artefact scatters in the Pilbara'. Veth (1993, 83–87) formulated predictions about the relationship between artefact assemblages from archaeological sites and regional site patterning with respect to water permanency. This in turn linked to a regional settlement/subsistence model of variation in group size and mobility among the Martu. This approach drew explicitly on hunter-gatherer land use models (Binford 1980; 1982) and a reduction model of stone tool manufacture (Flenniken and White 1985). It falls within an influential and ongoing research paradigm exploring how such models interact with the organisation of lithic technology to form archaeological assemblages of stone artefacts (e.g. Andrefsky 2009; Nelson 1991). Veth stressed that his approach provides a testable model of land use, and indeed argued that the archaeological correlates of the Martu seasonal pattern of aggregation and dispersal in the Great and Little Sandy Deserts differ from those typical of the Gibson Desert described by Gould (Veth 1993, 89–93, 101). However, in the absence of comparable model-building for the Pilbara, consultants working in the region have used Veth's model as a convenient, heuristic device when interpreting and explaining sites in terms of their function within a hunter-gatherer land-use system (Ryan and Morse 2009, 12).

Veth defined specific predictions for regional assemblage patterning and composition in terms of 'increased intensity of stone reduction with increasing group size, complexity and permanency, which in turn are mainly functions of water permanency' (Veth 1993, 84). Specific characteristics of site assemblages predicted to change with increasing water availability include:

- representation of more stages of the reduction sequence
- increased representation of specific artefact types as water permanency increases (such as adzes, backed pieces, grinding material)
- increased intensity of reduction of cores
- increased conservation of formal implements
- increased diversity in raw materials and artefact types.

Table 2.1 summarises the current working version of Veth's model as developed by Archae-aus (e.g. Hook, Dias and Rapley 2008, 12–13). It provides a heuristic framework for interpreting sites, particularly ubiquitous surface assemblages, in terms of mobility and group size. For example, small highly mobile groups (high residential and low logistic mobility) produce small sites with few artefacts, little diversity in artefact types and raw materials, and with early stages of reduction predominating. On the other hand, large sites with larger and more diverse assemblages, and dominated by middle and late stages of reduction, are thought to have been used by larger groups for longer periods (low residential and high logistic mobility). These archaeological correlates are clearly expressed in terms of a generalised reduction model of stone technology (Table 2.2). Although versions of this land-use model are widely referenced by consultants in the Pilbara, there has been little attempt to evaluate its applicability to the region (Ryan and Morse 2009).

Interpreting Pilbara surface scatters in terms of changes in mobility and group size assumes that such sites can be interpreted using an ethnographic frame of reference. As Binford notes (1980, 9), foraging results in two broad general categories of spatial context for the discard of archaeological remains: the residential base and the task-specific location. However, in practice, these may not equate simply with archaeological 'sites' as recognised by archaeologists. A substantial amount of activity in foraging societies inevitably takes place away from residential bases, and any resulting archaeological evidence may fall below the threshold of visibility or beyond the practical limit of site recording. This is especially true within the local compliance archaeology context. There is ample ethnographic evidence of low density of occupation and dispersal of activities within Australia's arid landscapes. This suggests that, with the exception of quarries, only residential base camps are likely to accumulate a sufficient quantity of observable archaeological remains, which could be meaningfully identified as discrete 'sites' (e.g. Hayden 1986). Furthermore, the fact that the archaeological record is a palimpsest resulting from the interaction of a range of long and short-term formation processes – both natural and cultural – cautions against the temptation to interpret 'sites' as if they directly corresponded to ethnographic scale behavioural categories (Holdaway and Fanning 2014, 17).

TABLE 2.1: Inland Pilbara land-use model, as developed by Archae-aus (Edwards et al. 2012, 37; after Veth 1993).

Attribute	High residential mobility/Low logistical mobility	Moderate residential mobility/moderate logistical mobility	Low residential mobility/High logistical mobility
Site size	Small	Generally small-medium to medium	Large
Assemblage size	Few artefacts	Small to medium number of artefacts	Many artefacts
Reduction stages	Few stages of reduction. Mainly early stages of reduction	Mostly early and middle stages of reduction	Mostly middle to late stage reduction. Multiple concentrations
Assemblage diversity	Few artefact types. Few raw materials	Moderate diversity in artefact types and raw materials	High level of diversity in artefact types and raw materials
Grinding material	Grinding material absent	Small amount of grinding material present	Grinding material common
Formal tools	Few formal tools	Some formal tools	Many formal tools.
Features	No discrete features or differentiation of activity areas	Multiple artefact concentrations and moderate differentiation of activity areas	Multiple features and differentiation of activity areas
Land use patterns			
Group size (after Binford 2001, Table 8.01) and mobility	Small groups of people (<16 people, mean of 11) during periods of higher mobility	Repeat visits of small groups or small aggregations (21–50 people, mean 31)	Larger groups (130–350 people, mean 245) and periods of lower mobility
Number of visits	Limited number of visits (one or two)	Limited number of visits	Many visits

TABLE 2.2: Summary of reduction sequence model as used by Archae-aus (Edwards et al. 2012, 37).

Attribute	Early stage reduction	Mid stage reduction	Late stage reduction
Cortex	High proportion of cortical flakes	Low proportion of cortical flakes	Few or no cortical flakes
Assemblage composition	Few cores Few retouched tools High proportions of debris	Moderate numbers of cores Moderate numbers of retouched tools Moderate proportions of debris	Many cores Many retouched tools Low proportions of debris
Flake shape	Mostly irregular Length:width about 1.0	Increasingly regular Length:width about 1.0	Mostly regular May show increased length:width ratio if blade technology is in use
Average artefact size	Mostly larger artefacts	Wider range of artefact sizes	Wide size range, with smaller artefacts common
Core reduction	Little reduction of cores, resulting in most cores single platform (SPC)	Increased reduction of cores, resulting in higher ratio of multi-platform cores (MPC) to SPC	High proportion of MPC and exhausted cores
Core preparation	Overhang reduction (OHR) rare Little evidence for platform preparation	Increasing evidence for OHR	OHR common
Retouch	Little evidence for retouch	Increased evidence of retouch	Large numbers of exhausted tools High proportion of edge retouched

The related concepts of mobility and sedentism are complex and elusive. Detecting them, or their proxies, in the archaeological record is far from straightforward (Andrefsky 2009; Close 2000; Kelly 1992; 2013). Andrefsky (2005, 225ff.) reviews various attempts to investigate mobility through the organisation of lithic technology. He notes that artefact and assemblage variability can sometimes be interpreted in terms of mobility, but in other situations factors such as access to or the quality of raw materials seem to have an overriding effect. As Andrefsky observes, 'We now know that lithic assemblages are created in peculiar contexts associated with human systems that have unique histories and unique sets of environmental contexts' (2009, 88).

In other words, the relationship between technological organisation and land use must be considered within specific environmental, cultural and historical contexts. It is now clear that much lithic assemblage variation relates to the interaction between 'raw material costs, residential mobility and forager risks', which are contingent on context, rather than site function or ethnic identity (Hiscock 2009, 91). Investigating the relationship between technological organisation and land use in the Pilbara should, therefore, start by exploring patterning in the archaeological record within regional and local contexts. One starting point for our study, therefore, is the evaluation of the relevance of a land-use model developed for a sandy desert, with uncoordinated drainage, to the inland Pilbara, with its coordinated drainage and stone-rich landforms. However, alternative approaches to investigating technological organisation and land use at different spatial scales will also be considered.

THE ARCHAEOLOGY OF LAND USE AND TECHNOLOGICAL ORGANISATION

Mobility is a key concept when considering hunter-gatherer settlement and subsistence. All hunter-gatherer societies solve problems arising from the uneven distribution of resources in space and time through movement. However, movement, by its very nature, is ephemeral and commonly does not leave direct archaeological evidence (Close 2000). Mobility is also complex, encompassing a range of different behaviours that can be considered at different ethnographic timescales, from daily foraging radius to annual rounds. Kelly (2013, 85) defines several different types of movement including:

- number of residential moves in a year
- average distance moved
- total distance moved each year
- total area used over the course of a year
- average length of a logistical foray.

Cross-cutting the movement of individuals and groups is changing group size, another major strategy used by hunter-gatherers. This in turn relates to motivations for movement that can be as much social as subsistence in nature. The establishment of a network of social relations, involving mutual rights and obligations, provides a flow of information between groups and a safety net in times of scarcity (Gould 1980; Whallon 2006). Clearly, the rich ritual and ceremonial life so evident in Aboriginal society is an example of this. One manifestation of information flow in material culture is, of course, exchange that involves the movement of objects rather than people. Exotic raw materials and decorative items can be interpreted as indicators of such long-distance networks, while rock art has also been used as a marker of information exchange (McBryde 1978; 1987; McDonald and Veth 2008a; Veth et al. 2011).

Binford's (1978; 1980; 1982) discussions about hunter-gatherer settlement systems and archaeological site formation have strongly influenced archaeological approaches to understanding past hunter-gatherer land use. Binford identified a continuum of hunter-gatherer strategies for solving the problems of uneven distribution of resources based on movement. He distinguished between foragers, who primarily use residential mobility to map onto resources, and collectors, who use logistical mobility to move resources to people. These contrasting strategies had predictable implications for the nature of the archaeological remains that resulted from them. Stone artefacts commonly dominate these archaeological remains. Since the procurement, use and discard of stone resources are usually embedded in other activities (Binford 1978), it follows that the distribution of these activities in the landscape can inform about hunter-gatherer land use.

Binford's insights provided the theoretical underpinning for linking stone artefact analyses to hunter-gatherer adaptive strategies through the study of technological organisation (Andrefsky 2009; Holdaway and Stern 2004, 71–2; Nelson 1991). The manufacture of flaked stone tools is a reductive process generating large amounts of waste, or debitage. For archaeologists, this has the advantage of providing information about the complete process of production. It is possible to describe complete reduction sequences from the selection of raw material to the discard of worn-out tools. Each stage – procurement, manufacture, use, maintenance, recycling and discard – can be identified from the distinctive products left behind.

For mobile hunter-gatherer groups, it is the embedded nature of use of stone that offers potential to explore the interaction of technological organisation and land-use at different scales. The investigation of raw material procurement, use and discard has been a particularly productive approach to investigating technological organisation in relation to land-use patterns. Consequently, the study of lithic technological organisation has been increasingly influential over recent decades, and there is now a large and complex literature dealing with aspects of stone tool production and its intersection with hunter-gatherer adaptive strategies (Andrefsky 2009).

A number of lines of enquiry are possible when investigating lithic technological organisation. Raw material is a common starting point and has long been used as an analytical proxy for mobility. Many analyses have used sourcing methods to investigate long-distance movements of exotic stone (McBryde 1978). Refitting can also, in theory, be used to demonstrate movement, though the practical difficulties usually militate against using it at scales other than within sites (Close 2000).

The idea of curation as a process has also been important in relating technological organisation and mobility (e.g. Andrefsky 2009; Bamforth 1986; Binford 1979; Shott 1996; Torrence 1983). While originally conceived primarily in terms of tools and a dichotomy between 'curated' and 'expedient' tools, curation can also be understood in terms of process and relationship between actual and potential use (Andrefsky 2009, 71). This allows the concept to be applied to cores and flakes as well as tools (Douglass 2010, 252ff; Holdaway and Douglass 2012).

Integrating the study of technological organisation in the archaeological record with hunter-gatherer settlement and subsistence has been strongly influenced by the work of Kuhn (1995, 18–37). He notes that solving the problems of maintaining the supply of tools and the raw materials with which to make them is closely linked to planning. Moreover, hunter-gatherer groups' solutions vary considerably, depending on a range of circumstances. A reliance on expedient tool making may be viable in some situations, particularly where raw materials are abundant, but the risk remains that suitable tool-stone may not be available when required. Therefore, some degree of advanced planning remains essential to addressing the problem of uneven distribution of resources in time and space, thus mitigating risk. Kuhn uses the term 'technological provisioning' to incorporate curation and expediency, as well as depth of planning. He further notes that different strategies have different costs and benefits, as well as different archaeological correlates. Kuhn outlines two contrasting strategies – provisioning individuals and provisioning places – and discusses the expected relationships between these, foraging and land use strategies. Broadly speaking, his model predicts that increasing mobility in terms of both frequency of residential moves and duration of occupation favours individual provisioning. Kuhn's model clearly relates to Binford's forager–collector continuum. The logistic mobility characteristic of collectors favours provisioning of places, while the residential mobility employed by foragers favours provisioning individuals. The effect of these alternative strategies on technological organisation in terms of the procurement, manufacture, maintenance and discard of stone artefacts produces different archaeological signatures.

Dibble and colleagues (2005) propose an approach to identifying mobility from the amount of cortex in an assemblage. This is an aggregate analysis that attempts to estimate any discrepancy between expected and observed cortex ratios to identify import or export of artefacts at sites, and thereby infer movement of people. The methodology has been successfully applied to assemblages from semi-arid western New South Wales (Douglass 2010; Douglass et al. 2008; Holdaway and Douglass 2012). In this case, deficits in cortex are explained by inferring the removal of large cortical flakes from sites. Holdaway and Douglass (2012) note that there is ample ethnographic evidence that Aboriginal people commonly transported unretouched flakes. They argue that, for mobile foragers, transporting large cortical flakes provided an efficient means to reconcile the competing parameters of weight and ongoing utility in terms of cutting edge. This methodology offers considerable potential for making sense of the large quantities of surface artefacts that characterise the archaeological record of the Pilbara region, assemblages which have proved difficult to analyse. The region is generally rich in raw material and local geology is often seen as a dominant influence on the structure of assemblages (Ryan and Morse 2009, 10). However, even in environments where raw material is abundant, movement of stone can be expected both in the normal course of foraging activities and planned provisioning strategies in anticipation of future needs (Holdaway and Douglass 2012; Lin, McPherron and Dibble 2015, 102). An important feature of the cortex ratio is that it lends itself to application at different analytical scales, from single flaking events to entire systems.

In Australia, ideas about technological organisation have long been influential in a number of research programs. These include investigating the movement of stone from source to discard (e.g. Bird 1985; Byrne 1980; Doelman, Webb and Domanski 2001; Hiscock 1986), determining the relationship between risk and mobility (Hiscock 1994), and predicting the archaeological correlates of different site functions within a regional land use system (Veth 1993). The generalised nature of lithic reduction sequences over much of the continent (Flenniken and White 1985) and the lack of diagnostic tool types present difficulties in disentangling temporal change. Nevertheless, ideas about technological organisation have been applied to a wide range of archaeological contexts (e.g. Barton 2003; 2008; Clarkson 2006; 2007; Doelman, Webb and Domanski 2001; Douglass 2010; Fanning and Holdaway 2001; Holdaway and Fanning 2014; Holdaway et al. 1998; Holdaway, Fanning and Rhodes 2008; Holdaway, Shiner and Fanning 2004; Robins 1998; Shiner 2008). Some of these studies explicitly make use of ecological models to explore evidence for variation in mobility and land use patterns (e.g. Barton 2003; 2008; Clarkson 2006; 2007).

Others incorporate Kuhn's provisioning model (e.g. Mackay 2005). A few are primarily concerned with site formation processes (e.g. Holdaway and Fanning 2014; Shiner 2008).

It is clear that complex relationships exist between aspects of technological systems (including raw material provisioning, technology and stone tool manufacture, and artefact discard) and hunter-gatherer land use strategies. A unifying theory for investigating stone artefact assemblages within a framework of technological organisation has not, so far, been achieved (Andrefsky 2009; Clarkson 2007, 22ff.). Indeed, specific relationships postulated by analysts between the archaeological record and past human behaviours often remain largely intuitive (Barton and Riel-Salvatore 2014).

SITES AS ARCHAEOLOGICAL CATEGORIES: ROCKSHELTERS AND SURFACE ARTEFACT SCATTERS

Although it is now widely recognised that the distribution of archaeological material is effectively continuous in many landscapes, the practical requirements of the administration of cultural heritage legislation still call for the delineation of 'sites', as discrete polygons on maps. This atomisation of the archaeological record, as discussed in Chapter 1, raises issues that influence site interpretation and assessment of significance. It is clearly in conflict with Aboriginal concepts of country and land use (Byrne 1996, 102) and also disconnects sites both from their landscapes and their relationships with one another (Tilley and Cameron-Daum 2017).

It is worth emphasising again here that sites are archaeological categories or constructs. Classifying them into types such as 'surface artefact scatter', 'rockshelter', 'stone arrangement' and so on is based on physical characteristics. These are not behavioural categories and it cannot be assumed that they are uniform as regards function, interpretation or significance.

Archaeologists commonly distinguish between relatively dense, localised concentrations of archaeological material, termed sites, and a background scatter of more sparsely distributed archaeological materials or isolated artefacts. The implications of this distinction between 'on site' and 'off site' or 'non-site' archaeology have been recognised and debated in archaeology since the late 1970s (Dunnell and Dancey 1983; Ebert 1992; Foley 1981a; 1981b; Thomas 1975). Archaeologists increasingly recognise that the low temporal resolution of much of the archaeological record is a product of long-term site formation processes, rather than directly reflecting human activity at an ethnographic scale. As we have already noted, rather than corresponding to sites at the ethnographic scale, archaeological sites are commonly palimpsest accumulations of artefacts that may have accumulated over considerable time periods. The definition of sites in terms of units of analysis and interpretation reflects both cultural and natural formation processes, as well as the archaeologist's recording scheme. Definitions of what constitutes a site can thus vary greatly and lack consistency. Indeed, defining a site is commonly dependent on contextual information and can differ locally or regionally.

The perceptions of rockshelters and surface artefact sites, and the different approaches taken to them in the compliance context in the Pilbara region, exemplify these issues. The evidence from excavated rockshelters or caves traditionally plays a prominent role in archaeological research, even though it is well recognised that such sites are not necessarily 'typical' of past occupation and commonly comprise a numerically small element of the regional archaeological record (Bailey and Galanidou 2009; Frankel 1991, 56). There are good reasons for this. Archaeologists generally place great importance on comprehensive study of relatively rich sites with good preservation and the capacity to provide dating evidence. The relatively confined space delimited by the walls of the shelter encourages the accumulation of sediments through repeated occupation of the same space by past people. The combination of stratigraphic sequences and preservation of datable materials means they are also important for their capacity to contribute to both relative and absolute chronologies.

In the Pilbara, surface artefact scatters dominate the regional archaeological record, and anecdotal ethnographic evidence is used to suggest that, in the past, shelters were infrequently used (Ryan and Morse 2009). Nevertheless, the undoubted archaeological value ascribed to rockshelters means relatively large numbers of shelters are tested in the course of compliance archaeology. Typically, shelter deposits in the region are shallow with a sparse suite of cultural remains and poor preservation. In practice, the limited evidence these small test pits reveal, together with the prevailing assumption that rockshelters were rarely used by Aboriginal people, mean that the results of most test excavations usually remain unpublished within the grey literature if old dates were not obtained.

The priority afforded to rockshelter excavation tends to reinforce and highlight the differences between rockshelters and surface scatters. However, like surface scatters, rockshelter deposits are time-averaged palimpsests. Rockshelter deposits accumulate within the physical constraints of the space defined by the shelter walls. Post-depositional processes mean that successive occupation episodes are commonly mixed together and temporal resolution is often very poor (Bailey and Galanidou 2009; Stern 2008). This recognition of time-averaging in rockshelter deposits is an important insight that conceptually minimises the difference between the two types of sites. Standard styles of data presentation in archaeology obscure this, both in publications and in consulting reports. Excavation data tends to be presented in fine-grained detail, emphasising individual excavation units. By contrast, surface assemblages are commonly summarised in more general terms. The presentation of data from the two different types of site can be characterised as extremes of splitting and lumping. This is particularly evident in consulting reports where the primary focus is on data presentation, rather than analysis or synthesis. This has important implications for interpretation because the choice of units for analysis is one that archaeologists impose on the primary data, and this in turn influences interpretations of change through time (Frankel 1988). Presenting data from small test pits using fine-grained excavation units highlights differences between the low-resolution deposits characteristic of most shelters and the time-averaged surface assemblages that occur in the surrounding landscape. For analytical and comparative purposes, most of these small rockshelter test pits would be better considered as single units or minimally subdivided.

Furthermore, rockshelters can themselves be thought of as surface sites. Many are associated with a range of surface archaeological features including surface artefacts, stone features and quarried outcrops, as well as art. These features may occur within the confines of the shelter or in the immediate vicinity. Not all shelters with such surface cultural remains have accumulated deposits. It is worth reiterating here that archaeological categories need not correspond to behavioural ones. We have already noted that surface accumulations of artefacts do not necessarily correspond simply to functional categories on an ethnographic timescale. Similarly, rockshelters with accumulated archaeological deposits should not be lumped together as a single functional site type wholly distinct from shelters without such deposits and surface scatters (Bird and Rhoads 2015). In practical terms, resolution and sampling issues mean that such distinctions may have little analytical or interpretive value.

PATTERNING IN THE SURFACE ARCHAEOLOGICAL RECORD

Investigating patterning in surface assemblages at a landscape scale, focusing on landform elements or other geographically defined analytical units, is one alternative to a site-based ethnographic approach (e.g. Barton 2003; 2008; Bird and Rhoads 2011; Hughes and Hiscock 2005; Hughes et al. 2011; Marwick et al. 2017; Robins 1998; Sullivan, Hiscock and Hughes 2014). Barton (2003; 2008), for example, uses distributional data to investigate the surface archaeological record and infer long-term behavioural patterns in the Simpson Desert. He uses foraging models to partition the landscape into landform elements with different foraging potential. Water sources are, of course, still a critical resource in this arid zone, but Barton characterises different landform elements in terms of resource productivity. This allows him to formulate a model of land use in terms of occupation span and varying levels of residential mobility associated with specific landform elements. The archaeological correlates of this model are broadly similar to those of Veth (1993) and also draw on concepts of technological organisation. They include the diversity and density of archaeological remains, measures of intensity of reduction, and indicators of tool production, recycling and repair. Rather than focusing on functional site categories, Barton relates these to length of occupation span and level of residential mobility at a landscape scale.

However, the assumption of long-term continuity and stability in land-use patterns remains difficult to avoid in landscape-scale analyses of surface assemblages. Integrating such landscape-scale analyses with a geoarchaeological approach to explore the formation of the archaeological record through time offers a possible solution (e.g. Holdaway and Fanning 2008; 2014; Holdaway, Shiner and Fanning 2004; Shiner 2008). Holdaway, Fanning and colleagues approach the problem from a geoarchaeological perspective, asking why archaeological remains are distributed as they are in the landscape, how old they might be and, as a consequence, what types of behaviour, inferences can be understood from the surface archaeological record (Holdaway and Fanning 2014, 163). Addressing these questions necessarily draws attention to the history of place use and thus explicitly concerns the interaction of behaviour, technology and site formation processes within a local context.

In practice, however, as we have noted, research of this sort is largely beyond the scope of compliance archaeology as currently practised in the Pilbara. The insights from such approaches certainly present challenges to heritage managers (Holdaway and Fanning 2014, 179). Nevertheless, it is important for archaeologists working in the compliance space to engage with the fact that surface archaeological remains make up such a large proportion of the record.

LANDSCAPE APPROACHES AND AN ARCHAEOLOGY OF PLACE

The intersection of technological organisation with the archaeology of place invites an integrated approach to interpretation of the archaeological record at a landscape scale, which can also incorporate contemporary Aboriginal understandings about country and the nature of the evidence. The concept of place in Aboriginal societies may be best associated with localities, rather than a particular point on the landscape (Pickering 2003). There is ample evidence of the large-scale and dispersed character of ethnographically observed camps, which are beyond the scale of what is usually considered a site (Memmott 2002; O'Connell 1987). For mobile foraging societies, such places form part of their social and economic interactions with larger scale landscapes, which thereby become enculturated and rich in meaning (Oetelaar and Meyer 2006; Whallon and Lovis 2016).

Ingold's notion of the 'taskscape' offers a way of thinking and talking about the archaeological record which is more congruent with a landscape-based than a site-based approach (Gamble 2006, 86; Ingold 1993). The idea of the taskscape considers the landscape not as backdrop or scenery, but as the collection of activities and interactions that took place there. The taskscape thus integrates disparate types of archaeological remains by considering them as related evidence of past activities and cultural interactions within the landscape.

Ingold (2007, 79) argues that the lives of hunter-gatherers can be portrayed as the sum of their journeys traced on the ground. The sum of the lives of many individuals forms a 'meshwork'. Places then, are the knots in the meshwork, connected and formed by the threads of many individual journeys as they cross and interweave, as individuals and groups move through their country. This useful metaphor is, of course, consistent with Aboriginal understandings of country and ancestral journeying (Bradley 2008). However, the metaphor also captures the idea of the distribution of archaeological remains in the landscape as a record of movement and tracing ancestral journeys. This record, in turn, documents the creation of a cultural landscape through generations of human agency (Oetelaar and Meyer 2006, 370).

We suggest that a perspective focusing particularly on the relationships between the distribution in time and space of archaeological remains and the landscape in which they occur, rather than on individual sites and categories of site, is crucial to developing a more nuanced approach to interpretation and assessment. Such a perspective actively encourages engagement with understanding the nature of the archaeological record – and particularly site formation processes associated with stone artefact production, use and discard – and how its characteristics might be interpreted in terms of past human behaviours (Holdaway and Fanning 2014, 166ff.).

Contemporary Australian archaeology has been shaped – and continues to be shaped – by engagement with the concerns of Aboriginal peoples (Griffiths 2018, 295). At a local scale, this is evident in the history of archaeology in the Pilbara. Aboriginal people are key stakeholders and, increasingly, decision makers with respect to heritage in the region, including archaeological sites. McDonald and Coldrick (in press) discuss the changing relationships between Aboriginal people and archaeologists in the Pilbara over time including changes in Aboriginal understandings and attribution of meaning to archaeological evidence. They point to emerging and developing 'communities of practice' with ongoing influences on assessment of archaeological sites. Our study, like other recent research in the inland Pilbara (e.g. Cropper and Law 2018a; Slack, Law and Gliganic 2018), arises directly from this emerging community of practice. The Cloudbreak–Christmas Creek study area is in Nyiyaparli country, where the landscape abounds in signs of both the creation of the land in the *Kukutpa*, or Dreaming, and the lives of their ancestors (Nyiyaparli Community, Bird and McDonald 2015, 34). This project, then, is supported by Nyiyaparli Traditional Owners as a way of finding out more about the lives of their ancestors. The approach taken here explicitly explores ways of moving between landscapes and sites to bring Aboriginal understanding of country and archaeological interpretation closer together.

INVESTIGATING THE ARCHAEOLOGY OF THE EASTERN CHICHESTER RANGE

The approach taken in this study is unquestionably influenced by the context of data collection and the prevailing general frameworks for interpreting sites documented during compliance fieldwork in the Pilbara region. No new data were collected specifically for these analyses, which therefore rely on the field records of assemblages or, in the case of excavated rockshelters, laboratory records. The site and assemblage attributes recorded by Archaeaus staff in the field were designed to characterise sites in terms of size, features, environmental context, raw material composition, reduction stages, technology, and formal tools (see Appendix 1 for description of methods and definition of terms). All consultants in the Pilbara use a broadly comparable set of attributes (e.g. Ryan and Morse 2009).

Sites identified during the fieldwork program were classified in accordance with definitions used by the Department of Aboriginal Affairs in registering sites under the *Aboriginal Heritage Act 1972* (WA), as well as standard practices in compliance archaeology in the region and elsewhere in Australia (e.g. Burke and Smith 2004, 202ff.). The following site types typical of the inland Pilbara were recorded in the project area: surface artefact scatter, reduction area, quarry, rockshelter, modified tree and structure. Isolated artefacts were also recorded in order to characterise the area's 'background scatter'. Rock art is absent from the area, most likely because the available banded iron formation rock surfaces are not suitable for the execution or survival of pigment or engraved art.

About 2000 sites were identified and recorded in the Cloudbreak–Christmas Creek area between 2006 and 2012. Nine hundred and fifty, including 19 rockshelters where test excavations were conducted, occur within the boundaries of the Christmas Creek study area as defined in Chapter 1. A substantial number of these contained more than one component, but surface artefact scatters were by far the largest single category of site (Table 2.3). More than 8000 isolated artefacts were also recorded within the boundaries of the Christmas Creek study area.

Three broad lines of enquiry are pursued in this study. First, surface artefact scatters are analysed to identify patterning with respect to environment, raw material and technology (Chapter 4). Our provisional inspection of the data suggested that assemblage sample size was generally small for many sites. Site definition followed threshold conventions established with reference to the requirements of compliance heritage survey in the region. However, as observed previously, these conventions serve as administrative devices to subdivide an effectively continuous cultural and archaeological landscape for management purposes. A pilot analysis (Bird and Rhoads 2015) suggested that sampling stone artefact assemblages at a landscape scale provided an analytical approach that could mitigate the problems of small samples and high levels of inter-assemblage variability clearly evident when analysing individual sites. Therefore, the analysis of surface scatters proceeds at different scales. An initial analysis looks at the overall characteristics and distribution of surface artefact sites in the project area in relation to vegetation formations. The analysis of stone artefacts then explores overall patterning in surface assemblages in the project area using landscape samples.

TABLE 2.3: Site types occurring within the Christmas Creek study area.

SITE TYPE	
Surface artefact scatter	827
Reduction area	234
Quarry	27
Stone feature	19
Rockshelter	42
Scarred tree	19

The second line of enquiry focuses on the use of rockshelters (Chapter 5). The results of test excavations in rockshelters allow a chronological framework to be developed for the study area and the identification of patterns in rockshelter use in time and space. A pilot analysis (Bird and Rhoads 2015) tested the conventional interpretation of rockshelters as ephemeral sites and explored the relationships between rockshelters and nearby surface scatters. This analysis is extended here to the full suite of rockshelters in the project area with a view to attempting to better integrate these sites with the surface archaeological record.

Finally, we explore the structure of the archaeological record at a landscape level through case studies (Chapter 6). These highlight how issues of scale, resolution and recording can influence site assessment and interpretation. Such description also, however, suggests how more comprehensive consideration of context can improve the interpretation of cultural material.

CHAPTER 3

NATURAL ENVIRONMENT AND CULTURAL CONTEXTS

THE STUDY AREA IS located in the sparsely populated, subtropical to semi-arid region of the inland Pilbara. Broadly-based pastoral activities have been the major commercial focus of the region since the mid-19th century. More recently, intensive iron ore mining has played a more dominant role. The environmental investigations associated with regulatory compliance requirements (e.g. Fortescue Metals Group 2013) and supported research (e.g. Skrzypek, Dogramaci and Grierson 2013) form the basis for some key understandings about the land and the people who once inhabited the region.

NATURAL ENVIRONMENT
CLIMATE
The Fortescue Marsh region is characteristically hot and drought prone, with some climate events lasting for long periods (Beard 1975, 64–70; Dogramaci et al. 2012; Fortescue Metals Group 2011; McKenzie, van Leeuwen and Pinder 2009; Skrzypek, Dogramaci and Grierson 2013; Van Vreeswyk et al. 2004). Rainfall averages about 350 mm per year and commonly occurs as scattered, localised showers or pronounced cyclonic storms. Annual pan

evaporation is high, almost ten times the yearly rainfall in the inland Pilbara. At Wittenoom, about 100 km west of the study area, mean annual rainfall is 472 mm. Skrzypek and colleagues (2013, 168) attribute this difference to the distance from ocean and the orographic effect or, in other words, the rise in an air mass as it is forced from a lower elevation.

The area experiences two distinct seasons, a dry winter/spring and a wet summer/autumn. During winter/spring (June–November), night time temperatures drop to 12 °C on average, and as low as zero. The hottest daytime temperature recorded during this season is 44 °C and the monthly average is 29 °C (Bureau of Meteorology Australia 2014a). About 80–90% of winter rainfall occurs as a result of cloud bands that build up over the Indian Ocean to the west and north-west of the study area (Wright 1997). On average, rain showers last about two days per month and total 17 mm over the season. Spring rainfall averages 5 mm per month, about half of which occurs in November, just before the wet season begins.

The summer/autumn wet season daytime temperatures average about 35 °C. Maximum monthly temperatures in summer are in the order of ten degrees higher. Temperatures at night average about 8 °C but can vary between 17 °C and 1 °C in summer and autumn, respectively. Summer rains mostly result from tropical lows and cyclones that develop off the north-west coast. Rainfall patterns vary from light scattered thunderstorms in isolated areas to infrequent and widespread light rain. Rainfall in summer averages 158 mm, with about half occurring in February; during autumn, precipitation averages 87 mm.

LANDFORMS AND GEOLOGY

The Fortescue Valley and Chichester Range (Figure 1.3) are the primary landforms in the Fortescue Marsh area (after Beard 1975, 62–7). Each of these can be further divided into several geomorphological units (Van Vreeswyk et al. 2004).

The Fortescue Valley consists of three units: the Fortescue Marsh (Martuyitha), the river channel and floodplains, and the sedimentary outwash plains. The Fortescue Marsh is the largest and extends westward from roughly Roy Hill Station to the Goodiadarrie Hills. This area is about 100 km

FIGURE 3.1: Samphire flats bordering the Fortescue Marsh.

long and 10 km at its widest point (Figure 3.1). It comprises primarily Quaternary alluvium. The second geomorphological unit, the river channel and associated floodplains, consists of Quaternary deposits and is mostly found upstream from the Marsh, beyond the eastern reaches of the study area. Sedimentary outwash plains border the Marsh on the north and form the third geomorphological unit (Figure 3.2). This landscape consists of Quaternary sand, silt and gravel alluvial and colluvial deposits. It is the product of overflow from the Marsh, as well as sheet-wash from the braided channels that crisscross the plains fringing the Chichester Range and flow into the wetlands.

The Chichester Range landform can also be divided into three units: stony hardpan plains, escarpment and plateau (Figure 3.3). The plains are situated along the base of the range and form a gently rolling land surface broken by 5–50 m wide drainage channels interspersed with low rises. A thin layer of partly cemented Quaternary alluvium/colluvium covers most of the plain and overlays Wittenoom dolomite bedrock. The upper layer of this formation occasionally surfaces and notably contains a carbonate

FIGURE 3.2: General view of the outwash plains.

FIGURE 3.3: The foothills of the Chichester Range.

layer rich in deposits of chert up to two metres thick, in addition to layers of bedded chert that occur lower down (Simonson, Hassler and Schubel 1993). The groundwater associated with the small creeks and alluvial plains bordering the Marsh is always fresh.

The escarpment of the Chichester Range is an erosion feature of the Marra Mamba Formation (Figure 3.4). This geological unit is primarily characterised by dominant layers of banded iron formation with significant silicate and carbonate content, as well as macrobands with varying proportions of dolomite, limestone and chert (Blockley et al. 1993). The landscape largely consists of plateaus and ridges up to 400 m high and steep scree slopes.

The plateau landform occupies the Chichester Range uplands. The Madinna Formation and more recent Jeerinah Formation comprise the underlying geology (Thorne and Trendall 2001, 115–42). The Jeerinah Formation is located immediately adjacent to the Marra Mamba Formation exposures along the escarpment and consists of dolomite, chert, various volcanic rocks, and fine-grained sedimentary rock (e.g. mudstone). The Madinna Formation lithology includes mudstone, fine to coarse-grained volcanics, quartz sandstone, and silicified carbonate.

Like much of the inland Pilbara, the area is rich in high quality stone suitable for flaking (Brown 1987, 5–6). This includes banded iron formation (BIF), a range of cryptocrystalline siliceous rocks (chert, chalcedony, mudstone), and basic igneous rocks (basalt, dolerite). In the survey area, primarily in the escarpment and plateau of the Chichester Range, raw

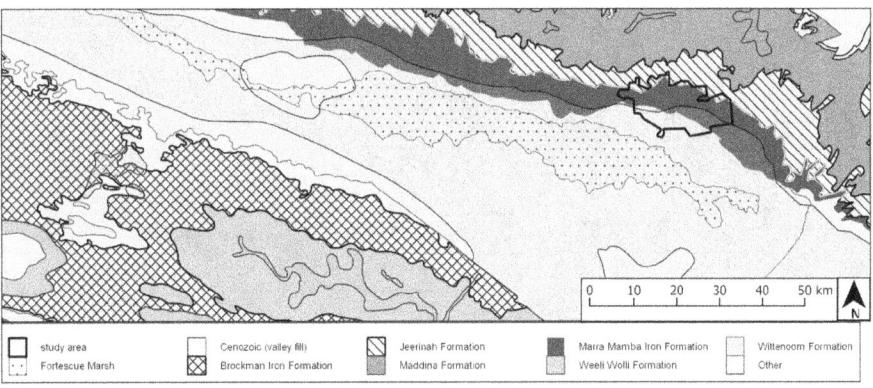

FIGURE 3.4: Geology of the Fortescue Marsh area.

material occurs as outcrops or seams, which can be quarried (Figure 3.5). Raw material can also be found on the outwash plains as part of the surface mantle of cobbles and pebbles. Creek lines are also rich in cobbles and pebbles (Figure 3.6). Banded iron formations are common and widely available. Chert, chalcedony and mudstone occur quite widely along the southern escarpment of the Chichester Range, mainly on top of knolls as small outcrops or isolated nodules. Cobbles of these materials also occur in creek lines. In this part of the Chichester Range, basalt occasionally occurs as outcrops and is more commonly found as cobbles in creek lines. This local material is very fine-grained and resembles chert in its flaking properties. Dolerite is mainly found as cobbles in the creek beds. Other raw materials occasionally occur in assemblages in the survey area (including silcrete, quartzite, and quartz) but no local sources have been observed. These materials thus presumably come from sources outside the survey area.

FIGURE 3.5: Quarried outcrops and exfoliating nodules: chalcedony – CB09-262 (top left); chert – CB09-106 (top right); banded iron formation – CB09-253.

Figure 3.6: Stone raw materials found as cobbles in creeks and on the outwash plains.

HYDROLOGY

The occurrence of surface water in the inland Pilbara becomes very sparse as one moves away from the major rivers. The Fortescue Marsh (Martuyitha) presents a notably different situation. There are two sources of fresh water feeding into the Marsh: the Fortescue River and, occasionally, the ephemeral creeks along the southern slope of the Chichester Range (Figure 3.7).

Rain falling in the Fortescue River headwaters, located in three distinct geographic regions – the south-east extent of the Hamersley Range, Ophthalmia Range and the western reaches of the Little Sandy Desert – contributes most of the fresh water arriving in the Marsh (Skrzypek, Dogramaci and Grierson 2013, 168–9, 171–2). Fresh water sits at or just below the surface of the Marsh, often appearing as small bodies of water perched above the more saline water that fills the Marsh's water table. Once flood waters cease to enter the Marsh, the high evaporation rate results in surface waters becoming brackish before disappearing altogether.

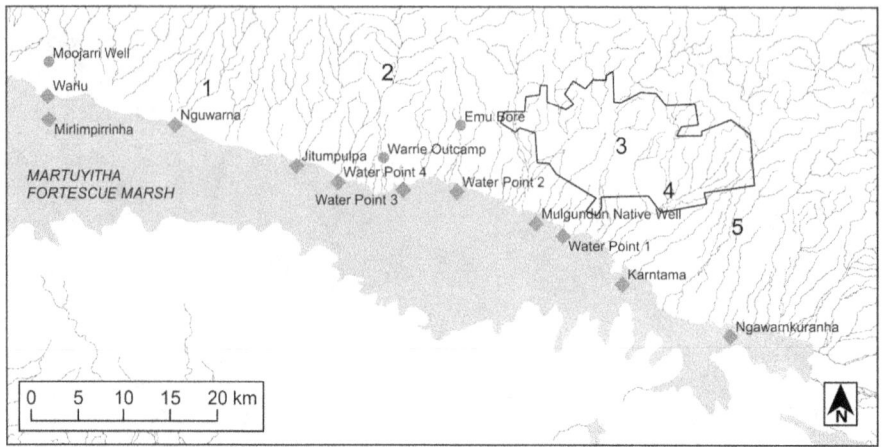

FIGURE 3.7: Hydrology of the study area, showing yinta and unnamed water points along the northern margin of the Fortescue Marsh. 1: Goman Creek. 2: Sandy Creek. 3: Marandu Creek. 4: Kakutungutanta Creek. 5: Christmas Creek.

The fall in elevation across the Marsh is close to zero, and water overflowing from the Marsh into the Lower Fortescue is rare, perhaps once every 1000 years.[1] The extent to which water normally covers the Marsh primarily relates to the intensity of rain events in the Fortescue River catchment, as shown in an analysis of flooding patterns over the last 100 years (Rouillard et al. 2015, 2063–6, see especially Figure 6). Rainfall of more than 75 mm in the river's upper catchment is sufficient for the Marsh's floodplains to become mostly inundated for one to three months during February to April. Rainfall events measuring less than 30 mm are generally insufficient to produce any flooding.

The two most reliable water sources are situated immediately southeast of the study area. Moorimoordinina Native Well (Karntama) and 14 Mile Pool are both located in the eastern reaches of the Marsh (Figure 3.7). Both recharge during the wet season through inflow of flood waters from the Fortescue River and, perhaps, from alluvial water inflows from nearby creek systems. Some recharge of the 14 Mile Pool waterhole via groundwater infiltration cannot be ruled out.[2] Both hold water for no more than a few months in seven out of ten years.

---

1 Skrzypek, personal conversation, September 2014.

2 Skrzypek, personal conversation, August 2013.

In the course of her research, Rouillard produced a model showing several other localities along the Marsh's northern margin where water predictably persists longest during flooding episodes (Figure 3.7).[3] These occur within the Marsh's inundation zone following very large flood events (Rouillard et al. 2015, Figure 6).

The first locality, referred to here as Water Point 1, is at the outfall of an unnamed creek draining the area of the Chichester Ranges just east of Mulgundun Native Well. Marsh flood waters are the major contributor of fresh water, and once flooding ceases, the waterhole probably retains water for several weeks. Alluvial creek flow may be an important factor sustaining fresh water entering the pool.

Water Point 2 is situated downstream from Emu Bore at the outfall of an unnamed creek. No pools are present, based on available aerial photos; however, the occurrence of dense vegetation indicates the likely presence of a pond during Marsh flooding. Modelling indicates the waterhole would reliably fill many times over a 100-year cycle.

Water Point 3 is situated south-east of Warrie Outcamp. No pools are visible in the available aerial photos, but again lush vegetation is visible along much of the creek's lower reaches, especially at a prominent circular feature. Once filled with flood waters from the Marsh, this feature and the channel downstream would be a relatively dependable source of water for a short time after.

Water Point 4 is located at the outfall of Sandy Creek (Figure 3.8). Aerial photo data indicates small pools occur along the creek channel. Marsh flood waters probably fill the channel regularly over a 100-year cycle but last only short periods.

The Cook Pool waterhole (Jitumpulpa)[4] has several distinguishable pools that fill with flood waters. They would be unlikely to retain water for very long.

Goman Pool (Nguwarna) is situated along the creek channel and becomes active as a result of stream inflow, rather than from Marsh floodwaters (Goode 2009, 30). The reliability of this waterhole over time cannot be estimated, but it is probably very low.

---

3 Rouillard, personal conversation, August 2013.

4 Goode (2009, 36) identified this place as Sandy Creek. This is mistaken, and the feature he discussed is situated at Cook Pool, based on a review of available aerial photography.

Figure 3.8: Sandy Creek in flood.

Mirlimpirrinha is situated west of the study area near the Marsh's north-west extent, and immediately south-east of Moojarri Well. It consists of three large playa lakes that are often filled by floodwaters. They all probably have water on many occasions, with the central one retaining surface water for the longest period.

Aside from waterholes, fresh water in the area may be found in the ephemeral creeks draining the southern slope of the Chichester Range. Water is available in ephemeral ponds, or from longer lasting alluvial water soaks. As Skrzypek and colleagues explain (2013, 167):

> Runoff from the rainfall on the flanks initially drains down a gradient as overland flow before concentrating into a defined flow channel. In steep areas … the runoff is rather rapid with relatively low losses and the drainage channels are typically in close proximity. In the lower slope areas of the marsh, runoff processes are rather slow with relatively higher evaporation losses and a greater distance between defined drainage channels …

High-volume rainfall events (>20 mm) recharge both shallow alluvium and fractured rock aquifers which, in turn, replenish the surface pools appearing along defined channels (Dogramaci et al. 2012). On the other hand, small or isolated rainfall events do not produce surface flows sufficient to recharge the water table. Nevertheless, they do contribute to the groundwater retained in the erosional depressions along creek lines.

In summary, the availability of potable surface water in the general vicinity of the study area is contingent on cyclonic storms occurring in the Fortescue River's headwaters, where rainfall amounts to 75 mm or greater. Smaller levels of precipitation enable the filling of pools near the Fortescue's outfall into the Marsh, but if rainfall in the catchment is less than 30 mm then the Marsh will suffer drought conditions. On these occasions and during winter, intermittent rain in the eastern Chichester Range comprises the only possible contribution of water to the study area.

VEGETATION

The Fortescue Marsh samphire flats, mulga woodlands and shrub steppe on the Chichester Range uplands form the primary vegetation regimes. A fine-grained picture of the area where we focus our archaeological investigations comes by way of the detailed flora studies associated with the Cloudbreak–Christmas Creek mine developments (FMG 2011; 2013).

The north-east shore of the Fortescue Marsh, near the study area (Figure 3.9, Table 3.1) is primarily vegetated by Low Shrubland (*Tecticornia indica* and *Nicotiana* over grasses). Low Halophytic Shrubland (*Tecticornia indica* spp.) also appears in patches along the shore and extends across the adjacent plains (Figure 3.1). Low Shrubland (*Muellerolimon salicorniaceum* and *Tecticornia indica*) vegetates large areas of the nearby Marsh. The calcrete platforms found near the shore are poorly vegetated with different grass species (Van Vreeswyk et al. 2004, 221) and *Acacia* spp. occasionally appear near their base, presumably where there are localised, natural 'wells' of freshwater.[5]

The river channel and associated floodplains, found upstream from the Marsh and just beyond eastern reaches of the study area, is covered with

---

5 Grierson, personal conversation, 2013.

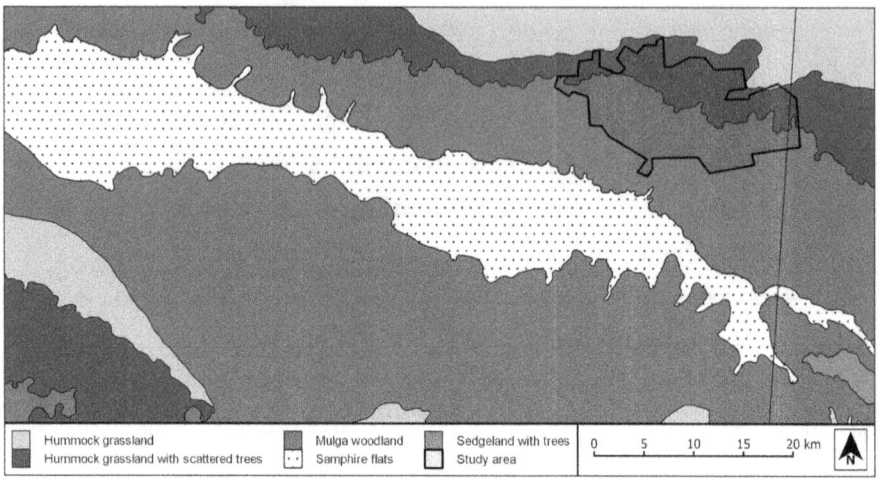

FIGURE 3.9: Vegetation communities (after Beard 1975; Beard et al. 2013).

eucalypt woodland consisting of scattered coolibah (*Eucalyptus victrix*) and whitewood (*Atalaya hemiglauca*) with a grass (*Eragrostis setifolia* and *Panicum* sp.) understorey. Coolibah woodlands closely fringe the Fortescue River channel and waterholes east of the Marsh.

The vegetation covering the plains to the north of the Marsh can be subdivided into four discrete units. The first only comprises a small portion of the plains, while the others cover about 85 per cent of the area in roughly equal proportions. Saline plains vegetated in Low Shrubland (*Tecticornia indica* and *Nicotiana* over grasses) and Low Halophytic Shrubland (*Tecticornia indica* spp.) border the Marsh. Stony, or gilgai (a mosaic of potholes and mounds), plains are situated inland for the most part. Gently undulating hardpan plains and low stony rises, carrying mulga woodlands (*Acacia* spp.), ranging from low woodland to open forest communities, fringe the Chichester Range and occasionally extend to the Marsh (Figure 3.10). Open woodland (*Acacia* spp.) appears along the creek lines crossing the outwash plains.

The rugged landscape of the Chichester Range and its southern escarpment is vegetated with hummock grassland (*Triodia* spp.) and a scattering of shrubs and trees – *Acacia* spp. and *Grevilla wickhamii* (Figure 3.11). Prominent, deeply incised creek channels also occur here and the primary vegetation community is Open Eucalypt Forest (Figure 3.12).

TABLE 3.1: Christmas Creek and environs vegetation communities (FMG 2010, 40–2, Figure 7).

Vegetation Community	Vegetation Community Code	% Christmas Creek Vegetation Assessment Area	% Study Area
SAMPHIRE FLATS AND FRINGES			
Low Halophytic Shrubland of *Tecticornia auriculata*, *Tecticornia indica* subsp. *leiostachya*, *Tecticornia halocnemoides* subsp. *tenuis* with patches of *Frankenia* species.	13	7.2%	0%
Low Shrubland of *Tecticornia indica* subsp. *bidens* and *Nicotiana occidentalis* over grasses with occasional stands of *Sesbania cannabina* and *Cullen cinereum*.	22	4.5%	0%
Low Shrubland of *Muellerolimon salicorniaceum* and *Tecticornia indica* subsp. *bidens*.	26	8.3%	0%
Low Shrubland of *Tecticornia indica* subsp. *bidens*, *T. auriculata* and *T. indica*, subsp. *leiostachya*.	31	7.2%	0%
Low Shrubland of *Muellerolimon salicorniaceum* over *Tecticornia indica* subsp. *bidens* and *T. indica* subsp. *leiostachya* with *Euphorbia* sp..	32	3.1%	0%
Low Shrubland of *Tecticornia indica* subsp. *bidens* and *Scaevola spinescens* with *Acacia synchronicia*.	33	0.4%	0%
Low Shrubland of *Muellerolimon salicorniaceum* over *Tecticornia indica* subsp. *bidens* and *T. auriculata* with *Heliotropium curassavicum* and *Atriplex flabelliformis*.	34	0.4%	0%
Low Shrubland of *Muellerolimon salicorniaceum* over *Tecticornia auriculata* with *Euphorbia* sp..	35	0.4%	0%

TABLE 3.1: *Continued*

Vegetation Community	Vegetation Community Code	% Christmas Creek Vegetation Assessment Area	% Study Area
FLATS AND BROAD PLAINS			
Low Woodland to Low Open Forest of *Acacia aneura* var. *aneura*, *Acacia pruinocarpa*, *Acacia tetragonophylla*, *Acacia tenuissima*, *Grevillea wickhamii* subsp. *aprica*, *Psydrax latifolia* over *Dodonaea petiolaris* and *Triodia* and *Aristida* species.	3	18.5%	19.9%
Low Open Woodland of *Acacia aneura* var. *aneura*, *Acacia pruinocarpa*, *Acacia xiphophylla*, *Acacia victoriae* over *Acacia tetragonophylla*, *Psydrax latifolia* and *Psydrax suaveolens* over *Ptilotus obovatus* and mixed *Maireana* and *Sclerolaena* species.	4	11.3%	22.3%
Low Open Woodland of *Acacia xiphophylla*, *Acacia victoriae*, *Acacia aneura* var. *aneura* over *Acacia tetragonophylla*, *Ptilotus obovatus*, *Senna* species and mixed species of *Maireana* and *Sclerolaena*.	10	11.2%	0%

Vegetation Community	Vegetation Community Code	% Christmas Creek Vegetation Assessment Area	% Study Area
CREEK LINES AND DRAINAGE			
Open Woodland of *Eucalyptus victrix*, *Eucalyptus camaldulensis* with pockets of *Acacia coriacea* subsp. *pendens* over *Grevillea wickhamii* subsp. *aprica*, *Petalostylis labicheoides* and *Acacia tumida* over *Triodia longiceps*, *Chrysopogon fallax*, *Themeda triandra*.	1	1.9%	2.6%
Low Woodland to Low Open Forest of *Acacia aneura* var. *aneura*, *Acacia citrinoviridis*, *Acacia pruinocarpa* over *Acacia tetragonophylla* and *Psydrax latifolia* over *Chrysopogon fallax*, *Stemodia viscosa*, *Blumea tenella*, *Themeda triandra*, *Triodia* and *Aristida*.	2	9.2%	13.4%
Closed Scrub to Tall Shrubland of *Acacia pruinocarpa*, *Acacia tumida*, *Acacia ancistrocarpa*, *Acacia maitlandii*, *Acacia kempeana*, *Acacia tetragonophylla* with occasional *Eucalyptus gamophylla* and *Corymbia deserticola* over *Triodia epactia*, *Themeda triandra* and *Aristida* species.	8	0.8%	0.6%
High Open Shrubland of *Acacia synchronicia* over *Aristida* species.	30	3.3%	3.6%
RANGES, HILLS AND HILLSLOPES			
Hummock Grassland of *Triodia basedowii* with pockets of *Triodia epactia* and *Triodia lanigera* with emergent patches of *Eucalyptus leucophloia*, *Corymbia deserticola* over *Acacia ancistrocarpa*, *Acacia pyrifolia*, *Hakea lorea* subsp. *lorea* over *Goodenia stobbsiana* and mixed *Senna* and *Ptilotus* species.	16 & 17	12.3%	37.6%

Figure 3.10: Mulga woodlands (*Acacia* spp.).

FIGURE 3.11: Hummock grassland, comprising spinifex (*Triodia* spp.) and scattered trees and shrubs.

FIGURE 3.12: Creek channels with eucalypt open forest.

ANIMAL LIFE

The research area has a rich and varied fauna, especially as regards birds and reptiles (see Table A3.1 in Appendix 3). When inundated the Fortescue Marsh 'supports up to 270,000 waterbirds, including more than 1% of the global populations of 14 species' (BirdLife International 2015). Resident bird populations mostly inhabit the mulga woodlands. Duck, swan and heron are found at the Marsh much of the year unless surface water becomes very scarce. Emu can probably be found throughout the area.

A wide range of reptiles live in the region with mulga vegetation having several species of lizard including skinks, geckos, legless lizards and one species of dragon. The medium-sized ridge-tailed monitor inhabits most parts of the study area with two other, smaller varanid species limited to particular habitats. The rare olive python is only found in the ranges near waterholes.

The two species of fish reported for the area probably migrate into the Marsh during flooding.

Thirteen species of mammals are found in the area. Most inhabit the spinifex grasslands and include the euro, northern quoll, spectacled hare-wallaby, two species of mouse and one type of dunnart. Red kangaroo are typically found in mulga woodlands, as are wallabies. Smaller mammals – *Antechinus*, *Planigale* and mouse – inhabit most vegetation communities. Rock wallaby and the great bilby are rare today but would previously have inhabited the ranges.

FORTESCUE MARSH AREA: MODELLED PALAEOENVIRONMENT

The following discussion presents a generalised model of past environments around the Fortescue Marsh from about the time humans first arrived here. The climatic and vegetation cover reconstructions are largely based on two indirect forms of information. This approach is necessary because, with one exception, there are no local proxies for the palaeoenvironment of the Fortescue Marsh area. The exception concerns the study by Rouillard and colleagues (Rouillard, Greenwood et al. 2016; Rouillard, Skrzypek et al. 2015; 2016) that documents palaeobotanical and sedimentological evidence from 14 Mile Pool at the eastern end of the Marsh. These data only pertain to roughly the last 2000 years.

Van der Kaars' palaeoenvironmental reconstructions for north-west Australia (van der Kaars and De Deckker 2002; van der Kaars, De Deckker and Gingele 2006) are the first and most important source of data to develop the model and are based on evidence from the GC 17 pollen core taken from the North West Shelf, offshore from the North West Cape. These data were used to reconstruct the vegetation cover for the area around the core site, as well as estimating the local rainfall and temperature conditions. Reeves, Bostock and colleagues (2013) provide useful complementary reconstruction relevant to the last 35,000 years through employing a full range of proxies to predict climatic conditions for different areas across northern Australia.

The second source we use to develop the model is the contemporary climate records for the Pilbara region (e.g. Bureau of Meteorology 2014a; 2014b). These data are relevant because we assume Pleistocene climatic conditions in the Fortescue Marsh area and around the North West Cape coast diverged in a comparable fashion to that occurring today. This conjecture is sustained on three grounds. First, there is little difference today in the seasonal and annual temperature patterns between the coast and the Marsh. Second, the exposed continental shelf was very narrow at the North West Cape during the last glacial period (van der Kaars and de Deckker 2002, 19); therefore, the effects of the Indian Ocean on this region's climate varied proportionally, much the same as those today, from the coast to the Marsh, some 650 km inland. Third, other key contributors to variability in rainfall, especially the orographic effect produced as the change in topography uplifts clouds of systems moving inland, were as important in the past as they are today.

These sources of information, when combined, support an approximation of rainfall and temperature patterns, as well as associated vegetation formations, over the last 40,000 years (e.g. see van der Kaars et al. 2006).

In addition, we follow the temporal frameworks proposed by Fitzsimmons and colleagues (2013, 90–3) and Gliganic and colleagues (2014) for the different Pleistocene and Holocene periods discussed in our palaeoenvironment model.

Appendix 3 presents a literature review of the current palaeoenvironmental reconstructions for areas of north-west Australia and the Pleistocene coastal plains.

40–30,000 YEARS AGO – CLOSE OF MARINE ISOTOPE STAGE (MIS) 3

Humid and cool conditions prevailed at the outset of this period. Mean maximum and minimum temperatures were lower than from those today, by 12% and 33% respectively. Total annual rainfall remained roughly unchanged from that 20,000 years earlier, roughly averaging 300 mm (about 160% less than today). Rainfall patterns, however, changed dramatically in this period. The greatest falls occurred in winter with a 135 mm average and ranged between 85 and 217 mm. Summer rainfall varied between 0 and 120 mm with an average of 65 mm.

These rainfall patterns and low temperatures suggest that the area of surface water on the Marsh would have probably reached 300 km^2 (Rouillard et al. 2015, Figure 6) more often than today. Also, flooding of the Marsh's north-eastern waterholes (a 40 km^2 coverage pattern) is likely to have occurred as often as drought conditions. Alluvial water in the creeks north of the Marsh would have been present more often and persisted for a relatively long time.

Open eucalypt woodlands with acacia and grass understorey occurred across the area. By the close of this period, it was replaced by a mixed eucalypt and *Gyrostemon* shrubland, with an understorey of broadleaf grasses and herbaceous groundcover.

30–18,000 YEARS AGO – LAST GLACIAL MAXIMUM

This period marks the driest time in the last 100,000 years. Temperature patterns varied little from those immediately before, but rainfall decreased by about 20%, or 100 mm, from the outset. At the peak of the Last Glacial Maximum, about 24–18,000 years ago, average annual rainfall was about 240 mm. Summer precipitation improved slightly and then effectively failed. Winter rainfall declined and then improved, but never re-established earlier averages. Surface water in the Fortescue Marsh diminished as droughts worsened and became common. Flood waters occurred from the occasional large winter rainfall events and lasted into March as low seasonal temperatures influenced a decrease in evaporation. Flooded areas in the Marsh were restricted to small areas along the north and east. The availability of potable water in the alluvium of the Chichester Range creeks was less predictable than today.

Mulga woodland with a grassy understorey covered the area until the time when rainfall reached its lowest levels. Then, grasslands consisting of chenopods, amaranths and asters became the prominent vegetation community in the region bordering the Marsh.

18–12,000 YEARS AGO – DEGLACIAL

This period was a time of dramatic climatic fluctuations. Annual rainfall averages returned to the same levels as those prior to the Last Glacial Maximum. Summer rainfall patterns similar to those of today became established and winter levels decreased to about 57 mm. Average temperatures increased only slightly and variability lessened.

The Fortescue Marsh probably experienced a greater number of flood events with the increased rainfall from monsoon events reaching the Fortescue River headwaters (Kuhnt et al. 2015), although the length of time floodwaters persisted in the Marsh, as well as their maximum extent, probably decreased. However, these matters and the periodicity of flood events are difficult to judge.

The primary vegetation in the area was open mulga woodlands.

Toward 12,000 years ago there was an upsurge in humidity. Temperatures increased. The rise in sea levels and sea surface temperatures promoted the establishment of summer monsoon weather patterns. Annual average rainfall was in the order of 490 mm, 50% greater than that today. Rainfall patterns were dominated by summer rains that probably averaged 140 mm. Winter rainfall continued to decrease.

Marsh flooding events mirrored those today. However, the increased rainfall probably produced more frequent and/or more intense events, and surface waters covering the eastern extents of the Marsh could have been common. Alluvial water in the creeks to the north of the Marsh became more regular.

12–8000 YEARS AGO – EARLY HOLOCENE

Temperatures continued to rise and rainfall, resulting from monsoon events, intensified and remained so until a thousand years or so after the close of this period, when substantial drier conditions returned (Ishiwa et al. 2019; Kuhnt et al. 2015). Surface water across many areas of the Fortescue Marsh would probably have been a recurrent feature at this time. Open eucalypt woodlands interspersed with mulga woodlands probably vegetated the area.

8–4000 YEARS AGO – MIDDLE HOLOCENE

Temperatures peaked about the beginning of this period and average precipitation was about 450 mm, ranging between 345 and 714 mm. The ratio of summer to winter precipitation was roughly three to one. Run-off and groundwater accumulation in the creek systems increased at this time. The Marsh would have continued to have substantial amounts of floodwaters. Open eucalypt woodlands dominated the region's vegetation.

By the close of the period, drier conditions returned, and temperatures moderated. Weather conditions and vegetation patterns began trending toward those today.

4000–PRESENT – LATE HOLOCENE

The mean temperature range decreased over the period. The general rainfall pattern changed with mean summer rainfall decreasing and winter rains increasing. Contemporary vegetation patterns were probably established during the late Holocene.

Rouillard's research (Rouillard, Greenwood et al. 2016; Rouillard, Skrzypek et al. 2016) indicates that a long period of extreme drought with only moderate flooding began sometime before about 2000 BP. These conditions changed around 1200 years ago by a 'boom/bust' cycle of high-volume flood events. These conditions persisted until about 400 years ago. This was followed by a period of regular Fortescue River flows into the Marsh broken by episodic flooding events. Current rainfall patterns began about 300 years ago, and since this time there have been several extreme flooding events.

It is important to note that recent research (O'Donnell et al. 2015) indicates that the contribution of the El Niño Southern Oscillation (ENSO) to rainfall in north-west Australia is more variable than is commonly thought to be the case elsewhere in Australia (e.g. Williams, et al. 2010).

CULTURAL CONTEXT

There are few anthropological records for most Pilbara Aboriginal groups. Early reports (e.g. Brown 1912, 1913; Clement 1903; Durlacher 2013; Yabaroo 1899), more contemporary and quite significant works (e.g. Brandenstein 1967, 1970a, 1970b, 1973; Tindale 1974) and recent Aboriginal remembrances (e.g. Guruma Elders Group et al. 2001; Juluwarlu Aboriginal Corporation 2007; Olive 1997) all provide information about various aspects of the region's Aboriginal peoples. Recently, our understanding has grown as a result of mining and exploration developments. Developers are now required to consult with Aboriginal elders in order to mitigate any impacts on places of special significance. This has resulted in a large number of anthropological reports; most, however, are not publicly available due to a range of restrictions. The native title process has also generated a substantial body of anthropological investigations, but these reports are also not generally accessible due to confidentiality concerns.

Published information about particular aspects of Nyiyaparli culture is sparse. Neighbouring groups living to the north and west of the Nyiyaparli have received considerably more attention (see Appendix 3). The Western Desert Martu peoples, who live to the east in the Western Desert, have, in particular, been carefully studied. The social systems of all these groups share much in common with the groups living in the Pilbara (Dench 1987; Tonkinson 1978, fn. 3 p. 45). The Martu subsistence patterns (e.g. R.B. Bird and D.W. Bird 2008; Codding 2011; Walsh 2008) are well-understood and, although the environment of the Pilbara differs in crucial ways from the Western Desert, there are some common elements. There continue to be close ties between the Martu and Nyiyaparli. Indeed, the longstanding Martu community of Jigalong is actually in Nyiyaparli country (Tonkinson 1974, 43, 112). Therefore, this documentary evidence, when combined with key anthropological studies and other cultural documentation of Pilbara Aborigines, provides a reasonable foundation for predicting the immediate pre-contact culture of the ancestors of the Nyiyaparli living in and around the study area.

MODELLED ABORIGINAL CULTURE FOR THE FORTESCUE MARSH AREA
COUNTRY AND LANGUAGE

Nyiyaparli country is around the headwaters of the Fortescue River near the present-day town of Newman (Nyiyaparli Community, Bird and McDonald 2015; Wangka Maya Pilbara Aboriginal Language Centre 2012, iii). It includes the Fortescue Marsh to the north, breakaway country to the northeast near the headwaters of the Oakover Creek and the rugged Ophthalmia Range to the west, and extends into the Little Sandy Desert to Jigalong (Figure 3.13). Nyiyaparli country thus lies around the boundary of the Pilbara region and the Western Desert. The Nyiyaparli speak a language belonging to the Ngayardic linguistic group found among people living across a vast region extending from the Pilbara coast into the Little Sandy Desert and south into the Hamersley Range.

MYTHOLOGY AND CEREMONY

For the Nyiyaparli all aspects of their life emanate from *Kukutpa* (the Dreaming), when the ancestors shaped the land and brought forth life during their travels (McDonald and Coldrick, in press; Nyiyaparli Community, Bird and McDonald 2015, 4). The Fortescue Marsh (Martuyitha) and the Fortescue River and its tributaries form the life-giving force the ancestors created to sustain the natural environment, its people and their culture.

Nyiyaparli country abounds with places belonging to *Kukutpa* and to stories about the ancestors. The Marsh's creation, as told by a Nyiyaparli elder, began when

> yurtupa [snake] come across the Dingo sing out at the side of the river. All the sea water went back and just left the salt what's in the Marsh now … [and] yurtupa turned to stone … The story comes from past Newman and comes right through the Marsh; it follows the water but is about the land as well. (Goode 2009, 18)

A mythological songline follows the northern shore of the Marsh and is marked by several freshwater pools, *yinta*, found there (see Brandenstein

1973) (Figure 3.7). The songs sung at these places form a part of rainmaking ceremonies for the renewal of Nyiyaparli territory.

Mangun (Law) was laid down by the ancestors during the Dreaming so that people understood how country came about and what teachings they must follow to protect the land. The Nyiyaparli maintained prime responsibility as caretakers for the significant places. In traditional times, young men undergoing initiation camped at these places, where elders taught them stories about Nyiyaparli country.

A major sacred site named Mankarlyirrkurra is situated in Nyiyaparli country. It was a focal point for significant Dreaming Tracks, as well as special places for both men and women.[6] It also served as a law ground where

---

6 Edward McDonald, personal conversation, 2016.

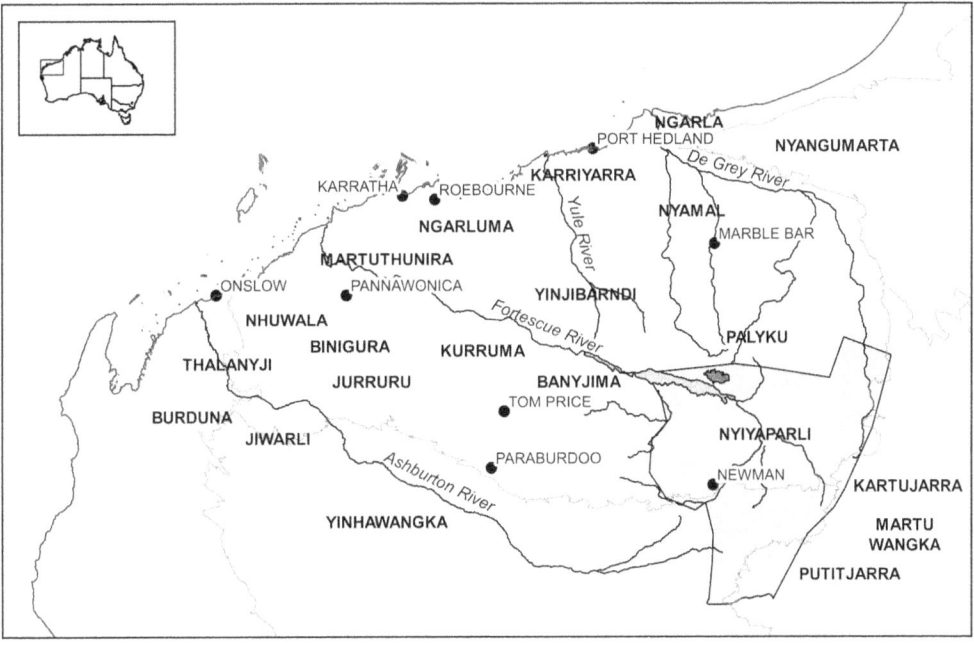

FIGURE 3.13: Language map of the Pilbara region showing the boundary of the Nyiyaparli Native Title Determination. Data from Wangka Maya Pilbara Aboriginal Language Centre (http://www.wangkamaya.org.au/pilbara-languages/indigenous-languages-of-australia) and the National Native Title Tribunal (http://www.nntt.gov.au/assistance/Geospatial/Pages/DataDownload.aspx).

young men from the Nyiyaparli, Banyjima and Palyku were initiated (Brandenstein 1972; Palmer 1977).

Numerous other ceremonial sites are recorded for the region (Brandenstein 1972; Green 2004, as cited in Goode 2009, 13; Palmer 1977). Many occur along the Marsh shores and are where specific rituals were performed to increase the numbers of plants and animals the people used for food.

SOCIAL SYSTEM

Kinship centred on relationships through the father's line (patrifiliation), and this formed the framework for virtually all interpersonal relationships. There was a strong desire for children to be born near a sacred site or a group of these sites with which their father was closely associated (e.g. Berndt 1959). Boys inherited responsibility to look after these sites and maintain totemic affiliation with them. They also retained access to the resources found within their father's estate. Therefore, a considerable portion of young men's lives was spent in and around their father's estate. Young girls moved to their husband's country after they were married and access to their father's country was often impractical. The kinship system also included a network of relations that extended well beyond where one lived and was sustained through siblings and cousins of the same sex, who referred to each other as brother and sister.

A complex arrangement of intergenerational 'cohorts', now referred to as 'sections' by anthropologists (e.g. Radcliffe-Brown 1931), formed the second major element of the social system. These associations were important to virtually every aspect of one's life. For example, people commonly referred to one another by their section, rather than personal, name when visiting a camp on a different estate. This practice allowed visitors arriving from distant estates to be easily linked to section members at the camp and ensured adherence to strict social conventions imposed by kinship practices. Section alignment took on different arrangements when several local groups came together for ceremonial, ritual or other important purposes (e.g. see Tonkinson 1978, Figure 3-5). The section system was, therefore, essential to sustaining a web of relationships extending well beyond one local estate to include other areas in the Pilbara and the Western Desert (Brown 1913;

Dench 1987; Tonkinson 1978, 45, fn. 3, 55–6). So, the Nyiyaparli and their neighbours were widely joined in a network of interdependence through kinship, marriage, friendship, trade and ritual, as was the case with many Aboriginal groups (e.g. Stanner 1965, 11). Moreover, all these peoples maintained communal totemic sites that comprised elements of a far-reaching and intertwined ritual landscape.

SETTLEMENT PATTERNS

The Nyiyaparli lived in several small groups scattered across their country, and usually near prominent waterholes. The settlement pattern followed by the people and members of their social network was very fluid. Each group consisted of six to 30 people belonging to one or more related families (e.g. Peterson 1983; Radcliffe-Brown 1931; Tonkinson 1978, 53). The married women in the group were commonly born and raised elsewhere, often among distant groups who frequently spoke different dialects, or even a different language.

A senior male elder led the group and was related to most men and unmarried women in the group through a common male ancestor. The core group area, commonly referred to as an 'estate' by anthropologists (e.g. Stanner 1965), included several waterholes. At least one of these was named and prominently known outside the estate. Totemic sites were also found in the area and initiated men living on the estate regularly conducted prescribed rituals to maintain these sites.

Tracts of land adjacent to an estate were also visited. This area, termed a 'range' (e.g. Stanner 1965), was a vital extension to a group's approach to accessing resources and critical when key resources in their estate became depleted or when severe climatic conditions prevailed.

Large gatherings of people formed the other primary type of group settlement. Seasonal factors often produced conditions where there was an abundance of food and water. The flooding of the Fortescue Marsh and the arrival of vast numbers of waterbirds would have been such occasions. The Nyiyaparli and their neighbours came together at these times for rituals and other ceremonial activities. When speaking about people living in the Western Desert, Berndt (1959, 103–4, fn. 79), for example, estimated upwards of possibly 200–300 people came together under such favourable 'economic' circumstances.

People lived at aggregation sites, such as the regional law ground Mankarlyirrkurra near the Fortescue Marsh, for as long as social relations remained generally friendly and food was plentiful. Male initiation and other men's rituals (e.g. celebration of events of the Dreaming associated with the area) often required a large number of participants and were, therefore, common occurrences at these gatherings. Intergroup gift exchange, celebrations and dancing were also important activities.

PLANT AND ASSOCIATED INSECT FOOD RESOURCES

The people living in the Fortescue Marsh area used a wide range of plant resources across several environmental zones. There are too many to review here and the following discussion concentrates on those plant communities found in the study area today, as documented by vegetation mapping associated with the Christmas Creek–Cloudbreak development (Figure 3.9). While there seem to be abundant resources (Tables 3.2, A3.1), economic plants are on the whole relatively scarce in and around the Fortescue Marsh area, and where they do occur they appear as patches (FMG 2013, Appendix F–G).

Three economic plant species – *Acacia aneura* (mulga), *Eucalyptus victrix* (coolibah) and *Ipomea muelleri* (poison morning glory) – probably comprise the most reliable plant foods in the study area. *Acacia* species make up the dominant source of plant and associated insect food in the area. Possibly not all *Acacia* species were exploited for starch (e.g. O'Connell and Hawkes 1984). Nevertheless, of the nine *Acacia* species present today, *Acacia aneura* seems most likely to have been a principal food source in the past. The seeds (*parrkala*), which were ground to make flour, are ready for harvest late spring to early summer. They are widely reported as a food source, and mulga occurs in abundance across more than 50% of the study area, along creek lines in the hills and plains, as well as covering much of the plains (Table 3.1). Various species of yam (e.g. *Ipomoea*) have been recorded as important in the diet of various Aboriginal groups across the Pilbara and Western Desert (e.g. Bindon 1998, 161–2; Hayes and Hayes

2007, 18–9; Walsh 2008). In the study area, *Ipomoea muelleri* is common along creeks and across the adjacent plains. There is no specific information about the use of *Ipomoea muelleri* for the region, although Crawford (1982, 69) recorded its use at Kalumburu in the Kimberley. Its tubers probably served as another important starch resource. *Triodia epactia* (spinifex) seeds, which ripened in spring, may have formed a starch resource. This plant is limited to small isolated patches in the ranges and, therefore, would probably not have been an abundant food source. Different species of spinifex, however, also had a range of non-food uses (Nyiyaparli Community, Bird and McDonald 2015, 14).

Honey, gum and lerp were supplementary foods sourced from many plants found across much of the area. Eucalypts, especially *E. victrix*, which commonly grow along the creeks in the hills, would have been a major source for these delicacies.

Along the Marsh, just south of the study area, there are several other important plant foods. These include the bush onion (*Cyperus bulbosus*), which is plentiful across the flats, and *Typha* sp., mostly found near waterholes. If present in sufficient quantities, *Typha* was very likely to have been among the staple food resources for Aboriginal people (e.g. Young and Vitenbergs 2007, 137), while bush onion (*ngarlku*) is well documented as a staple resource throughout the region (e.g. Bindon 1998, 97; Nyiyaparli Community, Bird and McDonald 2015, 12; Walsh 2008, 172).

ANIMAL RESOURCES

There is a variety of animal resources in the Fortescue Marsh area. The hills and ranges were important hunting areas. Euro (hill kangaroos), spectacled wallaby and northern quoll were among the most sought-after game animals. Fire drives were used to concentrate euros at particular localities where they could be easily dispatched (e.g. Durlacher 2013, 18). The people probably also used fire when hunting lizard. Other quarry – emu, quail and cockatoo – was caught by means of blinds, traps and lures (e.g. Clements 1903; Durlacher 2013, 77).

Fishing was not a prominent activity in the study area. However, the nearby Marsh would have become an important resource area when in

TABLE 3.2: Plant species occurring in the study area and their documented uses for food and material culture in the Pilbara and adjacent areas. Species listed are those whose area coverage within the sample localities in different vegetation communities totalled more than 10% (see FMG 2013, Appendix F).

Species	Common Name	Study Area Vegetation Community (See Table 3.10)
Acacia ancistrocarpa	Fitzroy wattle	8, 17
A. aneura	broad leaf mulga	1, 2, 3, 4
A. citronoviridis	black mulga	2, 3
A. coriaceae	weeping wire-wood	1
A. kempeana	witchetty bush	8
A. maitlandii	spiky wattle	8
A. pruinocarpa	gidgee	2, 3, 8
A. pyrifolia	kanji or ranji bush	17
A. synchronicia	bardi bush	2, 3, 30
A. tetragonophylla	dead finish	2, 3, 4, 8
A. tumida	pindan wattle	1, 2, 8
A. victoriae	gundabluey wattle	4
A. xiphophylla	snakewood	4, 30
Corymbia deserticola	desert bloodwood	8, 17
Corymbia [hamersleyana]	Pilbara bloodwood	8, 17
Cyperus bulbosus	bush onion	8
C. vaginatus	stiff flat-sedge	8
Enchylaena tomentosa	barrier saltbush	2

Ethnographic sources: (1) Bindon 1998; (2) Clement 1903; (3) Crawford 1982; (4) Guruma Elders Group et al. 2001; (5) Hayes & Hayes 2007; (6) Juluwarlu Aboriginal Corporation 2007; (7) Nyiyaparli Community et al 2015; (8) Pitman 2010; (9) Veth and Walsh 1988; (10) Walsh 2008; (11) Young and Vitenbergs 2007.

Documented Food Part Eaten	Documented Material Culture	Ethnographic Sources
seeds		4, 5
seeds, fruit, gum, gall	spears, boomerangs, spear throwers, clubs, digging sticks, firesticks	1, 4, 6, 11
grubs	fighting sticks, boomerangs, spears, spear throwers,	5, 11
seeds		1, 5, 10
grubs		1
gum		4
gum, sap		4, 6, 10, 11
seeds, gum		4, 6
lerp, grubs		5, 11
seeds	clubs, boomerangs	1, 4, 5, 10
seed pod, ? seeds, grubs	hunting spears	1, 4, 6, 10
seeds, grubs		1
seeds, gum, grubs	boomerangs, spear shafts (roots)	1, 4, 5, 6, 10
honey		5
fruit, honey, gum, galls, lerp		6, 11
tuber		1, 4, 7
tuber	fibre	11
fruit		11

TABLE 3.2: *Continued*

SPECIES	COMMON NAME	STUDY AREA VEGETATION COMMUNITY *(See Table 3.10)*
Eucalyptus camaldulensis	river gum	1
E. gamophylla	blue mallee	8
E. leucophloia	snappy gum	17
E. victrix	coolibah	1
Grevillea wickhami	holly leaved grevillea	1, 3
Hakea lorea	corkwood hakea	17
Hibiscus panduriformis	yellow hibiscus	1
Ipomea muelleri	poison morning glory	1, 2, 3
Panicum sp.		17
Psydrax latifolia	native plum or native currant	2, 3, 4
P. suaveolens	wild currant	4
Scaevola spinescens	prickly fanflower	2
Trioda basedowii	hard spinifex	17
Triodia epactia	spinifex	8, 17
Triodia pungens	soft spinifex	4
Triodia wiseana	buck spinifex	17
Triodia spp.	spinifex	2, 3

Ethnographic sources: (1) Bindon 1998; (2) Clement 1903; (3) Crawford 1982; (4) Guruma Elders Group et al. 2001; (5) Hayes & Hayes 2007; (6) Juluwarlu Aboriginal Corporation 2007; (7) Nyiyaparli Community et al 2015; (8) Pitman 2010; (9) Veth and Walsh 1988; (10) Walsh 2008; (11) Young and Vitenbergs 2007.

NATURAL ENVIRONMENT AND CULTURAL CONTEXTS | 87

Documented Food Part Eaten	Documented Material Culture	Ethnographic Sources
seeds, honey, gum, grubs, lerp	spears, shields	1, 4, 6, 10
seeds, nectar		1
honey, gum, gall, lerp	shields, boomerangs, digging sticks, bowls	1, 4, 6, 11
honey, gum		4, 6
gum		1, 6
nectar	boomerangs, water container	4, 5, 6, 11
flower stamen		1
tuber		3
seeds		9
fruit		4, 5, 6, 11
fruit		11
fruit		1
?seeds	resin	5
?seeds	resin	5
	shelters, resin	1
seeds		1
seeds	resin	2, 4, 8, 11

TABLE 3.3: The distribution of ethnographically documented plant resources in different vegetation communities in the Christmas Creek study area. Number of species indicated in parentheses.

Vegetation community (code)	Widely available: plant foods	Patchy availability: plant food
RANGES AND HILLS (INC. CREEK LINES)		
Open Eucalypt Woodland (1)	seeds (1), tuber (1), fruit (1), honey (1), gum (2), gall (1)	seeds (1), ? seeds (1), seed pod (1), honey (1), flower stamen (1), lerp (1), grubs (2)
Hummock Grasslands (17)	nil	seeds (4), fruit (1), honey (3), nectar (1), gum (3), lerp (2), galls (2)
CREEKS AND DRAINAGE LINES (PLAINS)		
Low Mulga Woodland (2)	seeds (1), tuber (1), fruit (1), gum (1), gall (1).	seeds (2), ? seeds (1), fruit (3), sap (1), lerp (1), gum (1), grub (1)
Closed Mulga Scrub/Tall Shrubland (8)	nil	tuber (2), seeds (4), ? seeds (1), seed pod (1), fruit (1), nectar (1), sap (1), gum (2), lerp (1), grubs (2), gall (1)
FLATS AND BROAD PLAINS		
Low Mulga Woodland/Open Forest (3)	seeds (1), tuber (1), fruit (1), gum (1), gall (1)	seeds (2), ? seeds (1), fruit (2), sap (1), lerp (1), gum (2), grub (1)
Low Open Mulga Woodland (4)	seeds (1), tuber (1), fruit (1), gum (1), gall (1)	seeds (4), fruits (3), gum (2), grub (2), gall (1)
High Open Shrubland (30)	nil	lerp (1), grubs (1)

Widely available: plant materials – cultural uses	Patchy availability: plant materials – cultural uses
spears (1), boomerangs (1), spear (1), throwers (1), clubs (1), digging sticks (1), firesticks (1)	hunting spears (1), shields (1)
nil	shields (1), boomerangs (1), digging sticks (1), bowls (1), water container (1), resin (1)
spears (1), boomerangs (1), spear throwers (1), clubs (1), digging sticks (1), firesticks (1)	spears (1), boomerangs (2), spear throwers (1), clubs (1), fighting sticks (1), resin (1)
nil	hunting spears (1), boomerangs (1), clubs (1), resin (1), fibre (1)
spears (1), boomerangs (1), spear throwers (1), clubs (1), digging sticks (1), firesticks (1)	spears (1), spear throwers (2), boomerangs (2), fighting sticks (1), clubs (1), resin (1)
spears (1), boomerangs (1), spear throwers (1), clubs (1), digging sticks (1), firesticks (1)	spears (1), spear throwers (1), boomerangs (2), clubs (1)
nil	nil

flood. Fish were more commonly found in pools further upstream along the Fortescue River. Netting fish was common, as was the use of fish 'poison' (*Tribulus suberosus*) (Guruma Elders Group et al. 2001, 105; Young and Vitenbergs 2007, 98) to stun fish that were scooped up from the water (Clement 1903).

MATERIAL CULTURE

Plants suitable for the production of wooden tools occur across much of the study area. The mulga woodlands were the best sources for raw materials for the manufacture of different types of spears, spear throwers, boomerangs, clubs, shields, digging sticks and musical instruments (Table 3.3). Ceremonial boards (Tindale 1974, 289) and message sticks (Durlacher 2013, 10) were among the other important wooden items in the inventory of material culture. Eucalypts, especially snappy gum (*Eucalyptus leucophloia*), and snakewood (*Acacia xiphophylla*), which commonly grow in the hills along creek lines and near water, were the source of wood to manufacture *yandi* – long, shallow containers also used for winnowing seeds. Spinifex fibre was collected from the hummock grasslands in the ranges and used to produce cord for general use (e.g. making bags), and for nets used to fish and trap birds (e.g. Guruma Elders Group et al. 2001, 96). Spinifex resin also provided glue for a range of purposes, such as attaching spear heads to their shafts. Spinifex was also used for making shelters (Nyiyaparli Community, Bird and McDonald 2015, 14).

Nyiyaparli people also used a variety of flaked stone and ground stone tools (e.g. Clement 1903; Guruma Elders Group et al. 2001, 87–88; Nyiyaparli Community, Bird and McDonald 2015). Spear heads were probably manufactured using freehand percussion techniques; however, Clement (1903, 4) mentioned Aboriginal peoples in the coastal Pilbara area using a kangaroo bone for pressure flaking. Stone scrapers or adzes were hafted to a spear thrower (*walparra*) with spinifex resin. This tool was commonly employed when carving or shaving wood. Ground stone tools included axes (*pulpu*) and whetstones (Guruma Elders Group et al. 2001, 87). Axes were used in the manufacture of a range of wooden items, including boomerangs. There were two stones used for seed grinding: millstone and top stone. These were often left at or near campsites, sometimes close to one another (Guruma Elders Group et al. 2001, 87).

CONCLUSION

From a traditional Aboriginal perspective of resource usage, the key environmental units in the study area would have been the ranges and the adjacent escarpment, the Quaternary outwash plains and the Fortescue Marsh. Each contains a suitable range of resources that could be the focus for small-scale human activities, but these would have been intermittent and mostly constrained to particular seasons.

For example, the Fortescue Marsh has plentiful fish, plant tubers and fresh water resources in early spring. This typically happens one year in four, when large rainfall events occur in the Fortescue River's upper catchment and the Marsh and its northern shoreline is flooded. When the Marsh experiences extensive flooding, on less frequent occasions, large quantities of waterfowl visit the area. This would have attracted large numbers of Aboriginal peoples. At other times, however, the Marsh's food resources are, at best, scarce, and sources for making stone and wooden tools are for the most part absent. In the ranges, on the other hand, plant and animal foods are commonly available off and on throughout the year. Their occurrence, however, is widely distributed. Raw material – stone and suitable timbers – for the manufacture of tools was abundant. Sources of potable water are commonly small pools found in isolated localities, and available only at the best of times. Key resources are most reliably present in the mulga woodlands, which dominate the outwash plains. Water in this area would be available as soaks or, seasonally, in pools along watercourses.

Therefore, the study area's environment would have been capable of supporting small, transient Aboriginal groups. We would expect Aboriginal occupation of the region during the entire possible period of Aboriginal habitation. The Last Glacial Maximum, however, was the only time when Aboriginal visitation to the Fortescue Marsh region was probably so infrequent that the associated cultural remains would be archaeologically invisible.

CHAPTER 4

SURFACE ARTEFACT SCATTERS

As discussed in Chapter 2, surface artefact scatters are the most common site type in the survey area, and indeed most of Australia. Archaeologists have struggled to develop effective methods to analyse surface artefact scatters and to integrate them into broader archaeological research programs. As their name implies, these are aggregations of stone artefacts visible on the ground surface. In many areas the occurrence of stone artefacts on the surface forms a more or less continuous distribution, commonly referred to as the background scatter. Distinguishing between concentrations of surface artefacts that can be identified as sites and the general background scatter is problematic and depends on characteristics of the local and regional archaeological record. The definition of a site is contingent on a range of local factors that include not only locations of past activities, but also natural processes of exposure and visibility, administrative and legal requirements and research design. Since this project is framed within compliance archaeology, it is based on those discrete sites that could be assessed in relation to the requirements of Western Australia's Aboriginal Heritage Act.

Reduction areas are a specific class of surface artefact scatter. The term reduction area refers to a cluster of artefacts that can be inferred to represent the flaking of a core. Often, some or all of the artefacts in a reduction area can be refitted, indicating that the artefacts may represent an individual knapping event. Alternatively, characteristics of the raw material, such as colour, grain size and cortex, indicate that the artefacts are derived from the same source material. This grouping of artefacts by distinctive raw material features is sometimes called Minimum Analytical Nodule Analysis (MANA) (Andrefsky 2009, 84–5). Reduction areas may form part of a broader surface artefact scatter, or may occur in isolation. The presence of discrete reduction areas can generally be taken to indicate that the surface artefact scatter is relatively undisturbed by processes such as sheet-wash. About 20% of surface artefact scatters in the analysed sample included one or more reduction areas. These records are relatively rare in the archaeological record, which can more commonly be described as a time-transgressive aggregation of numerous unrelated individual events (Stern 2015).

This analysis of surface artefacts in the Christmas Creek study area focuses on surface artefact scatters, reduction areas and isolated artefacts (see Appendix 1 for specific definitions and description of attributes recorded). Our discussion considers the evidence at different scales and from different perspectives, and is presented in two parts: a site-based distribution analysis and a locality-based assemblage analysis. We begin with a conventional site-based description of the distribution of archaeological remains in the whole project area in relation to the natural environment. Here, we discuss the characteristics and distribution of surface artefact sites defined according to the standard archaeological conventions used in the survey. However, a site-based approach to assemblage analysis presents practical difficulties because of the small size of most individual site assemblages and associated high levels of inter-site variability. Interpreting such assemblages is difficult. Indeed, they may simply be viewed as location markers of past activity, and consequently they are often characterised as having low significance. Therefore, we describe patterning in stone artefact assemblages in the survey area from the perspective of an analysis of sample assemblages defined on a locality basis. These assemblages were defined at a landscape scale and comprise all the stone artefacts recorded at a particular locality. This alternative approach takes advantage of the comprehensive survey coverage in the study area to allow conventional archaeological site-based data recorded for compliance purposes to be recombined for a landscape scale analysis using a non-site approach.

CHARACTERISTICS AND DISTRIBUTION OF SURFACE ARTEFACT SCATTER SITES

A total of 827 surface artefact scatters was recorded in the project area. Some formed part of multi-component sites that included reduction areas, rockshelters, quarries and scarred trees. Discrete reduction areas were also recorded in isolation. Adding these to the analysis gave a total of 911 artefact scatters.

In the course of primary field recording for most artefact scatters, a boundary was determined, length and width were recorded and a site plan drawn (see Appendix 1 for a description of recording methods and definition of attributes). Artefact density, including maximum, minimum and mean for large sites, was estimated in the field, and the total likely artefact population extrapolated. In this analysis, surface area is used as the primary indicator of site size. Artefact density is less consistently recorded and clearly varies considerably within sites. Density estimates also depend on the field selection of sample squares for detailed recording, and are susceptible to inconsistencies between observers. Archae-aus classifies sites into four size categories based on area determined from the polygon defining the site boundary:

- Small <2500 m^2
- Medium 2500 to <7500 m^2
- Large 7500 to <50,000 m^2
- Extensive >50,000 m^2.

Archae-aus records artefact density, based on field estimates, using four categories:

- Low <0.15/m^2
- Medium 0.15–1/m^2
- High 1–10/m^2
- Very High >10/m^2.

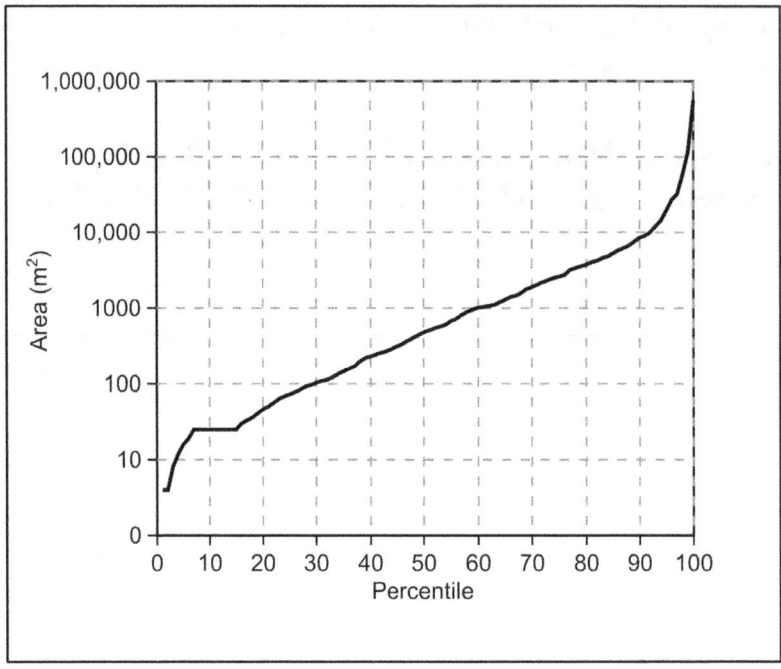

FIGURE 4.1: Log10 percentile distribution of area for surface artefact scatters. (Mean=5522±27,278 m²; median=479 m²; range 0.25–531,978).

Artefact scatters vary greatly in terms of area and the estimated number and density of artefacts. Most, however, are small with low artefact density. Site size and the number and density of artefacts all have skewed continuous distributions with many small low-density sites and relatively few large and dense sites (Figure 4.1).

The surface area of artefact scatters in the study area shows a continuous distribution with breaks at about 25 m² and about 10,000 m² (Figure 4.1). Log size classes are used here as an alternative to the original Archae-aus classification in order to determine whether any variation may be identified among small artefact scatters. Four classes were created (<100, <1000, <10,000, >10,000 m²). A very small number of sites (1%) were recorded as larger than 100,000 m².

The Christmas Creek study area can be divided into two parts: the ranges, comprising the rugged terrain of the Chichester Range escarpment, and the alluvial and colluvial plains. The overall distribution of artefact scatters and isolated artefacts in the study area suggests that, while artefacts are widely

TABLE 4.1: Distribution of surface artefact scatters in relation to major landforms.

	Ranges	%	Plains	%	Total	%
<100 m²	104	41.6	162	24.8	266	29.5
<1000 m²	68	27.2	208	31.9	276	30.6
<10000 m²	63	25.2	226	34.7	289	32.0
>10000 m²	15	6.0	56	8.6	71	7.9
Small	199	79.6	470	72.1	669	74.2
Medium	30	12	105	16.1	135	15.0
Large	17	6.8	64	9.8	81	9.0
Extensive	4	1.6	13	2.0	17	1.9
TOTAL	250		652		902	

distributed throughout, surface archaeological material is more densely distributed across the plains than in the ranges (Table 4.1). Surface scatters in the ranges tend to be smaller with higher proportions of scatters falling into the smaller size classes. The linear patterning of sites suggests a spatial association between sites and the numerous ephemeral watercourses (Figure 4.2).

The distribution of sites classified by size was analysed with respect to vegetation formations identified during detailed vegetation mapping undertaken in the Cloudbreak–Christmas Creek area as part of environmental compliance processes (see discussion in Chapter 3 and Appendix 2, and Table 3.1). In the ranges, Hummock Grassland dominated by spinifex (*Triodia* spp.) is the main vegetation community (VC 17), with Open Eucalypt Woodland (VC 1) and Low Mulga Woodland (VC 2) often occurring along creek lines. The plains are dominated by various Mulga Woodland formations (VC 2, 3 and 4), differentiated by the structure of tree cover and the occurrence of particular associations of tree and understorey species. The

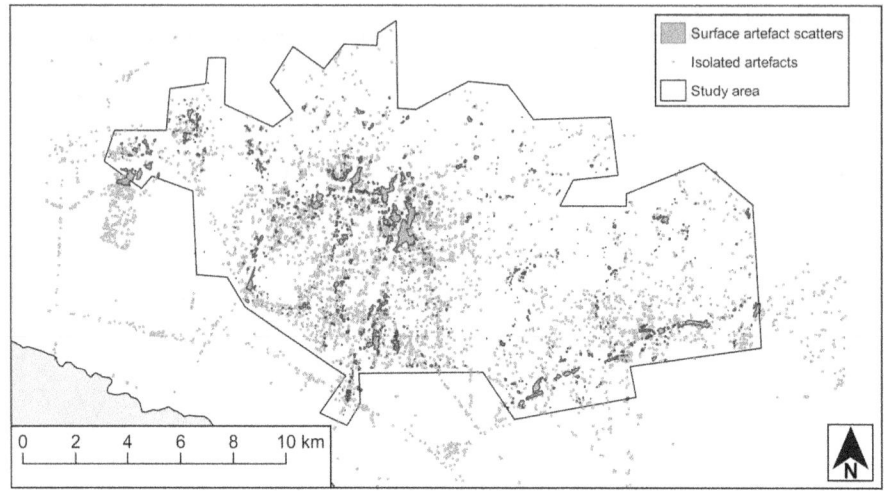

FIGURE 4.2: Map showing general distribution of surface artefact scatters and isolated artefacts.

general distribution pattern is related to distance from creek lines. Major creek lines also carry patches of Open Eucalypt Woodland (VC 1) and Mulga Woodlands (VC 2, 3 and 4). Closed Acacia Scrub to Tall Shrubland (VC 8) and High Open Acacia Shrubland (VC 30), both exhibiting sparse tree cover, appear across the stony hardpan plains.

Generally, sites in the Christmas Creek study area are preferentially associated with Low Mulga Woodlands and Open Forest (VC 3) and underrepresented in Hummock Grassland (VC 17) (Figure 4.3). This distribution effectively mirrors the generally denser distribution of sites in the plains, which mainly carry mulga woodlands, rather than in the ranges, where hummock grassland predominates (Table 4.2, Figure 4.2).

When site size is taken into account, this pattern also holds for the broader size classes used by Archae-aus. However, when the log size classes are used to investigate vegetation associations among smaller sites, those less than 100 m^2 in area are distributed in proportion to the occurrence of various vegetation formations (Table 4.2). While the distribution of the smallest sites appears effectively random, Figure 4.3 shows that larger sites are more likely to be associated with Open Eucalypt Woodland along creek lines (VC 1) and Low Mulga Woodlands and Open Forest (VC 3).

TABLE 4.2: Distribution of surface artefact scatters and isolated artefacts in relation to vegetation formations.

	1	17	2	8	3	4	30	
% survey area	5.2	22.7	15.7	0.8	29.3	21.2	5.1	
All sites	47	205	142	7	264	191	46	902
Archae aus size class								
Small	29	174	98	1	177	159	31	669
Medium	10	24	24	2	44	25	6	135
Large	6	6	18	2	34	7	8	81
Extensive	2	1	2	2	9	0	1	17
Log size class								
<100 m²	8	82	38	1	61	68	8	266
<1000 m²	14	65	41	0	77	64	15	276
<10000 m²	17	54	51	2	96	54	15	289
>10000 m²	8	4	12	4	30	5	8	71

Key to vegetation formation codes (see Table 3.1): 1. Open Eucalypt Woodland; 2. Low Mulga Woodland; 3. Low Mulga Woodland/Open Forest; 4. Low Open Mulga Woodland; 8. Closed Mulga Scrub/Tall Shrubland; 17. Hummock Grassland; 30. High Open Shrubland.

One possible interpretation of this result is that very small sites should be considered part of the background scatter. In other words, the result is an artefact of a continuous distribution of surface archaeological remains, subdivided for the purposes of analysis or recording in accordance with the prevailing compliance requirements. However, Figure 4.3 also indicates that distribution of isolated artefacts with respect to vegetation is similar to that of sites; that is, isolated artefacts are under-represented in spinifex grasslands (VC 17) and over-represented in mulga woodlands (VC 3 and

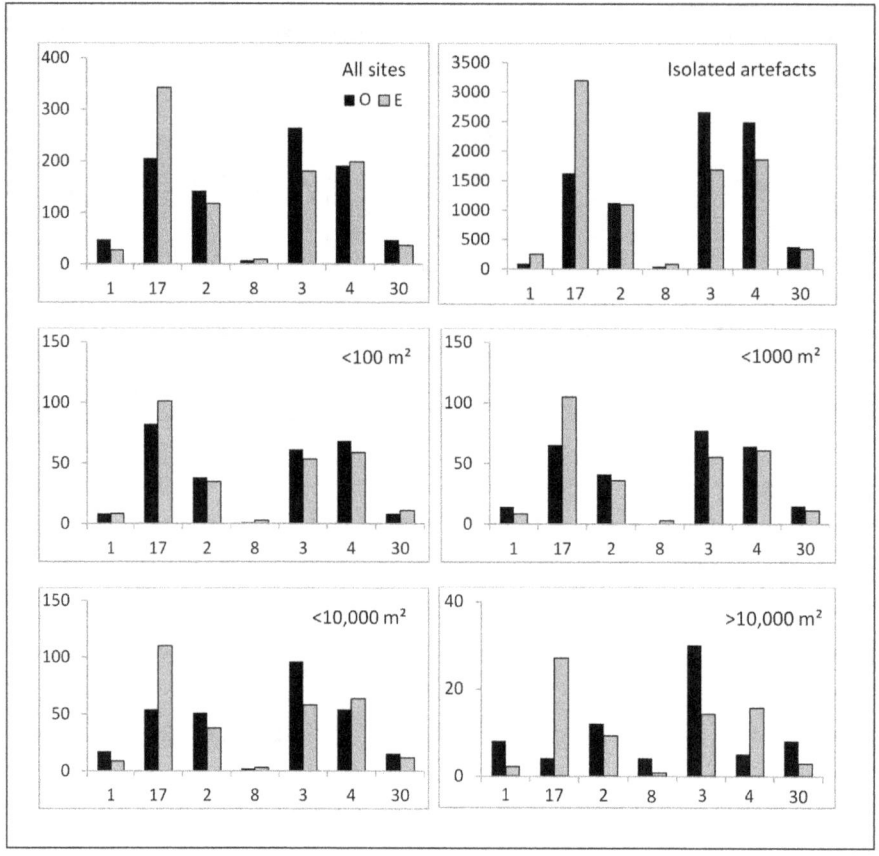

FIGURE 4.3: Observed (O) and expected (E) distribution of surface artefact scatters and isolated artefacts in relation to vegetation formations. Key to vegetation formation codes: 1. Open Eucalypt Woodland; 2. Low *Acacia* Woodland; 3. Low *Acacia* Woodland/Open Forest; 4. Low Open *Acacia* Woodland; 8. Closed *Acacia* Scrub/Tall Shrubland; 17. Hummock Grassland; 30. High Open Shrubland.

4). Since isolated artefacts are commonly thought to be the background scatter, it might be expected that, like small sites, their distribution would be essentially random. However, at the scale of the study area, the sample of isolated artefacts is very large, so the result may simply reflect the denser distribution of surface artefact material on the plains than in the ranges.

It is clear that overall distribution of archaeological surface artefacts, whether recorded as isolated artefacts or as sites, is denser on the plains than in the ranges. Surface archaeological material also seems to be more commonly associated with Open Eucalypt Woodland (VC 1) and Low Mulga Woodlands and Open Forest (VC 3) than with other vegetation communities. This is consistent with the occurrence of water sources along creek lines and with likely greater availability of food and other resources in the mulga woodlands on the plains (see Chapter 3). The noted preference for larger sites to be located in Low Mulga Woodlands and Open Forest (VC 3) is less easy to account for. However, shade may also be a factor attracting activity to these particular areas. This discussion highlights problems associated with the definition of appropriate analytical units and different scales of analysis. The issue will be explored further at the locality scale in Chapter 6.

SURFACE ARTEFACT ANALYSIS

Assemblages in the survey area are characterised by simple flake production using hard hammer percussion, with little evidence for core preparation. Most cores are single platform. Flakes show little evidence of platform preparation or overhang reduction. Retouch is rare. This seems to be typical of surface assemblages in the Pilbara where evidence of high levels of core preparation, or specialised flake or blade production is sparse (Ryan and Morse 2009, 10).

Disentangling the relationship between aspects of mobility and technological organisation in the archaeological record is no simple matter, as discussed in Chapter 2. It is increasingly clear that understanding the constraints imposed by the local socio-cultural, environmental and functional context is critical to making sense of the archaeological correlates of technological organisation (e.g. Andrefsky 2009; Bird 1985; Clarkson 2008; Holdaway, Shiner and Fanning 2004; Nelson 1991; Shiner 2009). In the study area, investigation of mobility through the procurement, use and discard of raw material thus proceeds from a situation of abundance rather than scarcity. Assuming that use of stone is embedded within subsistence activities, we can expect some movement of raw material into and out of the survey area, which only covers a limited part of what is now Nyiyaparli country (see Chapter 3), but local sources are likely to dominate archaeological assemblages. Veth (1993, 22) argues that, in the Rudall River area, the wide availability of raw material suitable for tool making and the absence of clear supply zones for particular materials meant that raw material could be regarded as a constant variable and need not be considered in the interpretation of site function. Ryan and Morse (2009) also argue that, while local raw material predominated at sites, other assemblage attributes, most notably diversity in raw material types and artefact types, were indicative of site function. Nevertheless, stone is still costly to procure and move, even over relatively short distances (Beck et al. 2002; Close 2000). Studies elsewhere in Australia have shown distance effects even at a very local scale (e.g. Doelman, Webb and Domanski 2001; Holdaway, Shiner and Fanning 2004).

Commonly used measures to investigate the relationship between technological organisation and mobility in the archaeological record include flake to core ratio, core rotation, amount of retouch, amount of cortex and size reduction in particular artefact classes. These all rely on the reductive nature of stone technology to look at how the residues of different stages of production are distributed in space and time in order to infer patterns of land use (Clarkson and O'Connor 2014, 177). In the Pilbara, a number of assemblage characteristics identified by Veth (1993, 84ff.) as indicating intensity of reduction and thus levels of mobility are often used to interpret sites (see Table 2.1). Decreasing levels of residential mobility are argued to be associated with increased numbers of artefacts, a wider range of artefact types, including the presence of grinding material, greater diversity of raw material and more intensive reduction of stone artefacts (e.g. Ryan and Morse 2009, 13). Cortex and volume ratios provide an alternative approach to inferring mobility by identifying if artefact transport occurred. These ratios indicate whether the products of reduction remain in place or whether they have been removed from or added to assemblages (Dibble et al. 2005; Ditchfield 2016; Douglass et al. 2008; Phillipps and Holdaway 2015).

The suggested relationship between levels of residential mobility and assemblage characteristics can also be linked to the distribution of water and other resources at a landscape scale (Barton 2003; 2008; Bird and Rhoads 2011; Clarkson 2006). In the Christmas Creek study area, core settlement can be expected to focus on the alluvial and colluvial plains, and particularly along the drainage lines. According to the land-use model, residential mobility in the plains should therefore be relatively low, and in the ranges should be high. As we have already noted, the distribution of archaeological material is clearly denser on the plains and this provides some support for the expectation that residential mobility will be lower on the plains than in the ranges. The margins of the Fortescue Marsh are also likely to be characterised by low residential mobility, at least during periods when the Marsh floods and resource productivity is particularly high (see Chapter 3). The Marsh margin is outside the boundaries of the intensively surveyed area and sites recorded there were not included in the site-based analysis above. However, some samples are available for comparison within the landscape analysis of surface artefacts (Figure 4.4). Their attributes should generally resemble samples from the plains, with the proviso that lithic resources are less available along the Marsh margins.

The land-use model can thus be reframed to predict overall assemblage characteristics in different parts of the survey area. Assemblages in the ranges should have low diversity of raw materials and artefact types, few formal tools and little grinding material and be characterised by early stage reduction. By contrast, plains assemblages should have high diversity of raw material and artefact types, more formal tools and grinding material and be characterised by middle and late stages of reduction. Marsh assemblages should be similar to those on the plains, but may show evidence of raw material conservation. Possible indicators of differences in degree of reduction specified by the model as signalling differences in level of residential mobility include: amount of cortex, size of cores and flakes, core to flake ratio, evidence of core rotation and the amount of retouch.

SAMPLING SURFACE ARTEFACTS AT THE LANDSCAPE SCALE

More than 50,000 artefacts were recorded from surface artefact scatters and reduction areas in the course of the entire field program for Christmas Creek–Cloudbreak. More than 10,000 isolated artefacts were also recorded. The site-based recording strategy and staged approach to recording meant that compiling and checking the records for this analysis was a major undertaking. Therefore, the final analysis of surface artefacts focused on a sample

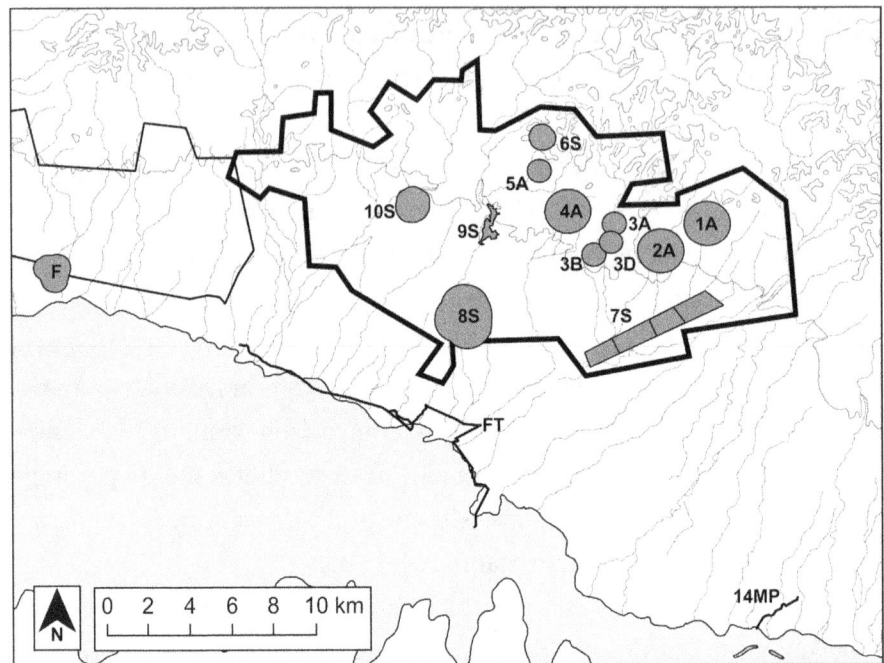

Figure 4.4: Christmas Creek survey area, showing location of group sample areas.

of 16,226 artefacts or approximately 25% of the artefacts recorded in the Christmas Creek study area.

A landscape-focused approach was taken to sampling surface artefacts for our analysis. This involved compiling suitable samples of adequate size associated with different landforms. The field data collection was not completely finalised when our analysis started. Consequently, several different methods were used to generate samples for analysis. In all cases, the overall aims were to maximise sample size, and ensure the primary land systems were assessed (Figure 4.4). In total, the group sample areas covered about 15% of the Christmas Creek survey area, evenly split between the ranges and the plains. An additional three sample areas were selected from close to the Fortescue Marsh outside the survey area boundary.

During the initial stage of our study we focused on analysing assemblages from excavated rockshelters. As part of these investigations, excavated assemblages were compared with surface assemblages from within an arbitrary 500-metre radius of each shelter, both as discrete sites and as grouped assemblages (Bird and Rhoads 2015). This analysis indicated that variability between grouped surface assemblages 'mirrored' variability between their associated rockshelter assemblages. The results suggested that locality-based surface artefact samples would be a promising avenue for investigating spatial patterning within the project area. This approach would mitigate the problem of small samples and permit exploration of variability at different spatial scales.

The samples selected for this analysis were defined in different ways depending on terrain. In the ranges, six samples (Groups 1A, 2A, 3B, 3D, 4A, 5A) included all artefacts recorded in sites whose boundaries were intersected by a buffer of 500 m radius around the rockshelter (or shelters) and all isolated artefacts recorded within the buffer. The buffer was expanded to 1 km radius where only a few artefacts were recorded. An additional surface sample (Group 6S) was selected close to the northern boundary of the survey area and immediately north of 5A along the same drainage line. This provided a surface sample from the ranges not associated with a rockshelter.

The plains samples were all defined differently. Group 7S was a transect approximately 500 m wide and 7 km long along a creek line crossing the plains in a south-westerly direction. The creeks where Groups 1A, 2A, 3B and 3D are located all drain into this creek line. This sample was subdivided into four subsamples for some analyses (7SA-D). Group 8S was centred on a large surface scatter (CB08-114) approximately halfway between the ranges and the Fortescue Marsh, and comprised all the recorded artefacts within a 1 km buffer of the boundary of the site. Group 9S consisted of the artefacts recorded within the boundary of a large and extensive single site (CB06-68). This group thus does not include any isolated artefacts, so a suitable comparative sample of isolated artefacts was compiled by selecting all the isolated artefacts within 500 m of the CB06-68 boundary. Group 9S is north of Group 8S on the same creek line, and close to the ranges. Both 8S and 9S were on the same creek line as 5A and 6S. The last Group, 10S, is situated east of Group 9S and, like Group 8S, centred on a large surface scatter (CB07-119). It included all the recorded artefacts within a 500 m buffer of the boundary of the site.

The Fortescue Marsh land system and the plains immediately fringing the Marsh did not fall within the Christmas Creek survey area. They were not archaeologically investigated with the same intensity. Nevertheless, it is possible to identify samples from close to the Marsh for comparison. These mostly came from less intensive surveys associated with mine infrastructure, such as access tracks. Group F lies east of the Christmas Creek survey area and consists of all the recorded artefacts from site CB12-64. Like Group 9S, it does not include any isolated artefacts. Group FT includes all artefacts recorded in 2010 along a transect close to the edge of the Fortescue Marsh. Group 14MP comprised all artefacts recorded along a 2.5 km length of access track running north-east of 14 Mile Pool.

As well as sampling different landforms, the use of analytical groups based on locality permits comparison between artefact samples recorded as part of sites and as isolated artefacts. This is relevant to the interpretation of the archaeological record in terms of whether sites and the background scatter are qualitatively different with respect to the record of human behaviour they represent, or whether they are both palimpsests, with sites differentiated from the background scatter by density alone (Shott 2008; Stern 1993). As discussed above (Chapter 2), it is commonly (if not always explicitly) assumed that sites in the Pilbara are qualitatively different from the background scatter and represent distinctly different activities. Our approach allows the structure of the local archaeological record to be described in terms of the relationships between sites and the background scatter within their local landscape context. It also facilitates comparison between site assemblages and the background scatter.

A pilot study used Principal Components Analysis (PCA) to explore variation in the landscape group samples with respect to key variables relevant to the predictions of the land-use model (Hammer, Harper and Ryan 2001). This preliminary analysis only used artefacts recorded as part of sites. Isolated artefacts were excluded because these data were not available for the separate samples comprising Group 7S, or for Groups 9S and F, which are exclusively site based. Each sample was characterised in terms of key predictions associated with the land-use model about raw material diversity and extent of reduction (Table 4.3). Raw material diversity was assessed for each group using the Shannon index (H) (Hammer 2013, 140) to account for sample size. This index is widely used as an estimate of heterogeneity, or a combination of richness and evenness. The value of H is open ended and increases as diversity increases, with zero indicating uniformity. The flake to core ratio and length of complete flakes were

TABLE 4.3: Summary data for group samples.

Group	% Cortex	mp:sp	Flakes:core	Length (mm)	Diversity (H)
1A	36	0.51	11	26	1.31
2A	53	0.45	9	32	0.87
3B	63	0.36	5	34	1.08
3D	51	0	12	32	0.73
4A	57	0.22	10	32	1.196
5A	40	0.33	8	26	1.27
6S	47	0.39	6	31	1.10
7SA	60	0.39	6	39	1.41
7SB	62	0.46	6	37	1.23
7SC	69	0.9	6	40	1.33
7SD	71	0.42	4	37	1.23
8S	61	0.62	8	39	1.18
9S	63	0.73	8	41	1.45
10S	68	0.38	7	40	1.42
F	64	0.43	5	35	1.4
FT	55	0.43	7	31	1.51
14MP	63	0.3	3.5	32	1.55

TABLE 4.4: Results of Principal Components Analysis on group samples.

	% VARIANCE			LOADINGS		
		% Cortex	mp:sp	Flakes:core	Length (mm)	Diversity (H)
PC 1	54.9	0.52419	0.37693	-0.44671	0.49961	0.36606
PC 2	19.5	0.40304	-0.21877	0.22988	0.47271	-0.71652
PC 3	16.7	-0.22926	0.76639	0.56298	0.20176	-0.04923

used as indicators of reduction intensity, while the ratio of multiplatform to single platform cores (mp:sp) was used to measure the extent to which cores were rotated. The percentage of cortical flakes in the assemblage provides an estimate of the amount of primary stage reduction. All these are widely used to infer levels of reduction in assemblages (Clarkson and O'Connor 2014; Ditchfield 2016).

The results of the PCA clearly differentiate between samples from the ranges and samples from the plains and Marsh margin (Figure 4.5, Table 4.4). Contrary to the predictions of the land-use model, assemblages in the ranges are characterised by greater levels of reduction, in terms of high flake to core ratios. Early stage reduction, on the other hand, indicated by greater numbers of large cortical flakes, is more prevalent in assemblages on the plains. This result is surprising. It seems unlikely that the inference that residential mobility is higher in the ranges than on the plains is incorrect. Rather, the result calls into question the assumptions about a general relationship between assemblage characteristics and mobility. It is therefore necessary to look more closely at the characteristics of assemblages with respect to the availability and properties of raw material. This permits us to explore what specific cultural and environmental parameters contribute to local variation in lithic assemblages, and how the use and discard of stone actually relates to the use of this landscape.

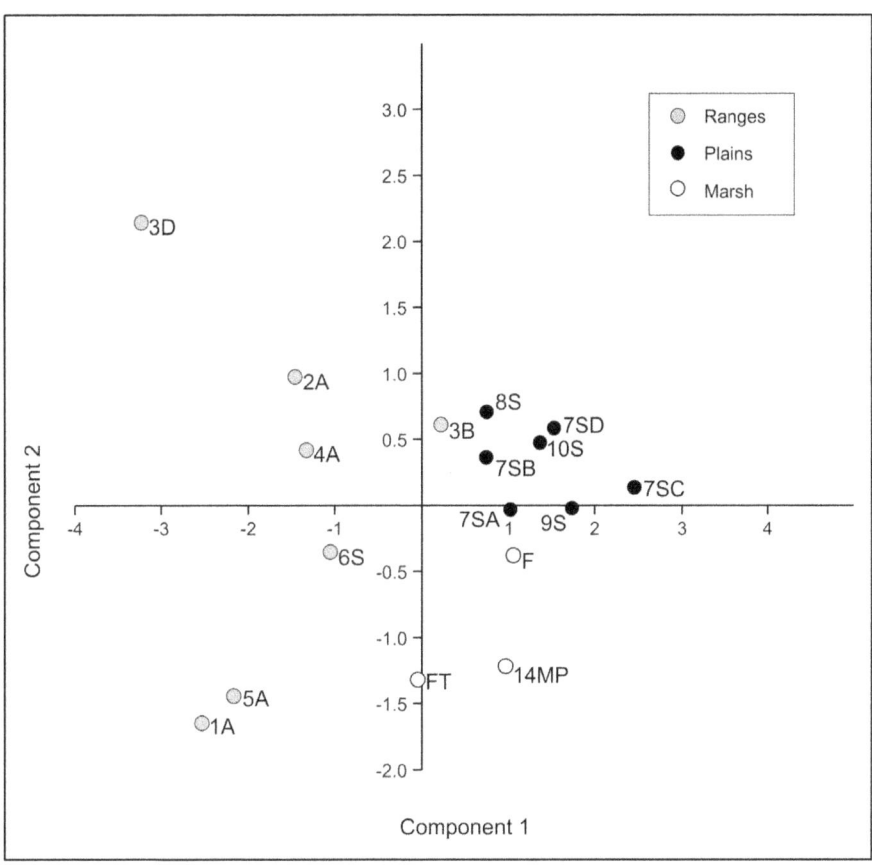

FIGURE 4.5: Results of Principal Components Analysis on group samples.

RAW MATERIAL DIVERSITY AND ASSEMBLAGE COMPOSITION

Up to 15 different types of lithic raw materials occur in flaked stone assemblages in the study area (Table 4.5). Nevertheless, just five account for 96% by number of all flaked stone recorded within the grouped samples. These are banded iron formation (BIF), basalt, chert, chalcedony and dolerite. Just over half of all flaked stone artefacts are BIF (51%) and basalt nearly one-third (28%), with much smaller amounts of chalcedony (8%), chert (5%) and dolerite (5%). The only other materials that occur in more than trace amounts are mudstone (1%) and quartzite (2%). Calculating the proportions of such an array of materials with different properties can be problematic. However, both the minimum number of flakes (MNF, calculated as the sum of complete flakes and proximal fragments) (Table 4.6) and the total estimated volume

TABLE 4.5: Raw material composition: all recorded flaked stone artefacts from group samples. 'Other' includes rhyolite, siltstone, granite and unidentified. Shaded rows=N; unshaded rows=%

Group	Basalt	BIF	Chalcedony	Chert	Dolerite	Ironstone	Mudstone
1A	149	447	45	60	29	12	3
	19.5	58.5	5.9	7.9	3.8	1.6	0.4
2A	26	403	13	28	3	1	13
	5.2	80.9	2.6	5.6	0.6	0.2	2.6
3B	67	582	63	61	3	0	26
	8.1	70.7	7.7	7.4	0.4	0.0	3.2
3D	24	118	0	7	3	0	0
	15.6	76.6	0.0	4.5	1.9	0.0	0.0
4A	88	412	24	72	15	10	5
	14.0	65.4	3.8	11.4	2.4	1.6	0.8
5A	171	485	17	93	26	8	3
	21.1	60.0	2.1	11.5	3.2	1.0	0.4
6S	18	184	23	74	0	5	0
	5.9	60.3	7.5	24.3	0.0	1.6	0.0
7S	709	2915	395	113	221	5	29
	15.4	63.2	8.6	2.4	4.8	0.1	0.6
8S	1365	716	177	40	121	0	7
	55.5	29.1	7.2	1.6	4.9	0.0	0.3
9S	930	719	167	62	173	9	40
	43.5	33.6	7.8	2.9	8.1	0.4	1.9
10S	328	366	108	66	70	0	0
	34.6	38.6	11.4	7.0	7.4	0.0	0.0
F	157	164	98	36	5	0	0
	33.7	35.2	21.0	7.7	1.1	0.0	0.0
FT	303	280	129	39	39	0	5
	37.2	34.4	15.8	4.8	4.8	0.0	0.6
14MP	12	75	30	8	13	0	0
	7.5	47.2	18.9	5.0	8.2	0.0	0.0
Total	4347	7866	1289	759	721	50	131
	27.9	50.5	8.3	4.9	4.6	0.3	0.8

Crystal quartz	Quartz	Quartzite	Silcrete	Other	Glass	Total
1	2	13	3	0	0	764
0.1	0.3	1.7	0.4	0.0	0.0	
0	3	8	0	0	0	498
0.0	0.6	1.6	0.0	0.0	0.0	
0	3	17	1	0	0	823
0.0	0.4	2.1	0.1	0.0	0.0	
0	0	2	0	0	0	154
0.0	0.0	1.3	0.0	0.0	0.0	
1	0	3	0	0	0	630
0.2	0.0	0.5	0.0	0.0	0.0	
3	0	3	0	0	0	809
0.4	0.0	0.4	0.0	0.0	0.0	
0	0	1	0	0	0	305
0.0	0.0	0.3	0.0	0.0	0.0	
6	17	162	30	12	0	4614
0.1	0.4	3.5	0.7	0.3	0.0	
1	1	17	5	1	9	2460
0.0	0.0	0.7	0.2	0.0	0.4	
2	2	7	26	0	0	2137
0.1	0.1	0.3	1.2	0.0	0.0	
1	1	8	1	0	0	949
0.1	0.1	0.8	0.1	0.0	0.0	
1	1	4	0	0	0	466
0.2	0.2	0.9	0.0	0.0	0.0	
0	0	15	4	0	0	814
0.0	0.0	1.8	0.5	0.0	0.0	
1	0	18	0	0	2	159
0.6	0.0	11.3	0.0	0.0	1.3	
17	30	278	70	13	11	15582
0.1	0.2	1.8	0.4	0.1	0.1	

TABLE 4.6: Raw material composition: MNF (complete flakes and proximal flakes) from group samples. 'Other' includes rhyolite, siltstone, granite and unidentified.

	Basalt	BIF	Chalcedony	Chert	Dolerite	Ironstone	Mudstone
1A	113	356	37	42	20	11	2
	19.1	60.1	6.3	7.1	3.4	1.9	0.3
2A	20	309	7	22	3	1	9
	5.3	81.3	1.8	5.8	0.8	0.3	2.4
3B	47	425	49	39	0	0	18
	7.9	71.2	8.2	6.5	0.0	0.0	3.0
3D	18	94	0	5	3	0	0
	14.8	77.0	0.0	4.1	2.5	0.0	0.0
4A	56	299	19	48	9	8	3
	12.6	67.3	4.3	10.8	2.0	1.8	0.7
5A	117	342	10	39	20	6	3
	21.8	63.7	1.9	7.3	3.7	1.1	0.6
6S	13	130	14	28	0	2	0
	6.9	69.1	7.4	14.9	0.0	1.1	0.0
7S	512	2283	319	76	179	3	20
	14.3	63.9	8.9	2.1	5.0	0.1	0.6
8S	1040	565	143	36	94	0	6
	54.7	29.7	7.5	1.9	4.9	0.0	0.3
9S	724	570	125	48	124	7	35
	43.6	34.3	7.5	2.9	7.5	0.4	2.1
10S	253	272	83	45	52	0	0
	35.4	38.1	11.6	6.3	7.3	0.0	0.0
F	104	114	67	24	4	0	0
	32.8	36.0	21.1	7.6	1.3	0.0	0.0
FT	231	214	105	26	31	0	2
	37.0	34.2	16.8	4.2	5.0	0.0	0.3
14MP	8	50	22	4	12	0	0
	7.3	45.5	20.0	3.6	10.9	0.0	0.0
TOTAL	3256	6023	1000	482	551	38	98
	27.7	51.2	8.5	4.1	4.7	0.3	0.8

Crystal quartz	Quartz	Quartzite	Silcrete	Other	Glass	Total
0	2	7	2	0	0	592
0.0	0.3	1.2	0.3	0.0	0.0	
0	2	7	0	0	0	380
0.0	0.5	1.8	0.0	0.0	0.0	
0	3	15	1	0	0	597
0.0	0.5	2.5	0.2	0.0	0.0	
0	0	2	0	0	0	122
0.0	0.0	1.6	0.0	0.0	0.0	
0	0	2	0	0	0	444
0.0	0.0	0.5	0.0	0.0	0.0	
0	0	0	0	0	0	537
0.0	0.0	0.0	0.0	0.0	0.0	
0	0	1	0	0	0	188
0.0	0.0	0.5	0.0	0.0	0.0	
2	14	127	27	10	0	3572
0.1	0.4	3.6	0.8	0.3	0.0	
0	1	9	5	1	1	1901
0.0	0.1	0.5	0.3	0.1	0.1	
2	2	4	21	0	0	1662
0.1	0.1	0.2	1.3	0.0	0.0	
1	1	6	1	0	0	714
0.1	0.1	0.8	0.1	0.0	0.0	
0	1	3	0	0	0	317
0.0	0.3	0.9	0.0	0.0	0.0	
0	0	12	4	0	0	625
0.0	0.0	1.9	0.6	0.0	0.0	
1	0	13	0	0	0	110
0.9	0.0	11.8	0.0	0.0	0.0	
6	26	208	61	11	1	11761
0.1	0.2	1.8	0.5	0.1	0.0	

TABLE 4.7: Raw material composition: volume (cm³) from group samples. 'Other' includes includes rhyolite, siltstone, granite and unidentified.

	Basalt	BIF	Chalcedony	Chert	Dolerite	Ironstone	Mudstone
1A	883	3284	146	354	715	132	13
	15.7	58.3	2.6	6.3	12.7	2.4	0.2
2A	269	5572	52	251	30	14	171
	4.1	84.3	0.8	3.8	0.5	0.2	2.6
3B	907	13367	545	672	44	0	404
	5.5	81.0	3.3	4.1	0.3	0.0	2.4
3D	163	1423	0	239	44	0	0
	8.7	75.8	0.0	12.7	2.4	0.0	0.0
4A	912	5190	147	276	273	95	48
	13.1	74.3	2.1	4.0	3.9	1.4	0.7
5A	1200	3968	124	456	234	83	18
	19.6	64.8	2.0	7.4	3.8	1.4	0.3
6S	80	2605	173	186	0	107	0
	2.5	82.5	5.5	5.9	0.0	3.4	0.0
7S	10955	71973	4773	1193	7320	80	569
	10.9	71.5	4.7	1.2	7.3	0.1	0.6
8S	32806	21224	1440	294	5468	0	99
	52.6	34.0	2.3	0.5	8.8	0.0	0.2
9S	19422	22330	2024	679	8616	154	908
	35.1	40.4	3.7	1.2	15.6	0.3	1.6
10S	6317	12027	1169	393	5325	0	0
	24.6	46.9	4.6	1.5	20.8	0.0	0.0
F	1501	2409	652	176	159	0	0
	30.4	48.8	13.2	3.6	3.2	0.0	0.0
FT	4710	7135	1005	285	1970	0	34
	30.8	46.7	6.6	1.9	12.9	0.0	0.2
14MP	186	1449	179	33	177	0	0
	8.4	65.2	8.0	1.5	8.0	0.0	0.0
TOTAL	80310	173956	12428	5487	30376	665	2265
	25.6	55.5	4.0	1.8	9.7	0.2	0.7

Crystal quartz	Quartz	Quartzite	Silcrete	Other	Glass	Total
2	9	86	8	0	0	5631
0.0	0.2	1.5	0.1	0.0	0.0	
0	199	51	0	0	0	6610
0.0	3.0	0.8	0.0	0.0	0.0	
0	61	490	17	0	0	16505
0.0	0.4	3.0	0.1	0.0	0.0	
0	0	8	0	0	0	1876
0.0	0.0	0.4	0.0	0.0	0.0	
1	0	39	0	0	0	6982
0.0	0.0	0.6	0.0	0.0	0.0	
18	0	26	0	0	0	6128
0.3	0.0	0.4	0.0	0.0	0.0	
0	0	7	0	0	0	3157
0.0	0.0	0.2	0.0	0.0	0.0	
65	262	2629	419	372	0	100610
0.1	0.3	2.6	0.4	0.4	0.0	
13	1	874	68	10	81	62376
0.0	0.0	1.4	0.1	0.0	0.1	
83	15	402	629	0	0	55263
0.1	0.0	0.7	1.1	0.0	0.0	
7	16	388	12	0	0	25653
0.0	0.1	1.5	0.0	0.0	0.0	
2	7	35	0	0	0	4942
0.1	0.1	0.7	0.0	0.0	0.0	
0	0	108	30	0	0	15279
0.0	0.0	0.7	0.2	0.0	0.0	
4	0	186	0	0	8	2223
0.2	0.0	8.4	0.0	0.0	0.4	
196	570	5327	1182	382	89	313234
0.1	0.2	1.7	0.4	0.1	0.0	

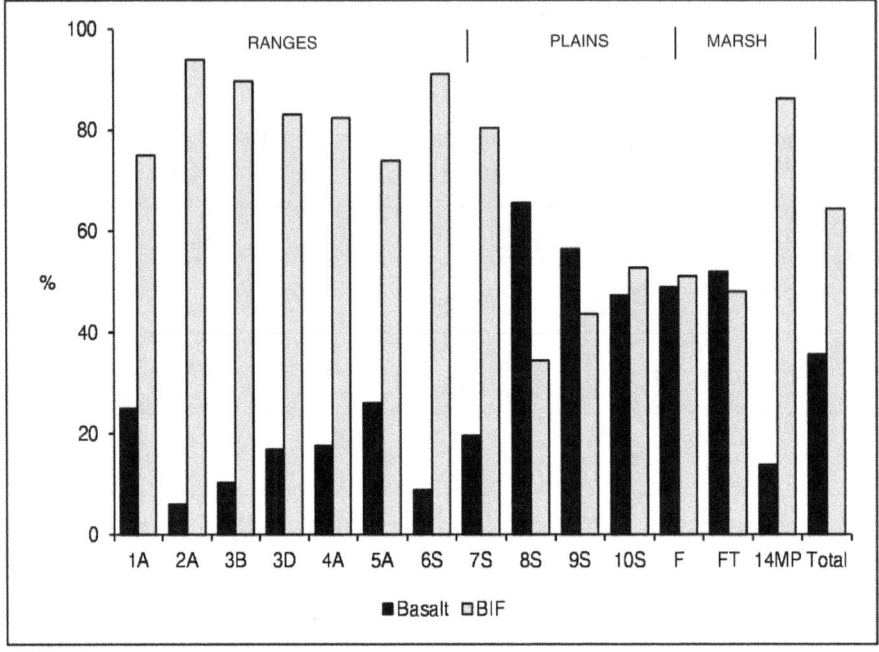

FIGURE 4.6: Ratio of basalt to BIF for each landscape sample group.

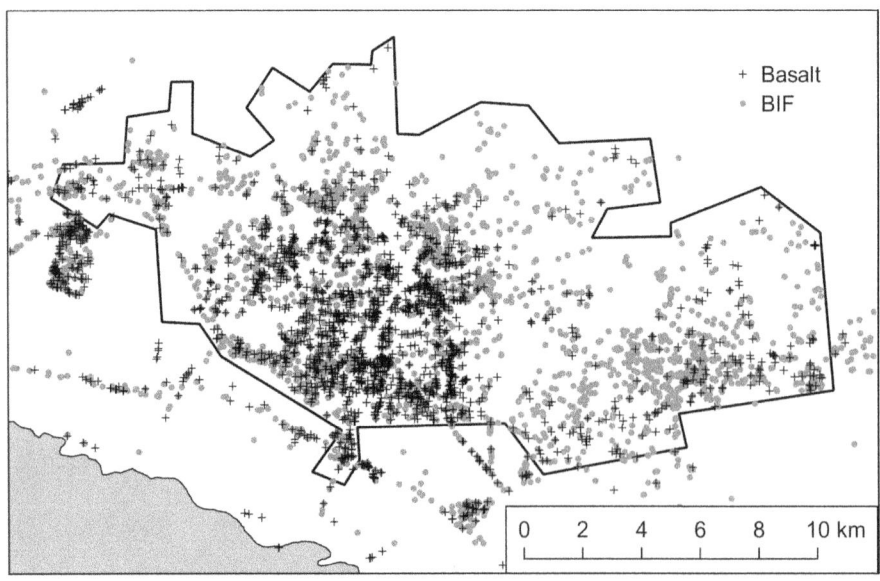

FIGURE 4.7: Distribution of basalt and BIF isolated artefacts.

(Table 4.7) give broadly similar results. The principal exceptions are chalcedony, chert and dolerite. Chalcedony and chert are slightly under-represented by volume, and dolerite is slightly over-represented. This result might be attributed to differences in the way these materials were used, perhaps through more intensive reduction of chert and chalcedony in comparison to the other materials. Alternatively, it may reflect differences in the initial 'packaging' of these materials; that is, the form in which they occur in the landscape.

As already noted (Chapter 3), BIF, basalt, chalcedony, chert and dolerite all occur locally and are widely available in the landscape as cobbles and pebbles in the creek lines, on the alluvial plains, and as seams, outcrops and exfoliating nodules in the ranges. Twenty-seven sites were formally recorded as quarries. All are limited in extent. Most are BIF or chert, with three chalcedony quarries, and one each of basalt and mudstone (see Appendix 4). However, these raw materials are not uniformly distributed throughout the analytical groups. BIF dominates all the ranges assemblages, Groups 7S and 14MP. The percentage of basalt is relatively high in Groups 8S, 9S and 10S and in two of the Fortescue Marsh samples. Thus, the ranges samples are clearly BIF dominated, while plains samples are split between the west of the study area, where basalt occurs in relatively high proportions, and the east (Groups 7S and 14MP), where the proportion of basalt is similar to the ranges (Figure 4.6). The east–west cline in basalt distribution is also evident in the distribution of isolated artefacts (Figure 4.7). Only one basalt quarry was recorded and it was situated on the north-west boundary of the study area, where other quarried basalt outcrops were seen immediately to the north.[1]

The percentages of chalcedony, chert and dolerite are quite variable (Tables 4.5–4.7). All three Fortescue Marsh samples have relatively high proportions of chalcedony. The only other sample where chalcedony exceeds 10% by number is Group 10S. There are relatively high percentages of chert (greater than 10%) in 4A, 5A and particularly in 6S. This is consistent with the presence of two chert quarries associated with CB09-249, immediately east of Group 5A (see Figure 5.6).

---

1 Stuart Rapley, personal communication, 2014.

All other raw materials occur in very small numbers. Only quartzite comprises more than 1% of the total and occurs in all samples. Quartzite exceeds 2% of the assemblage in Groups 3B, 7S and 14MP and is noticeably less prevalent in the western part of the survey area.

With the exception of the clear east–west cline in the distribution of basalt, the occurrence of raw material within assemblages varies little across the survey area. A local peak in the occurrence of chert in Groups 4A, 5A and 6S seems to be related to proximity to quarried sources. Generally, however, the same suite of raw materials appears throughout the study area in roughly the same proportions. The land-use model predicts

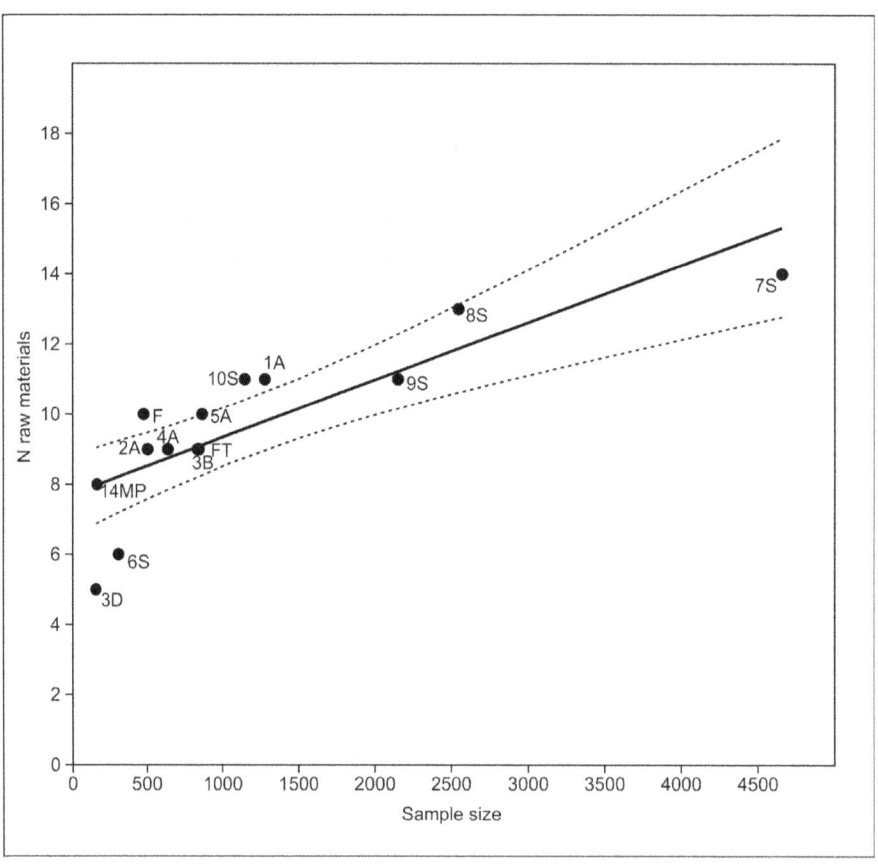

FIGURE 4.8: Group samples: linear regression between sample size and number of raw materials (r=0.83, p<0.001). Dotted lines indicate 95% confidence intervals.

that high diversity in raw materials should be associated with low residential mobility. However, there is little variation in diversity across the study area at a landscape level; only Groups 2A and 3D have noticeably lower values for H (Table 4.3). In fact, linear regression confirms that the number of raw materials is related to sample size (Figure 4.8). As sample size increases, so does the probability that rare raw materials will be represented in assemblages.

Shott (2008; 2010) notes that diversity in archaeological assemblages does not simply reflect activity and site function. Rather, it is commonly related to sample size effects resulting from the interaction of factors such as activity, occupation span, and tool use lives with natural formation processes. He advocates SHE analysis as a technique for examining sample size dependence through exploring the relationship between different components of diversity, namely assemblage richness, heterogeneity and evenness. Figure 4.9 presents the results of SHE analysis on both the sample groups and individual sites. In both cases, regression analysis indicates that richness (S) is strongly correlated with sample size (r=0.91 for Groups, r=0.96 for individual sites), while evenness (E) is negatively correlated with sample

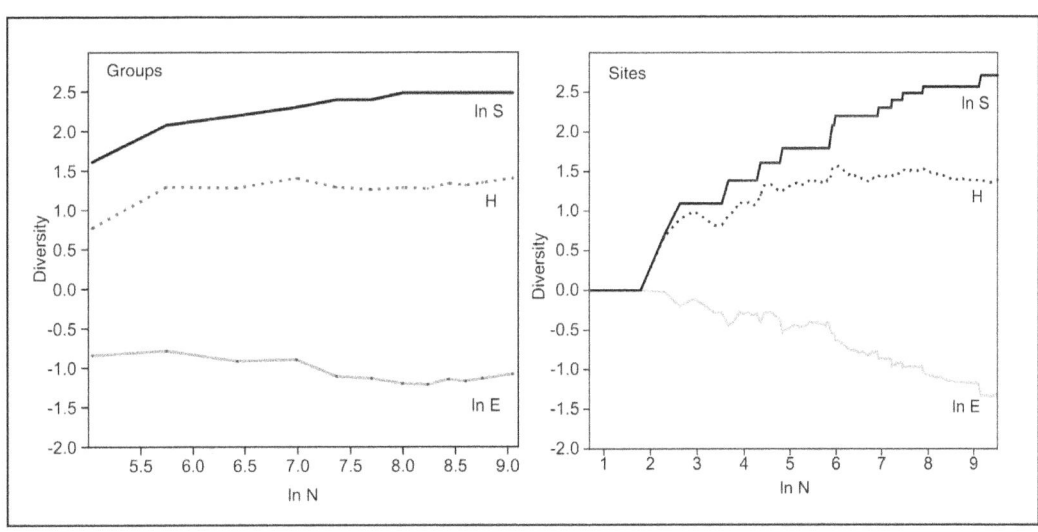

FIGURE 4.9: Results of SHE analysis of raw material diversity for group samples and individual sites.

size (r=-0.86 for Groups, r=-0.98 for individual sites. Heterogeneity (H) is also correlated with sample size in both cases (r=0.69 for Groups, r=0.69 for individual sites). The graph for the analysis of Groups (Figure 4.9, left) indicates that diversity is essentially uniform across the study area at a landscape level. In the analysis for individual sites (Figure 4.9, right), a clear sample size effect predominates, with the value for H levelling out once a sample size of about 50 is achieved.

CORTEX TYPE

Cortex provides evidence about the nature and source of particular raw materials. Because stone working is a reductive process, more cortical flakes are usually removed at the start of a reduction sequence than in subsequent stages. The characteristics and distribution of cortex within an assemblage can be used to infer stages of reduction and inform on the organisation of technology (Andrefsky 2005, 103–6; Clarkson and O'Connor 2014, 177–8; Holdaway and Stern 2004, 144–5; Veth 1993, 93).

The land-use model predicts that early stage reduction, as evidenced by cortical flakes, will mainly occur at sites used by small groups for short periods. With increasing occupation span, the intensity of reduction is also expected to increase, so evidence of middle and late stage reduction is likely to dominate assemblages at sites occupied for longer periods at a time.

Two types of cortex – riverine and terrestrial – were identified and recorded in the course of fieldwork. Riverine cortex indicates that the source material comes from cobbles and pebbles originating in creeks. Terrestrial cortex points to localities in the ranges, as the source material comes from either eroded nodules or from quarried outcrops or seams. It should be noted, however, that not all source material necessarily has cortex, and this is particularly true for terrestrial sources. Raw material that has been quarried may not have cortex. Terrestrial sources commonly also occur as heat-fractured boulders, outcrops and nodules. Thus, the outer surface of the source material, especially in the ranges, may not be completely cortical.

The overall percentage of cortex is high throughout the Christmas Creek survey area, with about 60% of all artefacts from the group sample areas retaining at least some cortex. The percentage of isolated artefacts retaining some cortex is slightly higher (63%). Table 4.8 indicates that there is some spatial patterning. Plains samples (Groups 7S, 8S, 9S and 10S) generally exhibit lower overall proportions of non-cortical artefacts than all but one of the ranges samples. Two out of three Marsh samples also have relatively low proportions of non-cortical artefacts.

Table 4.8: Amount of cortex by group.

	Non-cortical		<50%		>50%		100%	
	N	%	N	%	N	%	N	%
1A	462	63.3	167	22.9	77	10.5	24	3.3
2A	216	45.7	169	35.7	73	15.4	15	3.2
3B	288	37.1	314	40.5	141	18.2	33	4.3
3D	80	52.6	53	34.9	15	9.9	4	2.6
4A	260	42.6	223	36.5	95	15.5	33	5.4
5A	430	54.3	280	35.4	67	8.5	15	1.9
6S	150	50.2	109	36.5	37	12.4	3	1.0
7S	1545	35.5	1726	39.7	846	19.4	236	5.4
8S	870	36.0	899	37.2	480	19.8	170	7.0
9S	712	34.7	842	41.1	357	17.4	140	6.8
10S	312	33.3	420	44.8	162	17.3	44	4.7
F	242	52.6	152	33.0	52	11.3	14	3.0
FT	307	38.9	268	33.9	164	20.8	51	6.5
14MP	42	30.4	58	42.0	33	23.9	5	3.6
Total	5916	39.5	5680	37.9	2599	17.3	787	5.3

TABLE 4.9: Cortex type by raw material.

	Riverine	%	Terrestrial	%	None	%
Basalt	2015	46.4	470	10.8	1859	42.8
BIF	1847	23.5	3276	41.7	2738	34.8
Chalcedony	225	17.5	341	26.5	722	56.1
Chert	97	12.8	244	32.1	418	55.1
Dolerite	330	46.0	190	26.5	198	27.6

Table 4.9 (see also Figure 4.11) shows that BIF, basalt and dolerite artefacts have a relatively high proportion of artefacts with cortex, while most chert and chalcedony artefacts are non-cortical. Cortex on basalt and dolerite artefacts is mostly riverine and we may assume they are more likely to be made on pebbles and cobbles sourced from the intermittent watercourses. BIF artefacts, by contrast, have mainly terrestrial cortex. Where there is cortex on chert and chalcedony artefacts it is also more often terrestrial than riverine.

Clear spatial patterning emerges when the data is broken down by group sample areas. As we have noted, plains assemblages generally have higher proportions of cortical artefacts (Table 4.8). The overall proportion of riverine cortex is clearly higher for the plains samples (7S, 8S, 9S, 10S) than for those in the ranges (Figure 4.10). Marsh samples (FT, F and 14MP) are more varied. This pattern is also evident when basalt and BIF are considered separately. The proportion of riverine cortex is clearly higher in the samples from the plains (7S, 8S, 9S and 10S) and the Marsh (FT, F and 14MP) for both BIF and basalt (Figure 4.11). In the ranges samples, basalt is generally more likely to be non-cortical, although 4A and 6S are exceptions. Chert and chalcedony samples are more tightly clustered and therefore much more uniform (Figure 4.11). There is still a slight trend towards higher percentages of riverine cortex in the plains samples. Dolerite is by far the most variable. All plains Groups (7S, 8S, 9S and 10S) have high proportions of riverine cortex. Two samples (3B and 4A) have high proportions of terrestrial cortex.

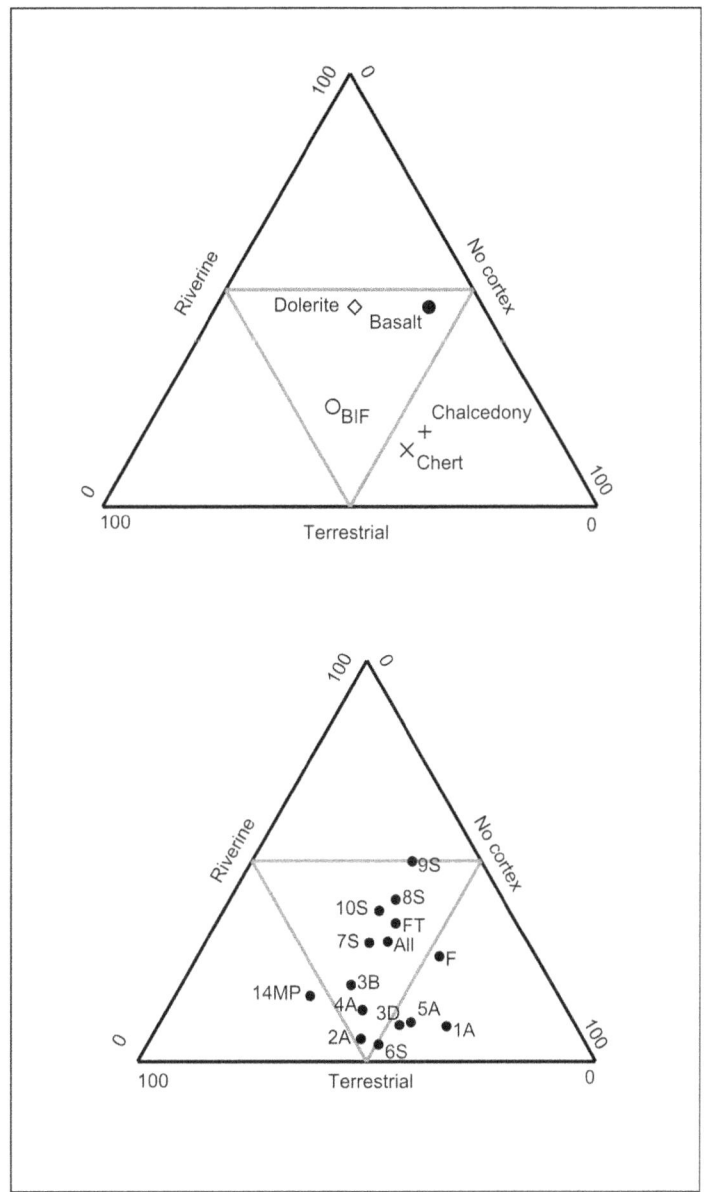

FIGURE 4.10: Cortex type by raw material (upper) and by group (lower).

The remaining ranges Groups and one Marsh sample (FT) are broadly similar to the chert and chalcedony samples.

The evidence from the analysis of cortex indicates that the use of stone is highly localised. In the ranges, terrestrial sources dominate assemblages, while on the plains cobbles and pebbles from the creeks provide the main sources of stone. This cuts across apparent variation in availability of particular raw materials, most notably basalt. The products of early stage reduction are therefore prominent in all samples, particularly plains samples.

With respect to the land-use model, cortex does not seem to discriminate between levels of occupation span and intensity at the landscape level. The density of archaeological remains is higher on the plains where residential mobility might be expected to be low. Nevertheless, the high proportion of cortical flakes in plains samples directly contradicts the expectations of the model. No doubt the fact that cortex is less prevalent in the ranges samples reflects primary use of quarried sources, outcrops and heat fractured nodules. Conversely, the relatively high percentage of cortex in plains samples demonstrates the importance of creek lines as a source of raw material. In this analysis, the nature of resource 'packaging' – as terrestrial or riverine resources – seems to be a primary determinant of assemblage variability. The occurrence and type of cortex present in archaeological assemblages in the Christmas Creek survey area is thus an indicator of highly localised use and discard of raw material in a landscape of abundant lithic resources. This interpretation casts doubt on the assumptions used in formulating the land-use model and highlights the need to modify general expectations in terms of local factors.

CORTEX AND VOLUME RATIOS

The evidence from the analysis of the distribution of cortex types suggests that local materials dominate artefact assemblages and that patterns of use of stone are strongly influenced by the form in which raw material occurs. The cortex ratio provides a method for determining whether or not all reduction and discard have occurred on site (Dibble et al. 2005). This method examines the characteristics of debitage assemblages in terms of volume, surface area and the occurrence of cortex to identify whether artefacts have been removed from or added to the assemblage. It involves calculating the expected cortical surface area for an assemblage and comparing it to the observed cortical surface area. These values should not differ if all cortical products remain in the assemblage and the value for the cortex ratio will be close to 1.0. Any discrepancy implies that cortical products have either been removed or added to the assemblage. This measure was originally

SURFACE ARTEFACT SCATTERS | 125

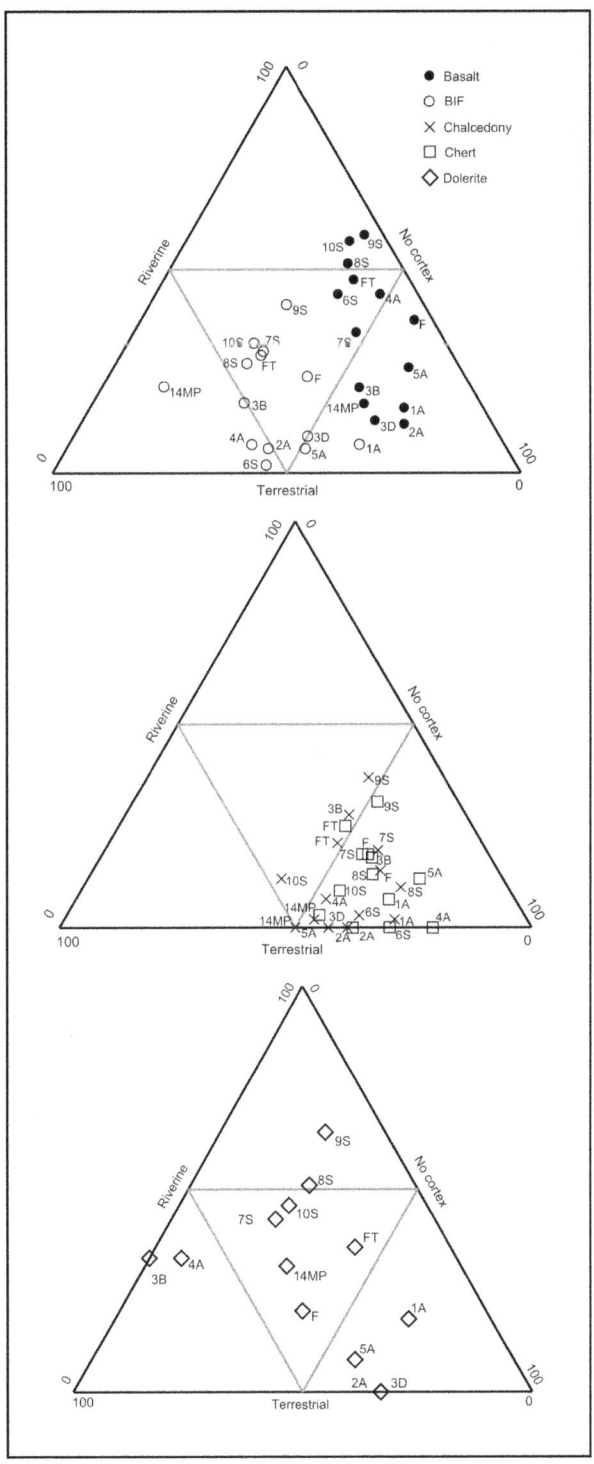

FIGURE 4.11: Cortex type by group for each raw material.

devised by Dibble and colleagues (2005) and evaluated based on experimental assemblages. Further experimental replication and simulation have confirmed the validity and usefulness of the method, which has also been applied to a range of archaeological assemblages in western New South Wales, the Pacific, France and Egypt (Ditchfield 2016; Ditchfield, Holdaway and Allen 2014; Douglass 2010; Douglass et al. 2008; Lin, McPherron and Dibble 2015; Phillipps 2012; Phillipps and Holdaway 2015).

Calculation of the cortex ratio involves some assumptions. It is primarily applicable to situations where assemblages are produced from fully cortical nodules. The volume ratio is similar to the cortex ratio, but uses estimates of assemblage volume rather than cortical surface area. Therefore, it does not assume fully cortical nodules as the form of the original raw material. Nevertheless, replication and simulation studies suggest that both measures provide reasonably robust estimates of loss or addition of artefacts to debitage assemblages, and, therefore, transport of artefacts (Dibble et al. 2005; Ditchfield 2016; Douglass et al. 2008; Douglass 2010, 111–12; Parker 2011, 90–91). In the study area, the attributes already recorded in the field can be used to calculate both ratios. The comprehensive nature of the survey means that the method can be applied at a landscape scale to investigate transport patterns of raw material.

In our study, the calculation of the cortex ratio generally followed the methodology set out in Douglass (2010, 105ff.):

- The number of nodules was estimated from the total of single and multiplatform cores.
- The mean nodule volume for each raw material was estimated by calculating the mean volume of cores with more than 80% cortex (Table 4.10).
- Expected assemblage surface area was calculated by using the result for estimated average nodule volume in an equation for a sphere. This result was then multiplied by the estimated number of nodules as approximated by the total of cores to give the expected cortical surface area for the whole assemblage.

- The surface area for flakes, flake fragments and debris was estimated by multiplying length and width.
- The surface area for cores and core fragments was calculated from length, width and thickness by inputting the relevant dimensions into an equation for the surface area of an ellipsoid (Douglass 2010, 106).
- Cortical surface area was then calculated for each artefact by multiplying the relevant surface area by the fraction of cortex recorded. Cortex was recorded in 10% increments in the field and these estimates were used directly. This differs slightly from the method used by Douglass who used fewer categories of cortex.
- The results for cortical surface area of each artefact were then summed to give the total observed cortical surface area.
- The cortex ratio was obtained by dividing the observed cortical surface area by the expected cortical surface area.

The calculation for the volume ratio was similar and generally followed the method described by Phillips and Holdaway (2015). Expected assemblage volume was calculated by multiplying the estimated average nodule volume, based on the mean volume of cores with more than 80% cortex, by the number of cores in the assemblage. The volume of cores was calculated

TABLE 4.10: Mean volume and surface area for all cores with 80% cortex or more.

	N	Volume (mm^3)	Surface area (mm^2)
Basalt	80	63879	7728
BIF	169	78734	8834
Chalcedony	6	49939	6558
Chert	10	81910	9121
Dolerite	21	132326	12558

using the formula for the volume of an ellipsoid. The volume of flakes, flake fragments and debris was simply calculated by treating them as rectangular prisms and multiplying length by width by thickness. This differs from Phillips and Holdaway, who calculated volume for different classes of flakes according to the geometric solid they most resemble (2015, Figure 6). The results for this study thus probably slightly overestimate the actual observed assemblage volumes. The volume ratio was calculated by dividing the observed volume by the expected volume.

Cortex and volume ratios were calculated for each of the sample groups for basalt, BIF, chert and chalcedony. Groups 7SA–D were combined as 7S because the isolated artefacts sample had not been subdivided by subsample. Only the transect sample from March was included in this analysis.

Tables 4.11–5 present the detailed results of the cortex and volume ratio calculations for each group. The cortex ratios are quite variable, but most are below 1.0. The value for chert from Group 3D is above 1.0, but the sample size for this group is small. For dolerite, the value for Group 10S is also above 1.0. This indicates that cortex has been removed from all assemblages.

Very few samples give results close to 1.0. Values above 0.8 occur in only nine samples. These are in Groups 8S and 9S for BIF, basalt and dolerite; in Group 10S for basalt; and for chert and dolerite in Group FT. It is worth noting that values are generally higher on the plains than in the ranges for both BIF and basalt. The values for both chalcedony and chert are very variable and generally do not show any particular spatial patterning (Figure 4.12).

The results for volume ratio calculations are also presented in Tables 4.11–5. Here again the results are variable, but nearly all are greater than 1.0. Only the results for chert in Groups 5A, 6S and 10S, and for dolerite in Groups 3B and 4A, are less than 1.0. Like the cortex ratio, a value of 1.0 indicates no transport. For the volume ratio, however, values greater than 1.0 indicate that volume has been removed from the assemblage. The high values in most samples demonstrate considerable loss of volume. It is also possible to calculate the expected number of cores by dividing the observed volume by the estimated mean nodule volume (see Table 4.10). The results clearly indicate that there are many fewer cores than would be expected in the assemblages. In most cases, the number of cores actually present is

Table 4.11: Banded iron formation: cortex and volume ratios.

Group	N	N of cores	Expected surface area (mm²)	Observed surface area (mm²)	CR	Expected volume (mm³)	Observed volume (mm³)	VR
1A	637	37	326858	103354	0.32	2913158	5207275	1.79
2A	403	33	291522	174586	0.60	2598222	5571789	2.14
3B	582	93	821562	455387	0.55	7322262	13366691	1.83
3D	118	7	61838	29081	0.47	551138	1422686	2.58
4A	412	35	309190	182060	0.59	2755690	5190194	1.88
5A	485	41	362194	95628	0.26	3228094	3968120	1.23
6S	184	24	212016	71744	0.34	1889616	2605097	1.38
7S	2915	455	4019470	2516808	0.63	35823970	71972658	2.01
8S	716	107	945238	811564	0.86	8424538	21223502	2.52
9S	719	88	777392	686641	0.88	6928592	22330420	3.22
10S	366	57	503538	378290	0.75	4487838	12026629	2.68
FT	280	52	459368	269403	0.59	4094168	7135319	1.74

two-thirds to half of the expected number of cores based on the volume of raw material present (Table 4.16).

One problem with interpreting these results is the likely presence of partially cortical nodules or source material quarried from bedrock seams. This may well account for the generally low values for the cortex ratio for chert and the lack of spatial patterning. As noted above, chert artefacts in general are mostly non-cortical. An additional sample from the ranges (Group 5Q) was analysed from shelters with quarried seams of chert in Group 5A. These assemblages were dominated by chert and had low percentages of cortex (16%). As one might expect, the cortex ratio was also low (0.15). However, the volume ratio of 2.62 also suggested a loss of volume. The expected number of cores was 45, compared to 17 actually recorded. The mean volume of chert cores in 5Q was 52,385 mm³, substantially smaller than the estimated chert nodule volume of 81,910 mm³ derived from cores in the project area with more than 80% cortex.

Another problem in interpreting the results is the assumption that one core is equivalent to one source nodule. This has obvious implications for the calculation of expected values of volume and cortical surface area. A related issue is how the estimated nodule volume is derived. Previous studies have used experimental data to examine the local form of raw material and test these assumptions (Dibble et al. 2005; Douglass 2010; Douglass et al. 2008; Lin, McPherron and Dibble 2015). Such experimentation was beyond the scope of this study, which sought to apply the methodology retrospectively to data already collected within a compliance context. Undoubtedly, future applications in the Pilbara should address this issue. Several indicators in this study, including the generally low levels of reduction, use of simple hard hammer percussion and the widespread occurrence of reduction areas indicating in situ flaking events, all suggest that the assumption that one core represents one nodule is reasonable. Estimating the size of the original nodules is more problematic. However, a high percentage of artefacts in the study area retain cortex. Cores with high proportions of retained cortical surface area can provide an estimate of the size of source material chosen for flaking. The mean volume and surface area of all cores from the survey area with 80% cortex or more were calculated to give an estimate of the size of source material.

A final issue concerns how the values of the cortex and volume ratios should be interpreted, in terms of statistically significant deviation from 1.0. This issue was discussed in detail by Lin, McPherron and Dibble (2015), who used experimental data and resampling to assign probabilities to cortex ratios derived from archaeological assemblages. No attempt was made to evaluate probabilities in this way, not least because, as already noted, experimental replication was beyond the scope of this study. It is clearly possible to alter individual values by changing the assumptions on which the calculations are based. However, the ratios are used here to identify differences between particular raw materials in different localities. Provided the assumptions are consistently applied, it is the differences in values that

TABLE 4.12: Basalt: cortex and volume ratios.

Group	N	N of cores	Expected surface area (mm²)	Observed surface area (mm²)	CR	Expected volume (mm³)	Observed volume (mm³)	VR
1A	204	11	85008	27781	0.33	702669	1558339	2.22
2A	26	2	15456	1969	0.13	127758	268912	2.10
3B	67	6	46368	19249	0.42	383274	906737	2.37
3D	24	0	0	3759	NA	0	163102	NA
4A	88	5	38640	23274	0.60	319395	911953	2.86
5A	171	8	61824	18085	0.29	511032	1200452	2.35
6S	18	1	7728	1101	0.14	63879	79593	1.25
7S	710	102	788256	291794	0.37	6515658	11380890	1.75
8S	1366	158	1221024	1186111	0.97	10092882	32830931	3.25
9S	930	96	741888	601603	0.81	6132384	19422367	3.17
10S	328	26	200928	183560	0.91	1660854	6316708	3.80
FT	303	39	301392	162986	0.54	2491281	4709678	1.89

are of primary interest, rather than the absolute values. Furthermore, the interpretation of the results relies on other contextual information.

The results of the analysis of cortex and volume ratios are broadly consistent with the spatial patterning in the occurrence and type of cortex. The relatively high values for cortex ratio on the plains are consistent with the greater prevalence of riverine cortex in assemblages here, while the lower values in the ranges are consistent with the likely occurrence of partially cortical source material. Nevertheless, the fact that cortex ratios are consistently below 1.0 suggests that there is a cortical deficit in assemblages, particularly in the ranges, indicating artefact transport. The assumption of fully cortical source material does not apply to the volume ratio. The volume ratio, in combination with the expected number of cores, confirms that there is indeed a deficit of material in the form of substantial numbers of cores missing from BIF, basalt and chalcedony assemblages in most samples from the project area. This result is surprising because we have suggested that the high values of cortex generally and the analysis of both cortex type and raw material diversity point to highly local use of raw material. Nevertheless, it seems that some stone procured in the study area was removed in the form of cores, perhaps for use in areas where stone material was less readily available as part of a 'place-provisioning' strategy. One possibility is that these cores were taken to the margins of the Fortescue Marsh for use there. There is some evidence, in the form of field observations of individual large cores associated with surface artefact scatters close to the Marsh, that this might be the case.[2]

Holdaway, Douglas and Fanning (2012, 287–88) suggest that cortex ratios can be further interpreted in terms of mobility by considering movement frequency and linearity by both individuals and groups. All things being equal, infrequent movement should result in higher cortex ratio values as more artefacts will be discarded at the place of manufacture. Linearity considers the distance over which movement occurs and can be expressed in terms of tortuosity. Point-to-point movement between specific places in the landscape has low tortuosity and high velocity. This can be contrasted with movement within areas, which has high tortuosity and low velocity. The latter may not result in the movement of artefacts far from their point of origin and will favour local deposition, and therefore higher values for cortex ratio. By contrast, movements with low tortuosity are more likely to result in transport of artefacts away from their point of origin and thus lower cortex ratios. In terms of the land-use model, then, high cortex ratio values might be expected on the plains, where low residential mobility equates to infrequent movement and high tortuosity, and thus more artefact discard close to point of origin. Conversely, in the ranges, low cortex ratios should correspond to more frequent movement and low tortuosity. The difference in cortex ratios in the study area between the ranges and the plains is

---

2 Stuart Rapley, personal communication, 2014.

TABLE 4.13: Chalcedony: cortex and volume ratios.

Group	N	N of Cores	Expected Surface Area (mm²)	Observed Surface Area (mm²)	CR	Expected Volume (mm³)	Observed Volume (mm³)	VR
1A	237	29	190182	36867	0.19	1448231	1771470	1.22
2A	13	1	6558	513	0.08	49939	52063	1.04
3B	63	4	26232	11668	0.44	199756	544637	2.73
3D	0	0	0	0	NA	0	0	NA
4A	24	2	13116	800	0.06	99878	147374	1.48
5A	17	2	13116	1192	0.09	99878	123579	1.24
6S	23	3	19674	10972	0.56	149817	173397	1.16
7S	395	42	275436	129497	0.47	2097438	4772702	2.28
8S	177	14	91812	45340	0.49	699146	1439723	2.06
9S	167	14	91812	58117	0.63	699146	2023750	2.89
10S	108	10	65580	24078	0.37	499390	1168569	2.34
FT	129	14	91812	38206	0.42	699146	1005420	1.44

consistent with longer residence times in the plains. In the ranges, terrain imposes more constraints on travel routes and therefore more point-to-point movement can be expected.

CORE REDUCTION

The land-use model suggests that more intensive reduction of cores and flakes signals limited mobility. Possible indicators of differences in degree of reduction include: size of cores and flakes, core to flake ratio, amount of cortex and evidence of core rotation.

The percentage of cores of different raw material is similar to the representation of those materials in the overall sample (Table 4.5, Table 4.17).

Table 4.14: Chert: cortex and volume ratios.

Group	N	N of Cores	Expected Surface Area (mm²)	Observed Surface Area (mm²)	CR	Expected Volume (mm³)	Observed Volume (mm³)	VR
1A	105	9	82089	15848	0.19	737190	489635	0.66
2A	28	3	21153	4577	0.22	167007	251158	1.50
3B	61	7	49357	25836	0.52	389683	672060	1.72
3D*	8	3	21153	26686	1.26	167007	425628	2.55
4A	72	5	35255	6239	0.18	278345	276086	0.99
5A	93	19	133969	17514	0.13	1057711	456072	0.43
6S	74	6	42306	6683	0.16	334014	185556	0.56
7S	113	17	119867	42214	0.35	946373	1192591	1.26
8S	40	0	0	2619	NA	0	294199	NA
9S	62	5	35255	16378	0.46	278345	679435	2.44
10S	66	8	56408	13597	0.24	445352	393440	0.88
FT	39	2	14102	13370	0.95	111338	284853	2.56

* One unusually large core has been omitted from calculations for Group 3D.

TABLE 4.15: Dolerite: cortex and volume ratios.

Group	N	N of cores	Expected surface area (mm²)	Observed surface area (mm²)	CR	Expected volume (mm³)	Observed volume (mm³)	VR
1A	43	3	37674	20440	0.54	396978	874630	2.20
2A	3	0	0	133	NA	0	30432	NA
3B	3	1	12558	780	0.06	132326	44282	0.33
3D	3	0	0	1248	NA	0	44336	NA
4A	15	3	37674	11744	0.31	396978	272758	0.69
5A	26	1	12558	5672	0.45	132326	234039	1.77
7S	221	31	389298	240770	0.62	4102106	7320353	1.78
8S	121	16	200928	195348	0.97	2117216	5467710	2.58
9S	173	25	313950	289300	0.92	3308150	8616127	2.60
10S	70	10	125580	174491	1.39	1323260	5324957	4.02
F	5	1	12558	4336	0.35	132326	159220	1.20
FT	39	5	62790	52614	0.84	661630	1970378	2.98

TABLE 4.16: Observed (O) number of cores and expected (E) number of cores based on total volume of raw material.

Group	BIF O	BIF E	Basalt O	Basalt E	Chalcedony O	Chalcedony E	Chert O	Chert E	Dolerite O	Dolerite E
1A	37	66	11	24	29	35	9	6	3	7
2A	33	71	2	4	1	1	3	3	0	0
3B	93	170	6	14	4	11	7	8	1	0
3D	7	18	0	3	0	0	3	5	0	0
4A	35	66	5	14	2	3	5	3	3	2
5A	41	50	8	19	2	2	19	6	1	2
6S	24	33	1	1	3	3	6	2	0	0
7S	455	914	102	178	42	96	17	15	31	55
8S	107	270	158	514	14	29	0	4	16	41
9S	88	284	96	304	14	41	5	8	25	65
10S	57	153	26	99	10	23	8	5	10	40
FT	52	91	39	74	14	20	2	3	5	15

SURFACE ARTEFACT SCATTERS | 137

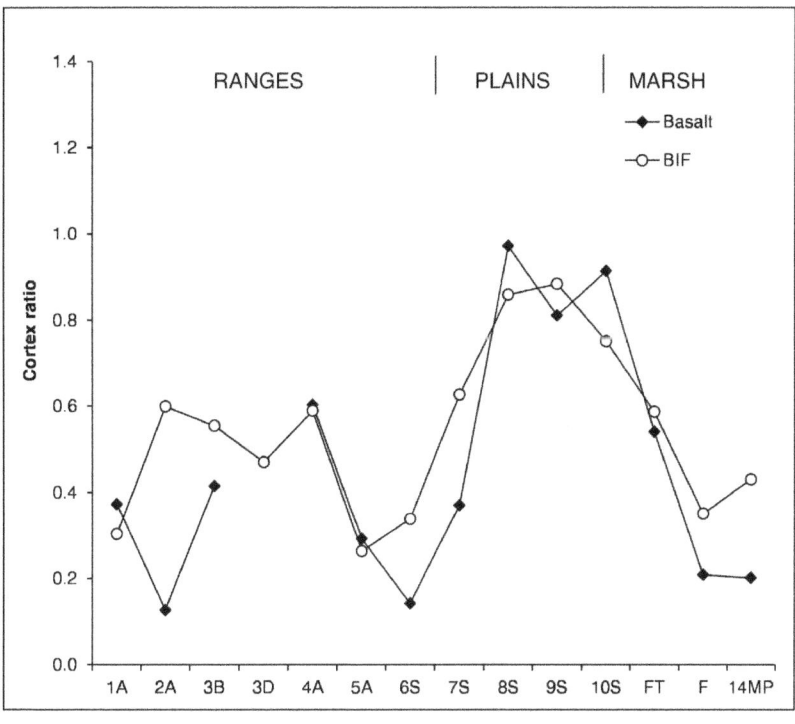

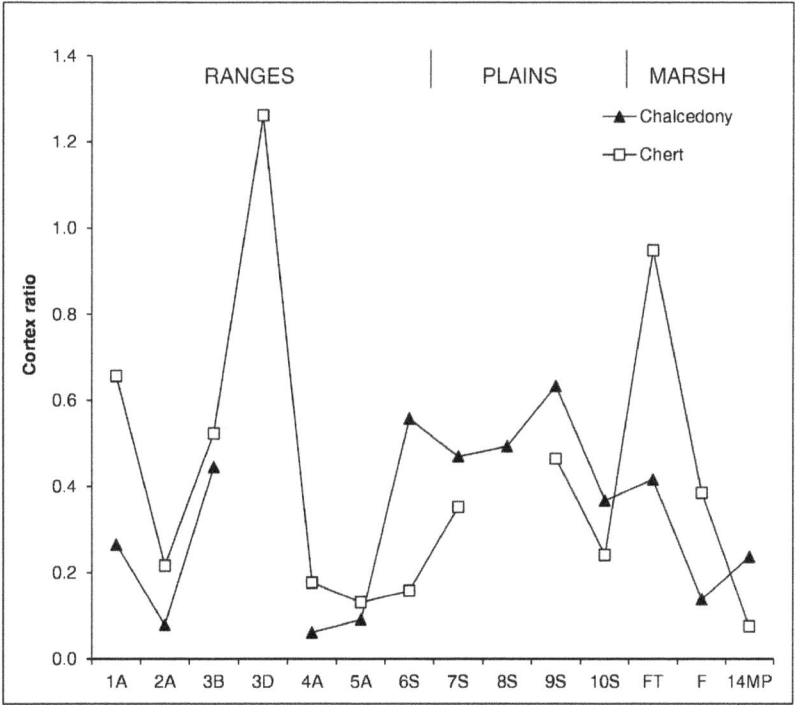

FIGURE 4.12: Cortex ratios for basalt, BIF, chalcedony and chert group samples in relation to landform.

More detailed analysis will be confined to cores of the five most common materials (BIF, basalt, chalcedony, chert and dolerite). Most cores are single platform flake cores. The remainder are rotated and worked from more than one platform (Table 4.17). The overall ratio of multiplatform cores to single platform cores is 0.51; that is, about a third of cores are rotated. Basalt and dolerite cores are slightly more likely to be rotated and BIF cores are least likely to be rotated. However, generally there is little evidence of much difference in the working of particular raw materials. There is also little evidence of systematic variation in the incidence of core rotation in relation to landform (Table 4.18). Both chert and dolerite multiplatform cores occur in relatively high proportions from near the Marsh. However, the sample size was small. Blade cores are rare; only three were identified, one chalcedony and two BIF.

Cores vary greatly in size, and this is clearly related to raw material type. Dolerite cores are the largest, BIF and basalt are smaller than dolerite cores and roughly the same size, while chalcedony and chert cores are the smallest and similar in size (Table 4.19). Core size also varies across the survey area (Table 4.20, Figure 4.13). Those recorded on the plains are generally larger than those near the Fortescue Marsh or in the ranges. The main exceptions are chert and dolerite, for which the largest cores are from near the Marsh. It is important to bear in mind that the sample size for both chert and dolerite from the Marsh is small. Nevertheless, it is clear that the expectation that cores will be more intensively reduced on the plains than in the ranges as a result of lower mobility is not met. Furthermore, the level of reduction is similar in both the Marsh and ranges for basalt, BIF and chalcedony cores.

Even more surprising is the fact that single and multiplatform cores are broadly similar in size; indeed, multiplatform cores are often larger. Core rotation is commonly interpreted as a strategy for extending the use life of cores, and therefore provides one indicator for intensity of reduction (Clarkson and O'Connor 2014, 178). The results of t-tests indicate that the differences in the attributes of single and multiplatform cores are not statistically significant in most cases. The exceptions are length and thickness for basalt cores, and length and volume for BIF cores. The dimensions of multiplatform cores are larger than single platform cores in all cases where differences are statistically significant. Clearly, length, width and thickness may not be directly comparable on single and multiplatform cores, given that cores were measured with reference to last flake scar (see Appendix 1). Whether the measurements are comparable depends on the direction and amount of rotation. Few cores show evidence of more than one rotation. One way of mitigating this is to use volume. This was estimated by applying axial measurements to the formula for an ellipsoid solid (Phillipps and Holdaway 2015). The results confirm that multiplatform cores do indeed tend to have larger mean volumes than single platform cores (Table 4.20).

Core rotation, therefore, does not seem to be an indicator of increased reduction. In the Christmas Creek study area, raw material is readily available and occurs in several forms including cobbles and pebbles in the creeks, thermally fractured pieces and outcrops. Reduction events typically involve production of a series of flakes by hard hammer percussion from a minimally prepared platform, often in a sequence resembling slicing a salami, rather than removal of flakes around the perimeter of a single platform core.

TABLE 4.17: Core type by raw material.

	MULTI-PLATFORM	SINGLE PLATFORM	TOTAL	%	MP:SP
Basalt	193	282	475	24.5	0.68
BIF	329	737	1066	55.1	0.45
Chalcedony	45	86	131	6.8	0.52
Chert	25	57	82	4.2	0.44
Dolerite	40	56	96	5.0	0.71
Mudstone	5	17	22	1.1	0.29
Quartzite	7	35	42	2.2	0.20
Other*	8	13	21	1.1	0.62
TOTAL	652	1283	1935		0.51

* ironstone, quartz, crystal quartz, silcrete, siltstone and unidentified fine-grained siliceous.

TABLE 4.18: Ratio of multiplatform to single platform cores (mp:sp) by raw material and landform.

	Ranges	Plains	Marsh
BASALT	28	390	67
mp:sp	1	0.70	0.60
BIF	264	718	96
mp:sp	0.38	0.49	0.32
CHALCEDONY	17	82	35
mp:sp	0.55	0.64	0.30
CHERT	64	30	5
mp:sp	0.36	0.67	1.50
DOLERITE	7	84	7
mp:sp	0	0.79	2.50

Larger pieces of raw material may simply have more capacity for reduction and therefore were more likely to be rotated. In a situation of raw material abundance, with varied original sizes of source material, it may not be worth attempting to maximise the production of flakes from smaller pieces. Rotation might even indicate re-use of a core sometime after the original reduction event, with a new individual choosing to begin a new reduction sequence from a different platform. In this scenario, cores might form a 'bank' of raw material available at frequently used locations. Consequently, core rotation might not be associated with more intensive reduction, but with variation in the original size of raw material packages. Larger source material simply has more capacity for reduction.

The amount of cortex is also an indicator of reduction intensity. Most cores (87%) retained some cortex (Table 4.21). Chalcedony and chert have the least cortex, with about a quarter being non-cortical. As core size decreases so does the amount of cortex (Figure 4.14). Figure 4.15 plots the mean volume of single and multiplatform cores in relation to amount of cortex for each raw material. This shows that both BIF and basalt multiplatform cores are larger than single platform cores of those materials. Chert single and multiplatform cores are similar in size. Only chalcedony single platform cores with more than 50% cortex are larger than multiplatform cores.

The amount and type of cortex also varies with raw material and in their spatial distribution. Terrestrial cortex is generally more common on BIF, chalcedony and chert cores, while dolerite and basalt more commonly have riverine cortex (Table 4.21). Plains assemblages have higher proportions of riverine cortex, while terrestrial cortex dominates in the ranges (Figure 4.16). This result is consistent with a highly local pattern of procurement of raw material. The primary sources of raw material in the ranges are terrestrial, while the creeks are key sources on the plains. Although type of cortex does vary with raw material, BIF, chert and chalcedony cores on the plains and the Marsh are clearly more commonly sourced from creeks than from terrestrial sources.

FLAKE SIZE

Flake size also varies systematically between raw materials. Dolerite flakes are the largest. Chert and chalcedony flakes are the smallest, while BIF and basalt are intermediate (Table 4.22). The mean size of complete flakes is generally larger on the plains than in the ranges, particularly for basalt and BIF. Flakes from the three Marsh samples are smallest on average, except for chalcedony. Figure 4.17 shows that the pattern of size variation also holds when examining individual samples, particularly for BIF and basalt. Chert and chalcedony are more variable, with mean length of chert flakes anomalously high in some ranges samples and in 14MP. In the case of groups 2A, 3D and 14MP, this result can probably be attributed to small sample size, while Group 3B is actually at the very edge of the ranges.

Comparing flake size in terms of the amount of cortex indicates that cortical flakes are larger than non-cortical flakes (Figure 4.18). This is consistent with the expectation that cortical flakes are mainly removed at an early stage of core reduction. As already noted, cortical flakes make up a greater proportion of plains assemblages and this could account for the

TABLE 4.19: Dimensions of single and multiplatform cores: summary statistics for five main raw materials.

	N	Length (mm)	SD	Width (mm)	SD	Thickness (mm)	SD	Volume (mm³)	SD
SINGLE PLATFORM									
Basalt	282	41.4	20.9	47.5	15.6	38.8	20.7	45708	48743
BIF	737	39.3	20.4	52.7	21.1	42.4	22.4	50403	55983
Chalcedony	86	35.4	15.6	43.5	17.2	30.1	16.6	31079	39957
Chert	57	31.3	22.5	38.1	17.3	22.7	11.5	19698	35466
Dolerite	56	49.7	25.2	62.9	26.9	55.4	33.0	101818	124702
TOTAL	1218	39.6	20.8	50.7	20.4	40.4	22.6	48879	59254
MULTI-PLATFORM									
Basalt	193	47.2	20.6	49.7	19.0	37.9	20.5	59680	75427
BIF	329	48.5	21.4	53.1	20.7	43.6	19.4	66996	66423
Chalcedony	45	37.1	19.1	40.6	16.1	27.6	13.9	29291	36646
Chert	25	37.4	22.7	37.6	12.7	27.1	14.1	25585	34120
Dolerite	40	63.4	29.3	61.4	29.7	55.1	25.4	154158	288220
TOTAL	632	47.8	22.2	51.1	20.9	40.8	20.6	65956	99815

TABLE 4.20: Volume (mm³) of cores, by type, raw material and landform.

	Single platform			Multiplatform			All cores		
	N	MEAN	SD	N	MEAN	SD	N	MEAN	SD
BASALT	282	45708	48743	193	59680	75427	475	51385	61320
Ranges	14	22307	32399	14	25539	39633	28	23923	35559
Plains	226	50852	51729	154	67759	80755	380	57704	65500
Marsh	42	25824	22968	25	29035	31812	67	27022	26423
BIF	737	50403	55983	329	66996	66423	1066	55524	59862
Ranges	190	37242	44132	73	43767	58956	263	39053	48670
Plains	474	57480	61309	233	74566	65773	707	63111	63281
Marsh	73	38711	36138	23	64035	79857	96	44778	50839
CHALCEDONY	86	31079	39957	45	29291	36646	131	30465	38719
Ranges	11	30264	25731	5	6535	8191	16	22849	24255
Plains	48	42308	48621	32	37528	40616	80	40396	45380
Marsh	27	11450	7629	8	10567	4052	35	11248	6931
CHERT	57	19698	35466	25	25585	34120	82	21493	34957
Ranges	37	22163	42809	10	18075	18596	47	21293	38791
Plains	18	14053	13337	12	30587	43886	30	20667	30045
Marsh	2	24901	24264	3	30605	36757	5	28323	28852
DOLERITE	56	101818	124702	40	154158	288220	96	123627	209233
Ranges	7	52069	74974	0	NA	NA	7	52069	74974
Plains	47	111912	131163	35	145827	300440	82	126388	218960
Marsh	2	38744	10784	5	212475	194509	7	162838	180078

TABLE 4.21: Cores: percentage of cortex.

	RIVERINE		TERRESTRIAL		NONE		TOTAL
	N	%	N	%	N	%	
BASALT	317	66.7	96	20.2	62	13.1	475
Ranges	14	50.0	10	35.7	4	14.3	28
Plains	258	67.9	80	21.1	42	11.1	380
Marsh	45	67.2	6	9.0	16	23.9	67
BIF	353	33.1	600	56.3	113	10.6	1066
Ranges	25	9.5	192	73.0	46	17.5	263
Plains	291	41.2	354	50.1	62	8.8	707
Marsh	37	38.5	54	56.3	5	5.2	96
CHALCEDONY	36	27.5	62	47.3	33	25.2	131
Ranges	2	12.5	8	50.0	6	37.5	16
Plains	25	31.3	38	47.5	17	21.3	80
Marsh	9	25.7	16	45.7	10	28.6	35
CHERT	16	19.5	46	56.1	20	24.4	82
Ranges	4	8.5	31	66.0	12	25.5	47
Plains	10	33.3	13	43.3	7	23.3	30
Marsh	2	40.0	2	40.0	1	20.0	5
DOLERITE	65	67.7	26	27.1	5	5.2	96
Ranges	3	42.9	3	42.9	1	14.3	7
Plains	58	70.7	21	25.6	3	3.7	82
Marsh	4	57.1	2	28.6	1	14.3	7
TOTAL	787	42.5	830	44.9	233	12.6	1850

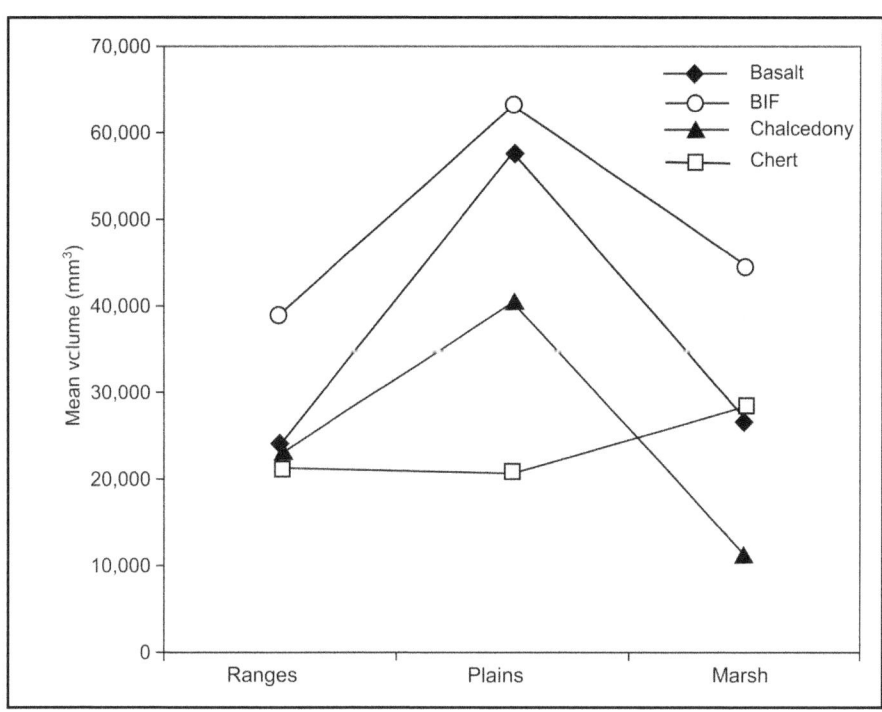

FIGURE 4.13: Mean volume (mm³) of cores by raw material and landform.

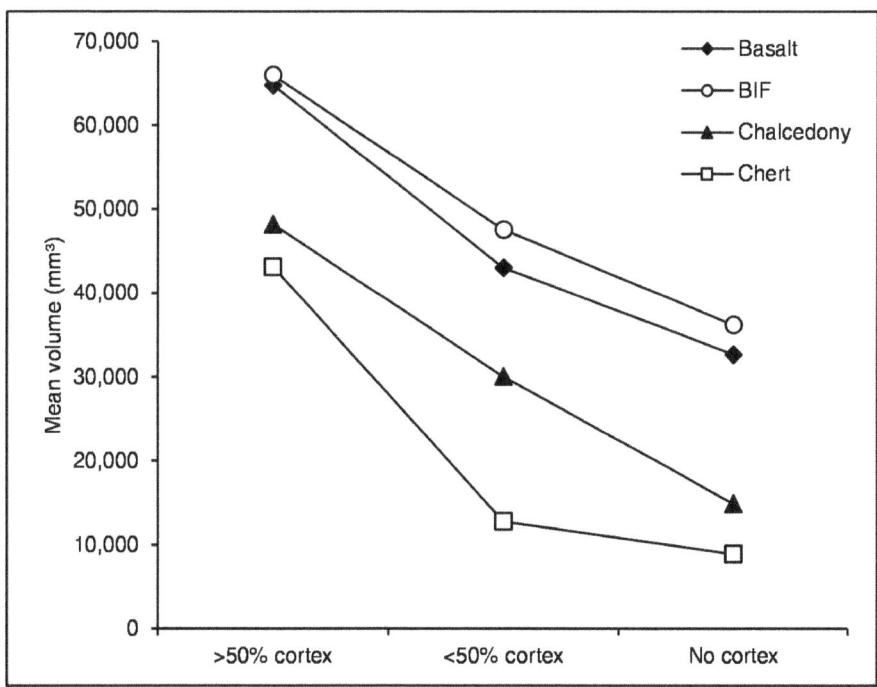

FIGURE 4.14: Mean volume (mm³) of cores by amount of cortex for each raw material.

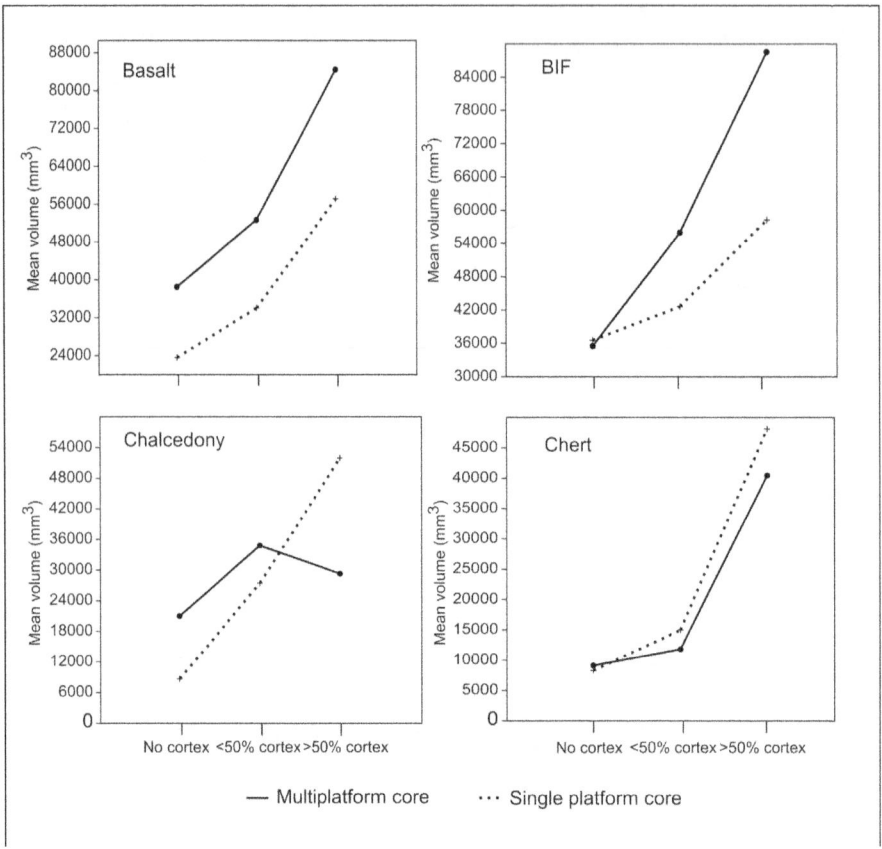

FIGURE 4.15: Mean volume (mm³) of single and multiplatform cores for each raw material by amount of cortex.

consistently larger size of flakes. However, when comparing flake length and different amounts of cortex for each raw material from different parts of the survey area, we find that the size difference between the ranges and the plains is repeated for each cortex group (Table 4.23). Flakes from the plains are consistently larger than those from the ranges regardless of raw material or amount of cortex. Table 4.24 indicates that flakes with riverine cortex are consistently larger than flakes with terrestrial cortex. This suggests that larger flake size on the plains may be related to the use of pebbles and cobbles from the creeks as the primary source of raw material.

There is little evidence of platform preparation. Most flakes (95%) have either cortical or plain platforms (Table 4.25), with approximately equal numbers of each. Cortical platforms are more common on dolerite flakes,

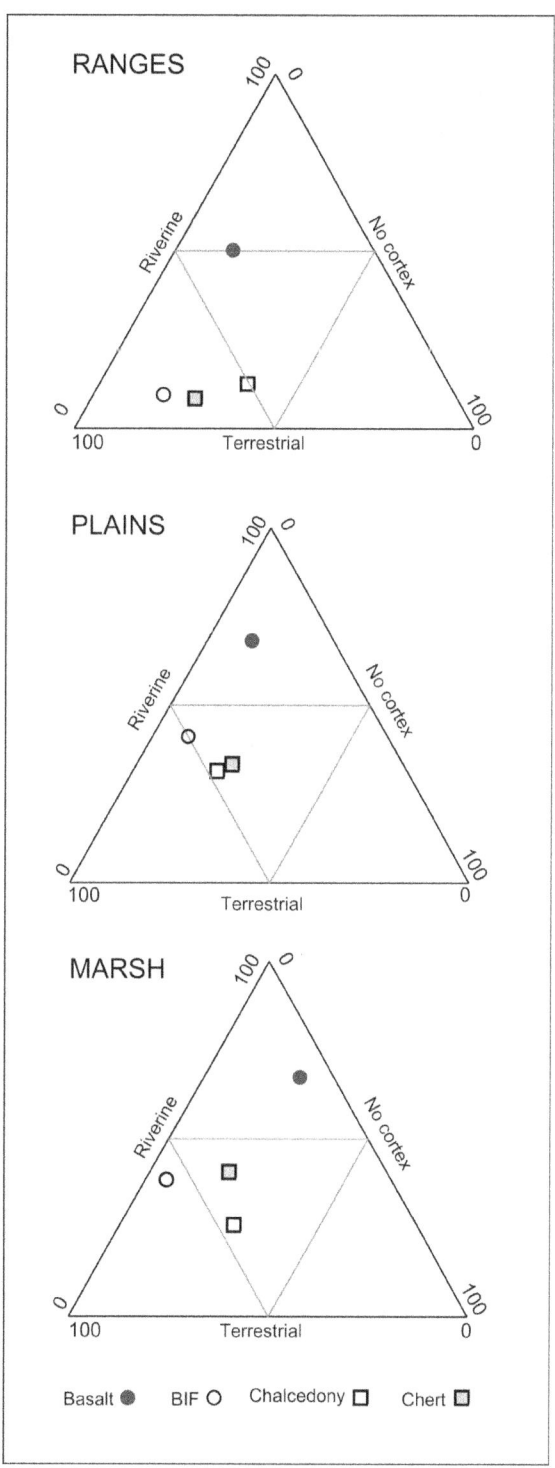

FIGURE 4.16: Proportion of different types of cortex, in relation to raw material and landform.

while chert and chalcedony flakes have much lower percentages of cortical platforms. This is consistent with the generally lower occurrence of cortex on chert and chalcedony flakes already noted. Overhang reduction is also uncommon; only 5% of complete and proximal flakes have any evidence of it and there is little variation between raw materials.

FLAKE TO CORE RATIO

The flake to core ratio is another possible indicator of reduction intensity. Assuming that reduction occurs in situ, the ratio should rise as reduction increases and more flakes are produced from each core. The ratio may also increase in situations where cores are removed from assemblages (Ditchfield 2016). The minimum number of flakes (MNF) was used to calculate the ratio (Hiscock 2002).

The flake to core ratio varies considerably between sample groups (Table 4.27). Overall, the highest ratios are in the ranges. Table 4.27 shows that the ratio also varies considerably between raw materials. Dolerite, chert and chalcedony are particularly variable, and this is likely to be sensitive to sample size. However, the chert assemblages from the Marsh Groups do have noticeably higher ratios. This may indicate more intensive reduction of chert in this part of the study area, given the limited natural availability of chert near the margins of the Fortescue Marsh. The ratios for basalt artefacts tend to be higher than for BIF artefacts, although the ratios for both are higher in the ranges.

This result is broadly consistent with those for size of both cores and flakes, which also indicated more intensive reduction in the ranges and near the Fortescue Marsh (see Figures 4.13, 4.17). Figure 4.19 shows that the plains samples are tightly grouped, with consistently larger mean length of flakes and flake to core ratios in the range 4–8. Ranges samples by contrast are much more variable for flake to core ratios (range 3–16), but mean length of flakes is consistently smaller. The Marsh samples resemble those from the ranges for mean length of flakes, but cluster with the plains samples for flake to core ratios. Group 3B has the lowest flake to core ratio of all the ranges groups, although the mean length of flakes is smaller than all the plains samples. This group is on the very edge of the ranges.

TABLE 4.22: Dimensions of complete flakes: summary statistics.

	N	Length (mm)	SD	Width (mm)	SD	Thickness (mm)	SD	LxW/Th	SD
BASALT	3006	39.1	16.1	30.5	11.4	10.1	5.2	129.3	71.6
Ranges	340	29.3	12.9	25.1	8.7	8.5	4.1	95.8	54.5
Plains	2356	41.0	16.1	31.6	11.7	10.5	5.3	135.2	72.9
Marsh	310	35.3	14.5	28.5	9.8	9.3	4.9	121.3	67.3
BIF	5565	38.0	14.9	33.5	14.0	11.3	5.7	122.0	63.7
Ranges	1728	32.0	12.9	30.2	16.8	9.9	4.8	105.5	60.3
Plains	3480	41.0	15.1	35.4	12.3	12.0	5.8	130.5	64.3
Marsh	357	37.8	13.3	32.1	10.4	11.4	6.7	119.7	58.2
CHALCEDONY	900	31.3	11.0	25.5	8.8	7.9	4.4	114.7	61.5
Ranges	125	25.8	9.7	21.6	7.1	6.9	3.4	90.0	43.0
Plains	596	32.9	11.2	26.6	8.9	8.0	3.7	121.0	62.7
Marsh	179	30.0	10.1	24.4	8.8	8.0	6.7	110.7	64.0
CHERT	413	27.2	11.8	25.0	10.0	7.8	3.8	93.7	52.2
Ranges	186	25.0	11.5	23.4	8.6	7.4	3.6	86.9	53.2
Plains	180	29.7	12.1	27.0	11.4	8.3	4.0	102.8	52.7
Marsh	47	26.1	10.2	23.9	8.2	7.7	3.4	86.1	40.1
DOLERITE	519	49.5	17.9	39.1	13.8	13.3	6.1	156.7	71.3
Ranges	46	38.5	14.2	29.7	8.6	9.4	3.1	131.1	71.8
Plains	429	51.4	17.9	40.4	13.7	13.9	6.2	161.5	71.6
Marsh	44	42.2	15.6	36.8	14.7	12.0	5.7	136.4	59.0

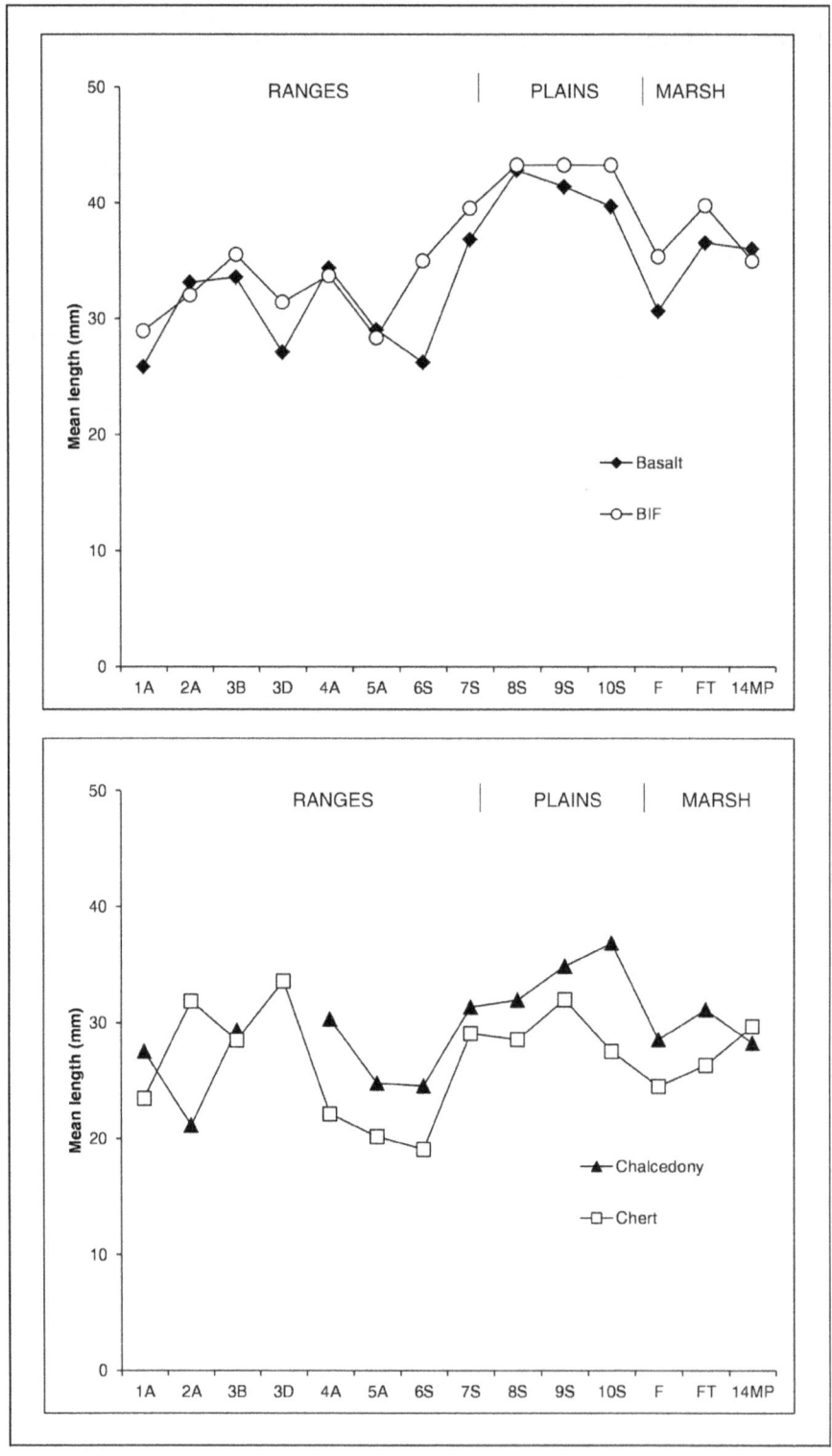

FIGURE 4.17: Mean length (mm) of complete flakes for individual sample groups.

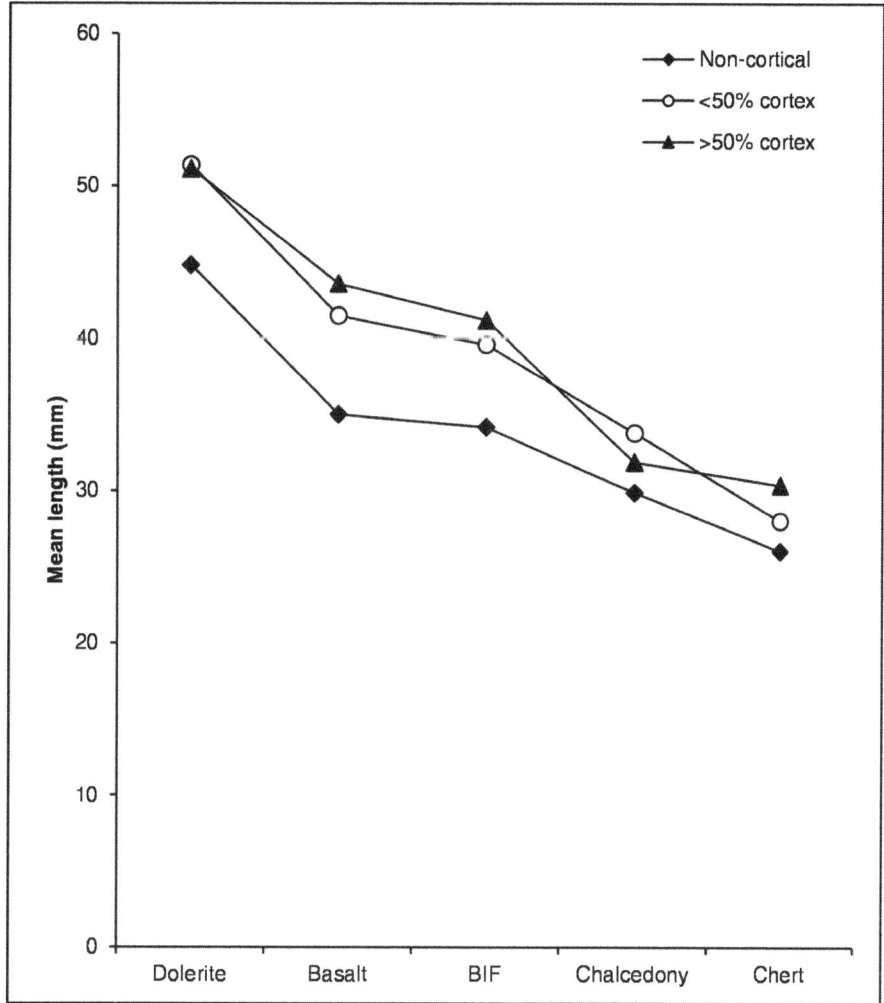

FIGURE 4.18: Mean length (mm) of complete flakes by cortex group.

TABLE 4.23: Mean length (mm) and standard deviation of complete flakes by cortex group.

	No cortex			<50% cortex			>50% cortex		
	N	LENGTH	SD	N	LENGTH	SD	N	LENGTH	SD
BASALT	1315	35.0	14.2	1116	41.5	15.7	575	43.6	18.5
Ranges	212	28.1	12.5	95	31.3	13.8	33	30.8	12.6
Plains	952	37.0	14.2	919	42.8	15.6	485	45.3	18.5
Marsh	151	32.4	12.8	102	39.0	14.4	57	36.7	17.1
BIF	1951	34.1	13.1	2387	39.6	14.2	1227	41.2	17.3
Ranges	755	29.3	11.3	668	33.8	12.7	305	34.8	15.3
Plains	1076	37.4	13.4	1574	42.1	14.3	830	43.5	17.5
Marsh	120	34.5	12.4	145	38.5	11.5	92	41.2	16.0
CHALCEDONY	507	29.8	10.2	276	33.9	11.4	117	31.9	12.6
Ranges	81	25.2	8.7	33	29.2	11.4	11	20.2	8.4
Plains	330	31.4	10.4	189	35.0	11.4	77	34.0	13.0
Marsh	96	28.3	9.4	54	32.8	10.5	29	30.6	10.4
CHERT	227	25.9	11.8	133	28.0	11.5	53	30.4	12.4
Ranges	108	23.3	10.6	55	25.7	11.1	23	31.0	14.4
Plains	95	28.6	12.3	63	30.2	12.3	22	33.4	10.3
Marsh	24	27.3	12.4	15	27.2	7.1	8	20.3	5.2
DOLERITE	145	44.8	15.5	220	51.4	18.4	154	51.1	18.7
Ranges	21	38.6	12.5	14	39.6	13.4	11	37.0	18.8
Plains	105	47.3	15.3	192	52.6	18.6	132	52.8	18.5
Marsh	19	37.9	16.2	14	46.2	14.5	11	44.5	15.3

TABLE 4.24: Mean length (mm) and standard deviation of complete cortical flakes by cortex type.

	Cortex type	N	Length	SD
Basalt	Riverine	1377	42.7	16.9
	Terrestrial	308	40.2	15.9
BIF	Riverine	1308	41.6	16.4
	Terrestrial	2298	39.3	14.6
Chalcedony	Riverine	161	34.6	13.2
	Terrestrial	230	32.4	10.6
Chert	Riverine	64	32.0	12.9
	Terrestrial	121	27.0	10.8
Dolerite	Riverine	223	52.5	17.1
	Terrestrial	147	49.6	20.4

TABLE 4.25: Percentage of platform types for each raw material.

	Cortex		Plain		Other*		Total
	N	%	N	%	N	%	
Basalt	1604	48.0	1572	47.0	167	5.0	3343
BIF	3208	50.2	2930	45.9	249	3.9	6387
Chalcedony	287	25.0	774	67.5	85	7.4	1146
Chert	119	17.4	503	73.8	60	8.8	682
Dolerite	361	62.1	193	33.2	27	4.6	581
TOTAL	5579	46.0	5972	49.2	588	4.8	12139

* Includes crushed, focal and faceted platforms.

TABLE 4.26: Percentage of complete flakes and proximal flake fragments with overhang removal.

	Overhang reduction		Total
	N	%	
BASALT	176	5.0	3494
Ranges	36	8.1	445
Plains	125	4.6	2693
Marsh	15	4.2	356
BIF	280	4.2	6611
Ranges	95	4.1	2299
Plains	171	4.4	3921
Marsh	14	3.6	391
CHALCEDONY	34	2.8	1199
Ranges	4	1.4	287
Plains	24	3.4	713
Marsh	6	3.0	199
CHERT	33	4.6	713
Ranges	17	4.0	427
Plains	10	4.5	222
Marsh	6	10.5	57
DOLERITE	20	3.3	605
Ranges	2	2.8	71
Plains	16	3.3	484
Marsh	2	4.3	47

RETOUCHED ARTEFACTS

Only a small percentage (about 4%) of artefacts shows any evidence of secondary modification or retouch. Of the five main raw materials, chert is clearly preferred for secondarily modified material, with 10% of all chert artefacts retouched. By contrast only 2% BIF, 7% basalt, 4% chalcedony and 3% of dolerite artefacts are retouched. The proportion of retouched material varies from 10% of all flaked stone in Group 1A to 1% in Group 2A. Overall, 5% of flaked stone in the ranges samples is retouched, while in the plains and Marsh samples 3.8% of flaked stone is retouched (Table 4.28).

Most secondarily modified artefacts are non-diagnostic retouched artefacts, rather than formal tools (Table 4.29). Formal tools included tula and non-tula adzes, and backed artefacts, all of which were geometric microliths. Fourteen retouched, pointed trigonal blades were also recorded, most of which were basalt. Both basalt and chert are more often retouched than their overall percentage in assemblages would suggest, while BIF artefacts are less frequently retouched. Chalcedony artefacts make up about the same percentage of the retouched assemblage as the overall assemblage. The relatively high proportion of chert retouched artefacts is largely due to a preference for using chert to produce adzes. About two-thirds (68%) of adzes were chert. All but two adzes (both tula) were recorded in sites, rather than as isolated artefacts. Similarly, the preference for basalt for manufacturing pointed trigonal blades contributes to the elevated percentage of basalt among the retouched artefacts.

DISCUSSION: RAW MATERIAL, ORGANISATION OF TECHNOLOGY AND THE LAND-USE MODEL

At a landscape level then, the predictions of the land-use model (see Table 2.1) are a poor fit with assemblages in the Christmas Creek study area. The model suggests that assemblages in the ranges, where residential mobility can be inferred to be high, should have low diversity of raw materials and artefact types, few formal tools and little grinding material, and be characterised by early stage reduction. By contrast, assemblages on the plains, where residential mobility would be low, should have high diversity of raw

TABLE 4.27: Flake:core ratios for individual sample groups by raw material.

	Basalt	BIF	Chalcedony	Chert	Dolerite	All raw materials
1A	14	14	6	8	10	11
2A	11	10	7	8	NA	9
3B	8	5	13	6	0	5
3D	NA	14	NA	2	NA	13
4A	12	9	10	10	4	9
5A	15	9	6	3	23	8
6S	14	6	5	6	NA	6
7S	5	5	8	5	6	5
8S	7	5	10	NA	6	6
9S	8	7	9	10	5	7
10S	10	6	9	6	5	7
F	4	5	4	26	4	5
FT	6	4	8	13	6	5
14MP	3	3	6	2	12	3

SURFACE ARTEFACT SCATTERS | 157

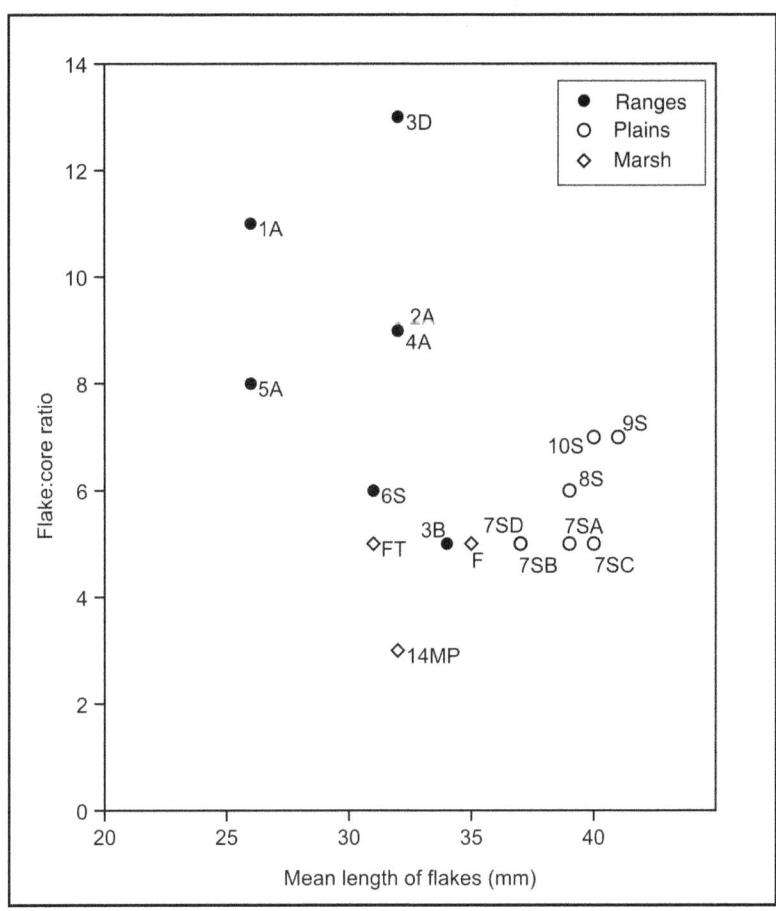

FIGURE 4.19: Relationship between flake size and flake to core ratio for sample groups.

material and artefact types, more formal tools and grinding material, and be characterised by middle and late stages of reduction. Marsh assemblages should be comparable to plains assemblages, but might show evidence of raw material conservation. None of these expectations are met by the exploratory multivariate analysis. Rather, the exploration of individual assemblage characteristics demonstrates that, in this stone resource-rich landscape, the highly localised pattern of raw material procurement and the form in which raw material occurs are critical influences on most aspects of assemblage composition. This suggests that the assemblage attributes highlighted by the

TABLE 4.28: Percentage of retouched artefacts for each sample group.

	% RETOUCHED
1A	10.1
2A	0.6
3B	2.2
3D	3.2
4A	6.7
5A	2.9
6S	1.6
7S	2.7
8S	4.8
9S	4.0
10S	5.4
F	6.1
FT	2.8
14MP	1.9
ALL	4.1

land-use model, and widely employed to interpret surface artefact scatters in the Pilbara, have little to say about mobility strategies within a land-use system. On the contrary, they clearly relate to the organisation of technology in relation to managing specific lithic raw materials. By contrast, the cortex ratio analysis, which was not included in the original predictions, did yield a result that was consistent with the expectation of high residential mobility in the ranges and low residential mobility on the plains.

Careful reconsideration of the assemblage attributes identified in the land-use model as related to mobility suggests that they are likely to be sensitive to sample size. The discussion of raw material diversity clearly demonstrates the relationship between diversity and sample size (Figures 4.8–4.9). Regression analysis was used to investigate whether sample size also affects the occurrence of specific artefact types (millstones, cores, retouched artefacts and adzes). Table 4.30 summarises the data used in the

TABLE 4.29: Retouched artefact types for each raw material.

	GEOMETRIC MICROLITH	NON-TULA	TULA	POINTED TRIGONAL BLADE	UNDIAGNOSTIC RETOUCHED	TOTAL	%
Basalt	0	1	3	9	285	298	44.3
BIF	0	0	3	3	178	184	27.3
Chalcedony	0	0	0	1	55	56	8.3
Chert	3	3	17	0	64	87	12.9
Dolerite	0	0	0	1	20	21	3.1
Ironstone	0	0	0	0	6	6	0.9
Mudstone	0	0	2	0	4	6	0.9
Quartz	0	0	0	0	2	2	0.3
Quartzite	1	0	0	0	8	9	1.3
Silcrete	0	0	0	0	4	4	0.6
TOTAL	4	4	25	14	626	673	

regression analysis and Table 4.31 outlines the results. Like raw material diversity, the occurrence of millstones, retouched artefacts and cores seems also linked with sample size, while adzes are the only artefact type whose presence appears unrelated (Figure 4.20). Unlike other artefact types, adzes occur almost exclusively at sites. Only two adzes were recorded as isolated artefacts – both from Group 10S. There seems to be no clear underlying pattern in the distribution of adzes. Group F is the most notable outlier, while Group 5A is the only ranges sample to have more adzes than might be expected. Only Group FT is an outlier for millstones (Figure 4.20). This anomalous result should be interpreted with some caution as the sample comes from a relatively narrow transect. Alternatively, it could be accounted for by a single millstone broken in several pieces.

These results show that as sample size increases so does the probability that relatively rare artefact types, such as millstones and retouched artefacts, will be recorded and that rare raw materials will also appear. This is entirely consistent with a view of the regional archaeological record as a time-averaged palimpsest comprising artefacts from many different behavioural episodes. This also raises the question of whether there are intrinsic differences between dense accumulations of artefacts recorded as sites and the background scatter, or do patches and scatters provide evidence for similar types of activities differing only in quantity of artefacts. More than 10,000 isolated artefacts were recorded in the Christmas Creek survey area. These can be compared to the sample of artefacts recorded as part of sites to assess whether the background scatter differs from the sites.

As noted above (Table 4.5), just five materials account for 96% by number of all flaked stone recorded within the survey area, although numerous other raw materials are found in small numbers. The overall percentages are generally similar for artefacts recorded within sites as for artefacts recorded as isolated artefacts (Table 4.32).

The picture is a little more variable at the local scale. Figure 4.21 compares raw material composition for artefacts recorded from sites and isolated artefacts within sample areas. Most pairs are broadly similar, particularly for the two main raw materials, BIF and basalt. Variability in the minor lithologies can probably be attributed to sample size. The isolated artefacts

TABLE 4.30: Summary data for each sample group used in the regression analysis.

	N	N RAW MATERIALS	MILLSTONES	CORES	TOTAL RETOUCHED	ALL ADZES
1A	1281	11	6	93	128	2
2A	504	9	0	43	3	0
3B	831	9	1	118	18	1
3D	156	5	0	10	5	0
4A	636	9	3	51	42	1
5A	861	10	4	71	25	3
6S	313	6	0	36	5	1
7S	4656	14	18	688	127	4
8S	2550	13	11	309	121	2
9S	2150	11	7	239	85	4
10S	1149	11	2	127	62	4
F	478	10	4	70	29	5
FT	840	9	18	116	23	1
14MP	163	8	1	35	3	1

from Group 1A are perhaps the most noticeably different from the artefact sample recorded from sites. Most isolated artefacts from Group 1A were complete flakes and the percentage of BIF was relatively small.

The overall percentage of retouched artefacts is also similar for both isolated artefacts (5%) and sites (4%) (Table 4.33). As with raw material, however, there is considerable variability at the local level and no particular pattern is evident. The relative proportion of major artefact classes is slightly different for sites and isolated artefacts (Table 4.34). Cores or complete flakes make up a higher percentage of isolated artefacts, while sites have higher percentages of debris and flake fragments. This difference is most likely a result of both obtrusiveness and level of intensity of recording. Debris and flake fragments, especially distal and medial fragments, are less easily recognisable as isolated finds and are thus more likely to be recorded if they are spatially associated with other artefacts. At the local scale, there is some variability (Figure 4.22). However, unlike the percentage of retouched artefacts, samples of isolated artefacts consistently have either more cores and complete flakes or similar proportions of these types than sites. Both cores and complete flakes recorded as isolated artefacts tend to be larger than those recorded as part of sites for each of the five main raw materials (Figure 4.23). This too is probably a result of the obtrusive character of these classes of artefacts.

CONCLUSIONS

The surface artefacts in the Christmas Creek area primarily provide evidence for activities relating to the procurement, manufacture, use, maintenance and discard of stone artefacts. These activities are broadly similar whether they occur at low or high density in the landscape. High density artefact occurrences thus more probably mark persistent places repeatedly occupied over longer periods, rather than discrete campsites with functional significance within a regional settlement model (Shiner 2009; Shott 2008; Stern 1993). These places occur primarily in association with Open Eucalypt Woodland and Low Mulga Woodlands along creek lines, and are more common in

TABLE 4.31: Results of the regression analysis.

Variable	Slope	Error	Intercept	Error	R	P
N raw materials	0.0016348	0.000319	7.7082	0.53139	0.82878	0.000249
Millstone	0.0036994	0.001006	0.97914	1.6774	0.72797	0.003159
Cores	0.14272	0.007746	-25.617	12.918	0.98278	3.62E-10
Total retouched	0.031998	0.006546	10.419	10.917	0.81588	0.000373
All adzes	0.00066829	0.000337	1.2806	0.56149	0.49716	0.070495

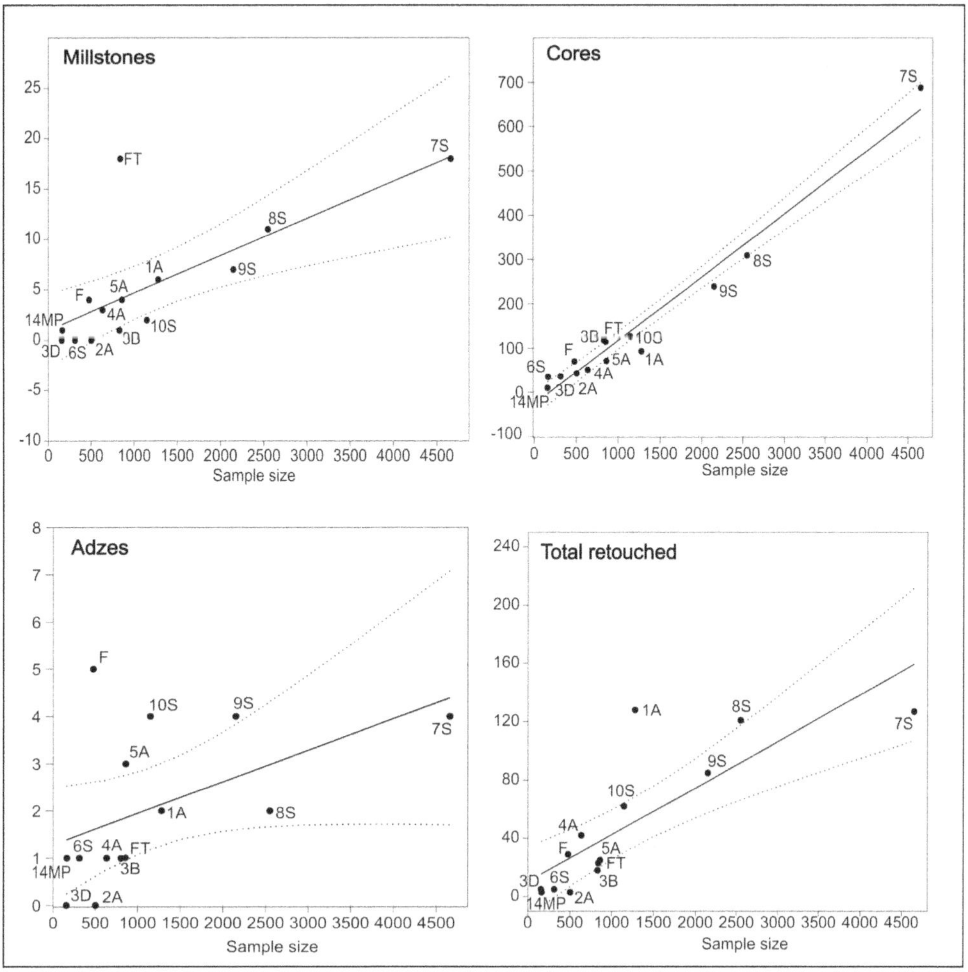

FIGURE 4.20: Linear regression: sample size and occurrence of individual artefact types (dashed lines indicate 95% probability)

the plains than in the ranges. The evidence from cortex ratios suggests that movement in the plains was less frequent than in the ranges. This would be consistent with longer residence close to the richer resources of the plains and shorter stays in the ranges. The evidence from cortex and volume ratios also suggests a deficit of raw material on sites in the survey area. Movement of material seems to have been largely in the form of cores.

This analysis highlights the fact that archaeological sites are constructs. In the context of compliance archaeology, the way sites are recorded is influenced by a range of factors which include both archaeological considerations

TABLE 4.32: Raw material composition: comparison between artefacts recorded as part of sites and all isolated artefacts. Other includes jasper, rhyolite, siltstone, granite and unidentified.

	Site		Isolated artefact	
	N	%	N	%
Basalt	3646	25.4	2899	27.6
BIF	7166	49.8	5456	52.0
Chalcedony	1395	9.7	618	5.9
Chert	1022	7.1	527	5.0
Dolerite	585	4.1	617	5.9
Ironstone	50	<1	29	<1
Mudstone	121	<1	111	1.1
Quartz and crystal quartz	47	<1	5	<1
Quartzite	266	1.9	124	1.2
Silcrete	58	<1	102	1.0
Other	21	<1	8	<1
TOTAL	14377		10496	

and non-archaeological project constraints. In the Christmas Creek area, the recorded sites are commonly small to medium surface artefact scatters which are highly diverse in their characteristics. Sample size is so small as to make interpretation of these sites very difficult. However, a consideration of these archaeological remains at a landscape scale indicates that there is patterning in the surface artefact scatters that can be interpreted at a lower resolution than the individual site. Collectively, individual artefact occurrences contribute to developing an understanding of land use at a local and regional scale.

This insight into the mismatch between units of archaeological recording and units of archaeological interpretation has obvious implications for assessment of significance in the context of site registration, and therefore decisions about management, preservation and further recording within the context of mitigating the impacts of development. Questions of scale and resolution

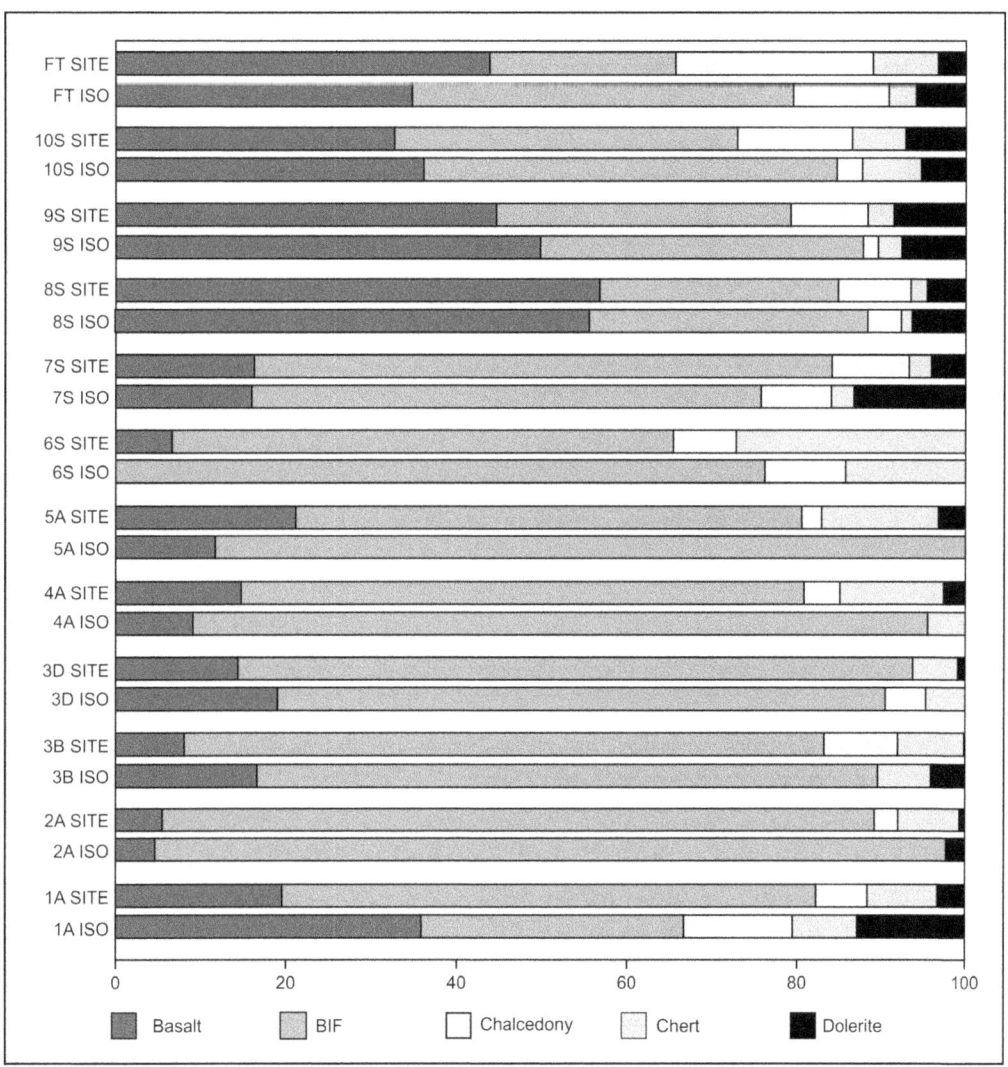

FIGURE 4.21: Comparison between artefacts recorded as part of surface artefact scatters and as isolated artefacts for each sample group with respect to raw material.

TABLE 4.33: Percentage of retouched artefacts recorded from sites and as isolated artefacts for each sample group.

	ISOLATED ARTEFACTS	SITES
1A	7.3%	10.2%
2A	4.5%	0.2%
3B	8.3%	1.8%
3D	9.5%	0.9%
4A	2.2%	7.0%
5A	0.0%	3.0%
6S	0.0%	1.7%
7S	4.5%	2.5%
8S	5.0%	4.7%
10S	9.9%	4.8%
FT	2.1%	3.8%
TOTAL	4.6%	4.0%

TABLE 4.34: Percentage of major artefact classes recorded from sites and as isolated artefacts for each sample group.

	ISOLATED ARTEFACTS		SITES	
	N	%	N	%
Debris	35	0.3	135	1.2
Complete flake	7975	76.0	7908	68.2
Flake fragment	907	8.6	2145	18.5
Core	1579	15.0	1407	12.1
TOTAL	10496		11460	

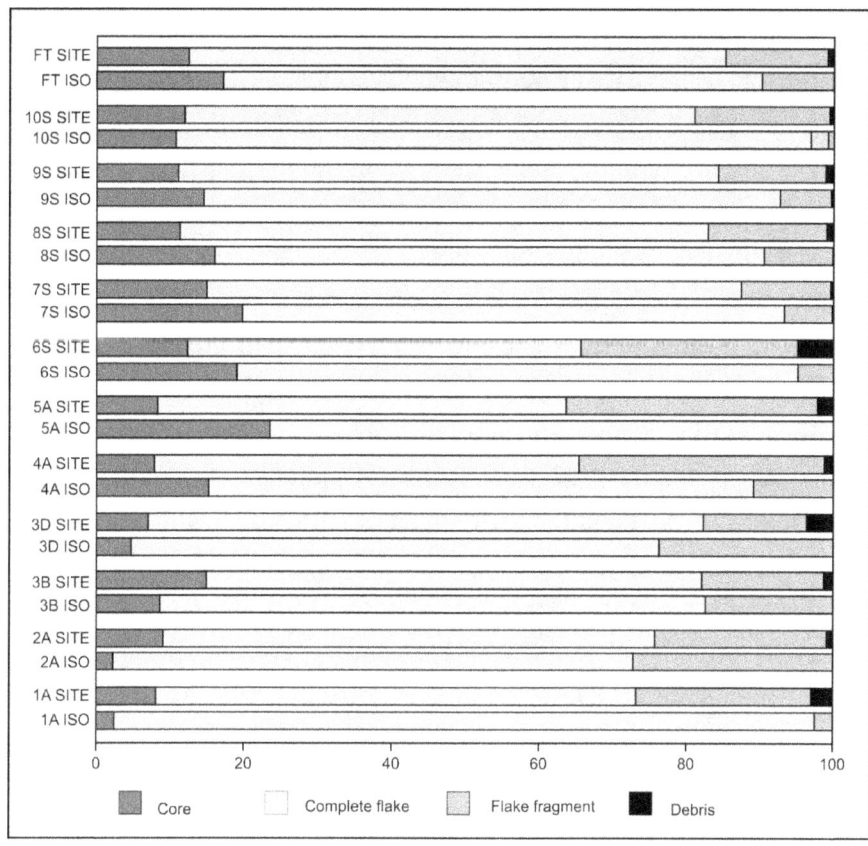

FIGURE 4.22: Comparison between artefacts recorded as part of surface artefact scatters and as isolated artefacts for each sample group with respect to major artefact class.

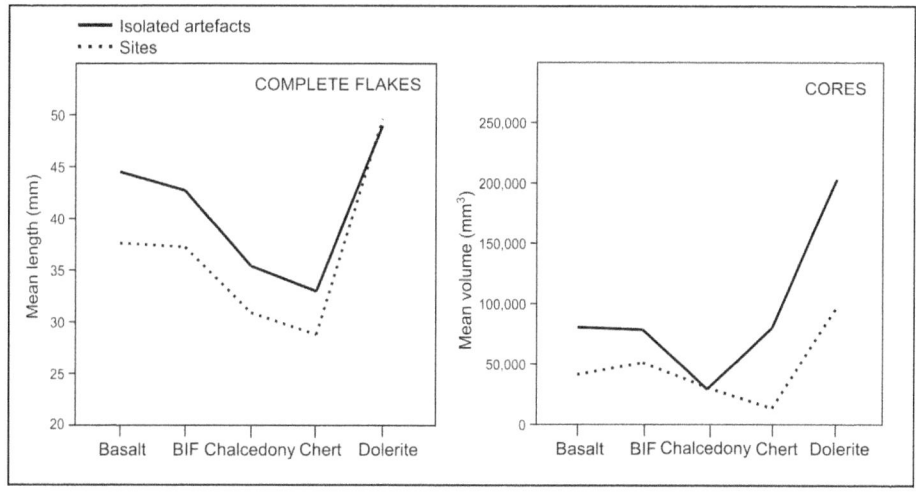

FIGURE 4.23: Comparison between mean sizes of complete flakes and cores of main raw materials, recorded as isolated artefacts or in sites.

in relation to interpretation will be taken up again in Chapter 6 with the presentation of locality-based case studies.

The analysis of surface artefact scatters always raises the issue of chronology. The absence of dating evidence is a common criticism of the surface archaeological record and commonly permits these data to be readily dismissed in discussions of site significance (Ryan and Morse 2009). The coherent patterns evident at a landscape scale in the Christmas Creek study area suggest that there is meaning and structure to be discerned in this record beyond the use of surface artefacts as markers of past human activity (Barton 2008; Bird and Rhoads 2011; Holdaway et al. 1998; Robins 1998; Shiner 2009). Studies of landscape formation processes are urgently required to better understand the formation of sites and the age of the land surfaces on which they occur (Holdaway and Fanning 2014). However, we suggest that the strong relationships evident between the distribution of surface artefacts and contemporary vegetation formations and the probable impact of frequent flood events on this surface record may indicate that much of the surface archaeological record is relatively recent. Moreover, artefacts showing evidence of weathering indicating prolonged surface exposure or redeposition by floodwater were occasionally recorded, but seem generally uncommon in the study area. It therefore follows that this record should be regarded as particularly significant to Aboriginal peoples today as a direct reflection of the lives of their immediate ancestors.

CHAPTER 5

ROCKSHELTERS

As well as providing a chronological framework for understanding the occupation of the Christmas Creek area, rockshelters provide an opportunity to investigate the nature of their use in the study area and to interpret them within their landscape context. In this chapter, we look at three aspects of the archaeological evidence from rockshelters. First, we describe the general characteristics of the rockshelters and the surface archaeological remains associated with them. Second, we consider the dating evidence from the shelters and analyse patterns of shelter occupation in time and space. Third, we discuss the excavated assemblages in relation to the predictions of the land-use model.

In an earlier analysis (Bird and Rhoads 2015), we concluded that rockshelters in the study area did not match their widespread characterisation as ephemeral on the basis of assemblage characteristics commonly associated with high residential mobility and low intensity of occupation (cf. Ryan and Morse 2009; Veth 1993, 86). Moreover, these sites showed differences in their characteristics and function. This casts doubt on the conventional interpretation of Pilbara rockshelters and highlights that rockshelters should not be assessed as a single uniform site type. This conclusion was based on evidence from six excavated rockshelters. Here we are able to expand this analysis to the full suite of excavated shelters in the Christmas Creek study area.

ROCKSHELTER CHARACTERISTICS

All rockshelters investigated occur in the foothills of the Chichester Range, commonly in outcrops of banded iron formation or conglomerate along ephemeral creeks (Figure 5.1). All those that could be safely accessed were inspected (Hook, Dias and Rapley 2008, 14). Roof fall was common. All cultural material on the surface was recorded. Shelters meeting certain criteria – accessibility, sufficient head room for a person to stand or crouch, and the occurrence of at least 10 cm of deposit – were recommended for test excavation (Dias and Rapley 2014).

More than 40 rockshelters were investigated. Nineteen proved to have archaeological remains when excavated, while a further 19 shelters, some with multiple chambers, were also identified as having cultural material or features or both, but were judged to have little or no excavation potential. There are also a number of overhangs, cavities or clefts that would not usually be regarded as habitable shelters, but which have stone features or other cultural remains found in association.

The 19 rockshelters judged to have excavation potential were test excavated as part of a significance assessment process prior to a possible application to disturb under section 18 of the *Aboriginal Heritage Act 1972* (WA). The aim of the test excavation program was to sample the deposits and provide age estimates to determine the nature and extent of subsurface archaeological remains. Test pits were placed in areas largely free of roof fall, with adequate ventilation and light, and where probing indicated that the deposit was likely to be deepest. The recording and excavation methods are outlined in Appendix 1. The results of most of the excavations were reported in a series of consultancy reports (Dias 2010; Dias and Rapley 2013; Edwards 2011; Edwards and Hook 2011; Hook, Dias and Rapley 2008). Some shelters have been preserved; others are now destroyed or are in areas scheduled for mining. No additional excavations were undertaken at any shelters for this analysis. Further excavations planned at CB10-93 were not conducted due to safety concerns. The documentation from all excavated shelters was reviewed and the stone artefact assemblage data were re-analysed as part of our study. Appendix 5 brings together the results of this review and provides a summary of the evidence available for each site.

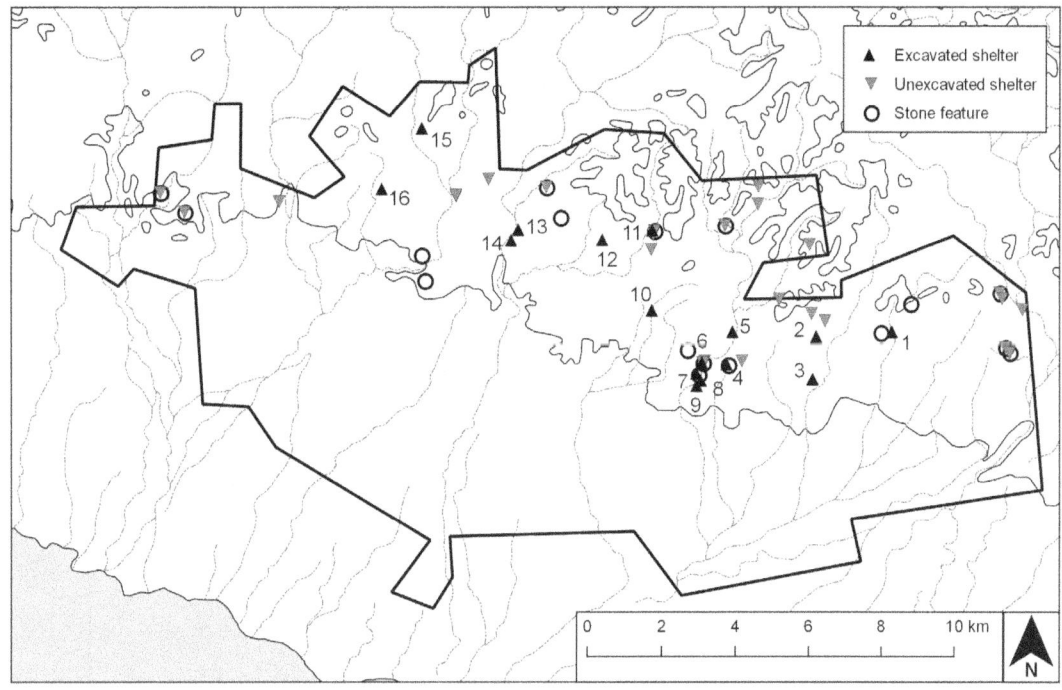

FIGURE 5.1: Rock shelters and stone features in the study area. 1. CB08-500, 2. CB10-123, 3. CB10-116 & CB10-117, 4. CB10-147, 5. CB10-133, 6. CB10-93, 7. CB10-88, 8. CB10-98, 9. CB10-92, 10. CB09-55, 11. CB09-249, 12. CB08-427, 13. CB10-41, 14. CB10-40, 15. CB11-89, 16. CB09-94.

Most shelters are small, although there appears to be little relationship between the characteristics of a shelter and its potential for excavated cultural material. Test pits in some small cramped shelters yielded relatively rich deposits (Dias and Rapley 2014). CB10-133 is unusual because it is a large and spacious shelter yielding substantial amounts of cultural material. Excavated and unexcavated rockshelters are similar with respect to size (Figure 5.2, Table 5.1). The aspect of excavated and unexcavated shelters, on the other hand, is clearly different (Figure 5.3). Excavated shelters face generally east or west, with a preference for a westerly aspect. Since shelters occur in drainage systems that flow roughly north to south, this might be considered an unsurprising result. Unexcavated shelters with cultural material, however, more commonly face north or south. All these shelters show evidence of use in the form of stone features, surface artefacts or both, but had no deposits or very shallow deposits judged unlikely to contain subsurface archaeological material. Many shelters were apparently used, at least occasionally. However, west-facing, and to some extent east-facing, shelters seem to have been used more intensively and regularly, thus resulting in accumulation of deposits with cultural material.

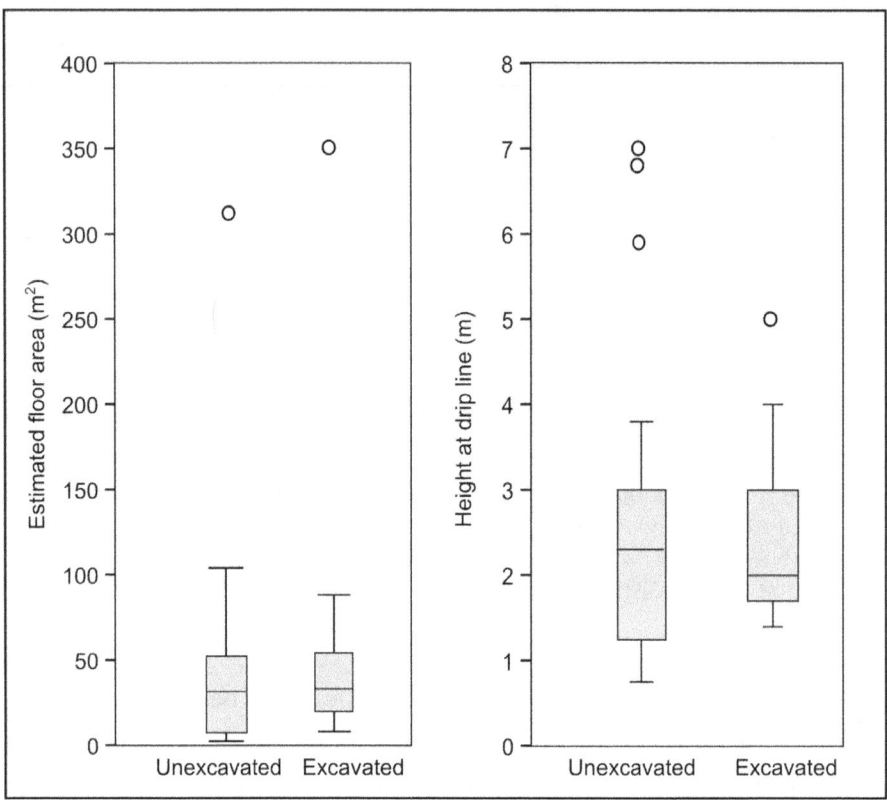

FIGURE 5.2: Comparison between excavated and unexcavated shelters with respect to estimated floor area (t=-0.366, p=0.715) and height at drip line (unequal variance, t=0.477, p=0.636).

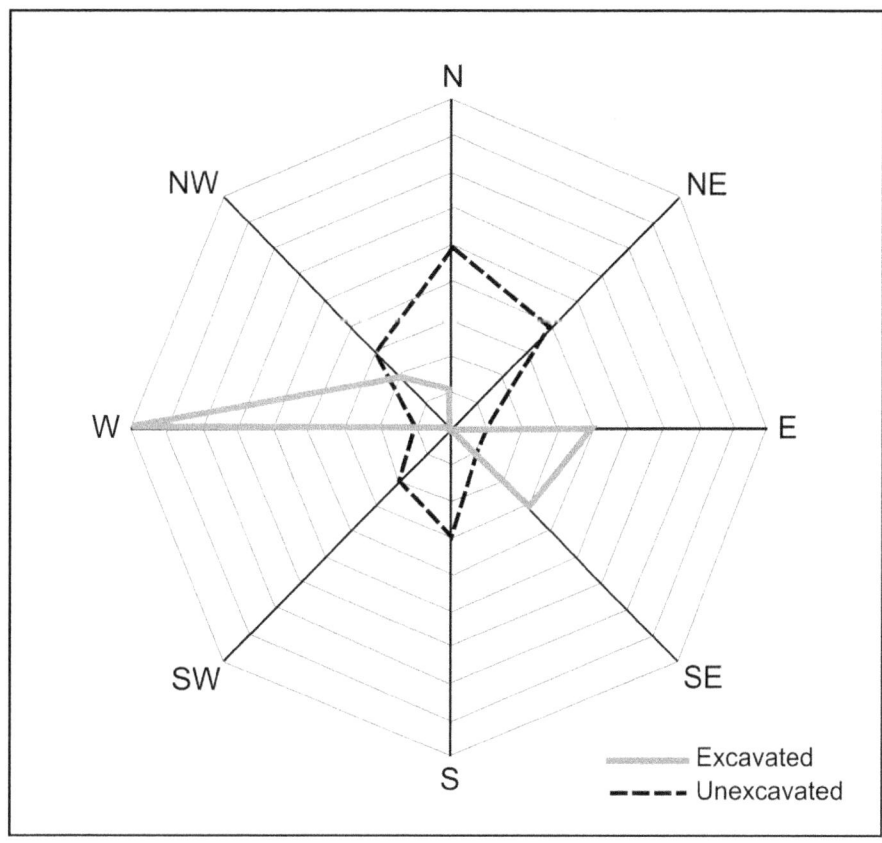

FIGURE 5.3: Aspect of excavated and unexcavated shelters (chi-square=21.055, df=7, p=0.004, Fisher's exact test p=0.001).

TABLE 5.1: Summary dimensions of rockshelters recorded in the Christmas Creek study area.

		N	MEAN	SD	RANGE
Surface area (m^2)	Unexcavated	24	44	65	1–312
	Excavated	19	52	76	8–352
Height at drip line (metres)	Unexcavated	24	2.6	1.8	0.8–7.0
	Excavated	19	2.4	1.0	1.4–5.0

SURFACE ASSEMBLAGES IN SHELTERS

There are a number of common features in the shelter surface assemblages. Surface artefact scatters throughout the study area are typically dominated by flakes and flake fragments. By contrast, flakes and flake fragments are rare in surface assemblages in excavated rockshelters, which typically comprise cores, manuports, grinding material or hammer stones. Only two excavated shelters (CB10-92 and CB10-116) have surface assemblages dominated by waste flakes (Table 5.2). Unexcavated shelters have more diverse surface assemblages (Table 5.3). Three have evidence showing they were used for quarrying seams of chert. Six have only waste flakes. The remainder are similar to the excavated shelters. Some only have stone structures and no other cultural remains. These are discussed below.

Millstones or mullers were found in several shelters (Figure 5.4). In one case (at CB09-83) a dolerite muller was cached in a niche within the shelter wall. Ethnographic evidence from the Western Desert indicates that millstones were often left in shelters or other regular camping places for future use (Gould 1980, 10, 71–2; Nicholson and Cane 1991; Tonkinson 1978, 33). This practice is also documented in the Pilbara (Guruma Elders Group et al. 2001, 87–8). Palmer (cited in Brown 1987, 45) suggests that women may have used rockshelters for milling seeds during windy conditions. Indeed, these items can be viewed as facilities, or site furniture, and indicate the intention to return.

The presence of cores and manuports seems to represent deliberate provisioning of these places with supplies of raw material for future use. The cores are clearly not fully exhausted. At CB10-98, for example, a dolerite core was apparently cached in the rear of the shelter (Appendix 5; Figure A5.75). Shelters at CB10-147 and CB08-427 have six and three BIF cores, respectively, while CB10-93 has five manuports – all BIF cobbles. At CB10-133, nine of the 36 flaked stone artefacts recorded on the surface were cores. Manuports and cores also occur in shelters without deposits. These include CB10-145, which contains a single river cobble, possibly used as a hammer stone, and CB11-108, where a single platform core was found. CB08-103 comprises two small shelters, neither of which is large enough to be used for occupation. Shelter A had two chambers, one of which contained a

TABLE 5.2: Summary of surface artefacts recorded at excavated rockshelters.

Site	Surface material
CB08-500	Dolerite muller and manuport, five cores (basalt, BIF, chert, dolerite, quartzite), retouched piece, surface scatter on terrace outside shelter
CB10-123	Millstone
CB10-116	Flakes only on surface
CB10-117	Chert core
CB10-88	Basalt core
CB10-147	Six BIF cores
CB10-92	Flakes only on surface
CB10-93	Five BIF manuports
CB10-98	Dolerite core cached in rear of cave, surface scatter on talus
CB10-133	Chambers 1 and 2: three millstones, a muller, hammer stone, baler shell fragment, nine cores (five BIF, two chalcedony, two chert), two geometric microliths. Chamber 3: several cached pieces of wood
CB09-55	Cached burnt wood, BIF core on surface
CB08-427	Three BIF cores
CB09-249	BIF millstone, chert core
CB10-40	Two single platform cores (one dolerite and one BIF), BIF manuport, two flakes
CB10-41/2	BIF core, dolerite manuport, surface scatter on talus
CB10-41/3	Muller, manuport, hammer stone, three cores (two dolerite, one basalt)
CB10-41/4	Three millstones, two manuports (dolerite cobbles), two cores (BIF, dolerite)
CB09-94	Two cores (one BIF, one chert)
CB11-89	Millstone, five pieces dark grey chert (debris, flake, proximal flake and core fragment)

TABLE 5.3: Summary of surface artefacts recorded at unexcavated rockshelters.

SITE	DESCRIPTION	SURFACE MATERIAL
CB09-266	Rockshelter and quarry	Two quarried seams of chert
CB09-267	Rockshelter	Three chalcedony flakes and eight BIF flakes
CB09-254	Rockshelter with cairn. Associated with CB09-255 (multiple walled enclosures)	Four BIF flakes and fragments, one with retouch
CB10-118	Rockshelter	BIF single platform core and eight flakes of BIF, chert, mudstone, chalcedony and dolerite
CB10-125	Rockshelter	BIF flake and BIF single platform core
CB10-127	Overhang	12 BIF artefacts including one multiplatform core
CB11-153	Rockshelter. Large stone placed to block hole on north wall of shelter	Two BIF flakes
CB10-145	Rockshelter	Manuport - river cobble possible hammer stone
CB10-94	Rockshelter (50 m north of excavated shelter CB10-93)	Two BIF flakes, one basalt flake, BIF manuport
CB09-239	Overhang with artefact scatter and quarry. Associated with CB09-240, CB09-250 (cairn) and excavated shelter CB08-249.	Quarry exploiting exfoliating bands of chert on the hill slope
CB09-240	Rockshelter with several overhangs, quarry and reduction areas. Associated with CB09-239, CB09-250 (cairn) and excavated shelter CB08-249.	Six discrete reduction areas on bedrock associated with exploitation of exfoliating chert nodules
CB11-108	Rockshelter, walled niche	Single platform core
CB11-111	Rockshelter	Seven BIF flakes and one chalcedony flake

Site	Description	Surface material
CB09-87	Rockshelter with discrete surface artefact scatter (CB09-83) 20 m to the south	BIF flake
CB09-83	Rockshelter	Five artefacts at the entrance (two dolerite manuports, three chert flakes and fragments) dolerite muller cached in niche inside shelter.
CB08-103	Site complex comprising two small shelters, artefact scatter with discrete knapping floors and stone arrangement on hill top above shelters	Shelter A: hammer stone, chert single platform core, BIF flake, and two hammer stones on the talus. Shelter B: five chert flakes.
CB08-128	Site complex comprising rockshelter with associated artefact scatter and BIF quarry, small overhang	Complete flake in shelter
CB08-239	Site complex comprising double chambered rockshelter with artefact scatter, quarry and stone arrangement on hill top above shelter	Millstone and chert distal flake

hammer stone, a BIF flake and a single platform core, and there were two additional hammer stones on the talus in front of the shelter. None of these assemblages are typical flaked stone assemblages, comprising mainly waste flakes. The cores do not seem to be simply discarded as they clearly still have potential for flake removal. Like the presence of grindstones, these cores and manuports indicate planned future use.

Pieces of wood were also found stored in some of these shelters. At CB10-133, several pieces of wood were found within Chamber 3. The size of these fragments and their location at the rear of the chamber or on a ledge suggest that they were deliberately cached. Two had cut marks, while one was charred and may have been used as a torch or firestick. A piece of charred wood was found in a niche at the rear of CB09-55.

Figure 5.4: Examples of artefacts stored in shelters. Top: Single platform core at CB09-94. Bottom: Lower grindstone at CB11-89.

FIGURE 5.5: Examples of stone features. CB08-239: stone arrangement (top left). CB09-250: cairn (top right). CB09-264: walled niche (bottom left). CB10-42: walled enclosure (bottom right).

STONE FEATURES

Twenty-two stone features were recorded at 17 sites (Figure 5.5) (see Appendix 4 for site descriptions). The stone features positively identified as cultural fall into five categories, based on form: stone arrangements, cairns, walled enclosures, niches and stone caches. Seventeen features were stone structures located in rockshelters, and most of these formed part of multi-component sites or site complexes. Walled enclosures were the most common type and occurred at eight rockshelters. Cairns and walled niches also occurred in rockshelters. No cultural material was recorded in association with any of these features. The two stone arrangements in the open were also part of site complexes that included rockshelters. Some enigmatic features also exist that are certainly not cultural. These are not discussed further here.

Possible functions documented or suggested for various types of stone feature in Pilbara rockshelters include storage, burial, structural modification of shelters and hunting (Wallis and Matthews 2016). Structural modification of shelters, resulting in stone features, includes clearing roof fall to create living space, use of stones to support brush windbreaks, and creating access to high niches. By far the most common documented use is storage, with walls or individual stones used to block access to areas of varying sizes. Where shelters have more than one entrance, blocking one with stones can also prevent prey from escaping. The use of caves and shelters for storage of ceremonial items is well documented in the region (Akerman 2006; Kimber 1981, 16; Native Welfare Department 1968; Smith 2002, 82; Tindale 1974, 239). Personal gear might also be stored in caves and there are also accounts of food storage, sometimes with stone walls built to keep out dogs (Bindon and Lofgren 1982; Brown 1987, 17; Smith 2002, 70–71; Wallis and Matthews 2016, 4–5). Comparable features are also reported from the Weld Range in the Murchison region further south, where storage of seeds wrapped in kangaroo skins is documented (Brown 2015, 39; Tindale 1974, 145). In the study area, the Nyiyaparli consider most features to have been used for storage, including walled enclosures, niches and some cairns. For example, Nyiyaparli Traditional Owners involved in the recording of the stone cairn at CB12-166 thought that it would have been used as a cache (Heritage Information Submission Form, lodged with the DAA). In at least two examples (CB08-509, CB08-513), blocking one of two entrances suggests the features were intended to act as traps to capture small game and the terrain in the vicinity of both these sites lends support to this interpretation. Storage might have been short-term with personal items and food perhaps stored during a day's absence from camp for foraging (Brown 1987, 17). However, some storage seems to have been long-term, for artefacts such as cores and grindstones , and particularly of ceremonial items. The existence of stone features can be viewed as an investment in facilities that could be repeatedly re-used. They indicate an intention to return and thus are one marker of long-term nodes in a network of planned visitation.

ASSOCIATIONS

Shelters typically occur as part of site complexes. At the very least, they are associated with a surface artefact scatter that occurs nearby or either continues well beyond the confines of the shelter. The configuration of surface artefacts in relation to shelters in some cases depends on local terrain. At CB08-500, for example, there is a surface scatter within the shelter and a small discrete scatter on a small gravel terrace about 20 metres to the north. At CB10-98, a cached dolerite core was the only artefact within the shelter, but a small artefact scatter was located on the talus slope (Appendix 5).

Obviously, the distribution of shelters is linked to surface geology and topography, and thus shelters with cultural material may be close together within the same landform (Figure 5.1). CB10-40 and the shelter complex at CB10-41 is one example, while CB10-116 and CB10-117 is another (see Appendix 5). Shelters with and without excavation potential may also be located near one another. There are several excavated shelters closely associated with stone structures (see Appendix 5). The association of occupied rockshelter CB10-147 and walled enclosure CB11-93 provides one example, while CB10-88 and CB10-89, and CB10-93 and CB12-180 are other instances of such associations. In the ranges, cultural remains are often highly clustered; arguably many of these localities should not be regarded as separate sites but as linked complexes. Figure 5.6 indicates the close association between shelters, stone features and other site types in the vicinity of excavated shelter CB09-249. This particular complex of shelters and associated archaeological features, including quarries, seems primarily focused on procurement of raw material.

CB08-103, in the west of the study area, constitutes another example of a site complex, this time at a more concentrated scale and recorded as a single site. It comprises two small rockshelters, a stone arrangement and a surface artefact scatter (Jimenez-Lozano and Edwards 2014, 379–86). The shelters occur on the north face of a prominent rocky hill, which commands a wide view of the surrounding terrain (Figure 5.7, Figure 5.8). Neither shelter is large enough for occupation. Shelter A is a small north-facing shelter with a secondary chamber. Two openings in the western wall of the main chamber have been blocked off by stacked stones. A hammer stone, a

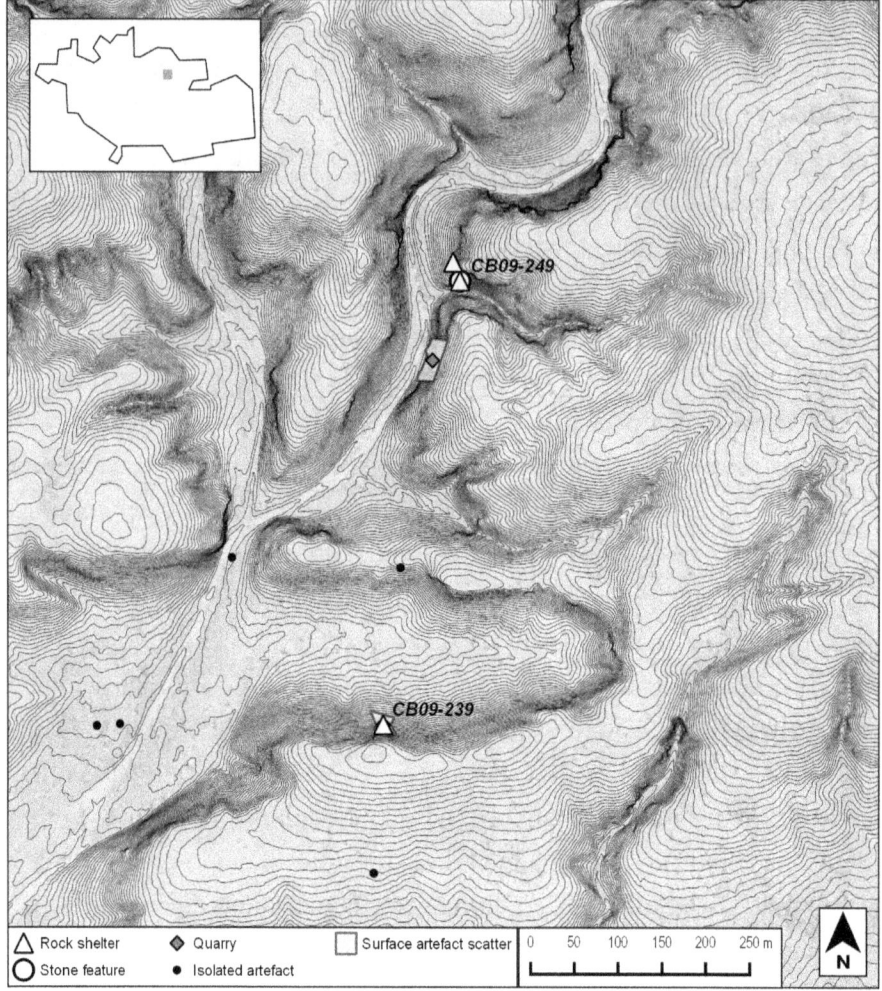

Figure 5.6: The site complex associated with CB09-249.

chert single platform core and a complete BIF flake were found within the shelter, and two additional hammer stones were found on the talus outside. Shelter B is a small, single chambered, north-east-facing shelter. Five chert flakes were recorded at the entrance to the shelter. The stone arrangement is on the hill top immediately above the two shelters. It comprises BIF cobbles and boulders up to 40 cm in size stacked to form an east–west aligned structure 8 m long, 5 m wide and about 0.5 m high (see Figure 5.7b). The artefact scatter is chert-dominated (95%) and was recorded as covering an area of 23,330 m². It includes several concentrations, including three

FIGURE 5.7: CB08-103 and its setting. Top left: General view of rocky hill looking towards shelters. Top right: View of surrounding country from stone feature above shelters. Bottom left: Cached hammer stone. Bottom right: Shelter A.

interpreted as reduction areas. The densest concentration was recorded about 25 m east of the rockshelters and included a dolerite anvil and three hammer stones. In this complex, the rockshelters apparently provide storage, shown by the stone features, core and hammer stone within Shelter A, while other activities clearly occurred through the general area. Switching focus to a lower resolution (Figure 5.9), within a kilometre radius of CB08-103 is a series of extensive surface scatters and chert quarries, primarily to the north and east.

DISCUSSION

Shelters that are close to one another often seem to represent different and complementary uses and they are also commonly clustered with other types of site, including surface artefact scatters and quarries. The distinctive character of rockshelter surface assemblages suggests provisioning places with supplies of raw material, as cores and manuports. Site furniture

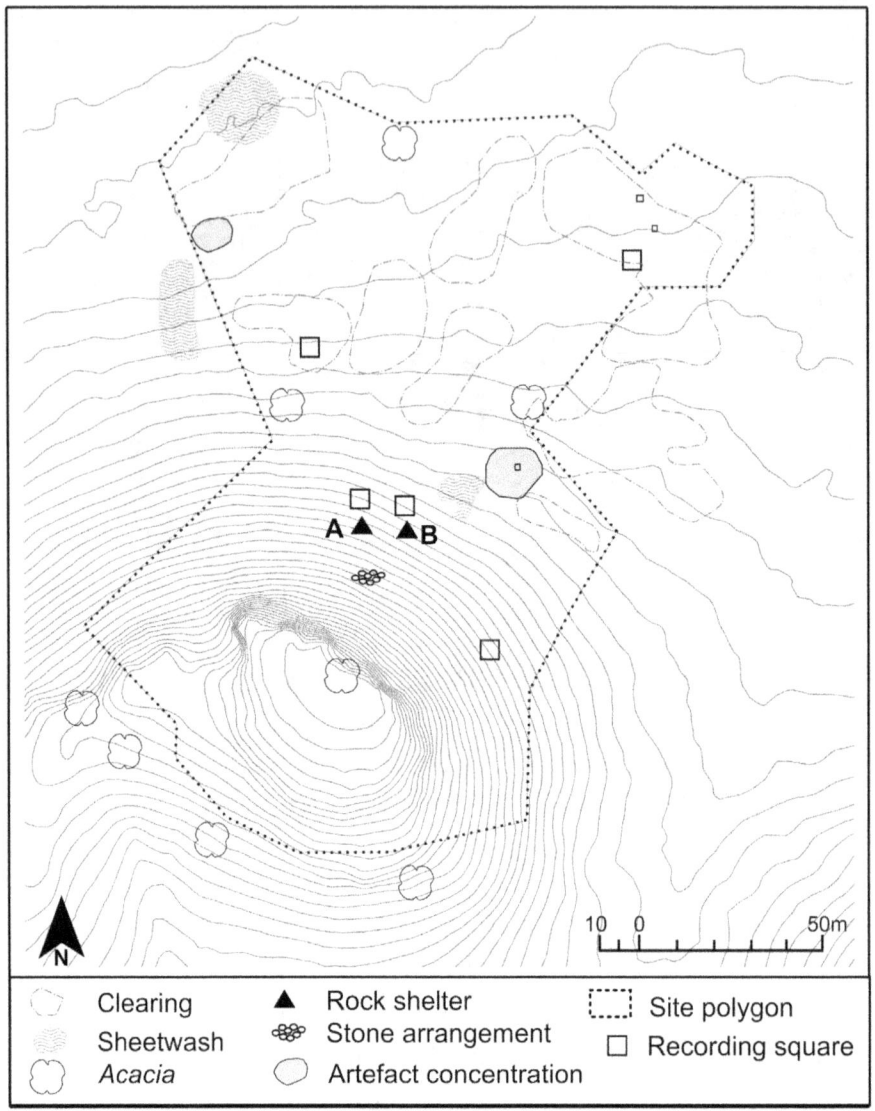

FIGURE 5.8: Plan of the CB08-103 site complex.

in rockshelters, represented by both grinding material and stone features mainly associated with storage, also implies place provisioning. Place provisioning indicates an intention to return and, we argue, provides evidence of a regular pattern of planned visitation to specific localities in the Christmas Creek survey area. Rather than necessarily being residential sites themselves, rockshelters can be regarded as fixed and prominent features in the landscape that afford convenient opportunities for shelter and storage.

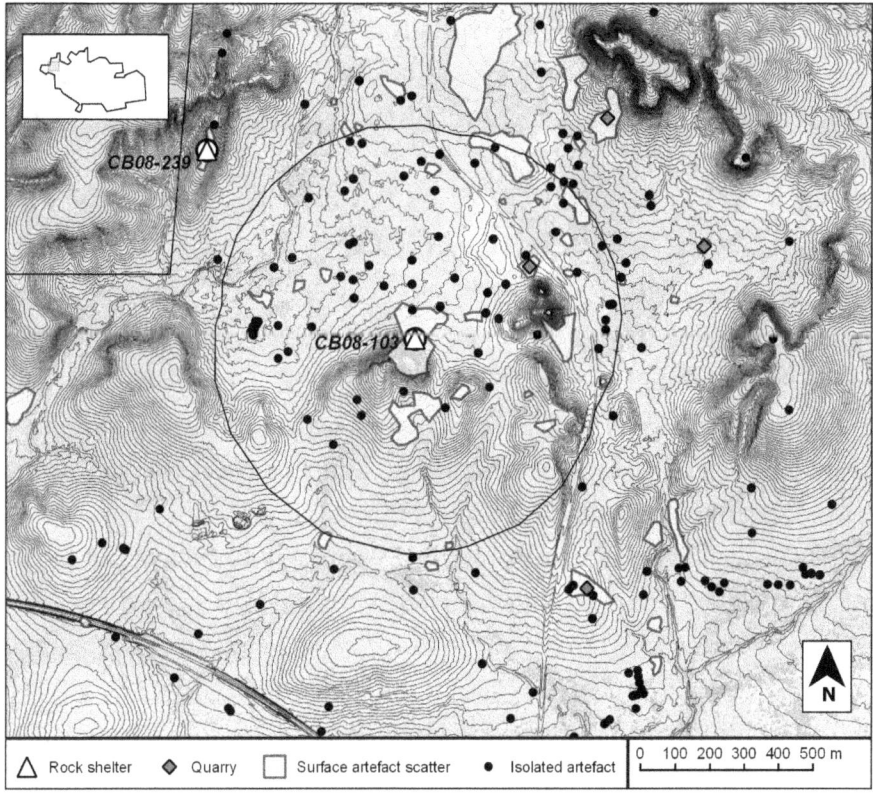

FIGURE 5.9: Distribution of archaeological remains in the vicinity of CB08-103, with 500-metre buffer shown.

The evidence for such place provisioning is not unique to Christmas Creek. Indeed, stone features are widespread in Pilbara rockshelters and storage is well recognised as a key function (Bindon and Lofgren 1982; Wallis and Matthews 2016). Grinding material and cores are also prominent in shelter surface assemblages elsewhere in the region. For example, three out of four shelters excavated by Brown and Mulvaney in the Packsaddle area also had surface assemblages dominated by grindstones and cores (Brown 1987; Brown and Mulvaney 1983). Similarly, the surface assemblage at Newman Orebody XXIX comprised an upper and lower grindstone and two flakes (Brown 1987, 23). At Newman Rockshelter, four cores were cached and enclosed by a stone feature in the western chamber (Brown 1987, 29–32). In the Paraburdoo area, evidence of storage of raw material (including balls of spinifex resin) and grindstones can be inferred from several shelters (Veitch, Hook, and Bradshaw 2005). One example is ERP-26 where a single quartzite muller was recorded on a rock shelf at the rear of the shelter, while two large ironstone slabs used as anvils made up the surface assemblage.

ROCKSHELTER CHRONOLOGY

Like many rockshelter deposits elsewhere in the Pilbara, those in the Christmas Creek area are mostly shallow with relatively poor preservation of organic material and sparse artefact assemblages. Deposits are generally dry and comprise fine sediments interspersed with gravels and occasionally larger rocks. Hearths occur in a number of shelters, but no other subsurface features have been found. Most deposits are acidic and, in the lower levels particularly, charcoal is poorly preserved. There was no evidence of scouring or flooding in any excavated shelter. Most deposits proved relatively shallow (mean depth 31±5 cm, range 11–87 cm) and in most cases cultural material occurred throughout (Dias and Rapley 2014).

The typically small size of test excavations associated with compliance archaeology means that the recovered sample of cultural materials is small. Assemblages are therefore difficult to interpret. Poor preservation of charcoal and cost pressures both mean that dating is also limited. However, the relatively comprehensive test excavation program undertaken at Christmas Creek produced data from a range of sites in the study area that would normally not be considered for excavation within a research program. These data have obvious limitations in that they have low temporal resolution. Nevertheless, considered collectively, they can contribute to an understanding of patterns of Aboriginal occupation of the eastern Chichester Range.

RADIOCARBON DATING

As part of the assessment of these shelters, 54 radiocarbon determinations were obtained from 19 rockshelters in order to establish the time span of site occupation (Table 5.4). Thirty-eight dates were originally reported in consulting reports (Dias 2010; Dias and Rapley 2013; Edwards 2011; Edwards and Hook 2011; Hook, Dias and Rapley 2008). More recently, excavations at CB09-94, CB11-89, CB10-40 and three of the five shelters at CB10-41, have yielded a further 16 radiocarbon determinations. The dates include one from CB08-500 Square 2, which the excavators considered unlikely to be cultural (Hook, Dias and Rapley 2008, 39) and four dates on pieces of wood collected from the surface at CB10-133 (Edwards and Hook 2011, 108–9).

Most sites have at least two radiocarbon determinations. CB10-88 has only a single date, while the two determinations from CB10-117 come from separate test pits. This scarcity partly reflects the context of the study, deriving as it does from test excavations aimed at site assessment within a compliance regime. Generally, samples for dating were chosen to provide dates for discrete features interpreted as hearths, and to estimate, as far as possible, the time span of occupation. Therefore, there is some bias towards samples that would provide basal or near-basal dates. In situ samples were selected if available. Otherwise, charcoal from the 6 mm sieve fraction was used. As noted above, however, the generally acidic nature of the deposits in this region means that charcoal is poorly preserved in these sites. It is common for the quantity of charcoal to decrease with depth, and other organic material is also commonly absent in lower levels. In some shelters, artefacts occur at a greater depth than charcoal.

The question of whether the charcoal samples are cultural in origin, or can be reasonably associated with cultural activity, must also be addressed. Hearth features are certainly recognisable in many sites, as are concentrations of charcoal that are probably degraded hearths. Apart from hearths, another possible source of culturally derived charcoal is from the ethnographically documented practice of burning spinifex to rid shelters of ticks (Clarke 1983, 24). Burning spinifex would not itself produce charcoal, but could result in burning or charring of wood present in the shelter. Charcoal not associated with cultural activity could have blown or washed into shelter deposits from natural or human-induced fires. This issue primarily applies to in situ samples not collected from features and to sieve samples. It could also account for some of the fine charcoal recovered from the 3 mm sieve fraction, but this charcoal was not used for dating.

It is worth noting that the distribution of charcoal in most shelters follows the distribution of cultural material, except where the occurrence of charcoal decreases with depth (see data for individual sites in Appendix 5).

TABLE 5.4: Radiocarbon date list.

Site	Lab code	Estimated age	Error	Median cal BP
CB08-500	Wk-24826	281	51	298
CB08-500	Wk-24828	159	35	113
CB08-500	Wk-24827	205	35	186
CB08-500	Wk-24829	1608	38	1458
CB10-116	Wk-30933	329	53	378
CB10-116	Wk-30934	234	60	198
CB10-117	Wk-30943	709	52	617
CB10-117	Wk-30942	7461	50	8255
CB10-123	Wk-34982	535	28	523
CB10-123	Wk-34983	5741	37	6483
CB10-88	Wk-33652	499	25	509
CB10-92	Wk-33646	1336	25	1226
CB10-92	Wk-33647	2167	25	2110
CB10-92	Wk-33648	2134	25	2064
CB10-98	Wk-33653	1721	32	1584
CB10-98	Wk-33654	4493	34	5101
CB10-93	Wk-33655	2473	30	2475
CB10-93	Wk-33656	36039	272	40692
CB10-133	Wk-30505	839	35	710
CB10-133	Wk-30506	423	38	451

1σ	2σ	Source	Context	Depth below surface (cm)
437–152	461–74	in situ	Sq.1, EU5	14
266–0	278–0	in situ hearth	Sq.1, EU7	17
286–143	298–0	in situ hearth	Sq.1, EU8	19
1515–1415	1537–1369	In situ	Sq. 2, base	19
446–300	491–155	6 mm sieve	EU1	0–2
313–12	438–0	6 mm sieve	EU3	5–11
665–564	684–549	in situ	Sq. A, EU2	8
8313–8188	8375–8061	6 mm sieve	Sq. B EU4	13–17
535–509	547–501	in situ	EU2	9
6530–6414	6632–6402	in situ	EU4	17
518–499	536–491	in situ	EU2	10
1271–1185	1285–1177	6 mm sieve	EU1	0–5
2151–2060	2299–2012	6 mm sieve	EU8	35–40
2091–2015	2148–2006	6 mm sieve	EU10	43–49
1687–1537	1701–1526	in situ	EU2	7
5274–4973	5288–4882	6 mm sieve (AMS)	EU4	15–21
2678–2361	2701–2353	6 mm sieve (AMS)	EU2	4–9
41025–40365	41324–40031	6 mm sieve (AMS)	EU5	20–27
731–681	765–670	Wood	Surface	
499–334	507–324	Wood	Surface	

TABLE 5.4: *Continued.*

Site	Lab code	Estimated age	Error	Median cal BP
CB10-133	Wk-30507	1012	39	860
CB10-133	Wk-30508	637	35	603
CB10-133	Wk-30937	455	25	488
CB10-133	Wk-30939	565	25	534
CB10-133	Wk-30938	2366	39	2344
CB10-133	Wk-30940	3221	47	3403
CB10-133	Wk-30941	3119	81	3272
CB10-147	Wk-33650	598	30	550
CB10-147	Wk-33651	4478	36	5040
CB09-55	Wk-30935	1146	59	1012
CB09-55	Wk-30936	1567	25	1401
CB09-249	Wk-28866	968	30	848
CB09-249	Wk-28867	973	30	850
CB09-249	Wk-28868	5862	30	6627
CB09-249	Wk-28869	4192	30	4692
CB08-427	Wk-28060	1371	30	1250
CB08-427	Wk-28059	5020	44	5707
CB08-427	Wk-28061	5917	33	6697
CB10-40	Wk-39781	241	25	198
CB10-40	Wk-39782	222	25	194

1σ	2σ	Source	Context	Depth below surface (cm)
925–806	955–791	Wood	Surface	
632–550	651–537	Wood	Surface	
505–470	514–338	in situ	Sq. A, EU2	9
546–523	555–509	6 mm sieve	Sq. A, EU3	9–13
2421–2212	2489–2180	6 mm sieve	Sq. C, EU1	0–5
3476–3356	3557–3251	in situ	Sq. C, EU4	18
3379–3174	3459–3007	in situ	Sq. C, EU5	23
623–530	631–518	6 mm sieve	EU1	0–5
5271–4892	5283–4872	6 mm sieve	EU3	9–15
1063–938	1178–919	6 mm sieve	EU2	4–10
1425–1365	1511–1351	6 mm sieve	EU4	13–15
905–792	920–769	in situ	EU1	5
905–796	920–772	in situ	EU2	9
6672–6564	6728–6507	in situ	EU3	10
4818–4615	4828–4569	in situ	EU3	12
1296–1188	1300–1185	6 mm sieve (AMS)	EU1	0–4
5843–5619	5891–5601	in situ	EU4	?
6739–6658	6790–6567	6 mm sieve (AMS)	EU5	15–19
295–154	304–148	6 mm sieve (AMS)	EU1	0–5
283–153	301–143	6 mm sieve (AMS)	EU2	5–10

TABLE 5.4: *Continued.*

Site	Lab code	Estimated age	Error	Median cal BP
CB10-41/2	Wk-39783	267	25	286
CB10-41/2	Wk-39784	323	25	384
CB10-41/3	Wk-39785	400	25	418
CB10-41/3	Wk-39786	219	25	194
CB10-41/3	Wk-39787	167	25	115
CB10-41/3	Wk-39788	113.2	0.004	
CB10-41/4	Wk-39789	520	29	517
CB10-41/4	Wk-39790	853	25	716
CB10-41/4	Wk-39791	1440	25	1303
CB11-89	Wk-39976	146	28	98
CB11-89	Wk-39977	549	25	528
CB11-89	Wk-39978	659	25	606
CB09-94	Wk-39979	470	25	498
CB09-94	Wk-39980	2583	25	2625

1σ	2σ	Source	Context	Depth below surface (cm)
309–155	320–151	6 mm sieve (AMS)	EU1	0–4
439–302	447–296	in situ (AMS)	EU2	5.5
489–332	495–325	in situ (AMS)	Sq. A, EU1	1
282–152	300–75	in situ (AMS)	Sq. A, EU2	6.5
270–0	278–0	6 mm sieve (AMS)	Sq. B, EU1	0–3
		6 mm sieve (AMS)	Sq. B, EU5	20–26
528–504	544–496	6 mm sieve	EU1	0–6
736–685	764–677	in situ (AMS)	EU3	15.5
1315–1285	1350–1274	6 mm sieve (AMS)	EU6	27–31
253–0	268–0	in situ (AMS)	Sq. A, EU1	5
540–516	550–505	6 mm sieve (AMS)	Sq. A, EU2	5–10
635–557	650–552	6 mm sieve (AMS)	Sq. B, EU1	0–3
513–487	523–545	in situ (AMS)	EU2	7
2744–2539	2750–2492	in situ (AMS)	EU4	18

There are no cases of shelters that have deposits with charcoal but lack cultural material. Unfortunately, the nature of compliance archaeology means that it is not possible to provide a comprehensive response to the question of cultural origin for all the charcoal. The priority given to features and in situ samples, and the exclusion of finely divided charcoal from the 3 mm sieves, does serve to increase the probability that the charcoal is cultural in origin.

Interestingly, there are no definite stratigraphic inversions. There are a few instances where dates are not in stratigraphic order based on the raw date or the median calibrated date. However, in each case, the calibrated ranges overlap and the dates can be considered the same.

Four shelter sites have more than one test pit (discussed in more detail in Appendix 5). The dating evidence for these sites commonly differs between pits – sometimes markedly so. In the case of CB08-500, the second excavated square (which was only 0.5 × 0.5 m) yielded very little cultural material and the excavators considered that the dated sample of charred wood might not be cultural (Hook, Dias and Rapley 2008, 39). At CB10-133, and probably also at CB10-117, the divergent results between test pits are best explained in terms of differences in depositional history between different parts of the shelter, with local preservation of older deposits in the more protected interior of the site. Similar observations have been made at other Pilbara sites (e.g. Morse, Cameron and Reynen 2014). This raises a number of questions about the site formation processes operating at inland Pilbara rockshelters, which are still poorly understood (Cropper and Law 2018b, 448ff.). The restricted scale and limited research focus of most excavations conducted within a compliance context militates against improving our understanding of site formation processes. Detailed geoarchaeological studies are rare for inland Pilbara rockshelters (Haberle, Hopf and Roberts 2018; Marsh et al. 2018; Reynen et al. 2018; Ward et al. 2017; Williams 2018). Clearly, the Christmas Creek examples caution against the current practice of assessing site significance from small test pits (Cropper and Law 2018b, 450–51). They also highlight the problems of extrapolating regional interpretations from small samples of cultural material from individual sites.

External characteristics of shelters in the study area do not correlate with age, or depth, of deposits. Similar observations have been made about the suite of shelters recorded and excavated at Hope Downs (Cropper and Law 2018b, 450–51). At Christmas Creek, all, with the exception of CB10-133, are small and have varying depths of deposit (Dias and Rapley 2014). CB10-133, however, is an unusually large and spacious shelter. It is also unusual because there are no surface artefact scatters within a radius of 600 metres. However, accumulation of shelter deposits does seem to be primarily associated with human occupation. In only one shelter (CB10-98) was there any accumulation of sediment without evidence of human occupation. All other rockshelters had cultural material to bedrock (see Appendix 5).

SITE OCCUPATION HISTORIES

Artefact discard rates, using corrections for area excavated and units of time, are commonly used as indicators of intensity of occupation (Attenbrow 2007, 120). Of course, discard rates need not be straightforward indicators of occupation intensity as they involve a series of assumptions about rates and continuity of sediment deposition (Attenbrow 2007, 103), while changes in technology and raw material use are other complicating influences. The number of artefacts discarded per century, corrected for area excavated, was estimated for each shelter. This result was calculated by estimating a maximum possible duration for the accumulation of deposits based on the distribution of radiocarbon determinations (Figure 5.10). Continuous deposition was assumed unless there were grounds for identifying a major break in use. The calculated rates must therefore be considered as broadly indicative only. Nevertheless, the results permit broad-brush comparison between sites.

The excavated shelters seem to fall into three categories based on artefact discard rates and whether occupation seemed to be relatively continuous or intermittent. The first type comprises sites where the pattern of occupation seems to be most intense. They seem to have been repeatedly and regularly occupied over hundreds or thousands of years. All of them have relatively large and dense flaked stone assemblages and have relatively high discard rates (Figure 5.10). These shelters have varying depths of deposit, with several radiocarbon determinations indicating their deposits have accumulated within, at most, the last 4000 years. This category includes CB10-133,

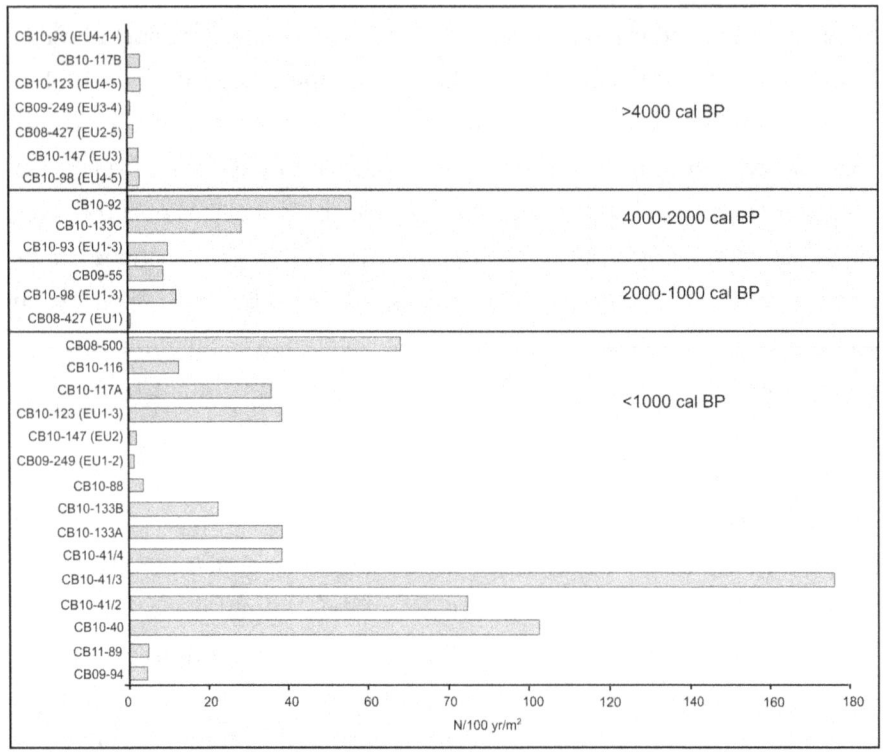

Figure 5.10: Estimated overall artefact discard rates (N/100 years, corrected for area excavated) for all shelters.

CB08-500, CB10-92 and CB10-116. CB09-55 can also be assigned to this group. This shelter has relatively shallow deposits, but the radiocarbon determinations indicate a relatively brief and intense episode of occupation 1000–1500 years ago. The shelter complex on Marandu Creek (CB10-40, CB10-41/2-4) seems to have particularly dense occupation with very high discard rates, dated to the last 1500 years or less.

The second category includes sites where the pattern of use seems to have been brief and episodic. These mostly have shallow deposits and radiocarbon determinations widely separated in time – typically indicating occupation in the early to mid-Holocene with a more recent episode of occupation within the last 1000 years. Overall, assemblages are sparse and artefact discard rates are very low (Figure 5.10). CB09-249, CB08-427 and CB10-147 all belong to this group. Three other sites may also be included. CB10-93 has low artefact density and radiocarbon determinations widely separated in time, although in this case the early date is Pleistocene rather than Holocene. Both CB10-88 and CB11-89 have shallow deposits, low artefact density and radiocarbon dates indicating occupation only within the last 1000 years.

The third category consists of sites which show a mixture of characteristics, but which, like the second group, probably indicate episodic use. At CB10-117, the discard rate in Square A is relatively high, although most of the flaked stone came from the sampled 3 mm sieve fraction. This material can be attributed to the last 1000 years. A second test pit (Square B) provides sparse evidence of an early Holocene, and very fleeting, episode of occupation within the shelter. CB10-123 also has shallow deposits and widely separated dates indicating episodes of occupation within the last millennium and early Holocene, but the artefact discard rate is relatively high. However, like CB10-117A, almost all the artefacts come from the sampled 3 mm sieve fraction and this probably inflates the estimate of artefact density. The deposits at CB10-98 are relatively deep (62 cm), but cultural material was only recovered from the top 26 cm. This was the only shelter tested where a significant depth of sterile deposits was encountered. However, the two radiocarbon determinations are widely separated in time and discard rate is low (Figure 5.10). CB09-94 has shallow deposits, widely separated dates and thus a low discard rate.

While there is clearly considerable variability in artefact discard rates, there seems to be a general trend of increasing activity through time (Figure 5.10). Better recovery and preservation of more recent sites could, in part, account for this trend (Marwick 2009). Nevertheless, it does seem that the intensity of shelter use prior to about 4000 years ago was low. The last 1000 years showed the most intensive shelter use, although there was still marked variation between sites. Between 4000 and 2000 years ago, few shelters were used, but discard rates were uniformly relatively high.

Discard rates are rarely reported for inland Pilbara rockshelters and uncertainties about chronology mean that they are difficult to calculate from the available data. Changes in site use are more commonly expressed in terms of artefacts per volume of sediment rather than unit of time, probably because chronological resolution in most rockshelters is very low. The results from the study area seem to be broadly characteristic of the inland

Pilbara, where published artefact densities (artefacts per m^3) for shelter deposits are usually low and increased quantities of artefacts are commonly reported during the last few thousand years. Where artefact discard rates have been calculated, these are generally low. At Watura Jurnti, for example, long-term discard rates were about 10.5 artefacts per 1000 years prior to the Last Glacial Maximum, falling to about 7.8 per 1000 years during the Last Glacial Maximum. The discard rate then fell even further to 1–1.5 per 1000 years until the last 1500 years, when it rose dramatically to 200–50 per 1000 years (Marsh et al. 2018). At Yurlu Kankala, on the Abydos Plain, estimated discard rates range from a peak of 62 artefacts per thousand years at around 18,000 years ago to 3 per thousand years for the period 17,600 to 10,000 years ago, with no artefacts at all deposited in Unit B (10,000–5400 years ago) (Reynen et al. 2018, Table 1).

Although chronological resolution is poor in many sites across the inland Pilbara, it is clear that their occupation histories are also varied. Some shelters have evidence for intermittent and episodic patterns of use, while others indicate more intense and regular occupation. This is particularly evident at some of the longer sequences such as Watura Jurnti (Marsh et al. 2018), Yurlu Kankala (Morse, Cameron and Reynen 2014; Reynen et al. 2018), Djadjiling (Law, Cropper and Petchey 2010; Law and Cropper 2018), Jundaru (Cropper 2018), Marillana A (Marwick 2005) and Yirra (Veitch, Hook and Bradshaw 2005), where the evidence suggests changes in the intensity of use of the shelter through time.

PATTERNS OF SHELTER USE IN TIME AND SPACE

The radiocarbon dataset from this study is small and localised. Nevertheless, it has the advantage of being comprehensive in that almost all rockshelters assessed as having excavation potential were tested. Here we examine the stratigraphic and cultural context of individual radiocarbon determinations in order to investigate temporal change in the use of this landscape.

The early date (40,692 median cal BP) from Kakutungutanta (CB10-93) is the first Pleistocene date reported from the Chichester Range (Dias and Rapley 2013; 2014). This confirms occupation in this area at an early date comparable to those from elsewhere in the Pilbara (Brown 1987; Edwards and Murphy 2003; Hughes and Quartermaine 1992; Law, Cropper and Petchey 2010; Marwick 2002; 2009; Morse 2009; Morse, Cameron and Reynen 2014; Slack, Fillios and Fullagar 2009; Veitch, Bradshaw and Hook 2005). It is difficult to say more about this early occupation because this is a single date associated with very sparse cultural material (see Appendix 5). Unfortunately, it has not been possible to return to the site to expand the excavation due to safety concerns.

The overall distribution of radiocarbon determinations for this study over the last 10,000 years is broadly similar to the distribution for the inland Pilbara as a whole, and more generally for the arid zone (Smith and Ross 2008; Smith et al. 2008; Williams, Veth et al. 2015). There is a marked increase in the number of dates through time, particularly from about 1500 years ago. The exponential increase in recent determinations is typical of many similar datasets. For Central Australia, Smith and Ross (2008) interpret the proliferation of dates in terms of evidence for environmental change to suggest significant population increase and expansion of settlement beginning around 1500 years ago. It is debatable whether this increase genuinely indicates significant changes in demography and/or land use or whether it can be accounted for by the greater preservation and recovery of more recent sites (Attenbrow and Hiscock 2015; Bird and Frankel 1991; Marwick 2009).

The distribution of Holocene dates in the study area shows marked patterning in both time and space (Figures 5.11, 5.12). Before about 4000 years ago, several rockshelters in the study area show evidence of use. About 4000 years ago, archaeological evidence of occupation contracts to a few shelters within the catchment of Kakutungutanta Creek. In contrast to the sparse evidence from earlier occupations, these sites were used more intensively. From about 1500 years ago, cultural remains indicate a more dispersed occupation of the Christmas Creek study area. Some shelters were used for the first time, while others were re-used after a period of abandonment. This pattern of reoccupation and use of new shelters continues into the last thousand years with widespread occupation throughout the area over the last 500 years. Some of these more recent sites have much denser accumulations of cultural material than previously seen in the study area (Figure 5.10).

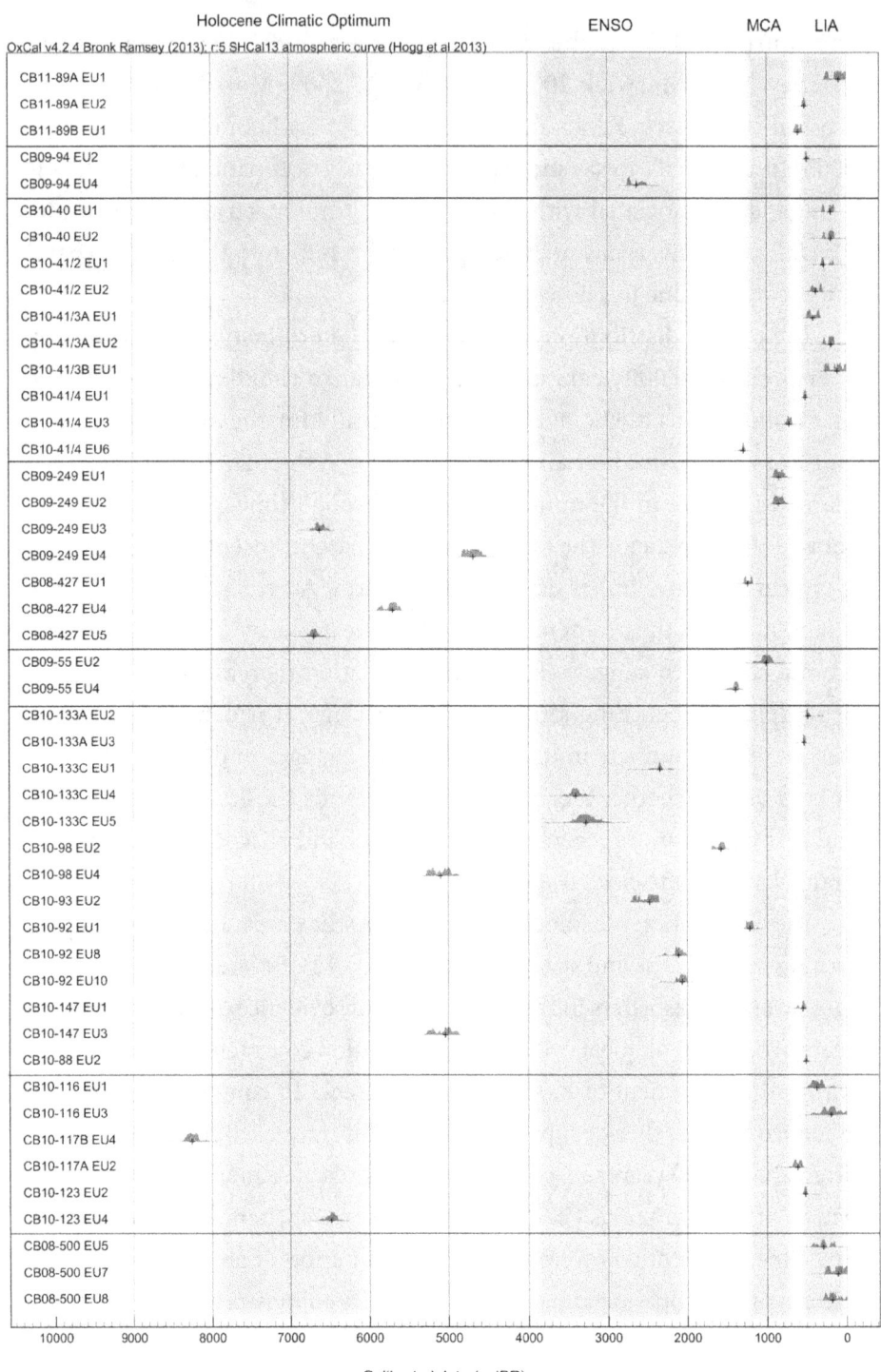

FIGURE 5.11: Distribution of calibrated radiocarbon dates in space and time. El Niño Southern Oscillation (ENSO), Medieval Climatic Anomaly (MCA), Little Ice Age (LIA).

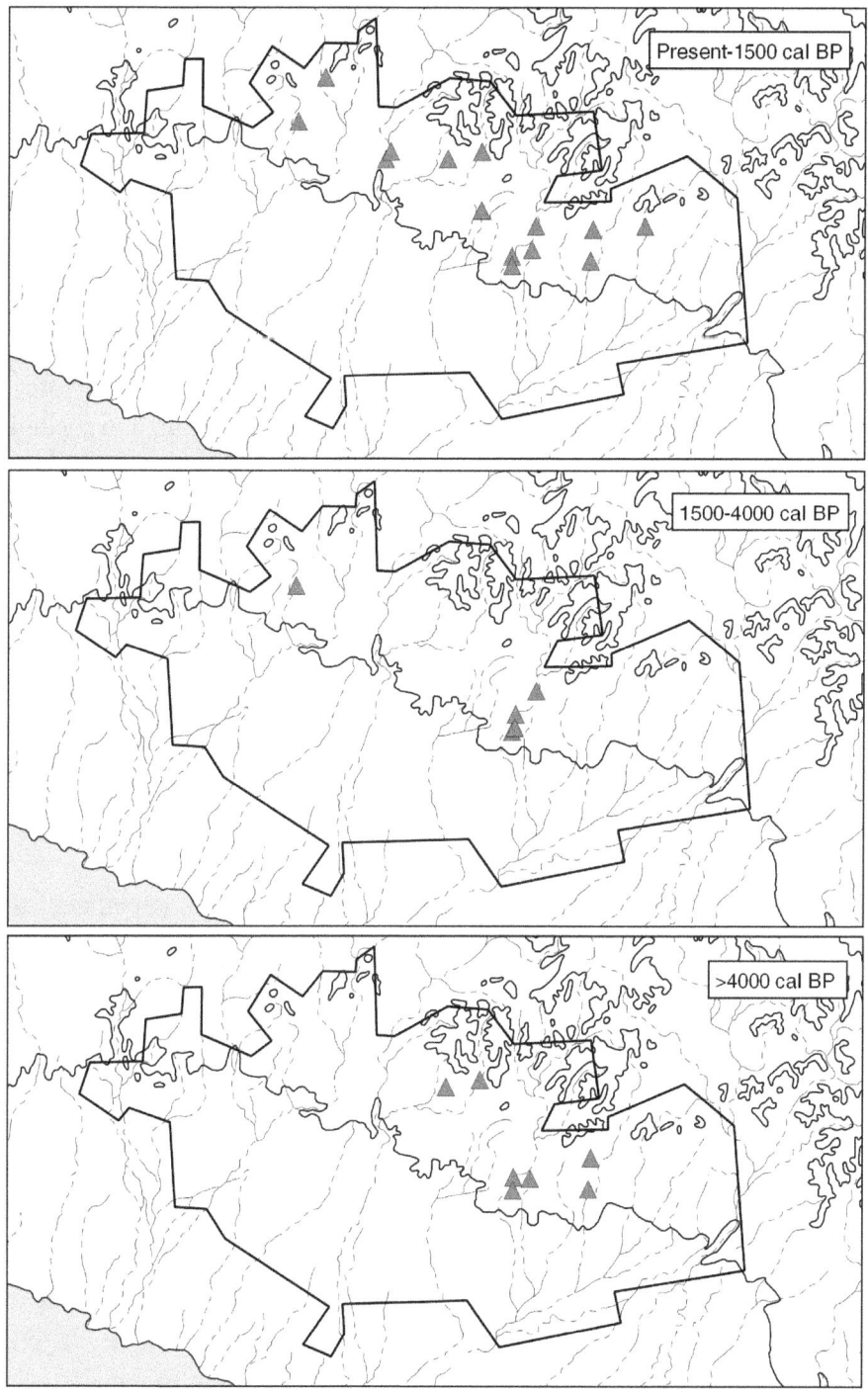

FIGURE 5.12: Summary of changes in the distribution of occupied rockshelters through time in the study area.

DISCUSSION

Palaeoenvironmental records for the arid zone and north-western Australia (Reeves, Barrows et al. 2013) show that hydroclimatic conditions were wetter than today during the early Holocene (see Chapter 3 for discussion). The sparse and dispersed occupation signal from the Chichester Range before 4000 years ago might indicate post-glacial population expansion out of refuge areas in the Hamersley Range. A relatively small population with a broad-based wide-ranging foraging pattern would have been able to take advantage of greater water resource availability across the landscape.

The contraction of evidence of occupation in the study area to shelters along Kakutungutanta Creek coincides with the onset of drier conditions in the mid-Holocene. Mid-Holocene aridity associated with the intensification of ENSO has been linked to changes in past land use and subsistence in both Australia and South America (Smith and Ross 2008; Sutton, Summerhayes and Ford 2015; Williams, Veth et al. 2015; Williams, Ulm et al. 2015; Williams et al. 2008). It is debatable how much impact ENSO would have had on climate in Western Australia (O'Donnell et al. 2015). But evidence for aridity in the mid-Holocene is quite widespread in northern Australia (e.g. Shulmeister and Lees 1995) and there is evidence for 'mega drought' from 2400 to 1300 years ago in the Kimberley (McGowan et al. 2012).

The local palaeohydrological record from 14 Mile Pool immediately to the south-east of the study area extends back about 2000 years and indicates extreme drought conditions on the Fortescue Marsh before about 1200 years ago. From about 1200 years ago, the 14 Mile Pool record shows a wetting trend with increasing frequency and reliability of flood events (Rouillard, Greenwood et al. 2016; Rouillard, Skrzypek et al. 2016). The recent expansion of use of the landscape documented in the archaeological record broadly corresponds to this return to wetter conditions from about 1200 years ago. Within the last 1000 years, settlement is once again spread throughout the ranges and new sites are occupied. The pattern of usage of individual shelters ranges from fleeting episodes to more regular visitation.

The evidence from dated rockshelter sequences in the Christmas Creek area thus suggests reorganisation of land use in response to changes in availability of surface water. The onset of arid conditions in the mid-Holocene saw a contraction of archaeologically visible occupation to a single creek system – indeed to a three-kilometre section of the creek. It is worth noting that this creek system is also the location of the single Pleistocene date. Several shelters, none of which were continuously used, thus attest to long-term continuity of usage in this locality.

The increasing frequency and reliability of flood events from about 1200 years ago, documented in the 14 Mile Pool sequence, provided opportunities for groups living near the Fortescue Marsh and resulted in an increasingly widespread and diverse archaeological signature, particularly over the last 1000 years. McDonald and Veth (2013a) argue for the intensification of ceremonial life in the Pilbara and Western Desert over the last 1500 years. More frequent and long-lasting flood events might well have facilitated such ceremonial intensification by providing more opportunities for large groups of people to gather for ceremonies.

EXCAVATED ASSEMBLAGES

Excavated rockshelter assemblages in the survey area typically comprise complete and broken flakes produced from a range of local raw materials using simple hard hammer percussion. Cores and pieces with secondary retouch are rare. Excavated cultural material from rockshelters is typically sparse in the Pilbara, while the limited size of most excavations means that small enigmatic assemblages with poor chronological resolution are usual. Well-dated examples of key artefact types (e.g. tulas, macroblades, grinding material) are scarce in the region (see Chapter 2 for discussion). Consequently, investigation of change through time in rockshelter assemblages is difficult and our understanding of changes in lithic technology is poor at a regional and local level.

In this study, mean sample size was 139 flaked stone artefacts, but only eight sites yielded more than 100, while five sites had fewer than 50. Sample size was further reduced when only the 6 mm sieve fraction was considered. The assemblages from two sites (CB10-117 and CB10-123) were overwhelmingly dominated by artefacts from the 3 mm sieve fraction; indeed, only material from the 3 mm sieve fraction was recovered from Square B at CB10-117.

TABLE 5.5: Summary of artefact assemblages likely to be from contexts older than about 4000 years.

CB10-93	EU4–14 Date uncertain. Pleistocene?	Twenty-one flakes, broken flakes and undiagnostic debris of BIF, basalt, chert, chalcedony and quartz, 14 of which came from the 3 mm sieve fraction. Chalcedony and chert only occurred in the 3 mm sieve fraction. Two flakes had evidence of secondary modification – a BIF flake from EU4 and a basalt flake fragment from EU7 – both undiagnostic.
CB10-117B	All EU Early Holocene	Fifteen artefacts were recovered from the excavation of test pit B and all came from the 3 mm sieve fraction. Five were chert flakes while the remainder were BIF complete flakes or debris.
CB09-249	EU3–4 Early Holocene	Eight artefacts, seven of which were complete flakes. Two BIF flakes come from the 3 mm fraction. Two BIF flakes, three basalt flakes and one basalt flake fragment came from the 6 mm fraction.
CB08-427	EU2–4 Early Holocene	Twenty-two artefacts all from the 6 mm fraction. All are likely to be associated with the remains of a degraded hearth in EU4. The assemblage comprises flakes, broken flakes and debris (8 each basalt and BIF, 5 chert and 1 quartzite).
CB10-147	EU3 Early Holocene	Ten flakes from the 6 mm sieve fraction (six BIF, three basalt, one chert), and a BIF distal flake fragment from the 3 mm sample.
CB10-98	EU4–5 Early Holocene	Six artefacts from the 3 mm fraction and four from the 6 mm fraction, all flakes, flake fragments or debris. BIF, chert and quartzite.
CB10-123	EU4–5 Early Holocene	Four BIF flakes from the 3 mm sieve fraction.

Subdividing these sparse assemblages for analysis is difficult. This is due to the generally uniform stratigraphy and limited dating evidence, particularly in the older levels. Any subdivision, of course, reduces a small sample even further. Most sites are therefore best viewed as single analytical units for comparative purposes. In a few instances, it is possible to partition site sequences. These include CB10-133 and CB10-117, where more than one test pit was excavated and each had a different depositional history. As discussed above, several sites (CB10-93, CB09-249, CB08-427, CB10-123 and CB10-147) with clearly episodic and discontinuous occupation histories could also be subdivided into early and later assemblages (Figure 5.10).

Twenty-six discrete assemblages can therefore be analysed, but some are quite small. Two assemblages (CB10-133C and CB10-93, EU1–3) are attributable to the period 4000–2000 cal BP and the basal excavation units at CB09-94 (EU3–4) also probably date to this time. CB10-92 spans the period from about 2500 to 1000 years ago. CB09-55, EU1–3 from CB10-98, EU1 from CB08-427 and perhaps the basal excavation unit at CB10-41/4 most likely date to between 2000 and 1000 cal BP. Material that is considered to be older than about 4000 years can be identified from seven shelters with some confidence (Table 5.5). All other assemblages date to the last 1000 years.

Unfortunately, it is difficult to generalise about the stone artefacts from older assemblages, other than to say they are all from very small samples and undiagnostic. They consist of flakes, flake fragments and debris of BIF, basalt, chert or quartz. Only two pieces show any evidence of secondary modification – both undiagnostic retouched pieces from CB10-93. There were no cores or grinding material. Cortical flakes occur in CB10-147, CB09-249, CB10-93, CB08-427 and CB10-98 (20%, 17%, 33%, 33% and 25% respectively of the 6 mm sieve fraction). All are BIF or basalt. All cortex is terrestrial except for two basalt flakes with riverine cortex from CB10-147.

ROCKSHELTERS AND MOBILITY INDICATORS

Rockshelters with evidence of cultural activity in the study area are clearly diverse both in terms of their surface features and intensity of occupation. Pilbara rockshelters are commonly characterised as ephemeral sites (Ryan and Morse 2009; see Veth 1993, 86). It follows that we might expect their assemblages to fit the characteristics of sites occupied only briefly by small, highly mobile groups. They should show low diversity of artefact types and raw material, low levels of reduction intensity, mostly early stage reduction, and few or no formal tools or grindstones. A pilot analysis of six excavated

TABLE 5.6: Summary of rockshelter assemblages in terms of mobility indicators.

	Key	Diversity (H)	Mean length of complete flakes (mm)	% cortical	6:3 mm
CB10-147, EU3	1	0.90	21.5	20	3.12
CB10-93, EU4–14	2	0.80	25.3	28.6	0.13
CB10-98, EU4–5	3	0.56	44.7	25	0.17
CB09-249, EU3–4	4	0.64	26.8	16.7	3
CB08-427, EU2–5	5	1.20	26.6	33.3	0
CB10-133C	6	1.44	21.3	57.5	0.08
CB10-92	7	1.36	20.1	28.0	0.41
CB09-94, EU4–5	8	0.76	18.0	18.2	0.5
CB08-500	9	1.40	15.0	11.6	0.32
CB10-123, EU1–3	10	0.00	12.0	50.0	0.01
CB10-116	11	0.52	21.2	35.0	0.19
CB10-117A	12	0.50	12.5	40.0	0.03
CB10-147, EU2	13	0.00	20.5	18.2	1.57
CB10-133AB	14	1.51	24.3	37.0	0.21
CB10-88	15	1.21	18.5	6.7	1.25
CB10-93, EU1–3	16	1.02	16.4	20.0	0.19
CB10-98, EU1–3	17	1.74	24.0	25.0	0.23
CB09-55	18	1.29	21.6	42.9	0.66
CB09-249, EU1–2	19	0.67	14.0	26.3	6
CB08-427, EU1	20	0.00	18.0	31.8	0
CB10-40	21	1.16	15.9	13.9	0.27
CB10-41/2	22	1.22	15.1	12.2	0.54
CB10-41/3	23	0.84	17.8	21.5	0.73
CB10-41/4	24	1.27	21.6	32.8	2.46
CB09-94, EU1–3	25	1.02	15.8	20.5	0.48
CB11-89	26	0.15	17.5	30.0	0.46

assemblages from rockshelters in the study area, using these indicators, instead suggested that they were functionally and behaviourally diverse (Bird and Rhoads 2015). The analysis also casts doubt on the interpretation of the mobility indicators suggested by the land-use model, and our discussion of the surface samples (see Chapter 4) further supports this conclusion. Here we complete the analysis for all the excavated assemblages.

The indicators used for excavated assemblages differ slightly from those used in the analysis of surface samples (Chapter 4). As for surface assemblages, raw material diversity, flake size (mean length of complete flakes), and percentage of cortical flakes were all calculated. The scarcity of cores in excavated assemblages means that it was impossible to calculate the flake to core ratio or the ratio of single to multiplatform cores, so these measures of reduction intensity were not used. Like the surface samples, retouch is rare in rockshelter assemblages and this measure of reduction intensity was also excluded. However, excavated assemblages offer additional data in the form of the relationships between the 6 mm and 3 mm sieve fractions (Bird and Rhoads 2015). Low proportions of flakes from the 3 mm sieve fraction suggest that stone knapping was not a prominent activity at the site (Hiscock 2005) while very high proportions can be interpreted as evidence for late stage reduction. Therefore, the ratio of flakes from the 6 mm to 3 mm sieve fractions, corrected for sampling where appropriate, was also calculated. A value greater than 1.0 indicates that flakes from the 3 mm sieve fraction are scarce and thus that stone flaking was probably not an important activity at the shelter. There are five sites with ratios greater than 1.0: CB10-88, CB10-147, CB09-249 and CB10-41/4. Ratios less than 0.2 indicate that the small flakes dominate the assemblage by more than five to one. Samples with this ratio or less include CB08-427, CB10-117B, CB10-123, CB10-116, CB10-93, CB10-133B and CB10-133C. However, in the case of CB08-427 and CB10-117B, the sample size was also very small and almost the entire assemblage came from the 3 mm residues.

Table 5.6 summarises each assemblage in terms of the mobility indicators. Classifying the excavated shelters in terms of discard rate (see Figure 5.10) effectively distinguishes between sites that show intermittent and ephemeral occupation by small groups, from those where occupation was more regular and frequent.

TABLE 5.7: Results of Principal Components Analysis on rockshelter assemblages.

		Loadings			
	% variance	Diversity (H)	Mean length	% cortical	6:3 mm
PC 1	30.7	0.011137	0.24856	0.6761	-0.69353
PC 2	28.0	0.75815	0.55979	-0.31953	-0.09869
PC 3	23.0	-0.48832	0.78376	-0.099935	0.37048
PC 4	18.2	0.43197	-0.10285	0.37048	0.60994

The results of a Principal Components Analysis of these mobility indicators (Table 5.7) were not clear cut. The first three components account for just over 80% of the variance, but the percentages are fairly evenly spread across these factors. The first component contrasts a high percentage of cortical flakes with a high value for the 6:3 mm sieve ratio. High values of this ratio indicate assemblages with very few small flakes and thus little evidence for on-site reduction. In terms of a reduction sequence model, one might expect high values to be associated with higher percentages of cortical flakes. The second component associates raw material diversity and mean length, and contrasts these variables with percentage of cortical flakes. According to the reduction model, assemblages with a higher proportion of cortical flakes should be less heavily reduced and thus have a larger mean size. The third component is most consistent with the relationship between reduction and mobility expressed in the land-use model as it contrasts diversity with mean flake length. High raw material diversity is also expected to characterise more heavily reduced assemblages, expressed in terms of smaller size flake.

Figure 5.13 plots component 1 with component 2, and component 2 with component 3. The assemblages are characterised with reference to degree of residential mobility – high versus low – based on occupation history. There is little clear evidence of discrete groupings. Assemblages with less intense occupation, indicating ephemeral sites with high residential mobility, tend to be outliers. These assemblages appear to be highly

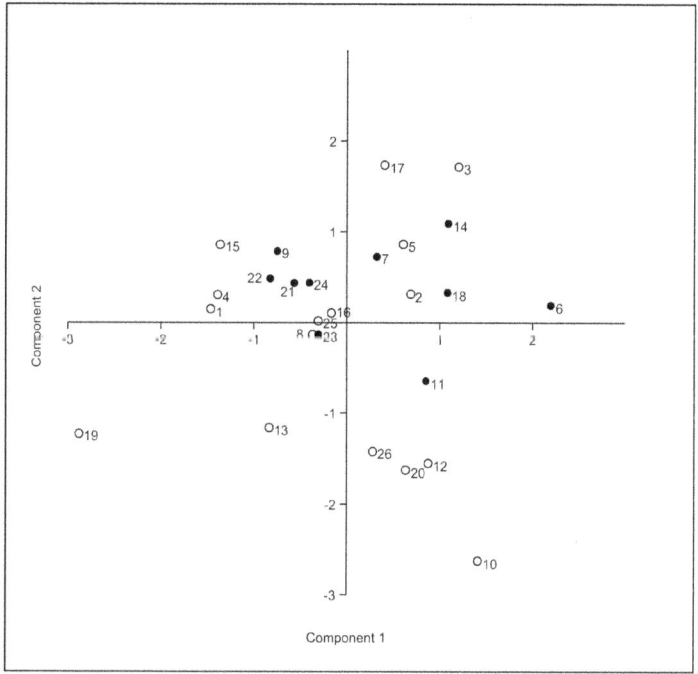

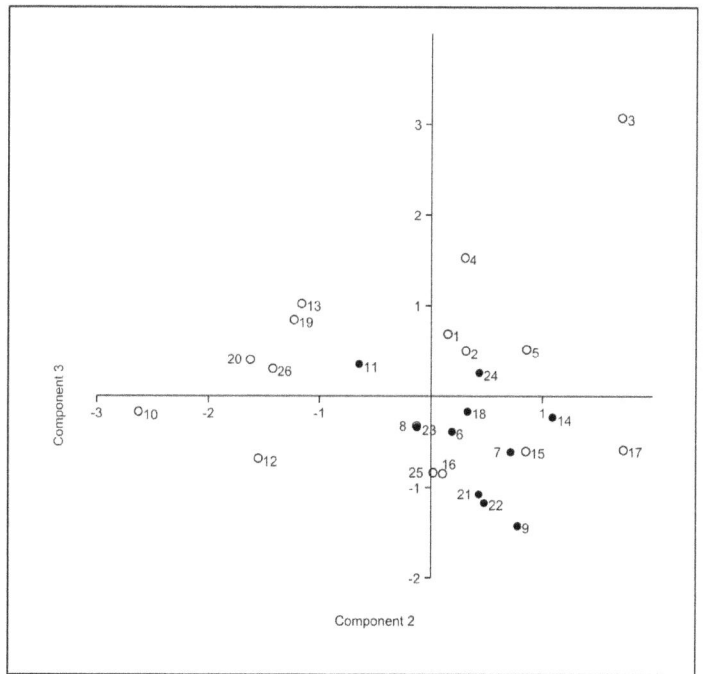

FIGURE 5.13: Results of Principal Components Analysis for shelter assemblages. For key to shelters see Table 5.6. Filled circles: low residential mobility. Open circles: high residential mobility.

variable, suggesting that sample size is a key influence on this result. The strong effect of sample size on various characteristics of assemblages has already been noted for surface samples (see discussion in Chapter 4, and Figures 4.8, 4.9 and 4.20).

As with the analysis of surface artefact scatters, the results of the PCA on rockshelter assemblages do not provide support for assemblage indicators used by the land-use model. It is therefore necessary to look more closely at the characteristics of excavated assemblages to tease out the nature of variability in rockshelters.

RAW MATERIAL DIVERSITY

A bewildering range of raw materials occurs in sites in the study area; ten different types were found in excavated shelter assemblages. However, like the surface assemblages, only five materials occur in more than trace amounts or in the majority of shelters (Table 5.8). Overall, BIF makes up about half of the total of artefacts by number and is found in all shelters. There is, however, substantial inter-site variability with the overall percentage of BIF ranging from 87% at CB11-89 to only 28% in Square B at CB10-133. The picture for chert is similar. Chert is found in all shelter assemblages and comprises about a fifth of the total by number. The representation of chert ranges from 46% at CB10-116 to 1% at CB11-89. Basalt and chalcedony occur in most shelters, and together make up a fifth of assemblages by number. Mudstone occurs in 11 shelter assemblages and makes up 7% overall. Quartzite comprises 6% of the assemblage in CB10-92, and is also present in four other shelters. Dolerite is also found in 11 shelters, but accounts for 1% overall. All other materials (ironstone, quartz, crystal quartz and silcrete) occur in trace amounts.

Raw material diversity, as measured by H, varies quite widely in individual rockshelter assemblages (Table 5.6). Surface assemblages are not directly comparable to excavated assemblages due to the greater recovery of small flakes through sieving. However, comparing only the 6 mm sieve fraction with the surface assemblages mitigates this to some degree. Overall, basalt and dolerite are both less common in shelter assemblages than in surface assemblages from the study area as a whole, while chert and mudstone are more common. However, excavated assemblages were more similar overall

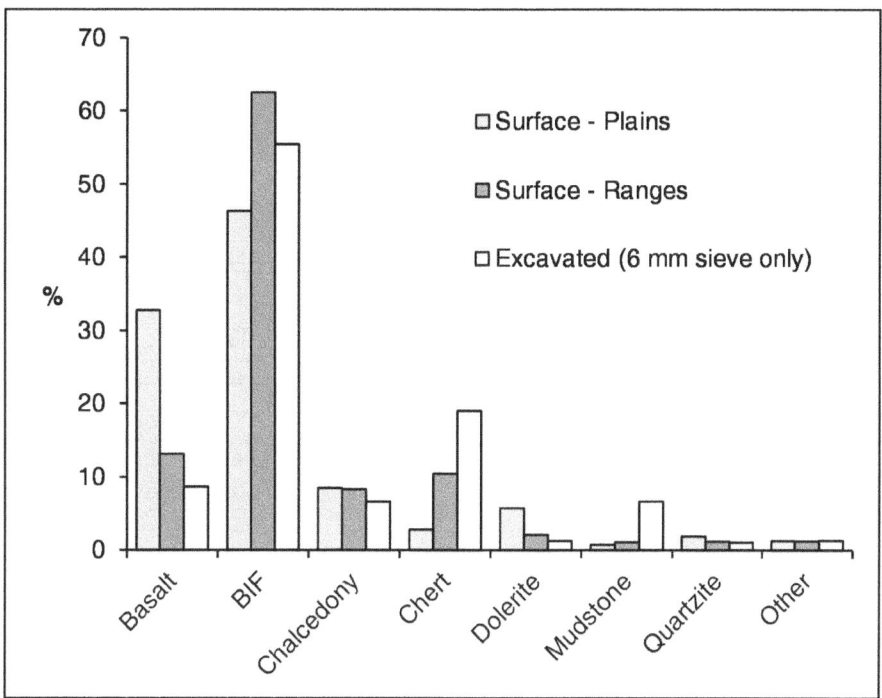

FIGURE 5.14: Representation of different raw materials in flaked stone assemblages from surface sites in the ranges and plains, and from excavated rock shelters (6 mm sieve fraction only).

to surface assemblages from the ranges, reflecting their location and suggesting local procurement and use of raw materials (Figure 5.14).

Table 5.9 summarises raw material composition for the 6 mm sieve fraction from individual rockshelter assemblages in comparison with analysed surface samples from the ranges. The table is arranged to group rockshelters with their nearby surface assemblages. Relatively high proportions of chert in excavated assemblages are matched in some of the grouped surface samples in the ranges. In general, however, the prominence of BIF and chert in the excavated assemblages simply reflects the location of rockshelters in the ranges. Mudstone occurs prominently in three shelter assemblages (CB08-500, CB10-133 and CB09-94) but is rare in surface samples. This raw material comprises 2.6% of the surface assemblage in Group 2A, and 3.1% in Group 3B, but is absent or only present in trace amounts in the other ranges surface assemblages. All other materials are variable in their occurrence.

TABLE 5.8: Summary assemblage composition from all rockshelter test pits (number of artefacts).

3 MM SIEVE FRACTION SAMPLE

	Basalt	BIF	Chalcedony	Chert	Dolerite	Ironstone	Mudstone	Quartz	Quartzite	Silcrete	3 mm Total
CB08-500	7	34	6	25	0	2	75	1	0	0	150
CB10-116	4	18	0	4	0	0	0	0	0	0	26
CB10-117A	0	53	0	3	0	0	1	0	1	0	58
CB10-117B	0	10	0	5	0	0	0	0	0	0	15
CB10-123	1	22	7	12	0	0	12	0	0	0	54
CB10-88	0	0	0	3	0	0	0	0	0	0	3
CB10-92	8	43	15	30	0	0	8	0	1	0	105
CB10-93	10	9	1	11	0	0	0	3	0	0	34
CB10-98	3	8	2	19	0	0	0	0	1	0	33
CB10-147	0	1	1	0	0	0	0	0	0	0	2
CB10-133A	9	19	18	2	7	0	12	1	0	0	68
CB10-133B	2	11	14	8	3	0	9	0	0	0	47
CB10-133C	0	69	29	8	9	2	5	0	8	3	133
CB09-55	1	8	2	2	0	0	0	0	0	0	13
CB09-249	0	2	0	0	0	0	0	0	0	0	2
CB08-427	0	0	0	0	0	0	0	0	0	0	0
CB10-40	2	11	8	22	0	0	0	0	0	0	43
CB10-41/2	4	13	26	5	0	0	0	1	1	0	50
CB10-41/3	7	36	16	62	0	0	0	0	0	0	121
CB10-41/4	4	15	9	16	0	0	0	0	0	0	44
CB09-94	5	59	7	10	0	0	0	0	0	0	81
CB11-89	2	46	3	1	0	0	3	0	1	0	56
TOTAL	69	487	164	248	19	4	125	6	13	3	1138

			6 mm Sieve Fraction								Total
Basalt	BIF	Chalcedony	Chert	Dolerite	Ironstone	Mudstone	Quartz	Quartzite	Silcrete	6 mm Total	Total
3	79	5	27	6	2	66	2	0	1	191	341
0	2	1	17	0	0	0	0	0	0	20	46
0	1	0	4	0	0	0	0	0	0	5	63
0	0	0	0	0	0	0	0	0	0	0	15
0	0	0	0	0	0	2	0	0	0	2	56
3	7	0	4	1	0	0	0	0	0	15	18
2	91	9	30	7	0	6	0	15	1	161	266
4	13	0	8	0	0	0	1	0	0	26	60
2	11	2	6	1	2	0	3	0	0	27	60
3	6	1	1	0	0	0	0	0	0	11	13
8	19	6	11	0	0	20	0	0	0	64	132
1	10	6	5	0	0	6	1	0	0	29	76
1	18	1	7	1	2	10	0	0	0	40	173
2	18	2	7	0	0	6	0	0	0	35	48
4	10	0	5	0	0	0	0	0	0	19	21
8	8	0	5	0	0	0	0	1	0	22	22
5	58	10	32	3	0	0	0	0	0	108	151
22	60	7	56	0	0	0	0	2	0	147	197
10	401	28	101	1	0	1	4	1	0	547	668
82	213	45	25	3	0	7	5	0	0	380	424
6	29	0	5	0	0	4	0	0	0	44	125
1	29	0	0	0	0	0	0	0	0	30	86
167	1083	123	356	23	6	128	16	19	2	1923	3061

TABLE 5.9: Raw material composition for the 6 mm sieve fraction in individual rockshelter assemblages, compared with composition of associated surface assemblages.

	Basalt		BIF		Chalcedony		Chert	
	N	%	N	%	N	%	N	%
1A	204	16.1	638	50.2	237	18.7	105	8.3
CB08-500	3	1.6	79	41.4	5	2.6	27	14.1
2A	26	5.2	405	80.4	13	2.6	32	6.3
CB10-116	0	0.0	2	10.0	1	5.0	17	85.0
CB10-117A	0	0.0	1	20.0	0	0.0	4	80.0
CB10-123	0	0.0	0	0.0	0	0.0	0	0.0
3B	67	8.1	584	70.7	64	7.7	61	7.4
CB10-88	3	20.0	7	46.7	0	0.0	4	26.7
CB10-92	2	1.2	91	56.5	9	5.6	30	18.6
CB10-93	4	15.4	13	50.0	0	0.0	8	30.8
CB10-98	2	7.4	11	40.7	2	7.4	6	22.2
CB10-133A	8	12.5	19	29.7	6	9.4	11	17.2
CB10-133B	1	3.4	10	34.5	6	20.7	5	17.2
CB10-133C	1	2.5	18	45.0	1	2.5	7	17.5
3D	24	15.5	118	76.1	0	0.0	8	5.2
CB10-147	3	27.3	6	54.5	1	9.1	1	9.1
4A	88	13.9	413	65.5	24	3.8	72	11.4
CB09-55	2	5.7	18	51.4	2	5.7	7	20.0
5A	176	20.6	503	58.8	19	2.2	114	13.3
CB09-249	4	21.1	10	52.6	0	0.0	5	26.3
CB08-427	8	36.4	8	36.4	0	0.0	5	22.7
6S	19	6.1	184	58.8	23	7.3	81	25.9
CB10-40	5	4.6	58	53.7	10	9.3	32	29.6
CB10-41/2	22	15.0	60	40.8	7	4.8	56	38.1
CB10-41/3	10	1.8	401	73.3	28	5.1	101	18.5
CB10-41/4	82	21.6	213	56.1	45	11.8	25	6.6
CB09-94	6	13.6	29	65.9	0	0.0	5	11.4
CB11-89	1	3.3	29	96.7	0	0.0	0	0.0

Dolerite		Mudstone		Quartzite		Other		
N	%	N	%	N	%	N	%	TOTAL
43	3.4	3	0.2	19	1.5	21	1.7	1270
6	3.1	66	34.6	0	0.0	5	2.6	191
3	0.6	13	2.6	8	1.6	4	0.8	504
0	0.0	0	0.0	0	0.0	0	0.0	20
0	0.0	0	0.0	0	0.0	0	0.0	5
0	0.0	2	100.0	0	0.0	0	0.0	2
3	0.4	26	3.1	17	2.1	4	0.5	826
1	6.7	0	0.0	0	0.0	0	0.0	15
7	4.3	6	3.7	15	9.3	1	0.6	161
0	0.0	0	0.0	0	0.0	1	3.8	26
1	3.7	0	0.0	0	0.0	5	18.5	27
0	0.0	20	31.3	0	0.0	0	0.0	64
0	0.0	6	20.7	0	0.0	1	3.4	29
1	2.5	10	25.0	0	0.0	2	5.0	40
3	1.9	0	0.0	2	1.3	0	0.0	155
0	0.0	0	0.0	0	0.0	0	0.0	11
15	2.4	5	0.8	3	0.5	11	1.7	631
0	0.0	6	17.1	0	0.0	0	0.0	35
27	3.2	3	0.4	3	0.4	11	1.3	856
0	0.0	0	0.0	0	0.0	0	0.0	19
0	0.0	0	0.0	1	4.5	0	0.0	22
0	0.0	0	0.0	1	0.3	5	1.6	313
3	2.8	0	0.0	0	0.0	0	0.0	108
0	0.0	0	0.0	2	1.4	0	0.0	147
1	0.2	1	0.2	1	0.2	4	0.7	547
3	0.8	7	1.8	0	0.0	5	1.3	380
0	0.0	4	9.1	0	0.0	0	0.0	44
0	0.0	0	0.0	0	0.0	0	0.0	30

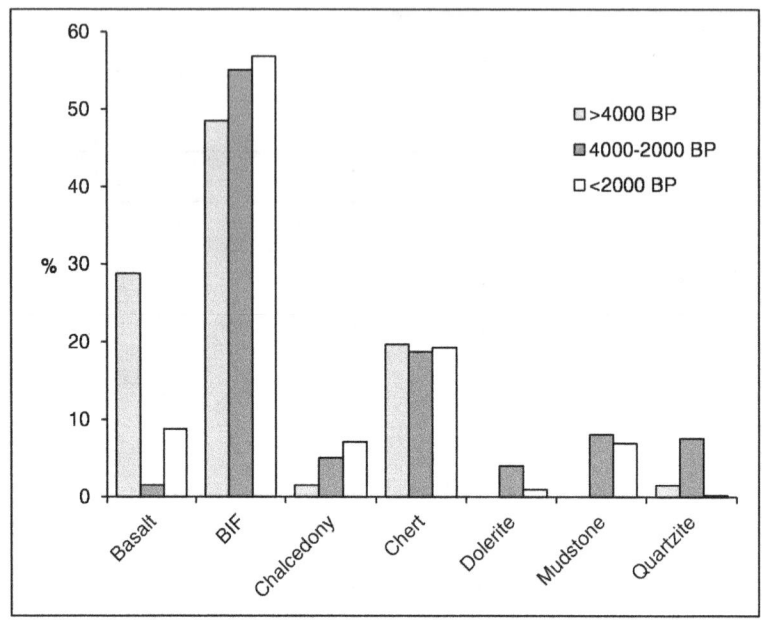

Figure 5.15: Excavated assemblages: raw material composition summarised by time period (6 mm sieve fraction only).

There is little evidence for trends in use of different raw materials over time. Figure 5.15 summarises assemblage composition by time period for the main raw materials from the 6 mm sieve fraction. The assemblages attributed to the periods 4000–2000 BP and <2000 BP are strikingly similar and reflect a general pattern of local use of lithic resources. There is a hint of a difference in the early assemblage, as it has a narrower range of raw materials and a higher representation of basalt. This might be taken to indicate a more wide-ranging and less localised use of the landscape. However, as with the surface assemblages, sample size and number of raw material types are highly correlated for both the 6 mm and 3 mm sieve fractions (Figure 5.16). The restricted range of raw materials in assemblages estimated to be older than 4000 years is, therefore, most likely a consequence of smaller sample sizes. Certainly, the evidence available from the few flakes with cortex indicates that raw materials from these older contexts were mainly sourced within the ranges. Only two basalt flakes from CB10-147 had riverine cortex. Cortex from younger assemblages is also predominantly terrestrial and reflects highly local usage of raw materials.

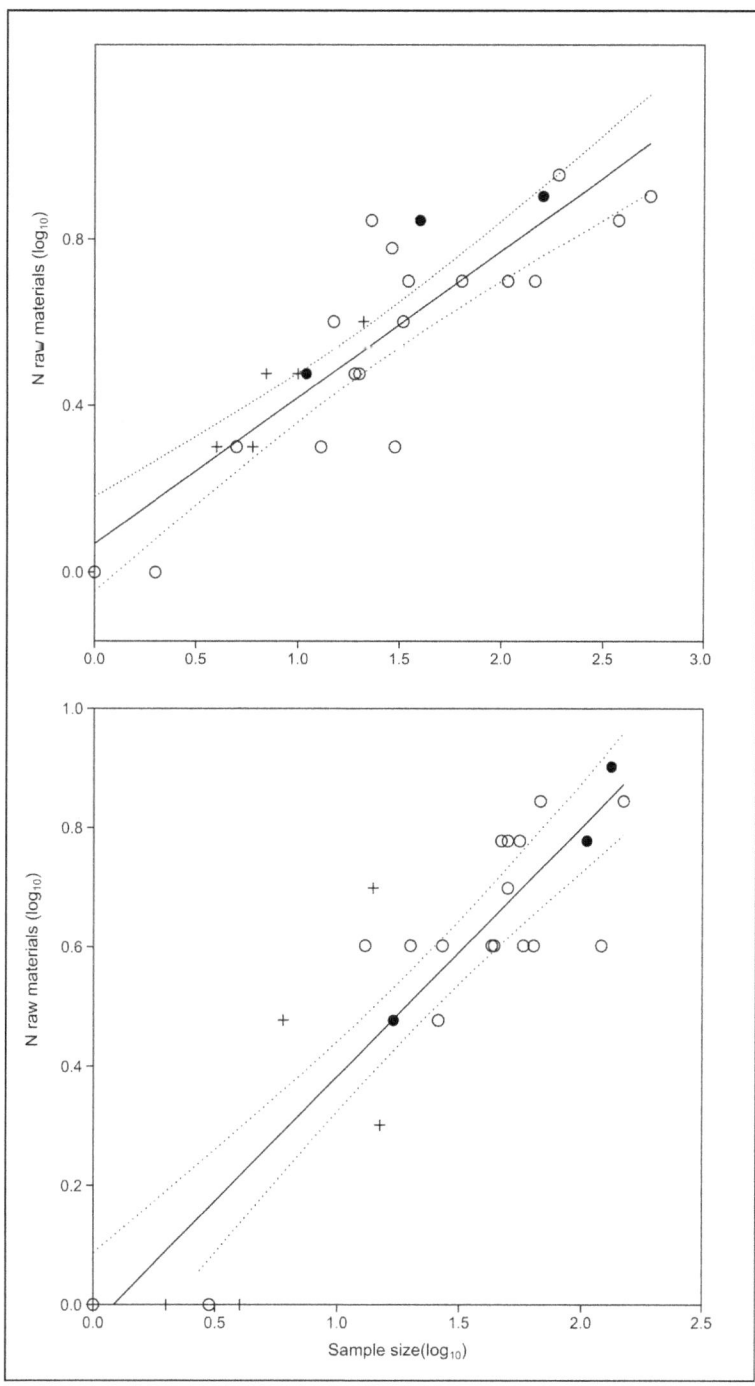

FIGURE 5.16: Relation between log10 sample size and log10 number of raw material types for individual rockshelter assemblages. Upper: 6 mm fraction (r=0.9, p<0.001). Lower: 3 mm sieve fraction (r=0.9, p<0.001). + Early assemblages >4000 cal BP; • 2000–4000 BP; o Late <2000 BP.

REDUCTION INTENSITY

Percentage of cortical flakes and size of complete flakes were used to assess reduction intensity. Table 5.6 indicates that both these measures are again variable. There is no obvious relationship with sites whose occupation histories suggest more intensive use.

Figure 5.17 plots the percentage of cortical flakes and mean size of flakes for assemblages dating to the last 2000 years. This suggests that there is generally a positive relationship between flake size and percentage of cortex in the collections. Assemblages with more cortical flakes also have a larger mean flake size, a result consistent with the reductive character of lithic technology. Assemblages are also characterised according to whether the raw material composition of the 3 mm and 6 mm sieve fractions differ significantly. Those with few or no artefacts recovered from the 3 mm sieve fraction noticeably diverge from this pattern. The absence of 3 mm sieve residues clearly indicates evidence for very limited span of

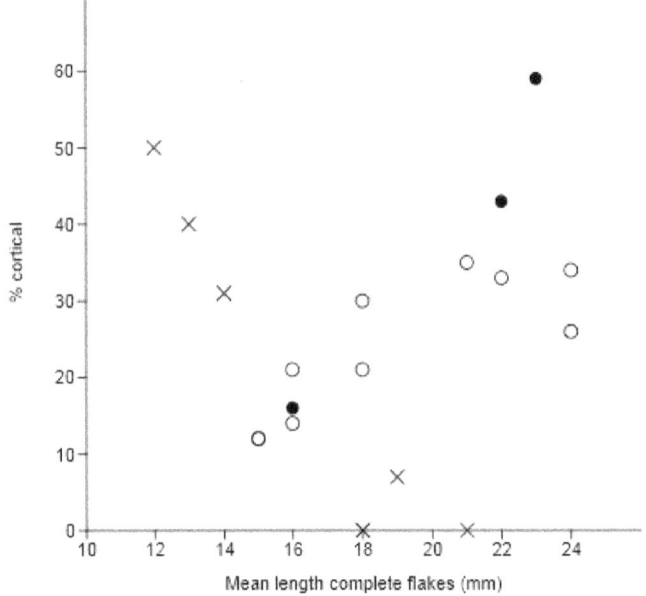

FIGURE 5.17: Size of flakes and percentage of cortical flakes for rock shelter assemblages (<2000 cal BP), categorised according to whether the difference in assemblage composition between 3 mm and 6 mm sieve fractions is statistically significant. Open circle=significant; closed circle=not significant; x=not applicable, few or no artefacts from the 3 mm sieve fraction.

TABLE 5.10: Length (mm) of complete flakes for each raw material with sample size >20.

Raw material	N	Mean	SD
Basalt	94	20.8	11.5
BIF	612	20.3	11.0
Chalcedony	58	16.2	7.5
Chert	180	14.8	9.2
Mudstone	83	15.1	8.0

occupation, with negligible stone-working activity. This divergence from the expected pattern can be seen as corroboration that these sites might be interpreted as task-specific sites rather than residential sites.

In most sites, sample sizes are too small for particular raw materials and individual artefact classes to be compared. For complete flakes from all sites, BIF and basalt are similar in size and consistently larger than chalcedony, chert and mudstone, which are also similar in size (Table 5.10). This pattern is generally consistent for individual sites where sample size is sufficiently large for meaningful comparison (see Appendix 5).

SIEVE FRACTIONS AND SMALL FLAKES

In terms of understanding site usage, rockshelter assemblages offer an additional line of enquiry in the recovery of artefacts through sieving. Small flakes are commonly absent from surface assemblages, primarily as a result of post-depositional processes such as sheet-wash, and are, in any case, difficult to identify and record consistently under field conditions during compliance surface surveys. Small flakes indicate late stage reduction and mainly result from tool maintenance, core preparation or incidental shatter fragments (Clark 1986; Eerkens et al. 2007, 586; Healan 1995; Hiscock and Mitchell 1993; Newcomer and Karlin 1987). Thus, most artefacts from the 3 mm sieve indicate stone-working activities on site. In excavated sites, particularly caves and rockshelters, controlling recovery by sieving means that the absence of small flakes indicates that stone knapping was not a prominent activity at the site (Hiscock 2005). By contrast, larger material may have been introduced and discarded as transported flakes or cores, rather than knapped on site. Thus, the representation of material in the different sieve fractions indicates whether stone working was a prominent feature of activities at the site, and if the manufacture and maintenance of a broad range of wooden tools was also important, since such activities are the main contributors to the consumption of stone resources.

The composition of the 3 mm sieve fraction may also relate to the length of occupation. An essential feature of the interaction between mobility and the reductive character of flaked stone technology is that different stages in the sequence of procurement, manufacture, use and discard of both tools and waste products can occur at different places. Thus, the disparity between the sieve fractions does relate to mobility in terms of the transport of artefacts. Raw material may be introduced into sites and then discarded through various processes. These range from late stage reduction of cores and resharpening of tools produced from materials brought from elsewhere, to early stage reduction of material procured locally. If the occupation span is short, the debitage resulting from these reduction events may differ markedly (Eerkens et al. 2007). At sites occupied for longer, more frequent and intensive reduction of a varied suite of raw materials is more likely to occur. As the occupation span increases, the different sieve fractions should become more similar, as material procured locally tends to numerically dominate assemblages (Kuhn 1995, 26). Moreover, the lifespan of technological elements is also a factor. Where the use life of some curated artefacts is longer than the duration of residence at particular sites, final discard may occur some distance from the place of manufacture. For example, small flakes may be discarded as a result of resharpening a tool used at the site. Neither the core and flakes associated with the manufacture of the tool, nor the discard of the tool at the end of its life, will be represented. In this case, the small retouch flakes provide evidence of transit in the form of raw material passing through the site as 'ghost' artefacts (Porraz 2009). We therefore suggest that marked differences in raw material representation in the 3 mm and 6 mm sieve residues are likely to indicate short-term occupation.

The representation of different raw materials within the different sieve fractions was compared for each site using chi-square (see Appendix 5 for details). Sites where the excavated assemblage came predominantly from one sieve fraction could not be analysed in this way. CB10-147, CB10-88, CB08-427 and CB09-249 all had little or no material in the 3 mm sieve fraction, while most of the artefacts from CB10-117 and CB10-123 were from the 3 mm sieve fraction. All these examples indicate a limited representation of particular stages of the reduction sequence and are best characterised as short-term episodes of site use. Most other assemblages did have statistically significant differences in the representation of different raw materials in the 3 mm and 6 mm sieve fractions. The exceptions include CB09-55, CB10-93, CB11-89 and CB10-92, while at CB10-133 the sieve fractions are significantly different only in the assemblage from Square B. Chi-square is sensitive to sample size and this is a possible influence on the results.

Nevertheless, the disparity between the 3 mm and 6 mm sieve fractions in most assemblages, together with the evidence for occupation intensity discussed above, supports a general conclusion that use of most shelters was episodic and short term. There seems to be no clear systematic relationship between either sample size or the categorisation of sites in terms of occupation history discussed above and significant differences in raw material composition of the different sieve fractions. Nevertheless, three of the five sites where the representation of raw materials in the different sieve fractions is similar, all have relatively large assemblages and high discard rates, suggesting more intensive occupation. It is intriguing that three of these sites are also located in the Kakutungutanta Creek system, which, as we have noted from the dating evidence, had long-term persistent occupation.

DIAGNOSTIC ARTEFACTS

Few artefacts from any shelter (2% of the total 6 mm sieve fraction) show evidence of retouch or use. The maximum was 12 from CB10-41/3, but all others had five or fewer. This percentage is lower than that recorded in surface assemblages (4%). However, better recovery of small unretouched flakes from excavated deposits probably explains this result. As with the surface assemblages (see Chapter 4), the presence of retouched artefacts in rockshelters seems mostly related to sample size. Eight shelters had no secondarily retouched material at all, including C10-40, which seems to have been one of the more intensively occupied sites.

Most retouched artefacts were undiagnostic (Table 5.11). It is also likely, of course, that at least some of the unretouched flakes would have been used for general cutting tasks without leaving macroscopic traces of edge damage. Two chert backed artefacts, both geometric microliths, were recovered from CB0-41/3. Two backed artefacts, also both geometric microliths, one chert and one chalcedony, were also found in the surface assemblage at CB10-133. The remaining eight formal tools were adzes. All came from contexts less than 2000 years old and all were tulas except for a single chert non-tula, or burren, adze from CB08-500. All adzes are discarded slugs and probably indicate retooling events where the stone components of woodworking tools were replaced.

Chert was used for more than half the retouched material. This is generally consistent with the preference for chert for retouched material in the surface assemblages. However, unlike the surface assemblages, half the excavated tulas were made of BIF rather than chert (see Table 4.29). Table 5.11 also suggests that chert was increasingly used for retouched artefacts through time. Although the chi-square value for this association is significant (chi-square=16.361, df=8, p=0.04, Fisher's exact test p=0.04), some caution is necessary. This is because assemblages older than 4000 are small. Similarly, preferential use of chert for formal tools, which occur only in assemblages younger than about 2000 cal BP, is also clearly a factor.

Blade technology is believed to occur at a late stage in the reduction sequence (Veth 1993, 85). Macroblades (see Hook 2009) feature in recent assemblages in the Pilbara, although, like other formal tools, they rarely occur in excavated assemblages. Blades are rare in the Christmas Creek survey area both in surface assemblages and rockshelters. There are no blade cores in any excavated assemblages. Macroblades were recovered from CB10-92 (two from EU5 and one from EU6) and one from CB10-41/4. The occurrence of blades in CB10-92 is interesting because they appear to date to the older levels of the site and may therefore be older than 2000 cal BP.

TABLE 5.11: Retouched artefact types by period and raw material.

	Basalt	BIF	Chert	Dolerite	Mudstone	Total
>4000 BP						
Undiagnostic use/retouch	1	1	0	0	0	2
TOTAL	1	1	0	0	0	2
4000–2000 BP						
Undiagnostic use/retouch	0	1	2	2	1	6
TOTAL	0	2	2	2	1	6
<2000 BP						
Geometric microlith	0	0	2	0	0	2
Tula	0	4	4	0	0	8
Non-tula adze	0	0	1	0	0	1
Undiagnostic use/retouch	2	5	10	0	0	17
TOTAL	2	9	17	0	0	28

Evidence of blade technology possibly of comparable age has been reported from only two sites (Djadjiling and Y02-12) in the Pilbara (see discussion in Chapter 2).

Another possible indicator for the use of blade technology is the presence of parallel ridges on the dorsal surface of flakes. Flakes and flake fragments with parallel ridges are rare (4%). The percentage of flakes and flake fragments with parallel ridges ranges from zero at 11 sites to 10% at CB10-133B, but is uniformly low in all periods.

Although grinding material and hammer stones were found on the surface in a number of shelters, these artefacts rarely occur in excavations (see Appendix 5). A granite hammer stone was recovered from EU7 in CB10-92. A basal grindstone was recovered from EU2 in CB10-41/2.

DISCUSSION

The rockshelter assemblages show little evidence for change through time, other than the appearance of small numbers of formal tools during the last 2000 years. Like surface assemblages in the study area (see Chapter 4), the shelter assemblages reflect highly localised procurement, use and discard of raw material. The analysis of surface assemblages suggested that spatial patterning at the landscape scale was primarily related to local use of raw material and different types of raw material 'packages' in the ranges from those found on the plains, rather than reflecting differences in mobility patterns. In terms of access to raw material, all the shelter sites occur in the ranges, so it is not surprising that these variables do not distinguish between sites. Inter-assemblage variation is strongly influenced by sample size and recovery, and is contingent on local circumstances.

The small assemblage sample size resulting from the limited extent of shelter excavations in the Christmas Creek study area suggests that the differences evident between rockshelters are comparable to the variability among small surface sites and can be regarded as 'noise'. Many small surface scatters probably represent individual or a small number of flaking events. It is not surprising that there should be considerable variability at the individual site level. The range of raw materials available in the Christmas Creek study area, and the nature of stone tool manufacture, mean that a single brief episode of reduction could generate a large amount of flaking debris, much of which would have been left in situ. The limited extent of the site area actually exposed in test pits means that such individual flaking events are less easy to recognise than in surface assemblages (see Appendix 5). Nevertheless, there are several examples indicating that comparable individual flaking events can be identified within rockshelters. One example is the grey chert adze and possible resharpening flakes recovered from the lower part of the excavation at CB08-500. Another concerns the two ironstone cores at CB10-133, one single platform core and one multiplatform core, both recovered from EU2, in Square C. Apart from two small flakes recovered from the 3 mm sieve, these were the only ironstone artefacts found at the site. These cores may well have been brought to the site and left for future use.

UNDERSTANDING ROCKSHELTERS IN A LANDSCAPE

It is clear that rockshelters in the Christmas Creek study area were widely used and commonly formed part of a varied pattern of visitation to particular localities. Patterns of use are represented by a complex of more or less discrete and diverse archaeological occurrences, rather than intense occupation of a single shelter. This finding is obscured by current practices that record individual archaeological elements as discrete 'sites' and thereby obscure the relationships between them.

The presence of grinding material is one signal of an intention to return to a place. As we have already noted, there is ample ethnographic evidence from elsewhere in Australia's arid zone that grinding equipment was commonly left behind for future use (Gould 1980, 10, 71–2; Guruma Elders Group et al. 2001, 87–8; Nicholson and Cane 1991; Tonkinson 1978, 33), and can be regarded as site furniture. There are a number of other indicators of planned future visits to shelters. Cores and manuports are common features of surface assemblages in shelters and seem to indicate provisioning of places with raw material for future use. Several shelters only have multiple cores or manuports in their surface assemblages (CB10-147, CB10-93). Sometimes these are carefully cached, such as the dolerite core in the rear of CB10-98. Like the presence of surface grinding material, this includes sites like CB10-147 and CB08-427, which by any other criteria would be regarded as ephemeral sites. There is other evidence for caching, for example, wood for unknown purposes at both CB10-133 and CB09-55. Similarly, many of the stone features seem to be associated with storage. Evidence for storage of grindstones and raw material, together with investment in facilities in the form of stone features, all signal that these places were repeatedly visited. This suggests that viewing the use of these sites as ephemeral is misleading. Rather, the use of shelters was primarily logistic. Thus, although the archaeological evidence of use of individual shelters may seem ephemeral in terms of accumulation of archaeological material, they nevertheless act as key nodes in the overall pattern of land use, marking localities revisited and re-used on numerous occasions (Bailey and Galanidou 2009, 4–5). From this viewpoint, the excavated shelters associated with Kakutungutanta

Creek are connected and, in tandem with other archaeological sites in the same locality, form a 'site complex', discussed in more detail in Chapter 6. This particular site complex provides evidence for occupation in this locality for thousands of years, and most particularly during the period 2000–4000 years ago, when use of the study area is not otherwise archaeologically visible. Other localities in the ranges also have aggregations of sites with long use histories, but these appear to be intermittent and less intense. By contrast, some places seem to be mainly used in the last few hundred years.

This alternative perspective of shelter use as logistic rather than ephemeral is likely to apply to other Pilbara site complexes. Evidence from the four Packsaddle shelters in the Hamersley Range, excavated by Brown and Mulvaney, suggests that they too constitute a longstanding site complex with complementary functions (Brown 1987; Brown and Mulvaney 1983). Coffee Table Shelter (P04623) had six lower grindstones, one with evidence of use as an anvil, with a seventh on the talus, and an upper grindstone. Two flakes and some pieces of charred or worked wood comprised the rest of the surface assemblage. In Bastion Shelter (P05315), there was a single lower grindstone in the rear of the shelter where the roof was only 15 cm high. A second lower grindstone was found in a small overhang three metres to the west. Phantom Shelter (P04627) had two lower grindstones and several fragments of grinding material all close to the wall at the western end of the shelter. The rest of the surface assemblage comprised a core, a core fragment, a flaked piece, a flake fragment and an adze. Brown and Mulvaney (1983, 75–77) note that the four shelters form a group within a single gulley, and that the location of the gulley is marked by a hill behind it, which is clearly visible from the ephemeral lake (Gundawana) about five kilometres to the south-west, which was a favoured spot for ceremonial gatherings following cyclonic rains. All of the Packsaddle shelters have different aspects and Brown and Mulvaney speculate that this might have offered shelter in different weather conditions. Evidence for occupation of the complex goes back some 8000 years in Bastion Shelter, while three of the shelters have dates of about 2500 years ago.

Integrating the interpretation of surface remains with rockshelter assemblages remains challenging. However, as we have already noted (Chapter 2), the differences in resolution between excavated and surface assemblages are commonly overstated. Through a comparison of shelter assemblages with grouped surface assemblages located within a 500-metre radius, we found that the shelter assemblages were actually more diverse in terms of raw materials and had lower percentages of cortical flakes than nearby surface scatters (Bird and Rhoads 2015). These surface assemblages, taken individually, ranged widely from small uniform scatters, to large and diverse surface artefact scatters. Most small uniform scatters probably represent a single event, related to raw material procurement. The large surface scatters, like the rockshelter assemblages, represent time-averaged palimpsests, comprising an accumulation of multiple individual events. However, when sampled at a landscape level, ignoring the individual elements of the surface palimpsest, the characteristics of the grouped surface assemblages tended to echo those of the associated shelter. This provides further support for considering relationships between sites within localities. It also suggests that focusing on the locality rather than the site might be the appropriate scale for understanding the archaeological record in this area. In the next chapter, we consider the patterning of the archaeological record and the nature of land use in the study area in more detail through specific place-based case studies.

CHAPTER 6

SITE AND LANDSCAPE

Two different scales of analysis were explored with respect to surface artefact scatters in the course of discussions so far. These archaeological remains comprise the most numerous site type in the Christmas Creek study area and are typically small, in terms of both site size and artefact numbers. The first analysis was positioned within a conventional site-based perspective that identified characteristics of, and variability among, different classes of archaeological remains in relation to the natural environment. The second explored patterning in surface artefacts at a landscape scale. Similarly, the discussion of rockshelters and associated artefact features (Chapter 5) considered patterning between individual site assemblages as well as their patterning in time and space at a landscape scale.

As we have already noted (Chapter 1), site-based analysis and recording is mandated under the Western Australian state heritage compliance regime within which the data were originally collected. We must also remember that archaeological sites are effectively constructs (see discussion in Chapter 2). These delimit local concentrations, or exposures, of archaeological remains, even though artefacts may form a more or less continuous, albeit low density, distribution at the regional scale. Consequently, sites recorded by archaeologists within a compliance context are neither necessarily nor intrinsically meaningful interpretive units of past human behaviour. In effect, sites reflect the particular requirements of the local heritage legislation that operates to atomise the Pilbara surface archaeological record into relatively small units or isolates for administrative convenience. This in turn has implications for how sites are assessed and managed (Dortch and Sapienza 2016). It also raises questions about how best to define archaeological sites, and how to place them within an interpretive framework.

The concept of a site within a compliance framework can also be at odds with Aboriginal peoples' understandings about country and land use (Byrne 1996). Heritage practice in Western Australia provides the context for this project and indeed for the vast bulk of archaeological investigation in the inland Pilbara. Many sites have both archaeological and ethnographic components. Furthermore, decades of heritage compliance in the Pilbara have seen Aboriginal groups increasingly engage with archaeologists and their methods and incorporate archaeological knowledge into their understanding of heritage. The result is an emerging 'community of practice' in response to the dynamic social context of heritage assessment (McDonald and Coldrick in press). It is thus important, in practice, for archaeologists to consider how their frames of reference relate to and interact with the frames of reference Aboriginal peoples use when speaking about sites.

Aboriginal beliefs about the landscape are integrated through the idea of the creative journeys and acts of the Dreaming. This, in turn, establishes a sacred geography that is both nourishing and must be cared for (Rose 1996, 9–10). This powerful integrating idea focuses not only on individual places, but the relations between them, often popularly expressed as 'songlines'. Mobility, expressed as travelling between places, is thus an essential element of inhabiting country. Human action, whether through performing ceremonies or living in, passing through, and caring for country, connects and reconnects people to the land (Holdaway and Allen 2012, 84; Morphy 1995). Ingold's (2007, 80ff.) apt description of how hunter-gatherers inhabit the world as a meshwork, with places representing the knots created by many interwoven journeys, highlights this focus on an integrative approach to both places and the connections between them.

Ethnographic mapping clearly shows that activity at individual places commonly occurs at a scale considerably larger than most conventional archaeological sites and exhibits complex use of space (Memmott 2002; O'Connell 1987; Pickering 2003, 70). Memmott, for example, describes the hypothetical formation of a large camp in terms of sub-camps and sub-camp clusters, made up of individual domiciliary units, together with a number of other place components such as one or more water sources, activity areas and public areas for dancing and ritual performance. In addition, the environs of the camp may also have specific sociospatial divisions, including ceremonial areas, with access restricted by gender. Depending on group size, length of occupation and season, the areas covered may be considerable. Among the Warlpiri, for example, Meggitt describes gender segregated country within a radius of three to four miles (Memmott 2002, 71). Pickering (2003, 68–9), in his study of the Garawa, whose traditional country is in the inland Gulf of Carpentaria, distinguishes between camp and locale (see also Gamble 2006, 68–76). A camp corresponds to an occupation event, while a locale is the 'setting or context for social interaction' (Johnstone et al. 1994, cited in Pickering 2003, 68). Pickering thus defines a locale as a named place, usually an environmental feature, such as a waterhole or rockshelter, around which individual camps were established. These locales varied in size from about a 20-metre radius to more than a kilometre depending on the season and the nature of the named place. A named place thus always included a hinterland within which individual camps were established. Similarly, O'Connell's study of Alyawarra camps (1987, 105ff.) concludes that 'patterns of site structure will often be apparent *only* in exposures of thousands or even tens of thousands of square meters, scales that are one or two orders of magnitude larger than those of the very largest excavations now undertaken'.

This observation is consistent with Aboriginal interpretations of archaeological sites in the Pilbara. Pilbara Aboriginal peoples do not commonly distinguish between individual sites as recorded by archaeologists. Instead they recognise a locality as a 'site', interpreted as a camp which may include a number of spatial components reflecting traditional camping behaviour. Such a locality might, at best, be recorded by archaeologists as a 'site complex', but is more commonly recorded in terms of its individual components, for which boundaries can be defined by the distribution of material remains (McDonald and Coldrick in press). This description of the structured use of space at particular locales can clearly be viewed in terms of a 'taskscape', or array of related activities (Gamble 2006, 86–7; Ingold 1993).

From an archaeological perspective, the issue of how to delimit and define sites is problematic, both in terms of the practical demands of the compliance context and the requirement to interpret and assess their significance. Do surface sites represent essentially different activities from the background scatter? Can functionally distinct types of sites be identified? Binford's (1980) widely used forager–collector continuum contrasts a collector strategy with high levels of logistic mobility and low levels of residential mobility with a forager strategy, which has high levels of residential mobility and low levels of logistic mobility. According to Binford, collectors can be expected to generate more varied types of sites than foragers, who only generate two types of sites – the 'residential base' and the 'location'. However, with reference to an 'archaeology of place', functional variation between site types may well be obscured by the re-use of particular places at different points in the seasonal round, as well as post-depositional transformations (Binford 1982). This functional interpretive framework is, of course, widely used by archaeologists. Nevertheless, it suffers from operating primarily at an ethnographic scale rather than taking into account the long-term cumulative nature of the archaeological palimpsest. Moreover, the focus is rather narrowly on settlement and economy rather than social interaction (Gamble 2006, 96).

Veth (1993, 83), in his Western Desert study, draws on Binford's forager–collector continuum and distinguishes between core habitation sites associated with permanent waters and satellite camps associated with ephemeral waters. He further identifies characteristics of the artefact assemblage as indicators of levels of logistic or residential mobility at different site types (see Chapter 2). We have already noted that, for the study area, the proposed indicators do not appear to apply at the landscape scale (Chapter 4), nor at the site scale with respect to rockshelters (Chapter 5). The differences between site types in Veth's study relate primarily to group size and occupation span, as well as the tethering effect of reliable waters in the desert environment. This in turn increases redundancy of place use and the resultant accumulation of archaeological material (Binford 1980, 7). This variation in group size and occupation span at particular sites associated with seasonal aggregation and dispersal is a typical feature of forager residential mobility.

Therefore, sites typically comprise an accumulation of co-located remains of individual past episodes of activity that form a relatively high density 'patch'. Patches may, in fact, result from repeated re-use of the same locale by past groups. However, various natural processes also create patches, and the occurrences which are recorded as sites may represent varying combinations of natural and cultural processes. The resulting palimpsest is a product of the interaction between the organisation of past social systems in relation to a dynamic environment (Binford 1982; Holdaway and Fanning 2014, 163). We have also seen (Chapter 4) that there is little difference in the Christmas Creek area between a more or less continuous low-density scatter of artefacts across the landscape, especially on the plains, and the artefacts occurring in concentrations recorded as sites. The patches here differ from the background scatter in terms of quantity; rather than representing different types of activity they mark 'persistent places' (Shiner 2009; Shott 2008; 2010; Stern 1993).

The idea of persistent places (Schlanger 1992; Shiner 2009) provides a possible approach to linking the long-term archaeological palimpsest to the taskscape. Persistent places represent 'the conjunction of particular human behaviours on a particular landscape' (Schlanger 1992, 97). They can be particular natural features, which attract and structure human activity; examples include water sources, rockshelters, specific resource patches and vantage points. Alternatively, once established, cultural features may themselves attract and structure subsequent use of the place; examples include bedrock grinding patches, fish traps and weirs, shell middens, earth mounds, hearths, rockshelters and storage features (Bird, Rhoads and Hook 2019). Surface artefacts accumulated from past occupations also have this effect, both as visible markers of past use and socialisation of the landscape, and as a source of raw material for future use (Bond 2009; 2013; Foley and Lahr 2015; Wragg-Sykes 2012).

Ingold (2007, 100) suggests that hunter-gatherer lives can be portrayed in terms of the sum of their journeys traced on the ground. The sum of the lives of many individuals forms a 'meshwork'. Persistent places then are the knots in the meshwork, connected and formed by the threads of individual journeys, crossing and recrossing at particular locales, where social interaction occurs. This metaphor invites us to think of the archaeological record in this study area as a record of movement (Holdaway and Fanning 2014, 177). It also emphasises connections between sites and between sites and landscape rather than narrowly focusing on attributes of individual 'sites'.

STRUCTURE OF THE ARCHAEOLOGICAL RECORD: CASE STUDIES

The comprehensive archaeological survey from which this study arises offers an opportunity to more closely examine the patterning and structure of archaeological remains at scales other than the usual scale of an individual site. The previous analysis of surface scatters (Chapter 4) demonstrates that, at the landscape scale, ranges and plains landforms differ in site density and size of sites, as well as associated vegetation formations. Moreover, the ranges and the plains also differ in the types of sites present. As one would expect, the variety of site types within the ranges is more diverse, reflecting the surface geology and more diverse topography. Site types in the ranges include rockshelters, stone features, quarries and surface artefacts, while sites on the plains are nearly all surface artefact scatters. The landscape-scale analysis of surface artefacts suggests that patterning can primarily be explained in terms of raw material characteristics and distribution rather than differences in site function.

In order to explore the structure of what seems to be a broadly continuous distributional record with localised higher density patches, primarily comprising stone artefacts, we describe in detail the archaeological record for four separate localities. These provide some of the landscape samples discussed earlier (Chapter 4): Group 1A, and Group 3B, both ranges localities; and Group 8S and Group 9S on the plains. All can be considered to be focused around a persistent place. Group 1A and Group 3B centre on individual rockshelters, while Group 8S is organised around a large, dense artefact scatter (CB08-114) along a prominent creek line. Group 9S, by contrast, corresponds to an extensive surface artefact scatter recorded as a single site, CB06-68, located north of CB08-114 along the same creek line. Group 9S is included to explore the nature of site definition and boundary delimitation in this project.

GROUP 1A

Group 1A is in the north-eastern reaches of the study area and is now heavily disturbed by mining. Rockshelter CB08-500 is at its centre and the area within a one-kilometre radius of the shelter, that is about 3.1 km², comprises the locality (Figure 6.1). The rockshelter deposits are interpreted as belonging to a single, very recent phase of occupation (see Appendix 5).

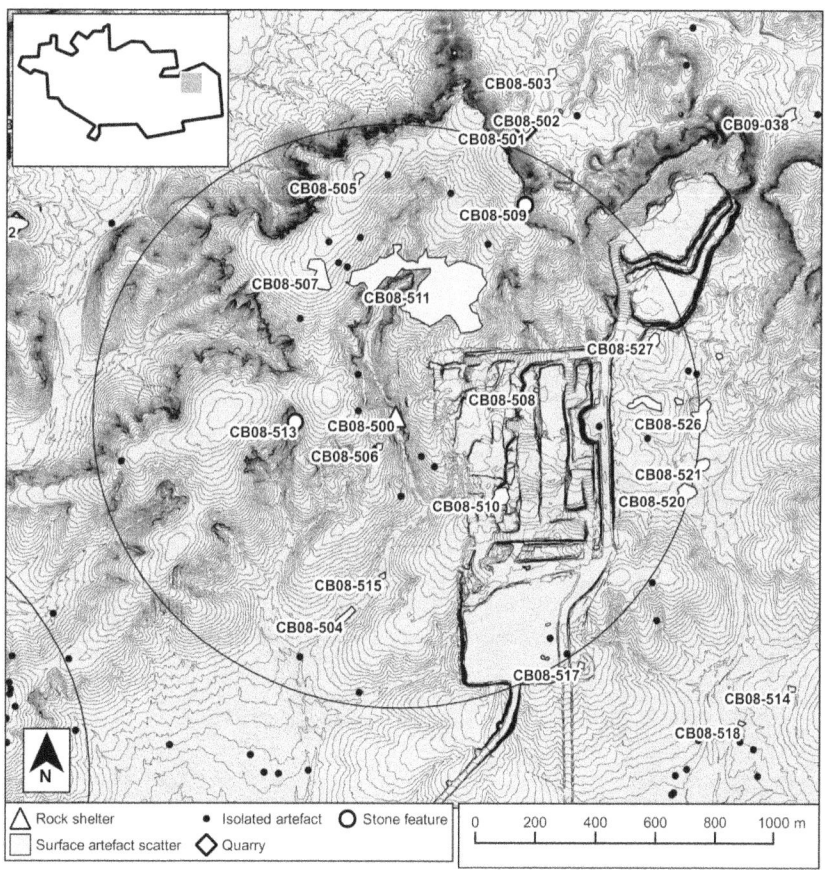

FIGURE 6.1: Group 1A: Site distribution. Circle defines group 1A (1 km radius from CB08-500).

TABLE 6.1: Group 1A: recorded artefact sites. AS: artefact scatter. RA: reduction area.

Site	Site type	Topography	Distance to potable water (m)	Site size (m^2)	Maximum recorded artefact density (N/m^2)
CB08-500	RS, AS	Gully slope	0	25	0.64
CB08-504	AS	Terrace	0	2634	0.56
CB08-505	AS	Hill top	200	871	0.28
CB08-506	AS, RA	Hill top	20	61	0.43
CB08-507	AS	Hill top	600	5884	0.36
CB08-508	AS, RA	Low hill	5	25	NA
CB08-510	AS	Mid-level plateau	20	3236	0.48
CB08-511	AS	Hill top	0	68984	5.25
CB08-515	AS	Terrace	0	570	0.40
CB08-517	AS, RA	Hill slope	100	25	0.60
CB08-520	AS, RA	Plain	0	4374	0.32
CB08-521	AS	Plain	10	3295	0.20
CB08-525	AS	Plain	20	3250	0.52
CB08-526	AS	Plain	0	3565	0.36
CB08-527	AS	Low hill	100	1410	0.64
CB08-529	AS, RA	Low hill	10	540	0.37

Recorded flaked artefact sample	Retouched	Non-flaked material
21	Three (BIF, basalt, dolerite)	Dolerite muller, manuport
58	12 (7 basalt, 2 BIF, one each of chalcedony, dolerite and ironstone)	Dolerite muller, 2 quartzite millstones, quartzite muller
28		
25		BIF millstone
50		
7		
47	3 retouched (2 basalt, 1 ironstone), chert tula	
648	85 retouched, basalt tula	Dolerite muller, 2 dolerite millstone fragments
21	3 retouched (basalt, BIF, chalcedony)	Dolerite millstone
15		
53	5 retouched (2 basalt, 2 BIF, 1 chalcedony)	
63		
50	1 BIF retouched	
52	1 BIF retouched	
38	3 retouched (2 chalcedony, 1 chert)	
20		

Group 1A was set within the ridges, hills and plateaus of the escarpment of the Chichester Range. A north–south seasonal creek in a broad, steep-sided valley was the main landscape feature, with the headwaters of two other creek systems to the east and west. Numerous small, ephemeral creeks drained the escarpment in the area. Rocky outcrops of the BIF and chert of the Marra Mamba Formation are common, with ironstone laterite capping in the northern portion. Detailed vegetation mapping is not available for this locality, because the area was burnt prior to the environmental surveys. Nevertheless, based on comparable areas nearby, eucalypt woodlands occurred along most of the creek's primary channel, while local small drainage lines carried mulga woodlands. Spinifex grasslands covered most of the rest of the locality. Waterholes were noted along the creek adjacent to the rockshelter.

Eighteen sites (Table 6.1) were recorded within 1 km of CB08-500. These are documented in several consulting reports (Ash, Di Lello et al. 2009; Bradley et al. 2014; Edwards and Rapley 2011; Hook, Dias and Rapley 2008; Martens and Craig 2015; Rapley, McHarg and Edwards 2009; Sinclair and Wright 2012; Wright and Craig 2011). Sixteen of the sites were surface artefact scatters and three also included reduction areas. A small surface scatter was associated with CB08-500, with some artefacts located within the shelter and a small scatter nearby. Five other scatters occurred within 500 metres of CB08-500. Most of the remainder formed a cluster of sites about one kilometre east of the rockshelter and were associated with the next major drainage system. The other two sites were stone features (CB08-509 and CB08-513). A chert quarry (CB08-501) was found in the north just beyond the one-kilometre boundary. There were also 41 isolated artefacts recorded for the locality.

Surface artefact scatters

The surface artefact scatters were mostly small to medium, low-density scatters situated on rises or gravel terraces (Figure 6.2). CB08-511 was by far the largest site recorded in Group 1A (Figure 6.3). It is situated about 500 metres north of the rockshelter and associated with the same seasonal creek. Another ephemeral creek borders the site to the west. The surface scatter covers the tops and slopes of three large silt and gravel hills, lying either side of the creek and surrounding an ephemeral rock hole. Stands of dense mulga (*Acacia aneura*) trees and shrubs line the water sources, with occasional eucalypts and a moderately dense spinifex understorey (*Triodia* spp.).

Grinding material is sparse in Group 1A. Six millstones and four mullers were recorded. All are associated with the main creek line (Figure 6.2, Table 6.1), although, apart from CB08-511, the individual sites with which they are associated are neither large nor dense. At CB08-500 a dolerite manuport was also recorded.

There are 128 artefacts with evidence of retouch or use, about 10% of the total. All are undiagnostic retouched flakes or fragments except for a basalt

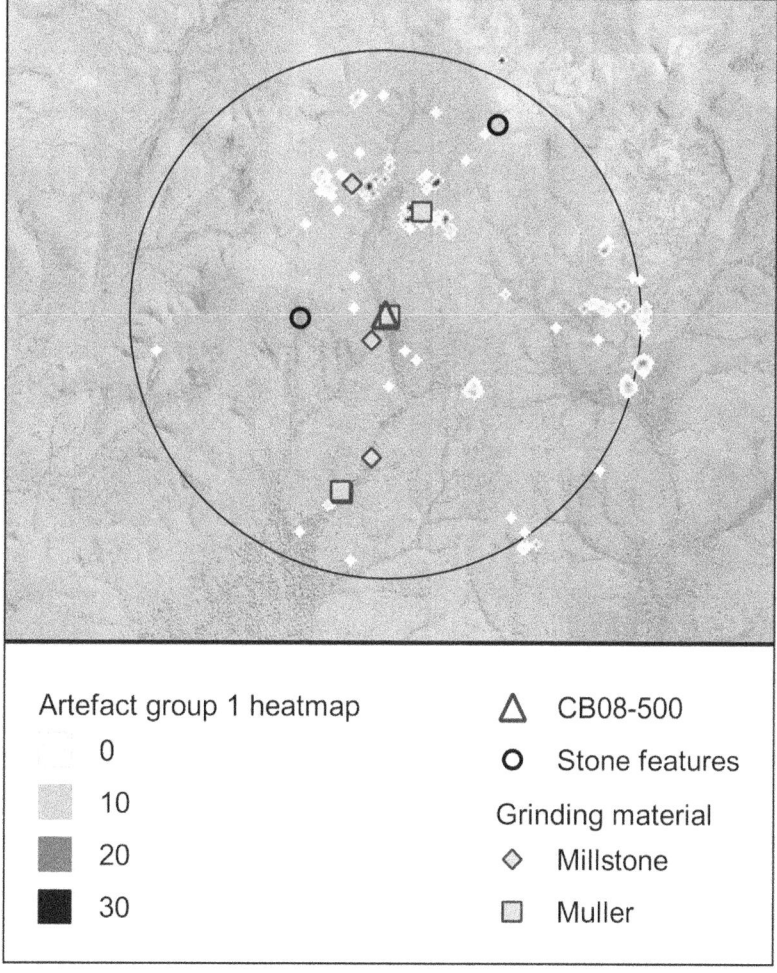

FIGURE 6.2: Group 1A: distribution of recorded surface artefacts and grinding material. Circle defines group 1A (1 km radius from CB08-500).

TABLE 6.2: Group 1A: raw material composition of individual artefact sites.

	Basalt	BIF	Chalcedony	Chert	Dolerite	Other
CB08-500	4	10	1	1	3	2
CB08-504	16	29	4	1	5	3
CB08-505	1	21	0	0	3	3
CB08-506	0	11	14	0	0	0
CB08-507	2	42	1	1	1	3
CB08-508	0	0	0	7	0	0
CB08-510	8	22	8	3	0	6
CB08-511	129	405	21	48	21	24
CB08-515	3	15	2	0	1	0
CB08-517	0	15	0	0	0	0
CB08-520	10	15	26	2	0	0
CB08-521	6	8	47	1	1	0
CB08-525	2	20	27	1	0	0
CB08-526	7	9	35	1	0	0
CB08-527	0	3	33	2	0	0
CB08-529	3	1	13	0	3	0
Isolated artefacts	14	12	5	3	5	2
TOTAL	205	638	237	105	43	43

SITE AND LANDSCAPE | 241

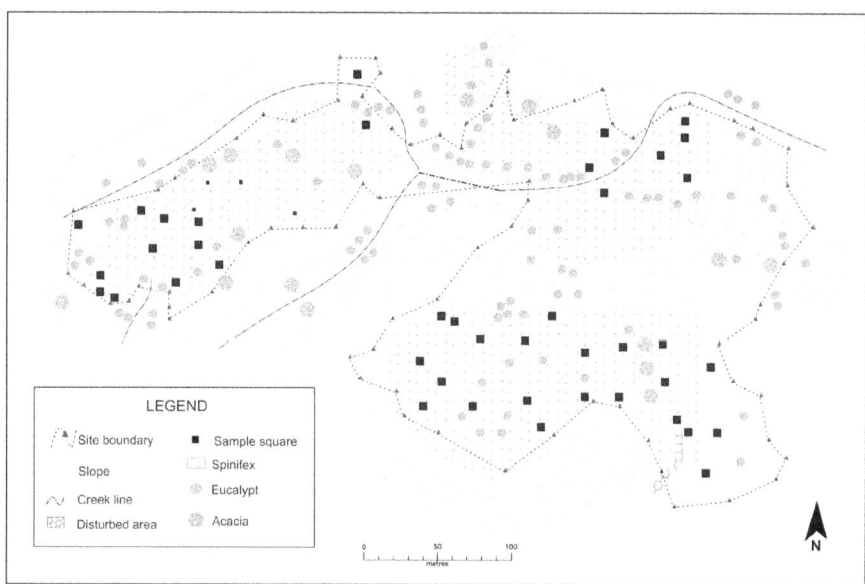

FIGURE 6.3: CB08-511: site plan.

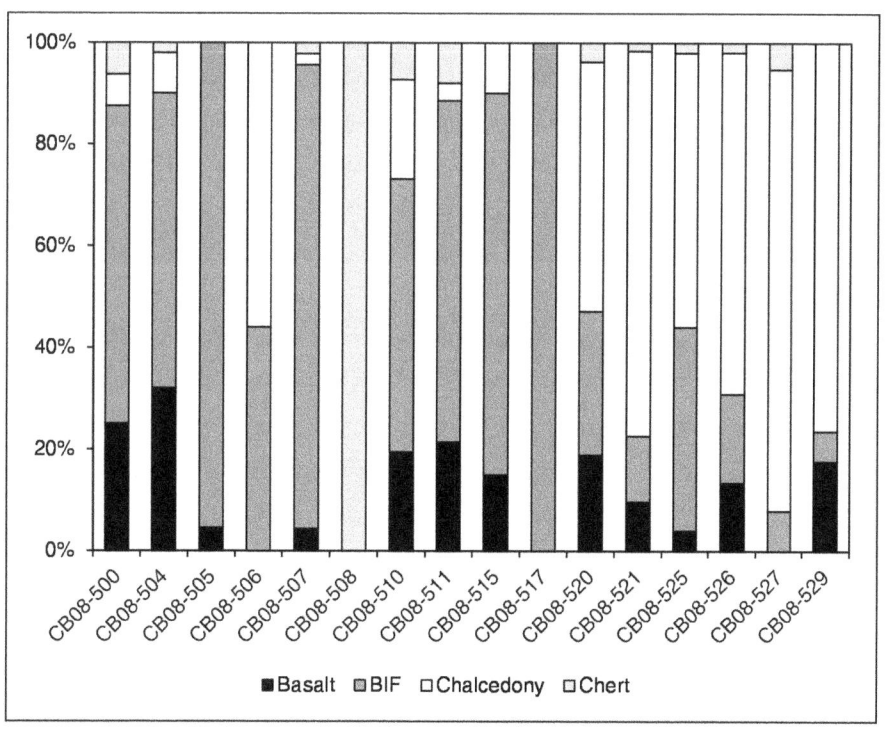

FIGURE 6.4: Group 1A: summary raw material composition for each site.

tula from CB08-511, a chert tula from CB08-510 and a large retouched basalt blade found as an isolated artefact. Most retouched material comes from CB08-511, which is also by far the largest site in terms of both area and artefact numbers.

Sites are variable in terms of assemblage composition. However, there is a clear trend for the group of sites at the eastern boundary to be dominated by chalcedony (Figure 6.4, Table 6.2). The other sites in Group 1A are more diverse, but BIF is the main raw material at most. There are three main exceptions. CB08-508 only consists of complete chert flakes and occurs in an area with natural heat-fractured chert nodules. CB08-517 comprises a BIF multiplatform core and 14 BIF flakes and flake fragments. CB08-506 has approximately equal numbers of BIF and chalcedony, together with a millstone fragment. The assemblage comprises two single platform cores, one each of BIF and chalcedony, and several flakes of each material, presumably associated with the reduction of the cores. The flakes are all non-cortical, possibly indicating that the largest flakes were removed for use elsewhere.

Cortex and volume ratios were calculated for each site, where possible, for basalt, BIF, chalcedony and chert following the methods outlined in Chapter 4 (Table 6.3). The results were extremely variable. Most individual values for cortex ratio were low, indicating a deficit of material; however, as discussed above (Chapter 4), these results should be interpreted with caution, given the likely prevalence of non-cortical surfaces or heat-fractured nodules in the ranges.

Volume ratios were also variable; most were greater than 1.0, indicating removal of material. On the other hand, some sites scored less than 1.0, so material was probably imported. Several sites with scores close to 1.0 had no net loss or gain of raw material. Most of the sites with scores close to 1.0 were chalcedony assemblages near the eastern boundary. This suggests that nodules of chalcedony were by and large collected and reduced in the immediate area. Flakes were then used and discarded on the spot. Two of these sites (CB08-525, CB08-527) had volume ratios greater than 1.0. In both cases there were fewer cores than expected to account for the assemblage, so it seems likely this represents procurement of raw material and that material was removed in the form of cores as well as flakes.

Figure 6.5: Group 1A: stone features. CB08-509 (top) and CB08-513 (bottom).

TABLE 6.3: Group 1A: cortex and volume ratios for individual artefact sites. NC not calculated (small sample); raw material no present.

	Basalt				BIF			
	CORES				CORES			
	VR	CR	O	E	VR	CR	O	E
CB08-500	1.41	0.32	1	1.4	3.90	1.21	1	3.9
CB08-504	NC	NC	0	2.1	1.30	0.24	4	5.2
CB08-505	NC	NC	0	0.0	3.37	0.58	1	3.4
CB08-506	--	-	-	-	0.70	0.07	1	0.7
CB08-507	NC	NC	0	0.4	NC	NC	0	3.8
CB08-510	NC	NC	0	0.7	1.33	0.51	1	1.3
CB08-511	2.03	0.25	4	8.1	1.56	0.26	22	34.2
CB08-515	NC	NC	0	0.2	2.82	0.71	1	2.8
CB08-517	-	-	-	-	1.30	0.24	1	1.3
CB08-520	0.82	0.10	3	2.5	3.22	0.37	1	3.2
CB08-521	0.90	0.10	1	0.9	0.56	0.11	1	0.6
CB08-525	NC	NC	0	3.8	2.22	0.12	1	2.2
CB08-526	0.59	0.01	1	0.6	0.84	0.11	1	0.8
CB08-527	-	-	-	-	1.03	0.37	1	1.0
CB08-529	NC	NC	0	0.2	NC	0	0	0.1

	Chalcedony				Chert			
		CORES				CORES		
	VR	CR	O	E	VR	CR	O	E
	NC	NC	0	0.0	0.73	0.41	1	0.7
	NC	NC	0	0.7	NC	NC	0	0.0
	-	-	-	-	-	-	-	-
	1.47	0.28	1	1.5	-	-	-	-
	NC	NC	0	0.2	NC	NC	0	0.1
	0.22	0.19	1	0.2	NC	NC	0	1.0
	NC	NC	0	0.9	NC	NC	0	0.0
	NC	NC	0	0.2	2.33	0.21	1	2.3
	-	-	-	-	-	-	-	-
	1.01	0.31	5	5.0	0.31	0.17	1	0.3
	1.01	0.08	5	5.1	NC	NC	0	0.1
	1.54	0.12	6	9.2	0.05	0.01	1	0.1
	0.91	0.21	8	7.3	NC	NC	0	0.1
	3.25	0.44	1	3.3	NC	NC	0	0.1
	0.76	0.09	2	1.5	-	-	-	-

For the whole Group 1A locality, volume ratios for basalt, BIF and chalcedony all exceeded 1.0, representing the removal of material, and generally fewer cores were recorded than would be expected. For chert, however, the volume ratio was less than 1.0 and more cores were recorded than expected. Sample size was small, although elsewhere in the ranges more chert cores than expected were also recorded for Group 5A, and the other ranges samples mostly had little discrepancy between observed and expected numbers of chert cores (see Table 4.16). This might indicate that chert was removed in the form of flakes rather than cores, as suggested above as an interpretation of CB08-506. Alternatively, chert cores were brought in from sources outside the immediate area and discarded where they could be readily replaced.

Stone features

Two stone features (CB08-509, CB08-513), both walled enclosures, occurred in this locality. Both were small chambers at the base of steep rocky slopes with two openings, one of which was blocked with stones (Figure 6.5). No other cultural material was associated with or near either site. The functions of these structures are unclear. One possibility is that they are caches, perhaps for ceremonial items (see Chapter 5 for discussion) (Day and McDonald 2008, 20). In the case of CB08-513, where one opening has been blocked, trapping animals is another possible use, as suggested by the Traditional Owners during initial field recording (Hook, Dias and Rapley 2008, 66).

Discussion

The patchy distribution of surface artefacts in the Group 1A locality is clearly related to topography (Figure 6.2). Artefacts are associated with rises and with terraces mainly along the drainage system. The relationship to topography is particularly evident at CB08-511, where the internal structure of the site is also patchy with artefact concentrations associated with each of the three rises (see Figures 6.2 and 6.3). The distribution of artefact concentrations at CB08-511, CB08-507 immediately to the west and the isolated artefacts recorded between these two sites, highlights the arbitrary character of site definition.

Most sites fall into two groups. The first group is a concentration of sites associated with the main creek line along which the rockshelter CB08-500 and the large surface scatter CB08-511 both occur. Grinding material is also concentrated along the creek. The second group of sites is on the eastern boundary. These are dominated by chalcedony cores and flakes and no ground stone artefacts were recorded. This group of sites clearly relates to the reduction of raw material, as do two others located elsewhere in the locality – BIF at CB08-517 and chert at CB08-508. CB08-505 could also be interpreted as a single reduction of a BIF core, with the associated discard of a few flakes of other materials. Clearly access to raw material has a strong influence on assemblage composition. At the landscape scale this is shown by the restricted distribution of chalcedony artefacts. At the site scale, CB08-511 shows internal variability. The different artefact concentrations are each distinct in terms of raw material composition. Although isolated artefacts occur widely, there is a noticeable concentration closer to the main creek line and to a lesser extent associated with the chalcedony-dominated cluster on the eastern boundary. Importantly, the two stone features are not closely associated with other archaeological remains.

Figure 6.6 represents the Group 1A taskscape. Lines connecting key activity locales and persistent places in the landscape represent the paths of journeys as people move though country forming a meshwork (Ingold 2007, 80–81). This meshwork can be interpreted in terms of two broad zones of activity (Figure 6.6). Along the main creek line there is evidence for activity focused on the water sources at CB08-511 and at CB08-500, but extending beyond those two localities. The presence of grinding material suggests regular visits and probably the presence of women. The cluster of chalcedony-dominated sites and the scattered individual reduction episodes, as well as the chert quarry immediately to the north (CB08-501), denote a more restricted range of activities primarily reflecting stone procurement. Aboriginal use of this landscape seems to be structured by topography and the distribution of key resources – water and stone. Central to the taskscape is a 'habitation zone' focused on the water and shade along the creek. Here, plant food resources were more diverse than among the nearby spinifex grasslands. Timber suitable for tool making was also readily available. The surrounding hills and gullies might be seen as a 'transit zone' and were primarily visited while hunting and travelling. Procurement of stone raw materials could be embedded in the course of these activities as sources could be reliably and predictably encountered. Much of the archaeological evidence in this zone primarily reflects this. The stone structures are also part of this broader transit zone, either in terms of trapping animals or perhaps storing ceremonial gear well away from frequently visited localities.

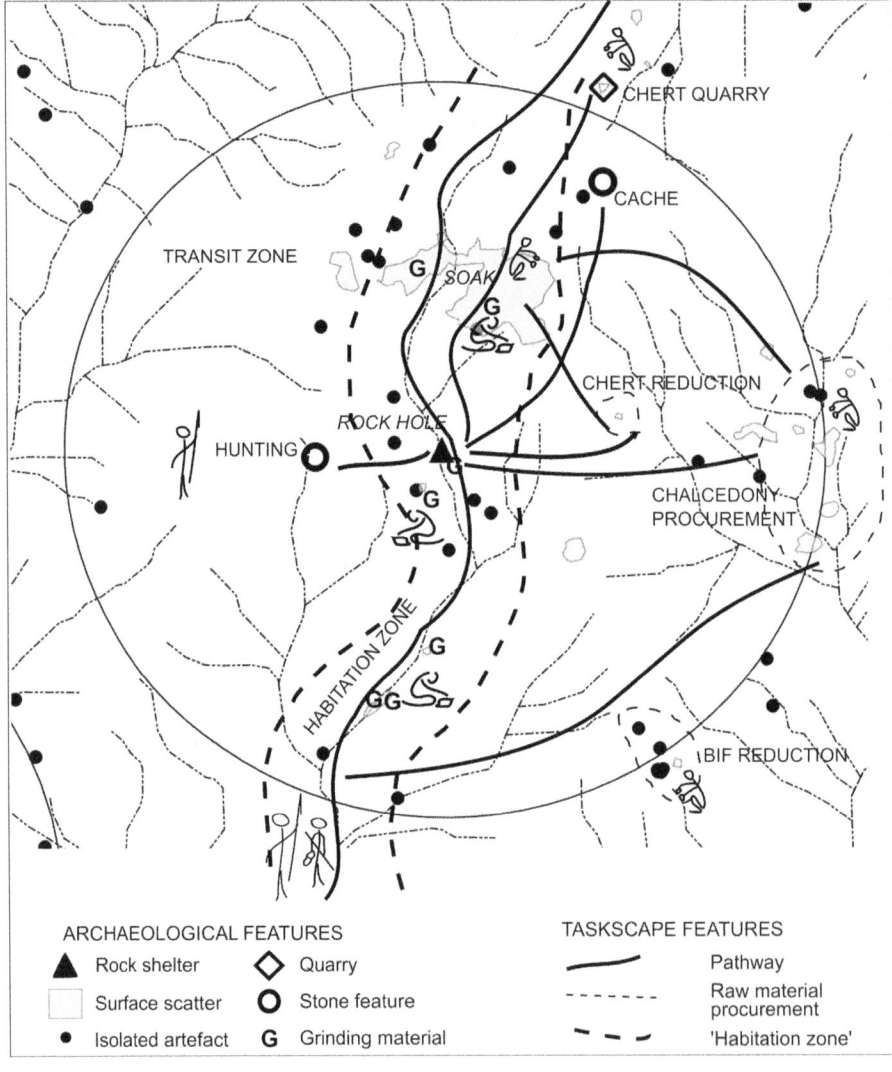

FIGURE 6.6: The Group 1A taskscape. Circle defines Group 1A (1 km radius from CB08-500).

GROUP 3B

Group 3B is defined by the area within a kilometre radius of the excavated rockshelter CB10-92 (Figure 6.7). It lies in the central portion of the study area within the foothills of the Chichester Range at the point where the valley of Kakutungutanta Creek emerges onto the outwash plains. Eucalypt woodland occurs along the creek, with some areas of VC 2 (Mulga Woodland), while spinifex grasslands cover the ranges (Figure 6.8). The outwash plains carry mulga woodlands, mainly VC 4 (Low Open Woodland).

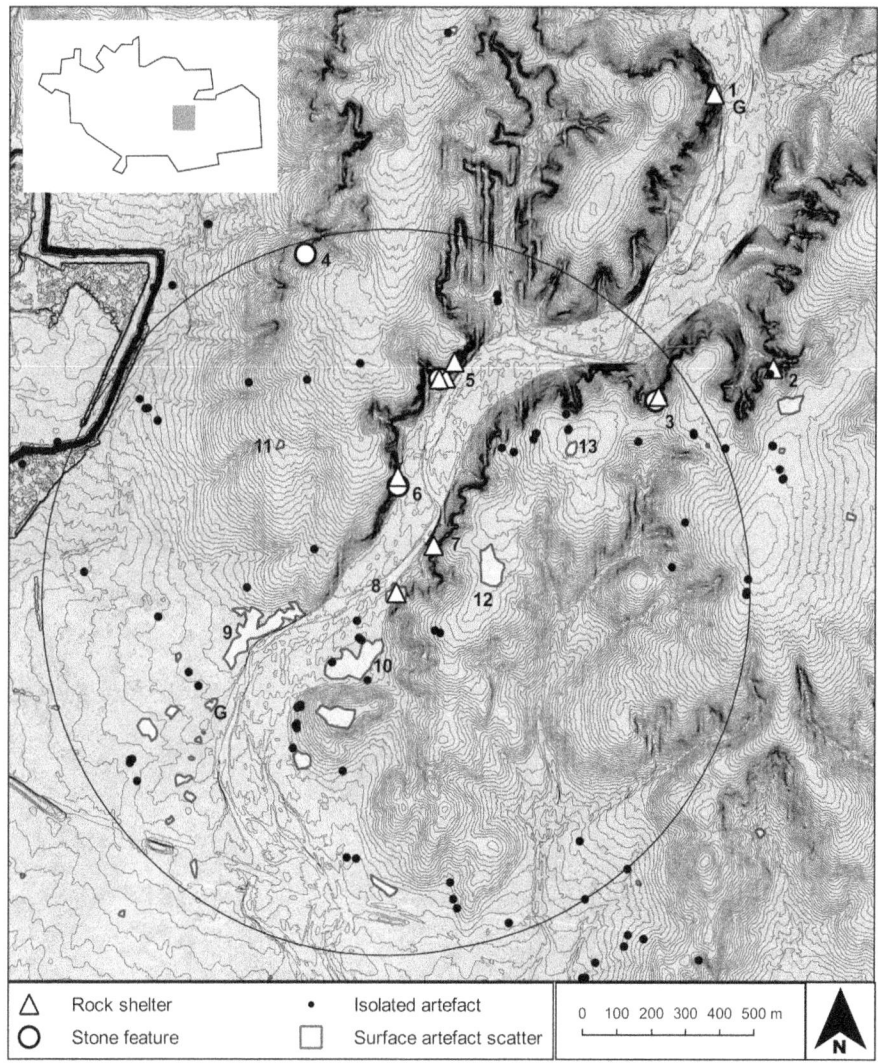

FIGURE 6.7: Archaeological features along Kakutungutanta Creek. (1) CB10-133. (2) CB10-145. (3) CB10-147, CB11-93 (4) CB10-91. (5) CB10-93, CB10-94, CB12-180. (6) CB10-88, CB10-89. (7) CB10-98. (8) CB10-92. (9) CB10-83. (10) CB10-90. (11) CB10-86. (12) CB10-97. (13) CB10-100. G=Millstone. Circle defines Group 3B (1 km radius around CB10-92).

Kakutungutanta Creek is a named place of significance to the Nyiyaparli, who believe water flowing through the creeks draining the ranges into the Fortescue Marsh is crucial to maintain the health of the country.

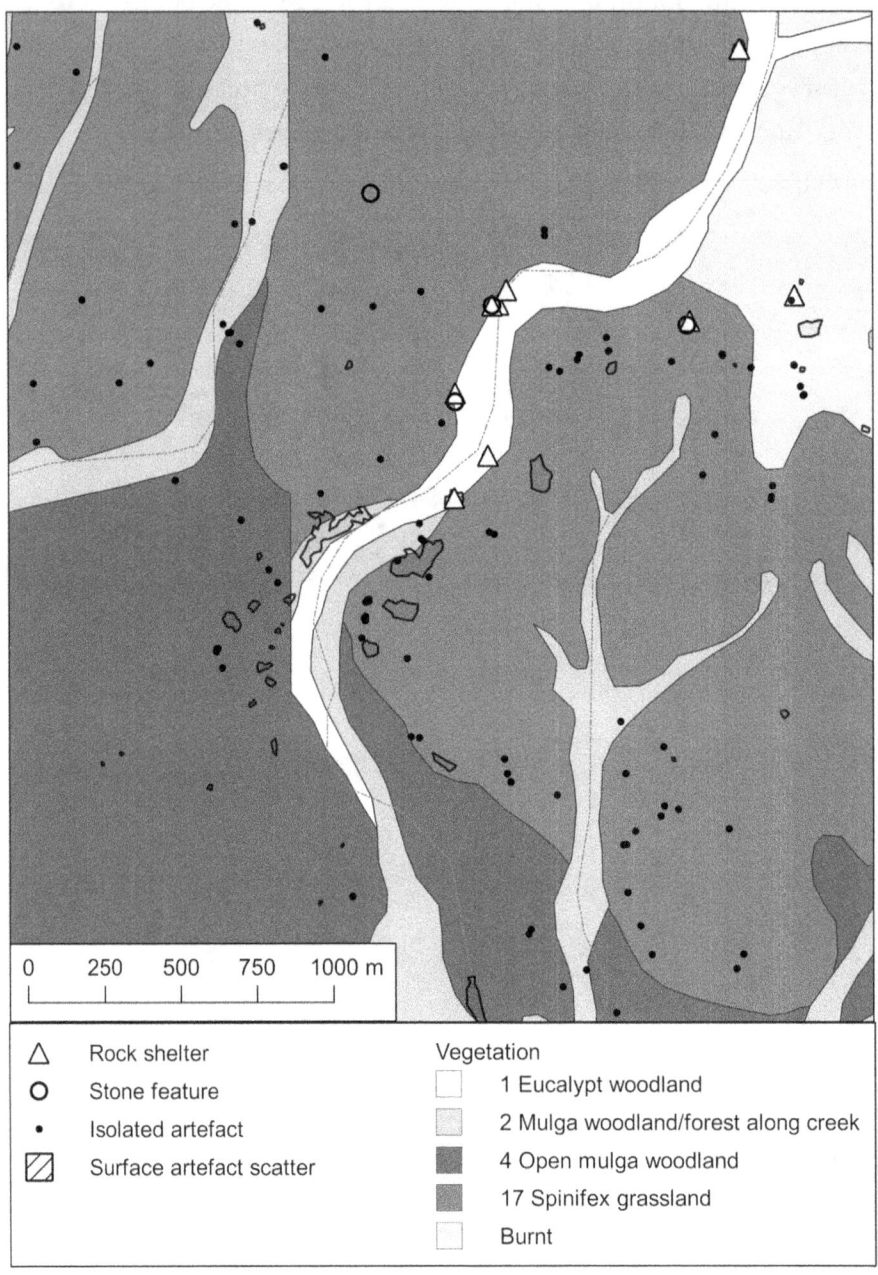

FIGURE 6.8: Kakutungutanta Creek: vegetation.

The sites within the area include five excavated rockshelters, five other rockshelters with cultural material or stone features, and 23 surface artefact scatters. Fifty-one isolated artefacts were also recorded (Figure 6.7). These are documented in various consulting reports (Dias and Rapley 2013; Edwards and Craig 2011; McHarg and Craig 2010; Wright and Tierney 2012). There are two other excavated rockshelters within 500 metres of CB10-92, namely CB10-88 and CB10-98. Further upstream and within a kilometre lie CB10-93 and CB10-147. There are several other shelters with cultural material, but these lack accumulated deposits. Some have stone features, most of which are walled enclosures. Most of the rockshelter sites form clusters, comprising excavated shelters and shelters with stone features or other cultural surface material. The walled enclosure at CB10-91 is an isolate. This site is about 500 metres north-west of CB10-93, overlooking the neighbouring creek system.

CB10-133 is situated another 700 metres further upstream from CB10-93. Although it is more than a kilometre from CB10-92, it seems clearly associated with this complex of sites on Kakutungutanta Creek and will be included in this discussion.

Twenty-three surface artefact scatters occur within the Group 3B locality, including those associated with the rockshelters at CB10-88, CB10-92, CB10-94 and CB10-98. Nine of these sites also include discrete reduction areas. The surface artefact scatters mostly cluster at the point where the creek leaves the ranges. Here, there are two more extensive surface scatters on the plains at the base of the escarpment (CB10-83, CB10-90). From here, several smaller artefact scatters are distributed downstream for about 500 metres, mostly along the west side. Some of these are also reduction areas.

There is a patchy distribution of surface artefact scatters and isolated artefacts throughout the rest of the area, mostly in the hills on the east side of the creek. Although there are no quarries in the locality, three surface artefact scatters with reduction areas occur on hill tops (CB10-86, CB10-97 and CB10-143). CB10-97 and CB10-43 to the east of the creek are both BIF dominated, while CB10-86 to the west is a chalcedony reduction area. These may represent opportunistic exploitation of raw material encountered during travel. Surface artefacts are largely absent from the valley floor. This does not indicate absence of activity, but rather can be reasonably explained by loss of cultural material through flood events.

All surface artefact scatters are small to medium in size. Excluding those associated with rockshelters, the remaining 19 artefact scatters range from 4 m^3 to 8161 m^3 in area, with a mean of 1469 m^3 and median of 495 m^3. Only seven are larger than 1000 m^3. In the Christmas Creek study area as a whole, larger sites are more likely to be associated with VC 1 (Open Eucalypt Woodland) or VC 3 (Low Mulga Woodland and Open Forest) (see Chapter 4, Figure 4.3); the latter element of the mulga woodlands mosaic is absent from Group 3B. The sites associated with eucalypt woodland along the creek valley are all rockshelters. Small to medium surface artefact sites cluster at the mouth of the valley at the ecotone between the mulga woodlands mosaic and the eucalypt woodland (Figure 6.8).

Sample size for individual artefact scatters is small in Group 3B. Mean recorded sample size is 33.9; however, the median is only 19 and 75% have 44 or fewer artefacts. Only one site (CB10-83) has more than 100 artefacts. Most artefacts are BIF (71%), with basalt, chalcedony and chert occurring in roughly equal proportions (7–8%). Other materials occur in trace amounts except for mudstone (3%) and quartzite (2%), which are found at a few sites. Unlike Group 1A there is no clear patterning in the distribution of raw materials. Variability seems to be attributable to sample size (Table 6.4).

Most flaked stone artefacts have cortex, with only 38% overall of artefacts from the four main raw materials having none. Terrestrial cortex is more common on BIF artefacts, while there is a more even split between terrestrial and riverine cortex on basalt, chalcedony and chert (Figure 6.9). This mixture of cortex type might reflect the position of Group 3B at the edge of the ranges, since materials from both the ranges and the creek have been sourced. About 2% of the flaked stone in Group 3B is retouched, which is relatively low for the study area generally (Chapter 4, Table 4.29). This contrasts markedly with Group 1A, where 10% of artefacts had evidence of retouch, the highest of any sample group in the study area. Most retouched artefacts are undiagnostic, with the exception of a BIF tula from CB10-82 and two geometric microliths from CB10-133.

TABLE 6.4: Group 3B: raw material composition.

	Basalt	BIF	Chalcedony	Chert	Dolerite	Mudstone	Quartzite	Other	Total
CB06-65	0	17	0	0	0	8	0	0	25
CB06-98	7	55	13	0	0	0	1	1	77
CB07-04	8	45	9	5	0	0	0	0	67
CB10-143	1	15	1	2	0	0	0	0	19
CB10-74	1	4	0	0	0	0	0	0	5
CB10-75	3	15	0	2	0	2	4	1	27
CB10-76	0	14	0	2	0	0	0	0	16
CB10-77	0	16	0	0	0	0	0	0	16
CB10-78	1	25	1	3	0	1	0	0	31
CB10-79	6	15	3	2	0	6	0	0	32
CB10-80	0	11	0	0	0	0	0	0	11
CB10-81	0	0	0	7	0	0	0	0	7
CB10-82	2	18	2	13	0	9	0	0	44
CB10-83	11	159	6	10	1	0	10	0	197
CB10-84	0	14	0	0	0	0	0	0	14
CB10-85	4	27	8	7	0	0	1	0	47
CB10-86	1	0	8	0	0	0	0	0	9
CB10-88	0	2	0	0	0	0	0	0	2
CB10-90	7	62	7	0	0	0	1	2	79
CB10-92	1	11	0	2	0	0	0	0	14
CB10-94	1	2	0	2	0	0	0	0	5
CB10-97	4	10	2	0	0	0	0	0	16
CB10-98	1	14	4	1	0	0	0	0	20
Isolated artefacts	8	35	0	3	5	0	0	0	51
TOTAL	67	586	64	61	6	26	17	4	831

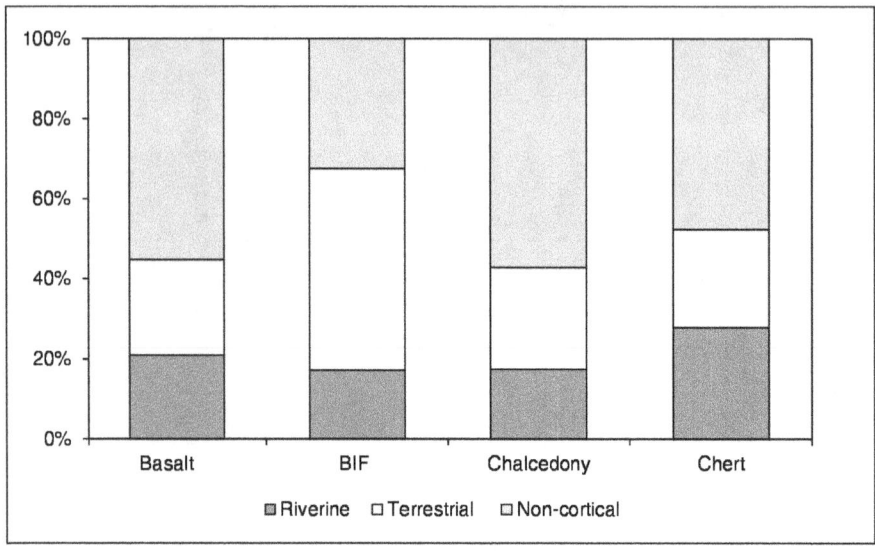

FIGURE 6.9: Group 3B: cortex type by raw material.

Grinding material is sparser in Group 3B than in Group 1A. There is only one millstone at CB10-82. None of the surface assemblages from the other rockshelters include grinding material, except for CB10-133 which has three millstones and a muller. A hammer stone was excavated from CB10-92 (Figure A5.69). Most of the shelters have cores or manuports indicating stockpiling of raw material and in several cases these make up the whole surface assemblage. In the case of CB10-98, a dolerite core was carefully cached in the rear of the shelter (Figure A5.75). At CB10-147, the surface assemblage comprises six BIF cores. At CB10-93, five manuports, all BIF cobbles, are the only surface artefacts. CB10-133 also has several cached pieces of timber, some charred or with cut marks.

Like Group 1A, the Kakutungutanta Creek taskscape (Figure 6.10) is centred along an ephemeral creek that provides both water and shade. Grinding material suggests regular and repeated visits, but unlike Group 1A, this activity is concentrated in two locations: at CB10-133 and at the point where the creek enters the outwash plains. CB10-133 is an unusually large and spacious shelter, and provides the only suitable camping place along this stretch of the creek. The excavated assemblage is relatively large and dense, and indicates long-term repeated use of the site (see Appendix 5). The second focus of activity occurs at the outfall of Kakutungutanta

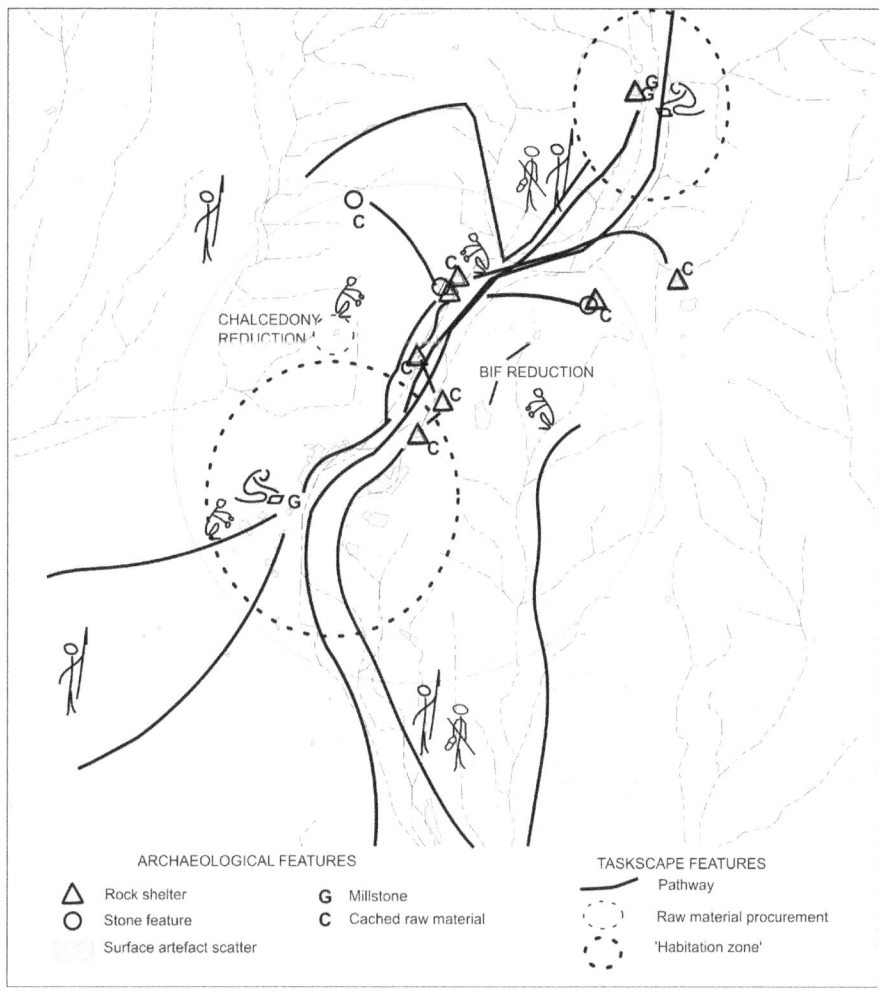

FIGURE 6.10: Group 3B: the taskscape along Kakutungutanta Creek. The light grey circle defines Group 3B (1 km radius from CB10-92).

Creek and seems likely to reflect the diversity of resources at this point in the landscape, as well as ready access to several different vegetation zones. CB10-92 is the first shelter encountered entering the valley. Although it is quite small, it has evidence for relatively dense and repeated occupation (see Appendix 5). Linking these two persistent places is a series of rockshelters with evidence for more ephemeral use, as well as caching and storage in the form of stone features, and surface finds of cores and manuports. By contrast to the main valley, the surrounding hills and ranges have only sparse evidence of activity. Like Group 1A therefore, the hills can be viewed as a transit zone. Although there are no quarries, reduction areas in the ranges suggest that opportunistic stone procurement was embedded in hunting and travelling in this zone. On the plains within Group 3B, archaeological evidence is sparse and largely restricted to the creek line. This highlights the role of creek lines in this area as a source of water and shade. Both habitation and travel routes therefore tend to be concentrated along them.

The evidence from the excavated shelters along Kakutungutanta Creek demonstrates that this area was used throughout the Holocene, and the early occupation at the Kakutungutanta rockshelter (CB10-93) indicates its history extends back some 40,000 years. During the arid period 4000–2000 years ago, this place provides the only visible archaeological evidence for use of the Christmas Creek study area (see Chapter 5).

GROUP 8S

Group 8S is situated on the stony outwash plains in the south-central portion of the study area (Figure 6.11). It is centred on a large artefact scatter (CB08-114) associated with a major north–south drainage line (Marandu Creek). The locality consists of the area within 1 km of the recorded boundary of CB08-114 – about 5.4 km^2 in total area. Primary reporting for sites recorded within this boundary is in a series of unpublished reports by Archae-aus for FMG (Archae-aus 2015; Craig and Bradley 2014; Edwards 2014; Hook, Di Lello and Ash 2008; Jimenez-Lozano and Edwards 2014; McHarg and Edwards 2010; Sinclair 2015a).

The landscape is typical of the alluvial plains between the ranges and the Fortescue Marsh, with the main topographic feature being a series of ephemeral drainage lines. The area carries a mosaic of different mulga woodland communities, with eucalypt woodlands concentrated along primary creek systems. The most widespread vegetation formations are the mulga woodland formations VC 3 (Low Mulga Woodland Open Forest) and VC 4 (Low Open Mulga Woodland), which cover 47% and 32% of the area, respectively.

In contrast to Group 1A, archaeological evidence in Group 8S comprises only surface artefacts. Not surprisingly, they are distributed in a linear fashion, clearly related to the ephemeral drainage (Figure 6.11). Fifty-two discrete sites were identified and recorded. Two were classified

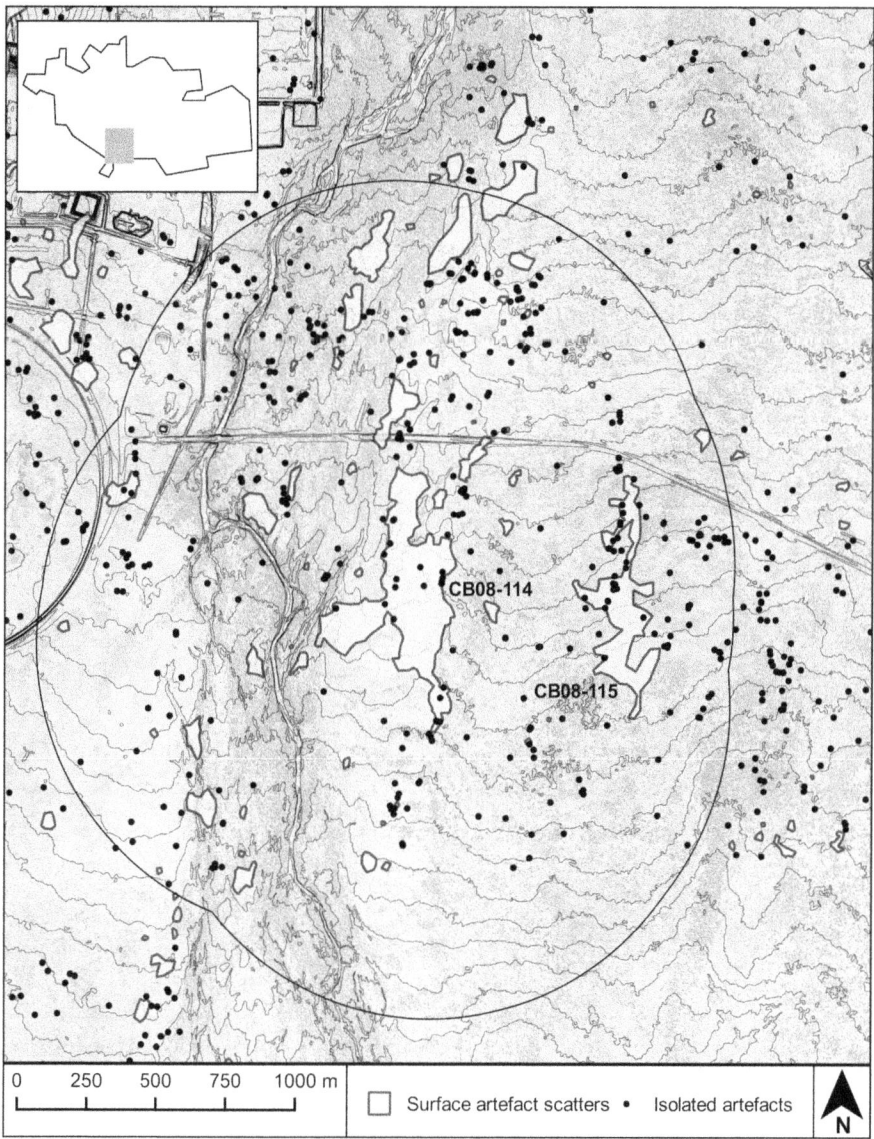

FIGURE 6.11: Group 8S: distribution of surface artefact scatters and isolated artefacts.

as reduction areas and the remainder were classified as artefact scatters. Eleven artefact scatters also included reduction areas. Two large and dense artefact sites were identified (CB08-114, CB08-115), but the remainder are all small or medium artefact scatters. Seven hundred and thirty-one isolated artefacts were also recorded.

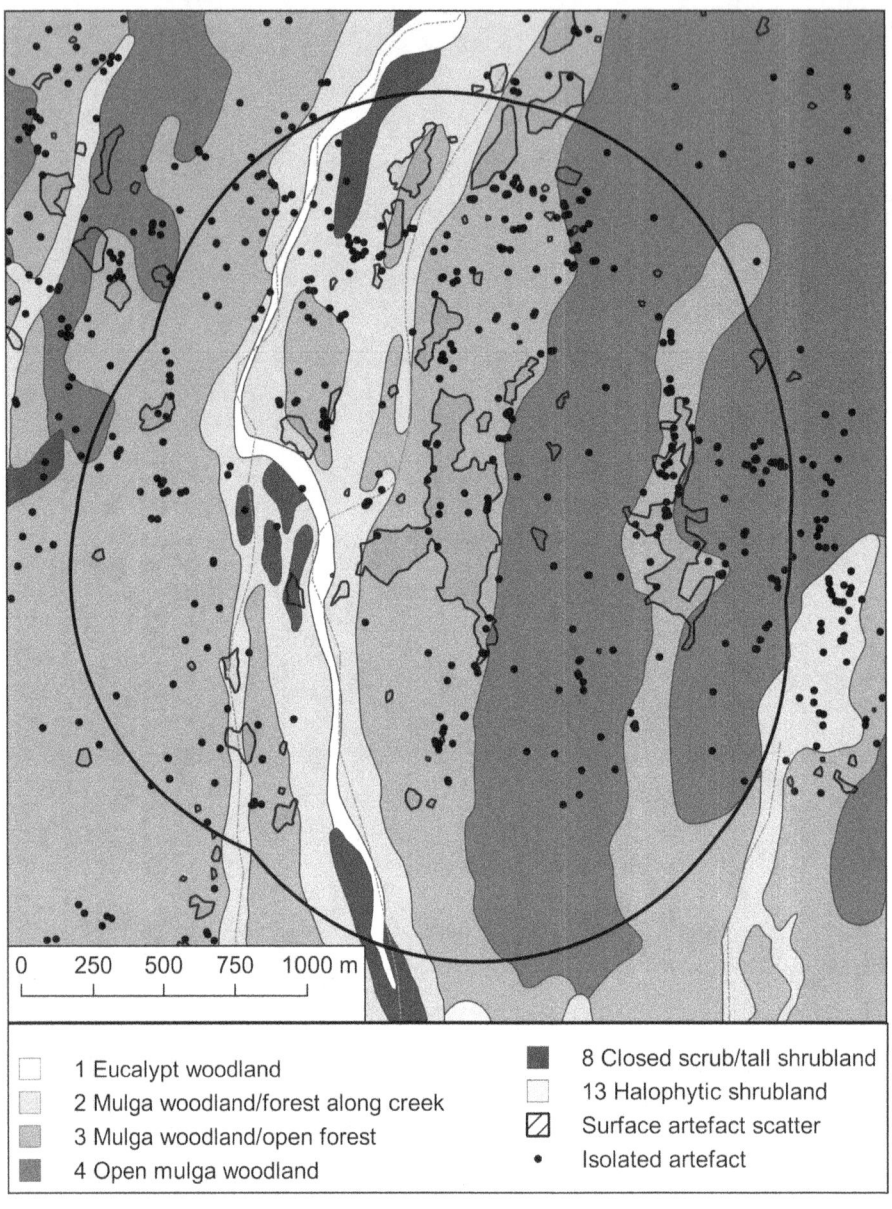

Figure 6.12: Group 8S: distribution of artefacts in relation to vegetation.

Surface artefacts appear widely distributed, but when mapped against vegetation types, there is a noticeable concentration of isolated artefacts associated with Low Mulga Woodland/Open Forest (VC 3). CB08-114 and CB08-115 are both associated with this vegetation community, as are almost all the ground stone artefacts (Figure 6.12).

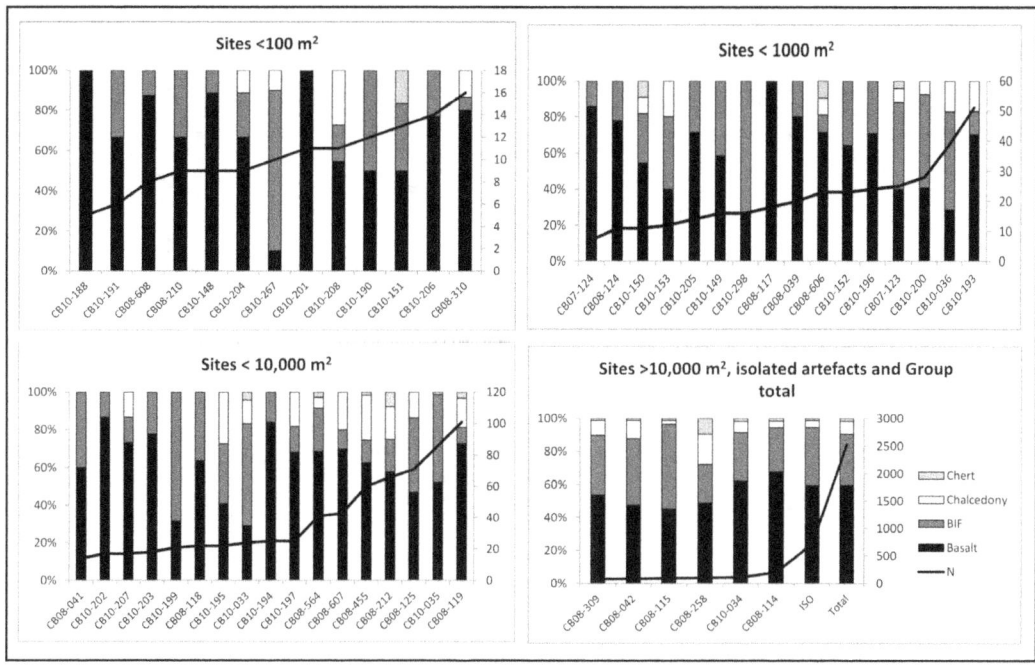

FIGURE 6.13: Group 8S: raw material assemblage composition for individual artefact scatters.

Assemblage composition is similar for both grouped site assemblages and isolated artefacts, with basalt making up about 60% of artefacts. However, the composition of individual site assemblages is variable. Sample size for small and medium sites is mostly small. Mean sample size is 32, but the distribution is skewed. The median is only 18.5, and 75% of samples have fewer than 39 artefacts. Figure 6.13 groups sites according to surface area and orders them by sample size. The sites fall into two broad categories. Sites less than 10,000 m² and with a recorded sample of fewer than 100 artefacts vary in raw material composition. They range from sites with one or two raw materials present to more diverse scatters with more even percentages of materials. The largest sites (>10,000 m²) are more uniform and approximate to the overall characteristics of Group 8S. This is not surprising. The large sites make a proportionally greater contribution to the characterisation of Group 8S, so are unlikely to diverge much from it. Many of the small sites, by contrast, are likely to reflect local and opportunistic procurement of raw material, which is distributed widely in the landscape.

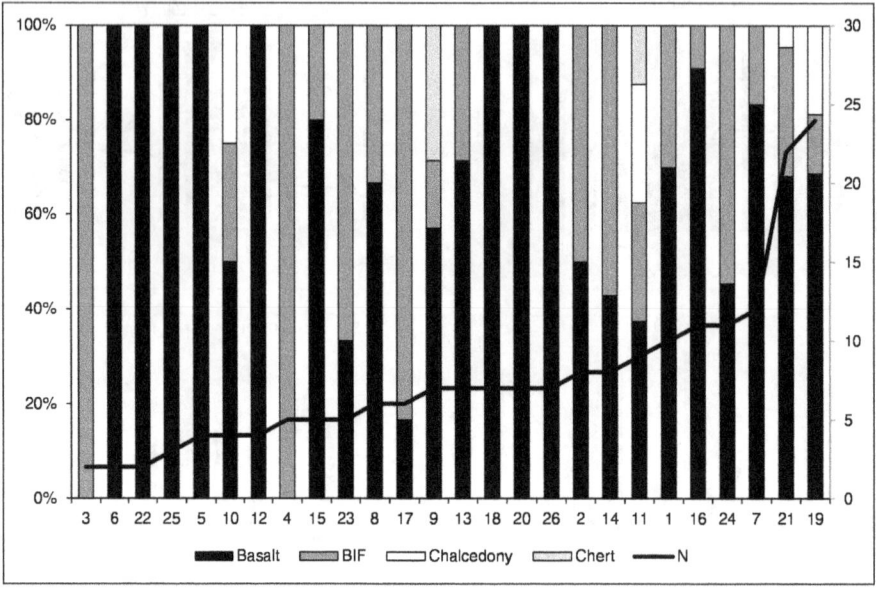

Figure 6.14: CB08-114: raw material assemblage composition for individual sample squares.

Within sites, assemblage composition by raw material is also variable. At CB08-114, sample size for the 26 individual recorded sample squares ranges from two to 24, with a mean of 8. Only six squares have a sample size greater than 10. Figure 6.14 orders squares by sample size and highlights the raw material variability between squares. This is comparable to that of the smallest sites within Group 8S (compare Figure 6.13).

There are differences in the way particular raw materials are distributed across the landscape. Basalt, BIF and chalcedony are widely and uniformly distributed. Chert artefacts, on the other hand, are concentrated in the northern part of the locality. No chert cores were recorded. All chert artefacts are flakes or flake fragments, most of which are non-cortical.

Cortex for both basalt and dolerite is mainly riverine, indicating that the creeks were the primary source for these materials. Terrestrial cortex was more common on BIF artefacts, although riverine cortex was also present on 23% of artefacts. Chalcedony and chert were mostly non-cortical, but, if present, the cortex was commonly from terrestrial rather than creek sources (Figure 6.15).

Cortex and volume ratios were calculated for assemblages with cores for basalt, BIF and chalcedony (Table 6.5). The results are very variable,

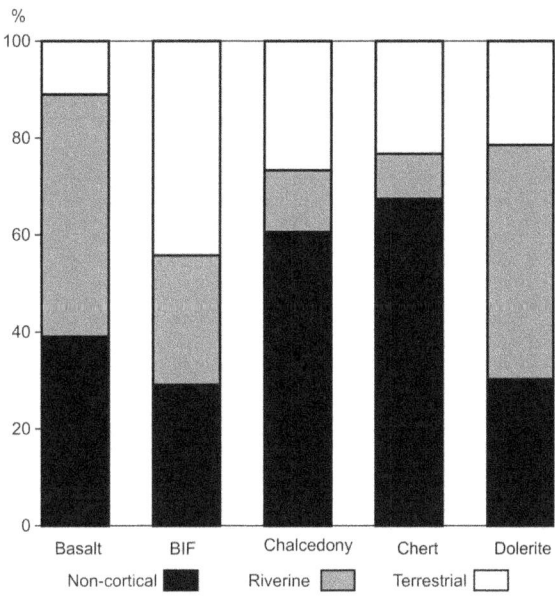

FIGURE 6.15: Group 8S: cortex type by raw material.

although generally values indicate a deficit of both cortical surface area and volume. Comparing the observed number of cores with the expected number indicates that, as for the overall analysis of the groups, there are noticeably fewer cores present than would account for the amount of flaked stone. In some cases, these deficits are very large. The relatively large basalt assemblage from CB08-114, for example, has a cortex ratio of 0.99. This suggests no net gain or loss of cortical surface area. However, the volume ratio is 4.27 and the number of cores present is about a quarter of what would be expected. Several individual sites show a similar pattern for basalt. CB08-258 and CB08-309 have high volume ratios for basalt and particularly large discrepancies between the number of cores expected than actually observed. The BIF assemblage at CB08-309 gives similar results. Cortex ratios at both sites are greater than 1.0. This is consistent with the removal of raw material in core form rather than as cortical flakes. Basalt cobbles obtained from the nearby creek were partially reduced on site, perhaps to produce flakes for immediate use which were largely cortical and discarded immediately. The resulting core was then carried away for use elsewhere.

TABLE 6.5: Group 8S: cortex and volume ratios for individual artefact sites. NC not calculated (small sample); - raw material not present.

	Basalt			N cores		BIF		
	N	CR	VR	O	E	N	CR	VR
CB07-123	10	0.67	2.08	1	2.1	12	1.80	4.26
CB08-114	120	0.99	4.27	7	29.9	47	0.76	4.23
CB08-115	27	0.75	3.70	2	7.4	42	0.49	2.10
CB08-117	18	0.88	2.42	1	2.4	-	-	-
CB08-119	70	0.70	2.07	9	18.6	8	0.68	1.37
CB08-124	7	1.51	3.62	1	3.6	2	NC	NC
CB08-125	31	0.49	1.46	7	10.3	26	1.65	7.33
CB08-210	6	0.72	3.59	1	3.6	3	NC	NC
CB08-212	37	0.71	2.78	3	8.4	11	0.77	1.92
CB08-258	46	1.81	11.79	1	11.8	22	0.38	2.31
CB08-309	42	3.08	13.76	1	13.8	28	2.73	10.20
CB08-310	12	0.61	1.47	2	2.9	1	NC	NC
CB08-39	16	0.46	4.40	1	4.4	4	0.83	1.22
CB08-42	39	0.74	2.04	7	14.2	33	2.00	7.95
CB08-455	37	1.32	3.58	5	17.9	7	0.77	1.57
CB08-564	24	0.29	1.10	3	3.3	8	NC	NC
CB08-606	15	NC	NC	0	2.2	2	NC	NC
CB08-607	28	1.29	3.43	3	10.3	4	0.53	1.11
CB08-608	7	0.23	1.09	1	1.1	1	NC	NC
CB10-148	8	NC	NC	0	3.2	1	0.55	0.86

N cores		Chalcedony			N cores	
O	E	N	CR	VR	O	E
1	4.3	1	NC	NC	0	0.0
4	16.9	7	NC	NC	0	0.8
6	12.6	2	0.57	0.86	1	0.9
-	-	-	-	-	-	-
4	5.5	15	0.21	1.66	3	5.0
0	0.5	9	NC	NC	0	0.9
1	7.3	-	-	-	-	-
0	0.6	-	-	-	-	-
2	3.8	10	NC	NC	0	2.0
3	6.9	17	NC	NC	0	1.7
1	10.2	7	NC	NC	0	0.9
0	0.1	2	NC	NC	0	0.2
1	1.2	-	-	-	-	-
2	15.9	8	0.42	1.44	1	1.4
2	3.1	14	NC	NC	0	1.0
0	2.8	2	NC	NC	0	0.2
0	1.9	2	NC	NC	0	0.3
2	2.2	8	NC	NC	0	0.7
0	0.1	-	-	-	-	-
1	0.9	-	-	-	-	-

TABLE 6.5: *Continued.*

	Basalt			N cores		BIF		
	N	CR	VR	O	E	N	CR	VR
CB10-149	7	NC	NC	0	2.5	5	0.87	2.32
CB10-150	6	0.75	2.70	1	2.7	3	0.65	0.83
CB10-151	6	0.64	1.73	1	1.7	4	NC	NC
CB10-152	9	1.08	2.14	1	2.1	5	0.28	0.77
CB10-153	2	0.07	0.27	1	0.3	2	NC	NC
CB10-188	5	NC	NC	0	0.9	-	-	-
CB10-190	6	NC	NC	0	1.1	6	0.25	0.53
CB10-191	4	NC	NC	0	1.2	2	NC	NC
CB10-193	33	2.93	9.76	1	9.8	6	NC	NC
CB10-194	21	1.29	7.71	1	7.7	4	NC	NC
CB10-195	9	NC	NC	0	1.3	7	NC	NC
CB10-196	17	0.65	1.72	2	3.4	7	0.89	2.01
CB10-197	15	0.87	3.91	2	7.8	3	NC	NC
CB10-199	6	0.08	0.28	3	0.8	13	0.51	1.29
CB10-200	11	1.04	2.33	2	4.7	14	0.81	1.72
CB10-201	11	1.31	3.31	1	3.3	-	-	-
CB10-202	13	0.55	2.88	1	2.9	2	NC	NC
CB10-203	14	0.93	3.37	2	6.7	4	NC	NC
CB10-204	6	0.48	1.10	1	1.1	2	NC	NC
CB10-205	10	NC	NC	0	1.8	4	1.75	4.95

N cores		Chalcedony			N cores	
O	E	N	CR	VR	O	E
1	2.3	-	-	-	-	-
1	0.8	1	NC	NC	0	0.2
0	1.6	-	-	-	-	-
4	3.1	-	-	-	-	-
0	0.1	1	NC	NC	0	0.1
-	-	-	-	-	-	-
1	0.5	-	-	-	-	-
0	0.3	-	-	-	-	-
0	0.7	8	0.30	0.91	2	1.8
0	1.0	-	-	-	-	-
0	1.7	6	NC	NC	0	0.7
3	6.0	-	-	-	-	-
0	1.1	4	NC	NC	0	0.5
2	2.6	-	-	-	-	-
2	3.4	2	NC	NC	0	0.2
-	-	-	-	-	-	-
0	0.4	-	-	-	-	-
0	0.6	-	-	-	-	-
0	0.6	1	NC	NC	0	0.1
1	5.0	-	-	-	-	-

TABLE 6.5: *Continued.*

	BASALT			N CORES		BIF		
	N	CR	VR	O	E	N	CR	VR
CB10-206	10	2.13	7.54	1	7.5	3	NC	NC
CB10-207	11	0.70	1.51	4	6.0	2	NC	NC
CB10-208	6	0.56	1.77	1	1.8	2	NC	NC
CB10-267	1	NC	NC	0	0.2	8	0.44	0.66
CB10-298	4	0.42	0.58	1	0.6	11	0.46	0.81
CB10-33	7	0.54	2.15	1	2.2	13	NC	NC
CB10-34	66	0.71	2.24	8	17.9	31	1.26	4.18
CB10-35	44	1.05	2.96	4	11.8	39	2.06	8.14
CB10-36	10	0.20	0.82	3	2.4	19	0.40	0.98
ISOLATED ARTEFACTS	395	1.19	3.92	58	227.6	233	0.86	2.16
GROUP 8S ALL	1365	0.97	3.27	157	513.6	716	0.83	2.43

Discussion

The descriptions of the two large sites in Group 8S exemplify how archaeological material is distributed across the plains landscape and illustrate how this distribution is recorded in the course of archaeological fieldwork. CB08-114 is located on a flat plain, characterised by raised gravel areas interspersed among numerous ephemeral soaks. The site is bounded by first order ephemeral creeks and large areas of the site are occasionally inundated. CB08-114 was originally identified in 2008 and fully recorded in 2010, when the site boundary was extended to include two surface artefact scatters previously recorded as separate sites. Artefact distribution is patchy with concentrations located on or near the raised gravel patches. CB08-115 has a similar history of recording and general characteristics. It was also first

N CORES		CHALCEDONY			N CORES	
O	E	N	CR	VR	O	E
0	0.4	-	-	-	-	-
0	0.3	2	0.42	0.68	2	1.4
0	1.5	3	NC	NC	0	0.2
4	2.6	1	NC	NC	0	0.2
2	1.6	-	-	-	-	-
0	2.1	3	NC	NC	0	0.3
3	12.6	7	0.31	1.65	1	1.6
1	8.1	1	NC	NC	0	0.1
8	7.8	6	0.24	0.67	2	1.3
48	103.8	27	0.59	2.10	2	4.2
111	269.6	177	0.49	2.06	14	28.8

identified in 2008 and fully recorded in 2010, when the site boundary was extended to incorporate two surface artefact scatters recorded as discrete sites. Artefacts are distributed in a series of concentrations on an undulating silt and gravel plain, associated with numerous soaks. At both sites, discrete reduction areas were identified (Jimenez-Lozano and Edwards 2014, 405–17). The numerous small artefact scatters in Group 8S are arguably equivalent to the individual artefact concentrations described within these two large sites. CB10-203, for example, is immediately to the south-west of CB08-114 and its mapped boundary is only 50 metres from the boundary of its larger neighbour. The site is described as a small artefact scatter on a silt and gravel plain, immediately adjacent to Marandu Creek. In this case, however, there is a single concentration of artefacts (a 'patch') within

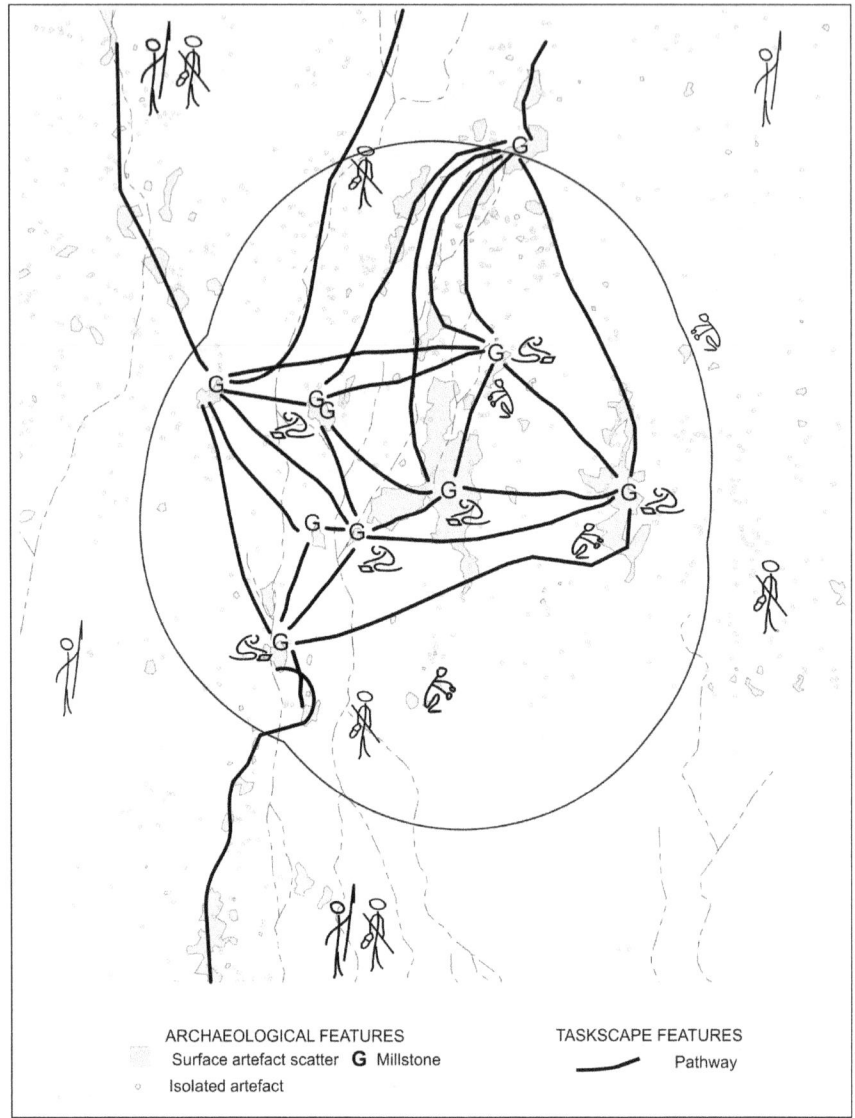

FIGURE 6.16: The Group 8S taskscape.

a lower density scatter of artefacts. The recorded artefact sample comprises two multiplatform cores and 12 flakes and flake fragments of basalt, four BIF flakes and a dolerite millstone (Edwards 2014, 518–22).

The staged recording of sites and isolated artefacts, and modification of boundaries with additional survey and ground inspection, highlights that archaeological sites are constructs of different field recording events. At the landscape scale, the distribution of archaeological material is roughly continuous although there are clearly concentrations or patches. These may reflect more intense past activity, although visibility and post-depositional processes should also be considered. In the study area, visibility on the plains is generally high, so this can probably be disregarded as a significant contributor to differential distribution of cultural material. However, the possible contribution of natural processes to the distribution cannot be ignored. Unfortunately, detailed consideration of geomorphological processes is beyond the scope of routine site recording for compliance archaeology in the inland Pilbara and would require a focused research program. What can be said is that evidence of sheet-wash was noted at many of the sites in Group 8S and a few examples of water-worn artefacts were recorded. However, the presence of discrete reduction areas also suggests that flowing water has had relatively little effect on the integrity of artefact scatters over the medium term, other than the predictable removal of the smallest artefacts (Holdaway and Fanning 2014, 82–83).

The Group 8S taskscape is dispersed along Marandu Creek (Figure 6.16). Here, lines representing journeys connect grinding material and artefact concentrations. These journeys form a closer meshwork than that in Group 1A as paths cross and recross, reflecting a more uniform environment and greater concentration of activities on the alluvial plains. Artefact distribution is sparse but continuous, with localised concentrations, many of which probably relate to individual reduction events. The nearby creek line provides ready access to stone resources in the form of cobbles and pebbles. However, more extensive concentrations of artefacts, including ground stone artefacts, can be identified, particularly in association with Low Mulga Woodland/Open Forest (VC 3). In terms of resources, the different elements of the vegetation mosaic of mulga woodlands that dominate the plains are broadly similar (see Chapter 3). The marked evidence of concentration of activity within the one particular mulga woodland and open forest formation is thus intriguing. It might be explicable in terms of factors such as shade, ease of movement and ready access to other vegetation communities. Clearly this evidence of patterning in the distribution of surface archaeological material at a micro scale should be further investigated.

GROUP 9S

Unlike Group 8S, Group 9S was reported as a single discrete site (CB06-68/DAA 23997) (Ash, McHarg et al. 2009; Sinclair 2015b). Like CB08-114, CB06-68 occurs on an undulating silt and gravel plain. The site is crossed by numerous ephemeral drainage lines that drain into Marandu Creek situated to the west. CB06-68 is about two kilometres north of Group 8S and extends for nearly two kilometres along the line of Marandu Creek. The recorded site polygon covers an area of 0.57 km^2 (Figure 6.17). The northern section has a series of small, raised gravel terraces while large ephemeral soaks occur in the southern section. The site comprises a series of low to medium density artefact concentrations, largely occurring on raised gravel terraces (Figure 6.18). Like Group 8S, vegetation in the area is primarily a mulga woodland mosaic and, also like Group 8S, the recorded site largely coincides with the Low Mulga Woodland/Open Forest formation mapped as VC 3 (Figure 6.19).

CB06-68 was first identified in 2006 and recorded in seven stages, between August 2006 and September 2009. Stages 2 to 6 all involved changes in the site boundary and in two cases this also involved the incorporation of artefact scatters previously recorded as distinct sites into CB06-68 (Sinclair 2015b, 12). Stage 7 involved detailed recording and salvage collection of artefacts. A total of 1856 artefacts was recorded from 388 5 × 5 metre sample squares. The number of artefacts in each sample square ranged from one to 26, with a mean of 4.8 and a median of 4. The distribution was strongly skewed; only 25% of squares had more than six artefacts. Several discrete reduction areas were noted in the field. Artefacts are thus fairly evenly distributed (Figure 6.20).

Group 9S is clearly similar to Group 8S, in that it documents the past use of Marandu Creek as a sparse but continuous distribution of artefacts with localised concentrations, many of which relate to individual reduction events. Comparison of the site description with that of the two large sites in Group 8S (CB08-114 and CB08-115) indicates that in all three cases individual scatters of stone artefacts extend over quite large areas with concentrated patches particularly associated with gravel terraces.

SITE AND LANDSCAPE | 271

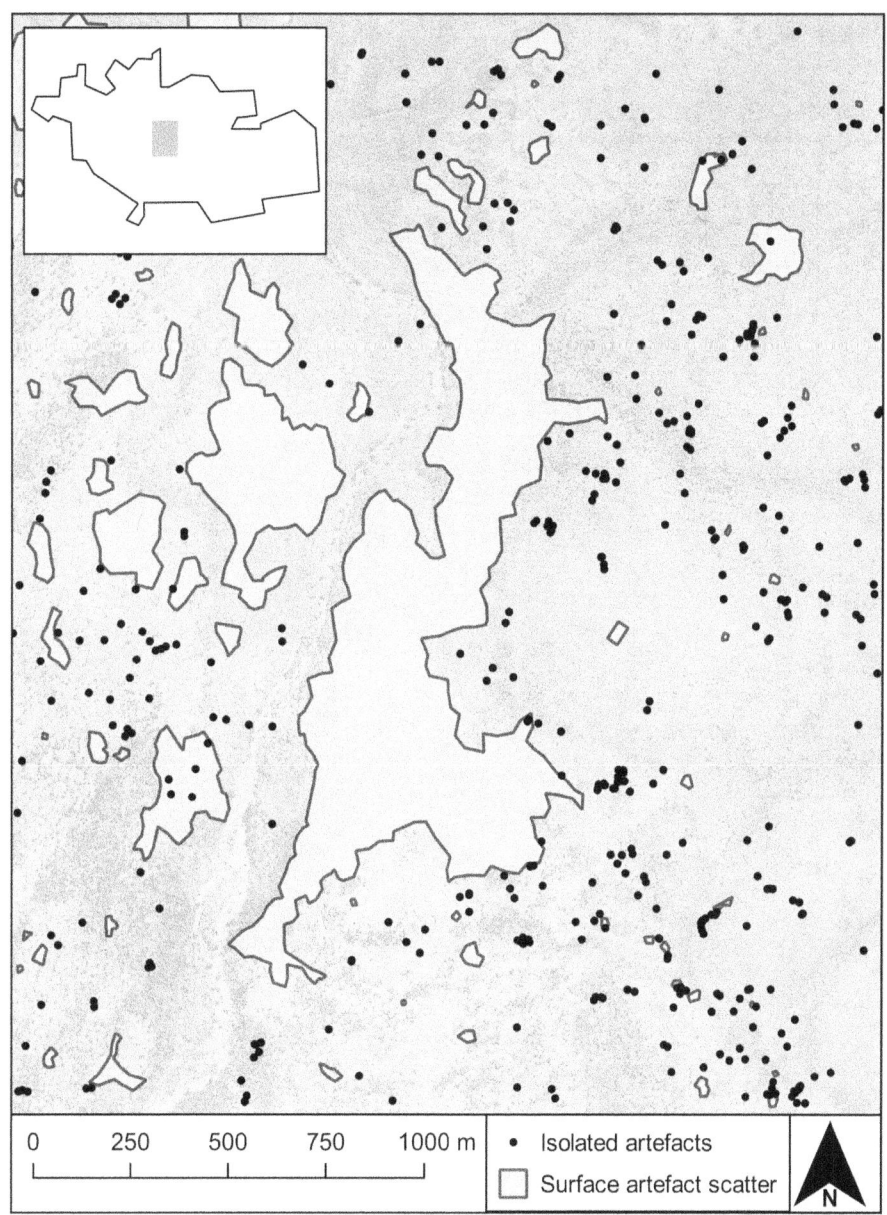

FIGURE 6.17: Group 9S (CB06-68): distribution of artefacts.

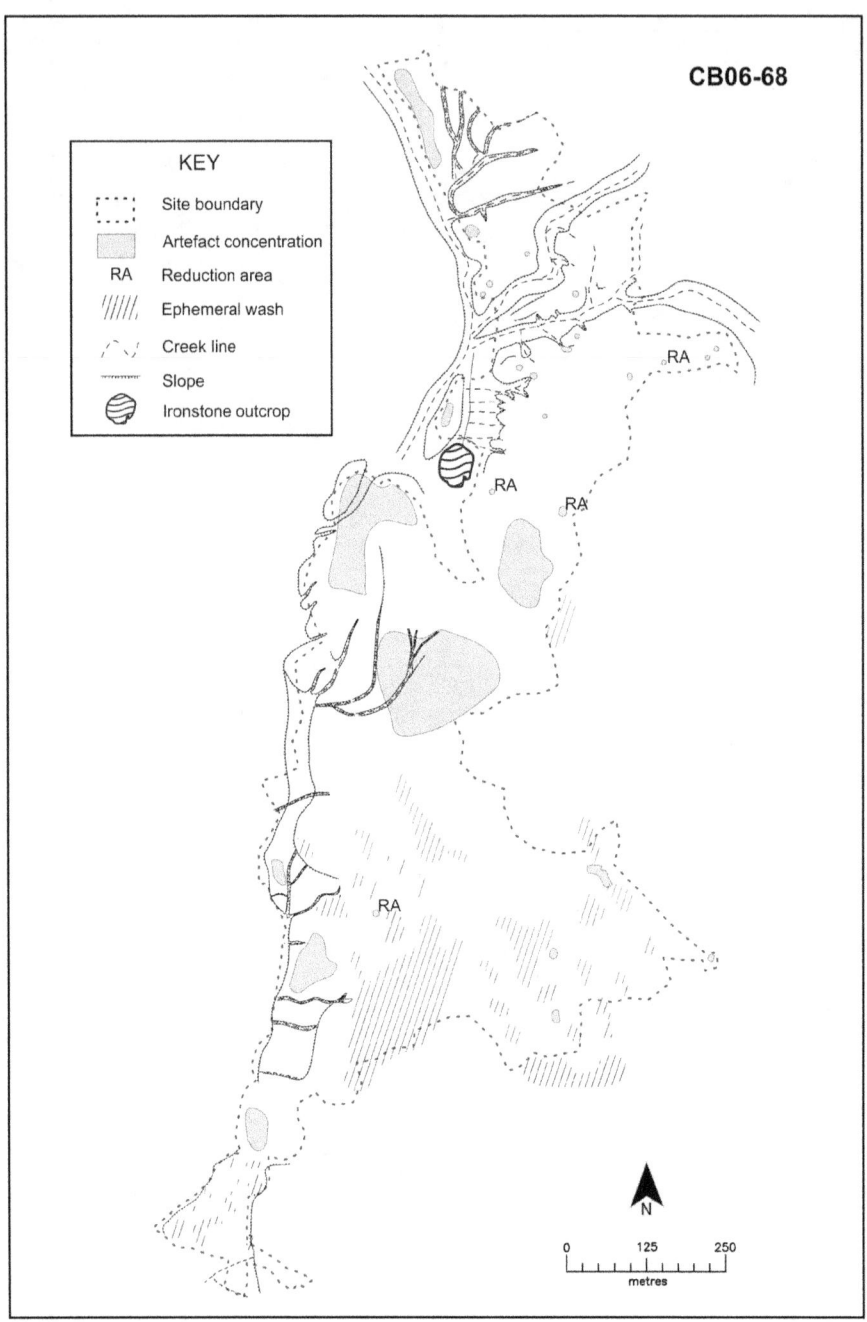

Figure 6.18: CB06-68: detailed site plan.

SITE AND LANDSCAPE | 273

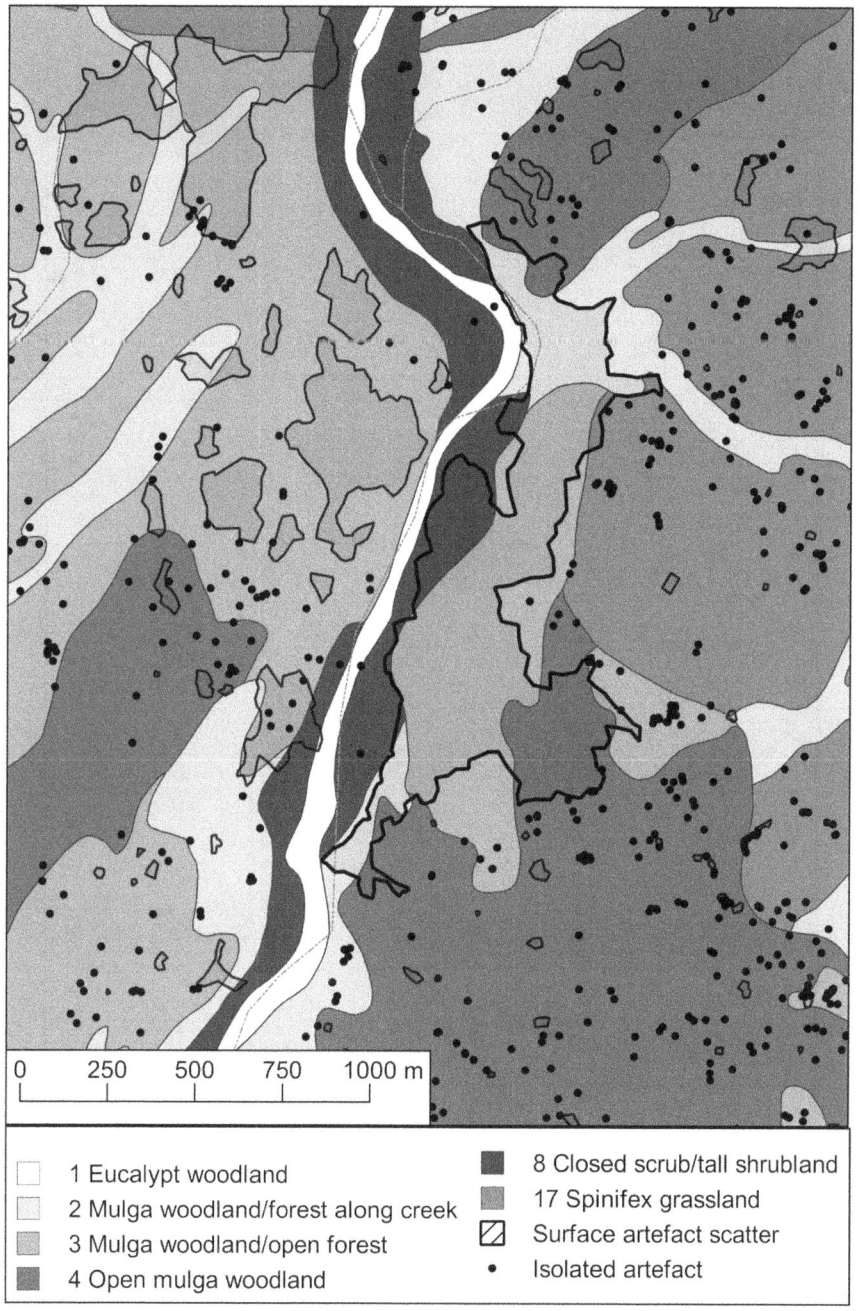

Figure 6.19: Distribution of surface artefact scatters and isolated artefacts in relation to vegetation in the vicinity of CB06-68 (Group 9S).

274 | CRAFTING COUNTRY

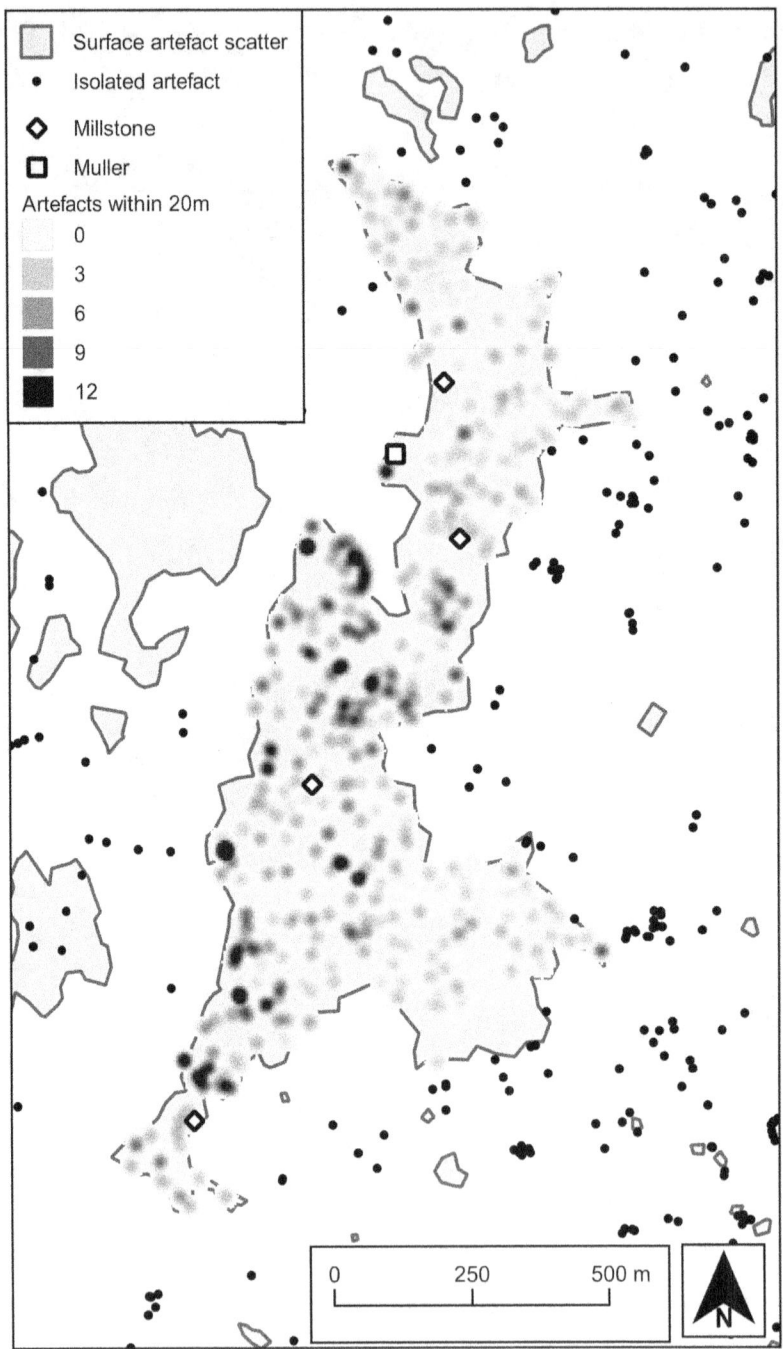

FIGURE 6.20: Group 9S: distribution of artefacts.

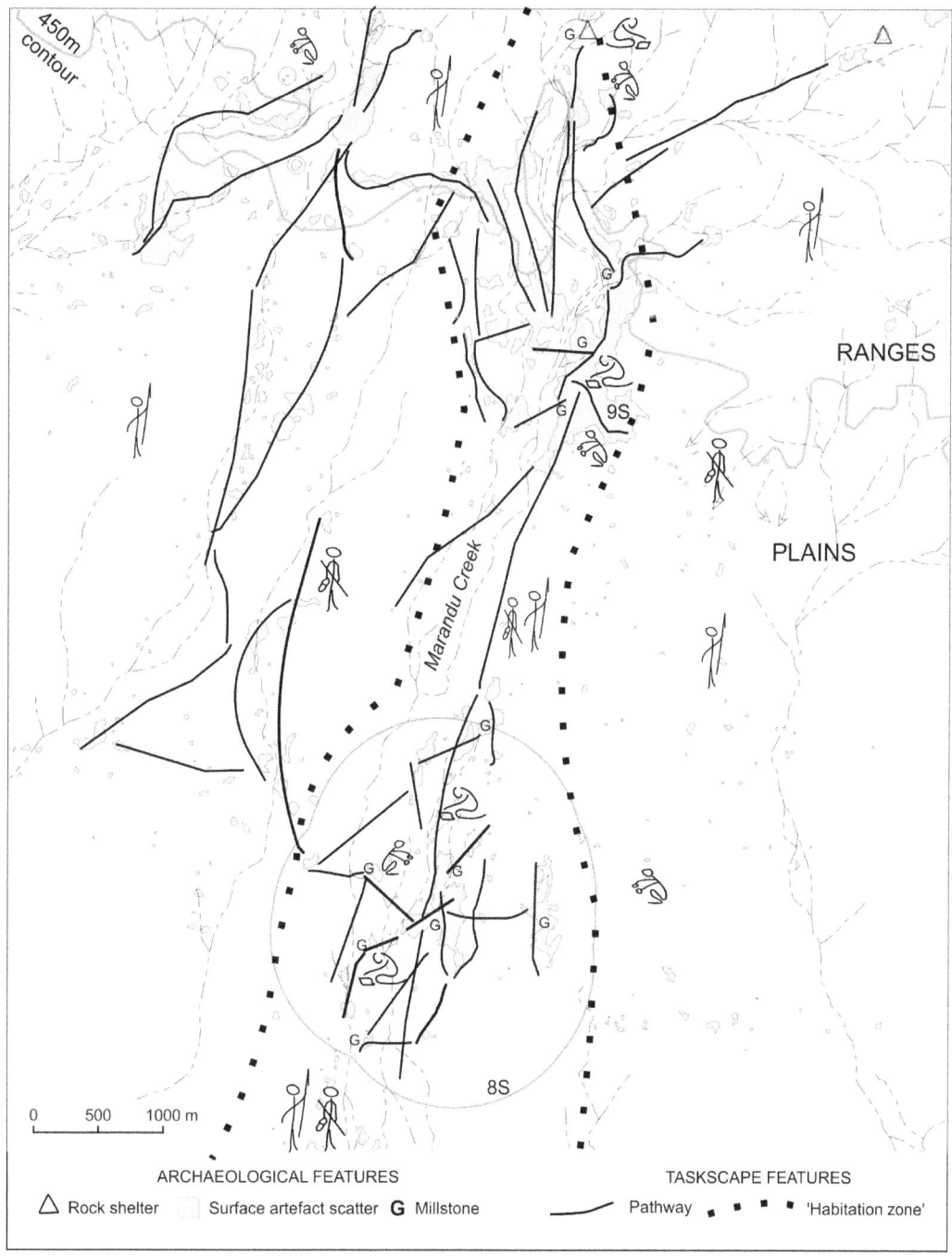

FIGURE 6.21: The Marandu Creek taskscape.

Together, Groups 8S and 9S sketch the Marandu Creek taskscape (Figure 6.21). At this scale, journeys represent the crossing and recrossing of pathways associated with dense artefact concentrations, as well as 'passing-through' country between persistent places. There is a tendency for artefact scatters to occur within a 'habitation zone' along the length of Marandu Creek. The large and dense artefact scatters with associated grinding material of Group 8S suggests a persistent place around this point on the creek, which is about midway between the Fortescue Marsh and the foothills of the Chichester Range, about 5 km from each. However, Group 9S is one of a group of large and dense artefact scatters around the outfall of Marandu Creek from the ranges. Thus, like the entrance to the Kakutungutanta Creek valley in Group 3B, the ecotone between the ranges and plains in this locality hosts a cluster of artefact scatters. About a kilometre further north into the ranges along Marandu Creek is the complex of rockshelters at CB10-40 and CB10-41. This group of shelters forms another persistent place, intensively used over about the last 1500 years.

PATTERNS IN THE ARCHAEOLOGICAL RECORD AT CHRISTMAS CREEK

These case studies show differences in land use in the study area's two major environments, as reflected in the surface archaeological record. Particularly on the plains, site definition is to a large extent arbitrary, although the overall distribution of archaeological remains is clearly patterned. Artefact distribution here is mostly linear, following creek lines. There is a tendency for denser 'patches', identified and recorded as archaeological sites, to be associated with Low Mulga Woodland/Open Forest (VC 3). At a micro scale, within the boundaries of a recorded site polygon, distribution of artefacts is also patchy. In the ranges, archaeological material is sparser, but more diverse in terms of site types, largely because of the occurrence of rockshelters and associated features. The distribution of these also appears patchy, as rockshelters with cultural material commonly occur as site complexes with different elements of the complex showing evidence of differential use (Bird, Rhoads and Hook 2019). Unsurprisingly, in this arid landscape, the association with creek lines is also clear, with the resulting distribution of

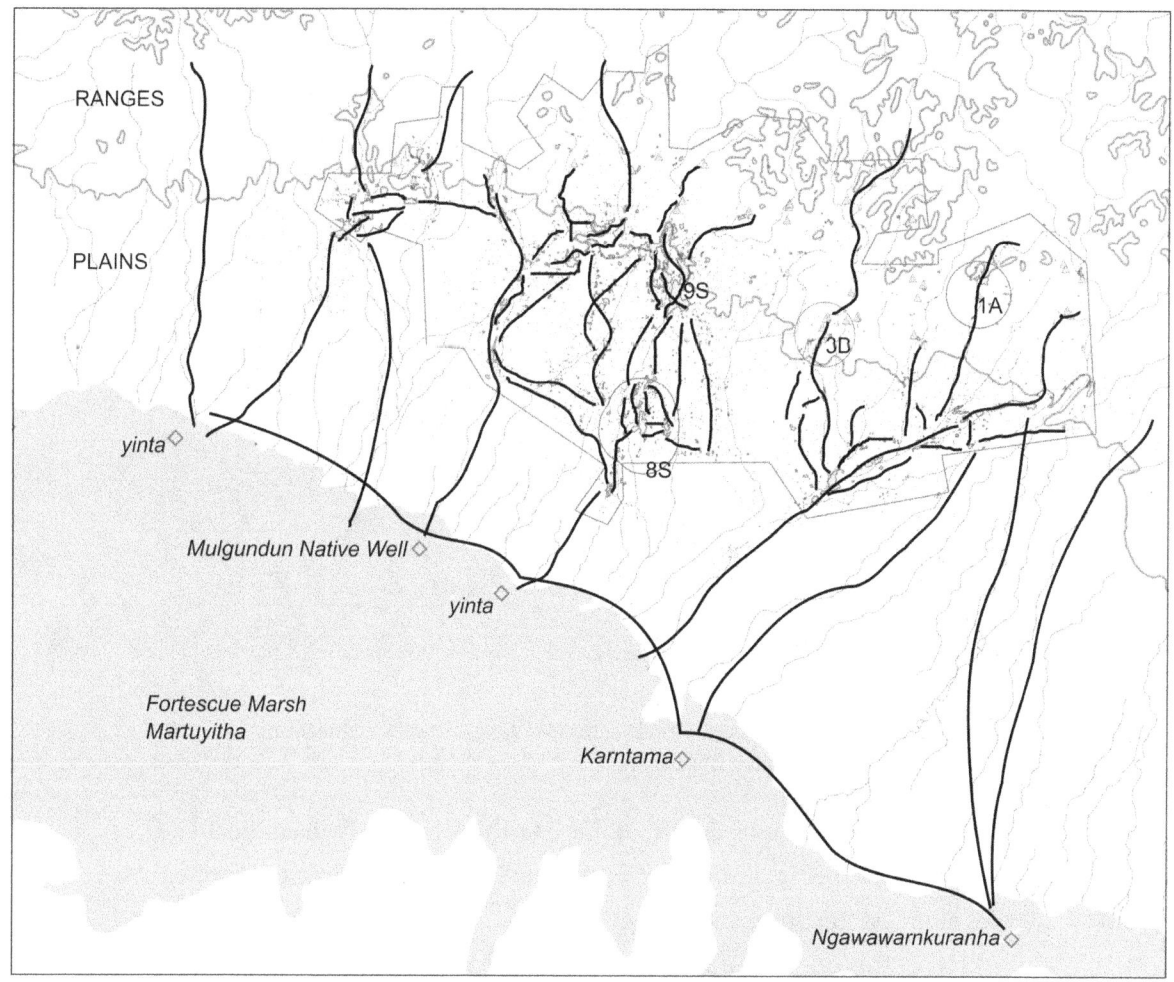

Figure 6.22: The Christmas Creek study area: local connections.

archaeological material structured by topography. In all four case studies, large surface artefact scatters show a similar pattern of patchy distribution of artefacts, with concentrations located on gravel rises and terraces interspersed with soaks. Individual concentrations within these sites are similar to small artefact scatters. Many of these individual concentrations seem to relate to procurement and reduction of raw material as it is encountered in the course of movement through the landscape.

We have already noted the general relationship between the distribution of archaeological remains and key watercourses (Chapter 4). At the scale of the Christmas Creek study area, the pathways between persistent places link

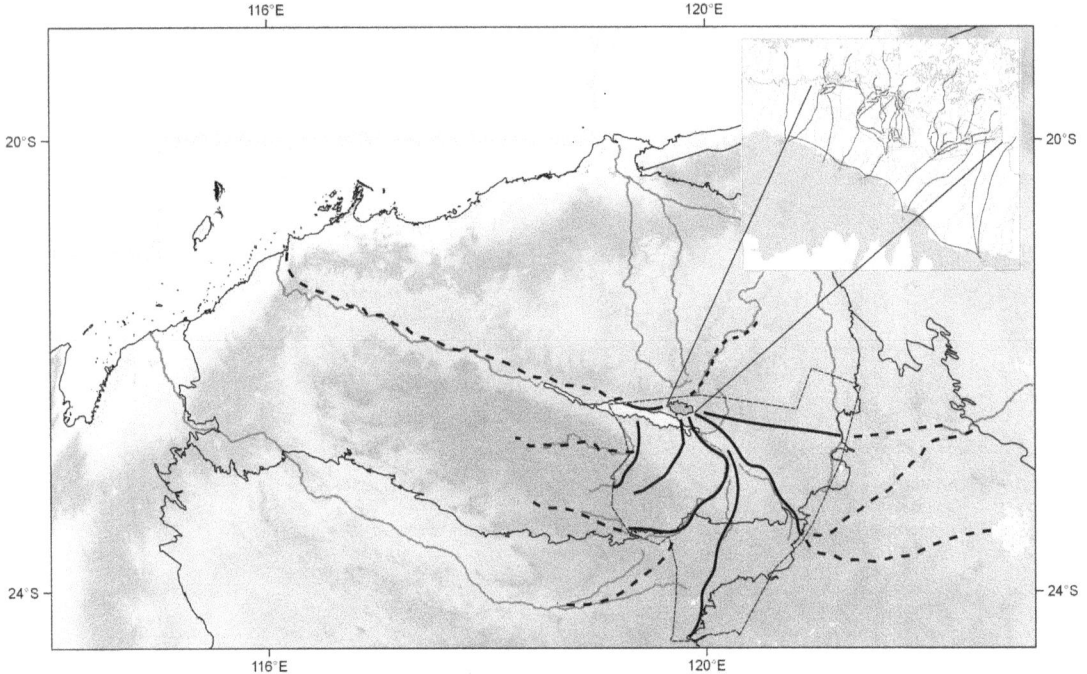

FIGURE 6.23: The Christmas Creek study area: long-distance connections within Nyiyaparli country and beyond.

the individual taskscapes described here to this broader hydrological and cultural landscape, including the Fortescue Marsh and the critical waterholes along its northern shore (Figure 6.22).

Placing this understanding of the archaeological record in time as well as space is, of course, problematic as the surface remains largely lack dating evidence. Detailed investigation of long-term site formation processes and geomorphology is generally beyond the scope of consulting archaeology as currently practised in the compliance context in Western Australia. Weathered and rolled artefacts have been recorded in the Christmas Creek area, but most appear relatively fresh. It seems likely, therefore, that much of the surface archaeological remains observed today relate to the most recent use of the area, and perhaps mainly to about the last 1500 years. At this time, climatic conditions and the flooding regime of the Fortescue Marsh were approaching those of the present following a period of aridity. The evidence from rockshelters suggests more widespread use of the area during this time, taking advantage of more reliable availability of water in the landscape. By

FIGURE 6.24: Baler shell (*Melo amphora*) from a surface artefact scatter in Nyiyaparli country.

contrast, between about 2000 and 4000 years ago, dated evidence of use of the area is almost entirely focused on a small group of rockshelters along Kakutungutanta Creek. This is also the location of the only surviving trace of Pleistocene occupation in the study area, and it is tempting to speculate that Kakutungutanta Creek itself is a long-lived persistent place perhaps dating back more than 40,000 years (Bird, Hook and Rhoads 2019).

Moving to the regional scale, we can consider how the Christmas Creek study area might be connected to the rest of Nyiyaparli country and beyond (Figure 6.23). Nyiyaparli country extends into the Hamersley Range through Weeli Wolli Creek, and eastwards to Jigalong and beyond into the desert. Songlines link the Christmas Creek area to Lake Disappointment. Archaeologically, finds of baler shell (Figure 6.24) link Nyiyaparli country to the coast. It is likely that people took stone from the study area with them, as they moved to stone-poor areas. There is almost no evidence for blade manufacture in the study area; the occasional finds of blades thus attest to movement of stone into the Christmas Creek area.

ABORIGINAL PERSPECTIVES ON LANDSCAPE USE

Consultation with Nyiyaparli elders at CB06-68 (Group 9S) highlights the cultural significance of this extensive artefact scatter and others like it. In this case, there was no objection to disturbance of the site by FMG's mining activities, with the proviso that the artefacts should be salvaged. The elders distinguish between different types of stone artefact scatters, characterising some as linked to the Dreaming through the use of tools by the 'Old People' for particular purposes, such as making boomerangs. In other situations, an artefact 'doesn't mean anything. It's just a thing that we use. It's a daily thing [that's] just been left as people been *travelling through*, you know?' (Coldrick and McDonald 2009, 11, emphasis added). Nevertheless, the elders emphasise that it is important to consult senior Nyiyaparli people about the specific significance of archaeological sites and that such sites should be salvaged. This particular consultation further linked archaeological material found at sites to songlines linking the permanent water sources, extending eastward into the desert as far as Lake Disappointment and west to the coast, as evidenced by finds of baler shells.

This interpretation is consistent with McDonald and Coldrick's (in press) account of the distinction made by Pilbara peoples generally between main sites or main camps, which can be characterised as persistent places, and small scatters comprising the by-products of tool making when the Old People were passing through. Main camps are considered culturally significant, while the small scatters are generally 'nothing to worry about'. Either of these categories, however, may contain individual artefacts (e.g. blades, grindstones) which themselves have intrinsic value. Veth (1993, 76–77) reports that the Martu of the Western Desert to the east of the study area make a similar emic distinction between main places and passing-through places and that these distinctions relate to permanency of water. For the Martu, main places are associated with permanent waters, which provide opportunities for aggregation, particularly at the end of the dry season.

Semi-permanent waters might be used for meetings at other times, but are usually characterised as passing-through places. Ephemeral waters are passing-through places, used only by small groups.

From an archaeological perspective, then, the surface archaeological record of the Christmas Creek study area reflects the distinction between main camps and passing-through places made by both Pilbara and Western Desert Aboriginal peoples. Many of the small scatters are essentially 'noise'. They represent individual events, some of which clearly relate to the embedded procurement of raw material as people move through the landscape. Patterning only emerges at a landscape scale, or when the palimpsest becomes dense and forms patches at persistent places. At this resolution, the differences between ranges and plains come into focus. The mulga woodlands of the plains primarily carry main camps, and the relative density of the archaeological record and the evidence from the analysis of cortex ratio at the landscape scale indicate relatively long visits and low residential mobility, focused particularly along the main watercourses. This concentration of archaeological evidence along watercourses reflects the role of these landscape features as preferred travelling routes (Walsh 2008, 65, 256–58). Much of the ranges, by contrast, is passing-through country, where residential mobility is higher. Here, activity is also focused on key watercourses, which serve as travel routes, with specific rockshelters and their associated site complexes acting as markers of persistent places and places of memory.

CHAPTER 7

CRAFTING COUNTRY

Landscape usefully connects archaeology with geography and anthropology, providing a long-term history of place and space and opening up a range of analytical possibilities (Gosden and Head 1994). Archaeological understandings of landscape range from ecological and economic perspectives, which view the environment as a stage for human activity or as a driver for human adaptation, to the idea of place and landscape as socially experienced and culturally constructed (David and Thomas 2008). The term 'cultural landscape' highlights the 'role of individuals who conceptualised these spaces and actively created and modified them in culturally specific ways' (Torrence 2002, 776).

Landscapes, then, are not passive backdrops to Aboriginal activity. On the contrary, they are shaped by ongoing social processes that produce 'taskscapes'. This heuristic device focuses our attention on how landscapes are perceived and experienced, not as scenery, but in terms of the collection of activities that occur there (Ingold 1993). Hunter-gatherer societies do not simply occupy space and use natural resources; rather, they actively transform the natural environment into an encultured territory. They accomplish this through interweaving the activities focused on meeting a range of economic, social and spiritual needs with the physical distribution of resources and landforms across their country. This perspective on the transformation of the natural world into a cultural landscape highlights the role of ongoing, active and creative engagement of people with the world around them (McDonald and Veth 2013b; Oetelaar and Meyer 2006). In this way, space is transformed into place through human action (Gosden and Head 1994, 115).

For hunter-gatherer groups, movement is a key strategy for addressing issues related to seasonal variations in resource abundance and distribution and thus travelling through country becomes a creative act. Ingold (2007, 83) describes how the act of inhabiting the landscape through travelling, or wayfaring, contributes to its weave and texture. The journeys of many individuals traced on the ground form a meshwork, with the knots in the meshwork forming places, as the consequence of the entanglement of many lives over time (Ingold 2007, 104). This imagery aptly describes the distribution of Aboriginal archaeological remains as the entangled knots, which comprise the threads of many individual lives through time that form persistent places (Schlanger 1992, 97). The sacred geography of the Dreaming in Australian Aboriginal culture is the epitome of the conceptual creation of a cultural landscape imbued with meaning, expressed as country that must be nurtured and protected through a network of rights and obligations (Gosden and Head 1994, 115). The travels of ancestral beings are, of course, the key agents in the creation of this sacred geography. The role of rock art in marking the land and signalling the socialisation of the landscape is well recognised (McDonald and Veth 2012; 2013b; Taçon 1994). Here we interpret the archaeological features of the Christmas Creek area as documenting the activities of past Aboriginal people as they travel through the land, thereby transforming the natural landscape into a socialised one – crafting country.

CREATING PERSISTENT PLACES

The idea that the activities of Aboriginal people transformed the land in a range of contexts and affected the distribution and productivity of resources is a familiar one. The best-known example is the acknowledged influence that human use of fire has on plant and animal populations (e.g. Bird et al.

2013; Hallam 1975; Head 1994; Jones 1969; Zeanah et al. 2017). Other comparable examples of niche construction have been explored with respect to human use of other forms of plant and animal resources (e.g. Atchison and Head 2012; Lullfitz et al. 2017; McNiven 2008).

We demonstrate that provisioning specific places comprises a key feature of the archaeology of the Christmas Creek area. Stockpiles of raw material, cores and manuports, as well as hammer stones for stone tool making and grinding material for food processing, were all regularly left at rockshelters, and often deliberately cached there. These fixed and prominent landmarks formed part of a meshwork of regularly visited places used logistically for storage and shelter. The structural modification of some shelters provided storage places, 'cupboards', to conceal important items and these places became incorporated into a socialised landscape (Bird, Rhoads and Hook 2019; see Taçon 1994). The visibility of rockshelters and their permanence in the landscape doubtless drew people's attention and they became places of memory, potentially charged with meaning (Bailey and Galanidou 2009).

It is more difficult to show that other places in the landscape were also provisioned. That this was indeed the case is borne out by how stone artefacts moved both into and out of the Christmas Creek study area. The analysis of cortex and volume ratios shows that stone artefact material, mostly in the form of cores, moved beyond the immediate Christmas Creek study area. Some cores were probably used to provision the relatively stone-poor margins of the Fortescue Marsh, arguably to underpin the exploitation of abundant resources following periodic flood events. Cores also formed part of the Aboriginal toolkit taken as portable supplies when visiting other areas, thus linking Christmas Creek to the larger social system of which it is known to have been a part. Archaeologically, provisioning of places with raw material has been demonstrated for the stone-poor dunes of Kinchega National Park in western New South Wales (Webb 1993), and for the Currawinya Lakes in south-west Queensland (Robins 1998). We note that there are also ethnographic accounts of transporting raw materials to particular places for future use. Gould, Koster and Sontz (1971, 163), for example, mention 16 pebbles carried 40 miles (64 km) from Partjar to Tika-tika where they were left for later use as hammer stones; they also note that individuals might carry stone with them from places to which they had a particular affinity. In Yanyuwa country, in the Gulf of Carpentaria, caches of glass and steel items can still be found (Bradley 2008, 634). The low proportion of retouched material observed in Christmas Creek assemblages is also consistent with a place-provisioning strategy (Barton and Riel-Salvatore 2014, 9). Some artefacts, such as adzes, did enter the study area as personal gear, and were sometimes replaced locally. The occasional presence of large blades at sites indicates the transport of these artefacts to the Chichester Ranges from blade quarries elsewhere in the Pilbara, also most probably as personal gear. However, the overall pattern is consistent with a strategy of provisioning places, albeit in a raw-material-rich environment and over relatively short distances.

The regular occurrence of grinding material along and near creek lines shows us that these artefacts were deliberately left for future use near regularly revisited places. Here, there were numerous features attractive for Aboriginal habitation, including shade, proximity to potential water in ephemeral creeks, raw material in the form of cobbles, and the resources of the fringing mulga woodlands, such as important plant foods and timber for artefacts and firewood. Again, ethnographic accounts report grindstones being stashed for future use at regularly visited camps (Guruma Elders Group et al. 2001, 87; Nicholson and Cane 1991, 340). Surface artefacts might themselves act as an attractor; cores and manuports left at repeatedly visited places offered a bank of raw material. The presence of artefacts then structures subsequent use of such locales, signalling that they have history and meaning as desirable places to camp (Bond 2009; 2013; Clarkson 2008; Hiscock 2014; Wragg-Sykes 2012).

Evidence for provisioning places with raw materials, tool-making gear and food processing equipment, as well as structural modifications of rockshelters directed towards storage, all demonstrate an active and cumulative transformation of the land that we characterise as 'crafting country'.

In the course of Western Australian compliance archaeological investigations, sites have necessarily been recorded as discretely bounded entities belonging to a particular type. Archaeological material present in the landscape at a density falling below an arbitrarily defined threshold is labelled as isolated artefacts, or part of a regional 'background scatter'. However, at Christmas Creek, where a comprehensive site survey was undertaken, such distinctions are more likely attributable to visibility and the obtrusiveness of particular types of archaeological remains. The implication is that similar activities occurred both on and off site and that the difference between them is quantitative not qualitative (Shott 2008, 59; Stern 1993). Therefore, it is a mistake to assume that variability in assemblage size necessarily indicates site function. Differences in sample size alone are a sufficient explanation.

So, what archaeologists commonly identify as 'sites' are places where activities frequently occurred or where natural processes reveal or preserve evidence of past activity. The main activity that is archaeologically visible at surface scatters is, of course, the manufacture of stone artefacts (Holdaway and Fanning 2014, 171). Many of these artefacts are 'just rubbish', the by-products of activities such as stone flaking or quarrying stone. Others represent making, using and repairing a range of equipment. Some artefacts are the result of encounters with raw material as people move through the landscape (Gamble 2006, 69–71). Other evidence marks the occurrence of deliberate actions – making fires or shelters. Some cultural remains represent deliberate constructive practices: producing art, leaving cores or grindstones at places to be used again, stone arrangements for ceremonies, fish traps, walled niches and the like. All are indicative of a taskscape – the lived and living landscape at the intersection between nature and culture.

In summary, Aboriginal archaeological sites are best viewed as concentrations, or patches within a broader distribution, or scatter, of cultural debris. Artefacts may be discovered anywhere, but the overall distribution of archaeological evidence is not uniform. In the Christmas Creek area, variability in the characteristics of the distribution of archaeological remains is evident in relation to landscape and topography, with the ranges and alluvial plains clearly differentiated. Concentrations of surface artefacts then commonly mark persistent places, revisited frequently. They are markers of a 'crafted country', the signs of a long-term socialised landscape.

SHARING ARCHAEOLOGICAL AND ABORIGINAL PERSPECTIVES

We explain how Christmas Creek's archaeological record serves as an example of the natural landscape's transformation into a cultural landscape. This crafted country reflects the journeys of past people as they inhabited, travelled through and interacted with the land, all of which contributed to 'the weave and texture of the world' (Ingold 2007, 83). Evidence for this resides within the country for the knowledgeable to read. For Aboriginal people, then, the whole land is imbued with meaning. The spiritual and ecological are inextricably intertwined and linked to country, thereby providing the basis for survival (Lewis 1976). Both stone artefacts and archaeological sites may be incorporated into these understandings. The Pilbara surface archaeological record is primarily formed by numerous individual events, which constitute a tangible record of past land use. This record can be observed and interpreted by archaeologists, and seen and understood by present-day Aboriginal groups as testimony of their connection to country.

There is now an ongoing sharing of ideas and practice between Aboriginal communities and archaeologists in Australia that results in a dynamic, evolving understanding of Aboriginal heritage (McDonald and Coldrick, in press). Bradley (2008), for example, describes the complex layers of meaning attributed to a stone quarry and the stone tools from it in terms of relationships between people, country and law in Yanyuwa country. Similarly, interpreting signs and marks on the land is central to the Aboriginal world view in both the sacred and secular spheres.

> These marks inform Aboriginal actors as to the nature of their food source and its environmental determinants, and the mythico-cosmological framework within which food-getting activities are defined. (Godwin and Weiner 2006, 125)

Archaeological remains constitute traces of the lives of ancestors and are commonly perceived in this way by contemporary Aboriginal peoples, who sometimes characterise artefact scatters as 'footprints of the ancestors' (Godwin and Weiner 2006, 130–31). McDonald and Coldrick (in press) highlight comparable views in their discussion of changing perspectives of Pilbara archaeological heritage. They note that some archaeological sites and materials are seen as an integral part of the ceremonial and mythological landscape and are strongly imbued with spiritual power. In particular, some quarries are the source of blades for use in male initiation ceremonies and retain special significance. Other archaeological sites are valued as the work of the ancestors, or Old People. Assessment of these sites may include information about how the land was used – sites in 'good camping country' distinguished from 'passing-through' country, such as the creek lines in the Chichester Ranges. Moreover, particular artefacts found at sites may also be valued for the stone from which they were made. Archaeological sites then remain important today because they are visible signs of how the Old People lived in the land for many thousands of years (Nyiyaparli Community, Bird and McDonald 2015).

Of course, archaeological remains were equally visible to the Old People. Discarded stone artefacts would arguably convey more information to individuals who, in the past, were well-versed in stone tool technology (Bond 2009; 2013; Hiscock 2014; Wragg-Sykes 2012). At the very least, these finds portray a socially constructed and enculturated landscape, marking places with a long history and meaning. These signals can be intuitively understood or deciphered by subsequent users of a locale, regardless of whether or not cultural continuity has occurred. In unfamiliar country, for example, evidence of past use is identified and interpreted in conjunction with other features of the landscape to indicate the presence of water (Lewis 1976, 277). Visible artefact accumulations also act as attractors for revisitation by marking places that were good for camping (persistent places) and by providing 'banks' of raw material easily scavenged and re-used (Bradley 2008, 634; Camilli and Ebert 1992). Tracing the distribution of stone artefacts in the landscape thus connects us with the travels and life histories of previous inhabitants. The taskscape, evidenced by these signs of past activities, denotes country crafted and socialised by the activities of past people.

The intertwined ideas of taskscape and crafting country present an interpretation of the archaeological record with inferred connections between persistent places and other key activity localities. From this perspective, the distribution of archaeological remains represents movement of both people and objects across country. Nyiyaparli understandings of this country are also expressed in terms of movement. Specifically, they describe the flows of water in the upper Fortescue catchment as being like blood passing through the veins and arteries of a person's body. The flow moves from the ranges to Martuyitha (the Fortescue Marsh) and its *yinta*, where creative spirits still live, and continues on down the Fortescue River to nourish and be nourished by other waters and communities downstream (Goode 2009; Nyiyaparli Community, Bird and McDonald 2015).

We maintain that archaeologists must learn to recognise a nuanced landscape, a crafted country, as a key means to communicate our own archaeological understandings to the Aboriginal community, as well as our own. This will allow us to develop significance assessments better grounded in archaeological theory and more in keeping with 21st century ideas about heritage practice. It requires us to think more deeply about the connections between and within sites, between site and landscape and how sites can be understood in terms of being in, travelling through and interacting with country. We can sum this up by advocating a shift in focus from individual 'sites' to an integrated understanding of places. This perspective on the archaeology stresses an active engagement with the land that is characteristic of Aboriginal experience of being 'on country'.

> Nyiyaparli country is full of the signs of the Kukutpa (Dreaming) when the ancestral spirits created the land. These places are very important to Nyiyaparli and many are very special and sacred. Over forty thousand years Aboriginal people have also left their mark on the landscape. All over Nyiyaparli country there are places with evidence of human activity. These places are special to the Nyiyaparli because they show how their ancestors lived in the land for many thousands of years. (Nyiyaparli Community, Bird and McDonald 2015, 34)

REFERENCES

Akerman, K. (2006). Cultural object stores project – preliminary investigations at Warburton Ranges and the Kimberley. In *For now and forever: an analysis of current and emerging needs for Aboriginal cultural stores and repositories in Western Australia*. G. Wallace and K. Akerman, eds. Appendix 1. Perth: Western Australian Museum.

Allen, H. (1997). The distribution of large blades: evidence for recent changes in Aboriginal ceremonial networks. In *Archaeology and linguistics: Aboriginal Australia in global perspective*. P. McConvell and N. Evans, eds. 357–76. Oxford: Oxford University Press.

Allen, H., S. Holdaway, P. Fanning, and J. Littleton (2008). Footprints in the sand: appraising the archaeology of the Willandra Lakes, western New South Wales, Australia. *Antiquity*, 82: 11–24.

Allen, J., and J.F. O'Connell (2014). Both half right: updating the evidence for dating first human arrivals in Sahul. *Australian Archaeology*, 79: 86–108.

Andrefsky, W. (2009). The analysis of stone tool procurement, production, and maintenance. *Journal of Archaeological Research*, 17(1): 65–103. http://doi.org/10.1007/s10814-008-9026-2.

Andrefsky, W. (2005). *Lithics: macroscopic approaches to analysis* (2nd edn). Cambridge: Cambridge University Press.

Archae-aus (2015). Report on the salvage of 25 Aboriginal archaeological sites and seven other heritage places in the Christmas Creek Windich and access road section 18, Christmas Creek project area (s18_038_NYI / 34-11186), Chichester Range, Pilbara, WA. Fremantle: Archae-aus Pty Ltd.

Ash, A., A. Di Lello, R. Stanger, J. Skippington and C.Y. Loo (2009). Report of an Indigenous archaeological assessment of the Fortescue Metals Group's Christmas Creek Overburden Area, Chichester Range, Pilbara. Fremantle: Archae-aus Pty Ltd.

Ash, A., K. McHarg, M. Wilson, C.Y. Loo, and J. Skippington (2009). Report of an Indigenous archaeological heritage assessment of the FMG Proposed Cathedrals Mining Area, Priority 1 – Christmas Creek, Pilbara. Fremantle: Archae-aus Pty Ltd.

Atchison, J., and L. Head (2012). Yam landscapes: the biogeography and social life of Australian *Dioscorea*. *The Artefact*, 35: 59–74.

Attenbrow, V. (2007). *What's changing: population size or land-use patterns? The archaeology of Upper Mangrove Creek, Sydney Basin*. Canberra: Australian National University E Press.

Attenbrow, V., and P. Hiscock (2015). Dates and demography: are radiometric dates a robust proxy for long-term prehistoric demographic change? *Archaeology in Oceania*, 50: 29–35. http://doi.org/10.1002/arco.5052

Australian Bushfoods (2019). Seed. www.ausbushfoods.com/map/resources/seed.htm.

Bailey, G. (2007). Time perspectives, palimpsests and the archaeology of time. *Journal of Anthropological Archaeology*, 26(2): 198–223.

Bailey, G., and N. Galanidou (2009). Caves, palimpsests and dwelling spaces: examples from the Upper Palaeolithic of south-east Europe. *World Archaeology*, 41(2): 215–41.

Bamforth, D.B. (1986). Technological efficiency and tool curation. *American Antiquity*, 51: 38–50.

Barton, C.M., and J. Riel-Salvatore (2014). The formation of lithic assemblages. *Journal of Archaeological Science*, 46: 334–52. http://doi.org/10.1016/j.jas.2014.03.031.

Barton, H. (2008). Expedient technologies and curated tools within a system of high residential mobility: an example using mass analysis of flakes from the Simpson Desert, Central Australia. *Lithic Technology*, 33(1): 51–71. http://doi.org/10.2307/23273620.

Barton, H. (2003). The thin film of human action: interpretations of arid zone archaeology. *Australian Archaeology*, 57: 32–41.

Beard, J. S. (1975). *Pilbara, 1:1 000 000 vegetation series: explanatory notes to Sheet 5: the vegetation of the Pilbara area*. Nedlands: University of Western Australia Press.

Beck, C., A.K. Taylor, G.T. Jones, C.M. Fadem, C.R. Cook, and S.A Millward (2002). Rocks are heavy: transport costs and Paleoarchaic quarry behavior in the Great Basin. *Journal of Anthropological Archaeology*, 21(4): 481–507. http://doi.org/10.1016/S0278-4165(02)00007-7.

Bednarik, R.G. (2006). *Australian apocalypse: the story of Australia's greatest cultural monument. Occasional AURA Publication 14*. Melbourne: Australian Rock Art Research Association.

Beesley, J. (1989). The scarred tree: a project for the Victoria Archaeological Survey. Unpublished report. Melbourne: Victorian Archaeological Survey.

Beesley, L.S. and J. Prince (2010). Fish community structure in an intermittent river: the importance of environment stability, landscape factors and within-pool habitat descriptors. *Marine and Freshwater Research*, 61: 605–14.

Bell D., P.L. Agar, J.R. Luyer and H.M. Robertson (2014). Winter bird assemblages of the Fortescue Marshes and surrounding vegetation, Pilbara Region, Western Australia. *Amytornis*, 6: 1–18.

Berndt, R.M. (1959). The concept of 'The Tribe' in the Western Desert of Australia. *Oceania*, 30(2): 81–107.

Berry, M. (2018). Murujuga desert, tide and Dreaming: understanding early rock art production and lifeways in Northwest Australia. Unpublished PhD thesis, University of Western Australia.

Bindon, P. (1998). *Useful bush plants*. Perth: Western Australian Museum.

Bindon, P., and M. Lofgren (1982). Walled rockshelters and a cached spear in the Pilbara region, Western Australia. *Records of the Western Australian Museum*, 10: 112–26.

Binford, L.R. (2001). *Constructing frames of reference: an analytical method for archaeological theory using hunter-gatherer and environmental data sets*. Berkeley: University of California Press.

Binford, L.R. (1982). The archaeology of place. *Journal of Anthropological Archaeology*, 1: 5–31. http://doi.org/10.1016/0278-4165(82)90006-X.

Binford, L.R. (1980). Willow smoke and dog's tails: hunter-gatherer settlement systems and archaeological site formation. *American Antiquity*, 45(1): 4–20. http://doi.org/10.2307/279653.

Binford, L.R. (1979). Organization and formation processes: looking at curated technologies. *Journal of Anthropological Research*, 35: 255–73.

Binford, L.R. (1978). Dimensional analysis of behavior and site structure: learning from an Eskimo hunting stand. *American Antiquity*, 43(3): 330–61. http://doi.org/10.2307/279390.

Biota Environmental Sciences (2003). Fauna habitats and fauna assemblage of the proposed FMG Stage B Rail Corridor and Mindy Mindy, Christmas Creek, Mt Lewin and Mt Nicholas Mine Area. Unpublished report for Fortescue Metals Group Pty Ltd, Perth, Western Australia.

Bird, C. (1985). Prehistoric lithic resource utilisation: a case study from the southwest of Western Australia. PhD thesis, University of Western Australia, Nedlands, WA.

Bird, C., A. Dias, F. Hook, M. Jimenez-Lozano, and H. Tierney (2014). Time and efficiency in data recovery: an experiment comparing wet and dry sieving in Pilbara rockshelter excavations. *Journal of the Australian Association of Consulting Archaeologists*, 1: 1–8.

Bird, C., and D. Frankel (1991). Problems in constructing a prehistoric regional sequence: Holocene southeast Australia. *World Archaeology*, 23(2): 179–92.

Bird, C., and S. Hallam (2006). *A review of archaeology and rock art in the Dampier Archipelago*. Perth: National Trust.

Bird, C., F. Hook, and J.W. Rhoads (2019). Tracing pathways: writing archaeology in Nyiyaparli country. Archaeology in Oceania 00:1–10. https://doi.org/10.1002/arco.5206

Bird, C., F. Hook, and J.W. Rhoads (2016). Reflections on CB08-500: alternative narratives, Aboriginal heritage and significance assessment in Western Australia. *Hunter Gatherer Research*, 2(3): 327–43.

Bird, C., and J.W. Rhoads (2015). Rockshelters as indicators of mobility patterns in the inland Pilbara. *Archaeology in Oceania*, 50: 37–46. http://doi.org/10.1002/arco.5055.

Bird, C., and J.W. Rhoads (2011). Topographic archaeology revisited: regional archaeological structure. In *'Fire and hearth' forty years on: essays in honour of Sylvia J. Hallam*. C. Bird and R.E. Webb eds. *Records of the Western Australian Museum*, 79 (Supplement): 109–22.

Bird, C., J.W. Rhoads, and F. Hook (2019). Persistent places and places of memory: archaeological evidence of long-term connection to country in the inland Pilbara, Western Australia. *Archaeological Review from Cambridge*, 34: 28-49.

Bird, R.B., and D.W. Bird (2008). Why women hunt: risk and contemporary foraging in a Western Desert Aboriginal community. *Current Anthropology*, 49(4): 655–93.

Bird, R.B., N. Taylor, B. Codding and D.W. Bird (2013). Niche construction and dreaming logic: Aboriginal patch burning and varanid lizards (*Varanus gouldii*) in Australia. *Proceedings of the Royal Society B*, 280: 20132297.

BirdLife International (2015). Important bird areas factsheet: Fortescue Marshes. www.birdlife.org/datazone/sitefactsheet.php?id=25148.

Blockley, J.G., I.J. Tehnas, A. Mandyczewsky, and R.C. Morris (1993). Proposed stratigraphic subdivision of the Marra Mamba Iron Formation and the Lower Wittenoom Dolomite. *Geological Survey of Western Australia Report*, 34: 47–63.

Bond, C.J. (2013). Experience and perception of memorable places: lithic scatters and mapping the British Neolithic. In *Place as material culture: objects, geographies and the construction of time*. D. Gheorghiu and G. Nash, eds. 86–122. Cambridge: Cambridge Scholars Publishing.

Bond, C.J. (2009). Biographies of stone and landscape: lithic scatters. *Internet Archaeology*, 26. https://doi.org/10.11141/ia.26.1.

Bowler J. M., K-H. Wyrwoll and Y. Lu 2001, Variations of the northwest Australian summer monsoon over the last 30,000 years: the paleohydrological record of the Gregory (Mulan) Lakes System. *Quaternary International*, 183–85: 63–80.

Bradley, J.J. (2008). When a stone tool is a dingo: country and relatedness in Australian Aboriginal notions of landscape. In *Handbook of Landscape Archaeology*. B. David and J. Thomas, eds. 633–37. Walnut Creek, CA: Left Coast Press.

Bradley, K., I. Piercy, M. Jimenez-Lozano, and L. Sinclair (2014). A report of the salvage of nine Aboriginal archaeological sites in the overburden section 18, Christmas Creek project area (S18_030_NYI / 22-05657), Chichester Range, Pilbara. Fremantle: Archae-aus Pty Ltd.

Brandenstein, C.G. von (1973). Place names of the north-west. *Western Australian Naturalist*, 12(5): 97–107.

Brandenstein, C.G. von (1972). The symbolism of the north-western Australian zig-zag design. *Oceania*, 42(3): 223–38.

Brandenstein, C.G. von (1970a). *Narratives from the north-west of Western Australia in the Ngarluma and Jindjiparndi languages*, Vols 1–3. Canberra: Australian Institute of Aboriginal Studies.

Brandenstein, C.G. von (1970b). The meaning of section names. *Oceania*, 41(1), 39–49.

Brandenstein, C.G. von (1967). The language situation in the Pilbara – past and present. *Papers in Australian Linguistics,* Vol. 2. Pacific Linguistics Series. Canberra: Australian National University.

Brown, A.R. (1913). Three tribes of Western Australia. *Journal of the Royal Anthropological Institute*, 43: 143–94.

Brown, A.R. (1912). The distribution of native tribes in part of Western Australia. *Man*, 12: 143–46.

Brown, S. (2012). Applying a cultural landscape approach in park management: an Australian scheme. *Parks*, 18(1): 99–110.

Brown, S. (2008). Mute or mutable? Archaeological significance, research and cultural heritage management in Australia. *Australian Archaeology*, 67: 19–30.

Brown, S. (1987). *Towards a prehistory of the Hamersley Plateau, northwest Australia*. *Occasional Papers in Prehistory* 6. Canberra: Department of Prehistory, Research School of Pacific Studies, Australian National University.

Brown, S.H., and K. Mulvaney (1983). Test pit excavations at Aboriginal Sites P4627, P4623, P5315 and P5316 Perth–Darwin National Highway Newman–Port Hedland Section. Prepared for the Main Roads Department. Perth: Main Roads Department.

Brown, V.A. (2015). Tool-stone resource management in the Weld Range, Midwest region, Western Australia. MA thesis, Department of Archaeology, University of Western Australia, Nedlands, WA.

Bureau of Meteorology Australia. (2014a). Climatic statistics for Australian locations: Newman. Canberra: BOM. www.bom.gov.au/climate/averages/tables/cw_007151.shtml.

Bureau of Meteorology Australia. (2014b). Climatic statistics for Australian locations: Wittenoom. Canberra: BOM. http://www.bom.gov.au/climate/averages/tables/cw_005026.shtml.

Burke, H., and C. Smith (2004). *The archaeologist's field handbook*. Sydney: Allen & Unwin.

Byrne, D. (1980). Dynamics of dispersion: the place of silcrete in archaeological assemblages from the Lower Murchison, Western Australia. *Archaeology and Physical Anthropology in Oceania*, 15: 110–19.

Byrne, D. (1996). Deep nation: Australia's acquisition of an Indigenous past. *Aboriginal History*, 20: 82–107.

Camilli, E.L., and J.I. Ebert (1992). Artifact reuse and recycling in continuous surface distributions and implications for interpreting land use patterns. In *Space, time and archaeological landscapes*. J. Rossignol and L. Wandsnider, eds. 113–36. New York: Plenum Press.

Cane, S. (2013). *First footprints: the epic story of the first Australians.* Sydney: Allen & Unwin.

Cane, S. (1987). Australian Aboriginal subsistence in the Western Desert. *Human Ecology* 15(4): 391–434.

Carver, M. (2011). *Making archaeology happen: design versus dogma.* Walnut Creek, CA: Left Coast Press.

Clark, J.E. (1986). Another look at small debitage and microdebitage. *Lithic Technology*, 15(1): 21–33. http://doi.org/10.2307/41999847.

Clarke, C. (1983). Adding figures to the landscape: an overlooked Aboriginal contribution to an archaeological survey, Pilbara, WA. In *Archaeology at ANZAAS 1983.* M.V. Smith, ed. 20–28. Perth: Western Australian Museum.

Clarkson, C. (2008). Lithics and landscape archaeology. In *Handbook of Landscape Archaeology.* B. David and J. Thomas, eds. 490–501. Walnut Creek, CA: Left Coast Press.

Clarkson, C. (2007). *Lithics in the land of the Lightning Brothers.* Terra Australis 25. Canberra: ANU E Press.

Clarkson, C. (2006). Interpreting surface archaeology in Wardaman country, Northern Territory: an ecological approach. In *An archaeological life: papers in honour of Jay Hall.* S. Ulm and I. Lilley, eds. 177–90. Brisbane: Aboriginal and Torres Strait Islanders Unit, University of Queensland.

Clarkson, C., Z. Jacobs, B. Marwick, R. Fullagar, L. Wallis, M. Smith et al. (2017). Human occupation of northern Australia by 65,000 years ago. *Nature*, 547(7663): 306–10. http://doi.org/10.1038/nature22968.

Clarkson, C., and S. O'Connor (2014). An introduction to stone artifact analysis. In *Archaeology in practice: a student guide to archaeological analyses* (2nd edn). J. Balme and A. Paterson, eds. 151–206. Chichester: Wiley-Blackwell.

Clement, E. (1903). Ethnographic notes on the Western Australian aborigines (with a descriptive catalogue of a collection of ethnographic objects from Western Australia by J. D. E. Schultz). *Publications of the Royal Ethnographical Museum at Leiden*, Series II (6): 1–29.

Close, A.E. (2000). Reconstructing movement in prehistory. *Journal of Archaeological Method and Theory*, 7(1): 49–77. http://doi.org/10.1023/A:1009560628428.

Clune, G. (2002). Abydos: an archaeological investigation of Holocene adaptations on the Pilbara coast, northwestern Australia. PhD thesis, University of Western Australia, Nedlands, Western Australia.

Clune, G., and R. Harrison (2009). Coastal shell middens of the Abydos coastal plain, Western Australia. *Archaeology in Oceania*, 44 (Supplement): 70–80.

Codding, B.F. (2011). 'Any kangaroo?': on the ecology, ethnography and archaeology of Australia's arid west. PhD thesis, Stanford University, Palo Alto, CA.

Coffey Environments (2014). Significant species management plan Wodgina DSO Project (north Chichester Range), unpublished report for Atlas Iron Ltd, Perth, Western Australia. www.atlasiron.com.au/IRM/Company/ShowPage.aspx?CategoryId=190&CPID=5391&EID=90163124.

Coldrick, B., and E.M. McDonald (2009). Report of an ethnographic survey and consultation regarding archaeological sites at FMG's Cathedrals Mining Area, Christmas Creek, Pilbara, Western Australia, FMG Survey Request ETH_NYI_069. Melville, WA: Ethnosciences.

Colley, S. (2002). *Uncovering Australia: archaeology, Indigenous people and the public.* Washington DC: Smithsonian Institution Press.

Comtesse, S. (2003). Mt. Newman sites re-analysed: Newman Orebody XXIX,

Newman rockshelter and P0959. University of Western Australia. BSc (Hons) thesis, Archaeology, University of Western Australia, Nedlands, Western Australia.

Contreras, D.A., and J. Meadows (2014). Summed radiocarbon calibrations as a population proxy: a critical evaluation using a realistic simulation approach. *Journal of Archaeological Science*, 52: 592–608.

Craig, T., and K. Bradley (2014). A report of the salvage of 17 Aboriginal archaeological sites within the Christmas Creek conveyor and infrastructure Section 18 area (S18_051 / 34-14490), Chichester Range, Pilbara. Fremantle: Archae-aus Pty Ltd.

Crawford, I. (1982). *Traditional Aboriginal plant resources in the Kalumburu area: aspects in ethno-economics*. Perth: Western Australian Museum.

Cropper, D.N. (2018). Excavations at Jundaru (HN-A9) Rockshelter. In *Rockshelter excavations in the East Hamersley Range, Pilbara region, Western Australia*. D.N. Cropper and W.B. Law, eds. 91–170. Oxford: Archaeopress.

Cropper, D.N., and W.B. Law, eds (2018a). *Rockshelter excavations in the East Hamersley Range, Pilbara region, Western Australia*. Oxford: Archaeopress.

Cropper, D.N., and W.B. Law (2018b). Summary and discussion of rockshelter investigations at Hope Downs 1. In *Rockshelter excavations in the East Hamersley Range, Pilbara region, Western Australia*. D.N. Cropper and W.B. Law, eds. 435–54. Oxford: Archaeopress.

Crowley, G.M. (1996). Late Quaternary mangrove distribution in northern Australia. *Australian Systematic Botany*, 9: 219–25.

David, B., and J. Thomas (2008). Landscape archaeology: introduction. In *Handbook of landscape archaeology*. B. David and J. Thomas, eds. 27–43. Walnut Creek, CA: Left Coast Press.

Davis, R.A., J.A. Wilcox, B.M. Metcalf, and M.J. Bamford (2005). Fauna Survey of Proposed Iron Ore Mine, Cloud Break, for Fortescue Metals Group. Perth: unpublished report.

Day, B., and E. McDonald (2008). Report on ethnographic consultation with the Karlka Nyiyaparli Association in relation to Fortescue Metals Group's proposed mine extensions, Christmas Creek, Pilbara, Western Australia. Melville, WA: Ethnosciences.

De Deckker P., T.T. Barrows and J. Rogers (2014). Land–sea correlations in the Australian region: post-glacial onset of the monsoon in northwestern Western Australia. *Quaternary Science Reviews*, 105: 181–94.

De Lange, Josara (2008). Time perspectivism and the structure of archaeological records. In *Time in archaeology: time perspectivism revisited*. S. Holdaway and L. Wandsnider, eds. 149–60. Salt Lake City: University of Utah Press.

Dench, A.C. (1998). What is a Ngayarta language? A reply to O'Grady and Laughren, *Australian Journal of Linguistics*, 18: 91–107.

Dench, A.C. (1996). Pilbara verbal morphology and the Western Desert: some first steps towards a comparative reconstruction. Paper presented at *Where did the Western Desert languages come from?* Workshop held at the Australian Linguistic Institute, ANU, Canberra, 10 July 1996.

Dench, A.C. (1987). Kinship and collective activity in the Ngayarda languages of northwest Western Australia. *Language in Society*, 16: 321–39.

Dias, A. (2010). Report of an archaeological test excavation of CB08-427 at Fortescue Metal Groups' Christmas Creek Resource, Chichester Range, Pilbara. Fremantle: Archae-aus Pty Ltd.

Dias, A., and F. Hook (2012). Report on the archaeological test excavation of DIA 9947 / Y02-12, DIA 20566 / Y02-16, DIA 22165 / JSE04-02 and DIA 2216 / JSE04-03, April 2012 for Rio Tinto Iron Ore. Fremantle: Archae-aus Pty Ltd.

Dias, A., F. Hook, and B. Veitch (2006). Report of the test excavation of four Aboriginal archaeological sites, on the West Angelas Mining Lease, Pilbara, Western Australia. Fremantle: Pilbara Iron and Archae-aus.

Dias, A., and S. Rapley (2014). New radiocarbon dates from the Chichester Range, Pilbara, Western Australia. *Journal of the Australian Association of Consulting Archaeologists*, 2: 9–14.

Dias, A., and S. Rapley (2013). A report of an Aboriginal archaeological assessment of six rockshelters (DAA 29117 / CB10-88, DAA 29118 / CB10-92, DAA 29119 / CB10 093, CB10-98, DAA 30390 / CB10-123 and DAA 29124 / CB10-147) within the Christmas Creek Resource, November 2013. Fremantle: Archae-aus Pty Ltd.

Dibble, H.L., U.A. Schurmans, R.P. Lovita, and M.V. McLaughlin (2005). The measurement and interpretation of cortex in lithic assemblages. *American Antiquity*, 70(3): 545–60.

Ditchfield, K. (2017). Pleistocene–Holocene coastal mobility patterns in the Carnarvon bioregion, North-Western Australia. Unpublished PhD thesis, University of Western Australia.

Ditchfield, K. (2016). An experimental approach to distinguishing different stone artefact transport patterns from debitage assemblages. *Journal of Archaeological Science*, 65: 44–56. http://doi.org/http://dx.doi.org/10.1016/j.jas.2015.10.012.

Ditchfield, K., S. Holdaway, and M.S. Allen (2014). Measuring stone artefact transport: the experimental demonstration and pilot application of a new method to a prehistoric adze workshop, southern Cook Islands. *Journal of Archaeological Science*, 50: 512–23.

Dixon, R.M.W. (2002). *Australian languages: their nature and development*. Cambridge: Cambridge University Press.

Doelman, T., J. Webb, and M. Domanski (2001). Source to discard: patterns of lithic raw material procurement and use in Sturt National Park, northwestern New South Wales. *Archaeology in Oceania*, 36(1), 15–33.

Dogramaci, S., G. Skrzypek, W. Dodson, W., and P.F. Grierson (2012). Stable isotope and hydrochemical evolution of groundwater in the semi-arid Hamersley Basin of subtropical northwest Australia. *Journal of Hydrology*, 475: 281–93.

Dortch, J., and T. Sapienza (2016). Site Watch: recent changes to Aboriginal heritage site registration in Western Australia. *Journal of Australian Association of Consulting Archaeologists*, 4: 1–12.

Douglass, M.J. (2010). The archaeological potential of informal lithic technologies: a case study of assemblage variability in western New South Wales, Australia. PhD thesis, University of Auckland, New Zealand.

Douglass, M.J., S.J. Holdaway, P.C. Fanning, and J.I. Shiner (2008). An assessment and archaeological application of cortex measurement in lithic assemblages. *American Antiquity*, 73(3): 513–26. http://doi.org/10.2307/25470502.

Dunnell, R.C., and W.S. Dancey (1983). The siteless survey: a regional scale data collection strategy. *Advances in Archaeological Method and Theory*, 6: 267–87.

Durlacher, J.S. (2013). *Landlords of the iron shore*. Perth: Hesperian Press.

Ebert, J. (1992). *Distributional archaeology*. Albuquerque: University of New Mexico Press.

Edwards, K. (2014). A report on the Aboriginal archaeological heritage assessments conducted in 2010 at Fortescue Metals Group's Cloudbreak and Christmas Creek Mining Resources and Nyidinghu/Marillana tenement and Horatio Exploration Areas. Fremantle: Archae-aus Pty Ltd.

Edwards, K. (2011). Report of an archaeological test excavation of CB09-249 in FMG's Eyre Pit East and North Treacheries

Pit project; Chichester Range, Pilbara. Fremantle: Archae-aus Pty Ltd.

Edwards, K., and T. Craig (2011). Report of an Indigenous archaeological assessment of the Fortescue Metals Group's Central Christmas Creek Mining area. Fremantle: Archae-aus Pty Ltd.

Edwards, K., and F. Hook (2011). A report on the archaeological excavation of CB09-55, CB10-116, CB10-117 and CB10-133 in FMG's Christmas Creek Central project area; Chichester Range, Pilbara. October 2011. Fremantle: Archae-aus Pty Ltd and Fortescue Metals Group.

Edwards, K., and A. Murphy (2003). A preliminary report on archaeological investigations at Malea Rockshelter, Pilbara region, Western Australia. *Australian Archaeology*, 56: 44–46.

Edwards, K., and S. Rapley (2011). Preliminary advice of an Indigenous archaeological assessment of survey request Areas NYI 143, NYI 161 and NYI 163, salvage within the Conveyor and Infrastructure Area and test excavation of two rock shelters and four walled niches. November, Stage 2. Fremantle: Archae-aus Pty Ltd.

Edwards, K., L. Sinclair, M. Jimenez-Lozano, T. Martens and N. Wright (2012). A report of the salvage of 21 Indigenous archaeological sites in the CCY2 and CC Airstrip Project Areas, Chichester Range, Pilbara. Fremantle: Archae-aus Pty Ltd.

Eerkens, J.W., J.R. Ferguson, M.D. Glascock, C.E. Skinner, and S.A. Waechter (2007). Reduction strategies and geochemical characterization of lithic assemblages: a comparison of three case studies from western North America. *American Antiquity*, 72(3): 585–97.

Fanning, P., and S. Holdaway (2001). Stone artifact scatters in western NSW, Australia: geomorphic controls on artifact size and distribution. *Geoarchaeology: An International Journal*, 16(6): 667–86. http://doi.org/10.1002/gea.1015.

Fitzsimmons, K.E., T.J. Cohen, P.P. Hesse, J.D. Jansen, G.C. Nanson, J.H. May et al. (2013). Late Quaternary palaeoenvironmental change in the Australian drylands. *Quaternary Science Reviews*, 74: 78–96. http://doi.org/10.1016/j.quascirev.2012.09.007.

Flenniken, J.J., and J.P. White (1985). Australian flaked stone tools: a technological perspective. *Records of the Australian Museum*, 36: 131–51.

Foley, R. (1981a). A model of regional archaeological structure. *Proceedings of the Prehistoric Society*, 47: 1–17. http://doi.org/10.1017/S0079497X00008823.

Foley, R. (1981b). Off-site archaeology: an alternative approach for the short-sited. In *Pattern of the past: essays in honour of David Clarke*. I. Hodder, G. Isaac and N. Hammond, eds. 152–84. Cambridge: Cambridge University Press.

Foley, R.A., and M.M. Lahr (2015). Lithic landscapes: early human impact from stone tool production on the Central Saharan environment. *Plos One*, 10(3): e0116482. http://dx.plos.org/10.1371/journal.pone.0116482.

Fortescue Metals Group (2013). Christmas Creek life of mine flora and vegetation assessment – update. https://consultation.epa.wa.gov.au/seven-day-comment-on-referrals/christmas-creek-iron-ore-mine-expansion/supporting_documents/Flora and Vegetation Assessment.pdf.

Fortescue Metals Group (2011). Significant flora, vegetation, fauna and fauna habitats of the Special Rail Licence. http://reports.fmgl.com.au/ENVIRO/Additional Rail EPBC/Appendices/Appendix 7 Flora Vegetation Fauna Report.pdf.

Frankel, D. (1991). *Remains to be seen: archaeological insights into Australian prehistory*. Melbourne: Longman Cheshire.

Frankel, D. (1988). Characterising change in prehistoric sequences: a view from Australia. *Archaeology in Oceania*, 23: 41–78.

Frawley, S., and S. O'Connor (2010). A 40,000 year wood charcoal record from Carpenter's Gap 1: new insights into palaeovegetation change and Indigenous foraging strategies in the Kimberley, Western Australia. In *Altered ecologies: fire, climate and human influence on terrestrial landscapes.* S.G. Haberle, J. Stevenson and M. Prebble, eds. 299–323, *Terra Australis 32.* Canberra: Australian National University.

Fullagar, R., and L. Wallis (2012). Usewear and phytoliths on bedrock grinding patches, Pilbara, north-western Australia. *The Artefact: Journal of the Archaeological and Anthropological Society of Victoria*, 35: 75–87.

Gamble, C. (2006). *The Palaeolithic societies of Europe* (2nd edn). Cambridge: Cambridge University Press.

Gammage, B. (2011). *The biggest estate on earth: how Aborigines made Australia.* Sydney: Allen & Unwin.

Geytenbeek, B. and Wangka Maya linguists (n.d). Nyiyaparli: language details. www.wangkamaya.org.au/pilbara-languages/nyiyaparli-overview.

Gliganic, L.A., T.J. Cohen, J.H. May, J.D. Jansen, G.C. Nanson, A. Dosseto et al. (2014). Late-Holocene climatic variability indicated by three natural archives in arid southern Australia. *The Holocene*, 24(1), 104–17. http://doi.org/10.1177/0959683613515732.

Godwin, L., and J.F. Weiner (2006). Footprints of the ancestors: the convergence of anthropological and archaeological perspectives in contemporary Aboriginal heritage studies. In *The social archaeology of Indigenous societies.* B. David, B. Barker and I. McNiven, eds. 124–38. Canberra: Australian Aboriginal Studies Press.

Goode, B. (2009). Report on an ethnographic Aboriginal heritage survey of Christmas Creek hydrological system, Western Australia. Melville, WA: Ethnosciences.

Gosden, C., and L. Head (1994). Landscape – a usefully ambiguous concept. *Archaeology in Oceania*, 29(3): 113–16.

Gould, R. (1980). *Living archaeology.* Cambridge: Cambridge University Press.

Gould, R.A., D.A. Koster, and A.H.L. Sontz (1971). The lithic assemblage of the Western Desert Aborigines of Australia. *American Antiquity*, 36(2): 149–69. http://doi.org/10.2307/278668.

Graesch, A.P. (2009). Fieldworker experience and single-episode screening as sources of data recovery bias in archaeology: a case study from the central Pacific Northwest coast. *American Antiquity*, 74(4), 759–79. http://doi.org/10.2307/20622474.

Green, N., F. Hook, G. Jackson, S. Mitchell, L. Shipley, and A. Walster (1994). The report of an Aboriginal heritage survey of the southern section (Wiluna to Kambalda) of the Goldfields gas transmission pipeline route and corridor, Western Australia, Vol. 2. Perth: Department of Indigenous Affairs.

Griffiths, B. (2018). *Deep time Dreaming: uncovering ancient Australia.* Carlton: Black Inc.

Guruma Elders Group, L. Brehaut, P. Stevens, and A. Vitenbergs (2001). *The Guruma story: Guruma-yharntu wangka.* Alice Springs: IAD Press.

Haberle, S., F. Hopf and P. Roberts (2018). Sedimentary, charcoal and palynological analysis of Djadjiling (HD07-1A-04), HD07-3A-PAD13, HD07-3A-03, HS-A1, Jundaru (HN-A9) Rockshelters, Pilbara, Western Australia. In *Rockshelter excavations in the East Hamersley Range, Pilbara region, Western Australia.* D.N. Cropper and W.B. Law, eds. 385–99. Oxford: Archaeopress.

Hallam, S.J. (1975). *Fire and hearth.* Canberra: Australian Institute of Aboriginal Studies.

Hamm, G., P. Mitchell, L.J. Arnold, G.J. Prideaux, D. Questiaux, N.A. Spooner, et al. (2016). Cultural innovation and megafauna interaction in the early settlement of arid Australia. *Nature.* http://doi.org/10.1038/nature20125

Hammer, Ø. (2013). *PAST: Palaeolontological statistics version 3.0 reference manual.*

Natural History Museum, University of Oslo.

Hammer, Ø., D.A.T. Harper, and P.D. Ryan (2001). PAST: Paleontological Statistics Software Package for Education and Data Analysis. *Palaeontologia Electronica*, 4(1): 9.

Harrison, R. (2004). *Shared landscapes: archaeologies of attachment and the pastoral industry of New South Wales*. Sydney: University of New South Wales Press.

Hayden, B. (1986). Resource models of inter-assemblage variability. *Lithic Technology*, 15(3): 82–9.

Hayes, A., and S. Hayes (2007). *Ngambunyjarri Thalanyjibarndi yininyjarri: Ngambunyjarri: Thalanyji plant names and uses*. Port Hedland: Wangka Maya.

Head, L. (2008). Geographical scale in understanding human landscapes. In *Handbook of Landscape Archaeology*. B. David and J. Thomas, eds. 379–85. Walnut Creek, CA: Left Coast Press.

Head, L. (2000). *Cultural landscapes and environmental change*. London: Arnold.

Head, L. (1994). Landscapes socialised by fire: post-contact changes in Aboriginal fire use in northern Australia and implications for prehistory. *Archaeology in Oceania*, 29: 172–81.

Healan, D.M. (1995). Identifying lithic reduction loci with size-graded macrodebitage: a multivariate approach. *American Antiquity*, 60(4): 689–99. http://doi.org/10.2307/282053.

Hesse P.P., J.W. Magee and S. van der Kaars (2004) Later Quaternary climates of the Australian arid zone: a review. *Quaternary International*, 118–19: 87–102.

Hiscock, P. (2014). Learning in lithic landscapes: a reconsideration of the hominid 'toolmaking' niche. *Biological Theory*, 9: 27–41.

Hiscock, P. (2009). Reduction, recycling, and raw material procurement in western Arnhem Land, Australia. In *Lithic materials and Paleolithic societies*. B. Adams and B.S. Blades, eds. 78–93. Oxford: Wiley-Blackwell. http://doi.org/10.1002/9781444311976.

Hiscock, P. (2008). *Archaeology of ancient Australia*. London: Routledge.

Hiscock, P. (2005). Artefacts on Aru: evaluating the technological sequences. In *The archaeology of the Aru Islands, Eastern Indonesia*. S. O'Connor, M. Spriggs and P. Veth, eds. 205–34. Terra Australis 22. Canberra: ANU E Press.

Hiscock, P. (2002). Quantifying the size of artefact assemblages. *Journal of Archaeological Science*, 29(3): 251–58. http://doi.org/10.1006/jasc.2001.0705.

Hiscock, P. (2001). Sizing up prehistory: sample size and composition of artefact assemblages. *Australian Aboriginal Studies*, (1): 48–62.

Hiscock, P. (1994). Technological responses to risk in Holocene Australia. *Journal of World Prehistory*, 8(3): 267–92.

Hiscock, P. (1988). Prehistoric settlement patterns and artefact manufacture at Lawn Hill, Northwest Queensland. PhD thesis, University of Queensland, St Lucia, Qld.

Hiscock, P. (1986). Raw material rationing as an explanation of assemblage differences: a case study of Lawn Hill, northwest Queensland. In *Archaeology at ANZAAS Canberra*. G.K. Ward, ed. 178–90. Canberra: Canberra Archaeological Society.

Hiscock, P. (1984). Preliminary report on the stone artifacts from Colless Creek Cave, northwest Queensland. *Queensland Archaeological Research*, 1: 120–51.

Hiscock, P., and C. Clarkson (2005). Experimental evaluation of Kuhn's geometric index of reduction and the flat-flake problem. *Journal of Archaeological Science*, 32(7): 1015–22.

Hiscock, P., and S. Mitchell (1993). *Stone artefact quarries and reduction sites in Australia: towards a type profile. Technical publications* (Vol. 4). Canberra: Australian Heritage Commission.

Hiscock, P., and L.A. Wallis (2005). Pleistocene settlement of deserts from an Australian perspective. In *Desert peoples: archaeological perspectives*. P. Veth, M. Smith and P. Hiscock, eds. 34–57. Malden MA: Blackwell Publishing.

Holdaway, S.J., and H. Allen (2012). Placing ideas in the land: practical and ritual training among the Australian Aborigines. In *Archaeology and apprenticeship: body knowledge, identity and communities of practice*. W. Wendrich, ed. 79–98. Tucson: University of Arizona Press.

Holdaway, S.J., and M. Douglass (2012). A twenty-first century archaeology of stone artifacts. *Journal of Archaeological Method and Theory*, 19(1): 101–31. http://doi.org/10.1007/s10816-011-9103-6.

Holdaway, S.J., M. Douglass, and P. Fanning (2012). Landscape scale and human mobility: geoarchaeological evidence from Rutherfords Creek, New South Wales, Australia. In *Landscape archaeology between art and science: from a multi- to an interdisciplinary approach*. S. Kluiving and E. Guttmann-Bond, eds. 279–94. Amsterdam: Amsterdam University Press.

Holdaway, S.J., and P.C. Fanning (2014). *Geoarchaeology of Aboriginal landscapes in semi-arid Australia*. Canberra: CSIRO Publishing.

Holdaway, S.J., and P. Fanning (2008). Developing a landscape history as part of a survey strategy: a critique of current settlement system approaches based on case studies from western New South Wales, Australia. *Journal of Archaeological Method and Theory*, 15(2): 167–89. http://doi.org/10.1007/s10816-008-9051-y.

Holdaway, S.J., P. Fanning, and E. Rhodes (2008). Challenging intensification: human–environment interactions in the Holocene geoarchaeological record from western New South Wales, Australia. *The Holocene*, 18: 403–18.

Holdaway, S.J. and N. Porch (1995). Cyclical patterns in the Pleistocene human occupation of southwest Tasmania. *Archaeology in Oceania*, 30: 74–82.

Holdaway, S.J., J. Shiner, and P. Fanning (2004). Hunter-gatherers and the archaeology of discard behavior: an analysis of surface stone artifacts from Sturt National Park, western New South Wales, Australia. *Asian Perspectives*, 43(1): 34–72.

Holdaway, S.J., and N. Stern (2004). *A record in stone: the study of Australia's flaked stone artefacts*. Canberra and Melbourne: Aboriginal Studies Press and Museum Victoria.

Holdaway, S.J., D. Witter, P. Fanning, R. Musgrave, G. Cochrane, T. Doelman, et al. (1998). New approaches to open site spatial archaeology in Sturt National Park, New South Wales, Australia. *Archaeology in Oceania*, 33(1): 1–19.

Hook, F. (2009). A tale of two blades: macro-blade manufacture and discard in Paraburdoo, Western Australia. *Archaeology in Oceania*, 44 (Supplement): 23–31.

Hook, F., and A. Di Lello (2010). Gurdadaguji stone arrangements: Late Holocene aggregation locals? In *Session C68 (Part II). Monumental questions: prehistoric megaliths, mounds, and enclosures*. D. Calado, M. Baldia and M. Boulanger, eds. 285–97. Oxford, England: Archaeopress.

Hook, F., and B. Veitch (1999). The report of an Aboriginal heritage assessment of the proposed Channar mine extension areas, near Paraburdoo, Western Australia. Perth: Hamersley Iron Pty Ltd and Archae-aus Pty Ltd.

Hook, F., A. Di Lello and A. Ash (2008). Report of an Indigenous archaeological assessment of the Fortescue Metals Group's Cloudbreak to Christmas Creek rail extension (NYI 040) and associated levees (NYI 047), Chichester Range, Pilbara. Fremantle: Archae-aus Pty Ltd.

Hook, F., A. Dias, and S. Rapley (2008). Report of an Indigenous archaeological assessment of the Fortescue Metals Group's initial mining and waste dump area at Christmas Creek (NYI 067 and NYI 069), Chichester Range, Pilbara. Fremantle: Archae-aus Pty Ltd.

Hughes, P.J., and P. Hiscock (2005). The archaeology of the Lake Eyre South Area. *Archaeology of the Lake Eyre South Region. Lake Eyre South Monograph Series* 6, 1–20. Adelaide: Royal Geographical Society of South Australia.

Hughes, P.J., and G. Quartermaine (1992). Investigations of Aboriginal archaeological sites in the Mesa J development area, Pannawonica. Perth: Department of Indigenous Affairs.

Hughes, P.J., G. Quartermaine, G., and J. Harris (2011). Pleistocene rockshelters J23 and J24, Mesa J, Pilbara, Western Australia. *Australian Archaeology*, 73: 58–61.

Hughes, P.J., M. Sullivan, P. Hiscock and B. Marwick (2011). Archaeological investigations at Olympic Dam in arid northeast South Australia, *Journal of the Anthropological Society of South Australia*, 34: 21–37.

Ingold, T. (2007). *Lines: a brief history* (2016 edn). London: Routledge.

Ingold, T. (2000). *The perception of the environment: essays on livelihood, dwelling and skill*. London: Routledge.

Ingold, T. (1993). The temporality of the landscape. *World Archaeology*, 25(2): 152–74. http://doi.org/10.1080/00438243.1993.9980235.

Ishiwa, T., Y. Yokoyama, L. Reuning, C. McHugh, D. de Vleeschouwer, and J. Gallagher (2019). Australian summer monsoon variability in the past 14,000 years revealed by IODP Expedition 356 sediments. *Progress in Earth and Planetary Science*, 6: 6–17.

Jimenez-Lozano, M., and K. Edwards (2014). A report on Aboriginal archaeological heritage assessments conducted in 2008 at Fortescue Metals Group's Cloudbreak and Christmas Creek mining resources. Fremantle: Archae-aus Pty Ltd.

Johnson, C.N., and B.W. Brook (2011). Reconstructing the dynamics of ancient human populations from radiocarbon dates: 10,000 years of population growth in Australia. *Proceedings of the Royal Society B*, 278: 3748–54.

Johnson, I. (1980). Bytes from sites: the design of an excavation data recording system. In *Holier than thou: proceedings of the 1978 Kioloa conference on Australian prehistory*. I. Johnson, ed. 91–118. Canberra: Department of Prehistory, Research School of Pacific Studies, Australian National University.

Johnstone R.E., A.H. Burbidge and J.C. Darnell (2013). Birds of the Pilbara region, including seas and offshore islands, Western Australia: distribution, status and historic changes. *Records of the Western Australian Museum*, Supplement 78: 343–441.

Jones, R. (1969). Fire-stick farming. *Australian Natural History*, 16: 224–28.

Juluwarlu Aboriginal Corporation. (2007). *Ngurra warndurala buluyugayi: exploring Yindjibarndi country*. Roebourne: Juluwarlu Group Aboriginal Corporation.

Kelly, R.L. (2013). *The lifeways of hunter-gatherers: the foraging spectrum*. Cambridge: Cambridge University Press.

Kelly, R.L. (1992). Mobility/sedentism: concepts, archaeological measures, and effects. *Annual Review of Anthropology*. http://doi.org/10.1146/annurev.anthro.21.1.43.

Kendrick, P. (2002). Pilbara 2 (PIL2 – Fortescue Plains subregion). In *A biodiversity audit of Western Australia's 53 biogeographic subregions*. N.L. McKenzie, J.E. May and S. McKenna, eds. 559–567. Perth, WA: Department of Environment and Conservation.

Kimber, R.G. (1981). Some thoughts on stone arrangements. *The Artefact*, 6(3–4): 10–8.

Kuhn, S.L. (1995). *Mousterian lithic technology*. Princeton: Princeton University Press.

Kuhnt, W., A. Holbourn, J. Xu, B. Opdyke, P. De Deckker, U. Rhöl, and M. Mudelsee (2015). Southern Hemisphere control on Australian monsoon variability during the late deglaciation and Holocene. *Nature Communications*, 6: 5916. http://doi.org/doi: 10.1038/ncomms6916.

Langley, M.C., C. Clarkson, and S. Ulm (2011). From small holes to grand narratives: the impact of taphonomy and sample size on the modernity debate in Australia and New Guinea. *Journal of Human Evolution*, 61: 197–208.

Law, W.B., and D.N. Cropper (2018). Excavations at Djadjiling Rockshelter (HD07-1A-04). In *Rockshelter excavations in the East Hamersley Range, Pilbara region, Western Australia*. D.N. Cropper and W.B. Law, eds. 245–86. Oxford: Archaeopress.

Law, W.B., D.N. Cropper, and F. Petchey (2010). Djadjiling rockshelter: 35,000 14C years of Aboriginal occupation in the Pilbara, Western Australia. *Australian Archaeology*, 70: 68–71.

Lees, B.G. (1992). Geomorphological evidence for late Holocene climatic change in northern Australia. *Australian Geographer*, 23(1): 1–10.

Lewarch, D.E., and M.J. O'Brien (1981). The expanding role of surface assemblages in archaeological research. *Advances in Archaeological Method and Theory*, 4: 297–342.

Lewis, D. (1976). Observations on route finding and spatial orientation among the Aboriginal peoples of the Western Desert region of Central Australia. *Oceania*, 46(4): 249–82.

Lin, S.C., S.P. McPherron, and H.L. Dibble (2015). Establishing statistical confidence in cortex ratios within and among lithic assemblages: a case study of the Middle Paleolithic of southwestern France. *Journal of Archaeological Science*, 59: 89–109. http://doi.org/10.1016/j.jas.2015.04.004.

Lock, G., and B.L. Molyneaux (2006). Introduction: confronting scale. In *Confronting scale in archaeology: issues of theory and practice*. G. Lock and B.L. Molyneaux, eds. 1–11. New York: Springer.

Long, A. (2005). *Aboriginal scarred trees in New South Wales: a field manual*. Sydney: Department of Environment and Conservation.

Lorblanchet, M., and R. Jones (1979). Les premières fouilles à Dampier (Australie Occidentale), et leur place dans l'ensemble australien. *Bulletin de La Société Préhistorique Française*, 76: 463–87.

Lourandos, H. (1997). *Continent of hunter-gatherers: new perspectives in Australian prehistory*. Melbourne: Cambridge University Press.

Lullfitz, A., J. Dortch, S.D. Hopper, C. Petterson, R. (Doc) Reynolds, and D. Guilfoyle (2017). Human niche construction: Noongar evidence in pre-colonial southwestern Australia. *Conservation and Society*, 15: 201–16.

Mackay, A. (2005). Informal movements: changing mobility patterns at Ngarrabullgan, Cape York, Australia. In *Lithics 'Down Under': Australian perspectives on lithic reduction, use and classification*. C. Clarkson and L. Lamb, eds. 95–107. Oxford: British Archaeological Reports S1408.

Manne, T., and P. Veth (2015). Late Pleistocene and early Holocene exploitation of estuarine communities in northwestern Australia. *Quaternary International*, 385: 112–23.

Marsh, M., P. Hiscock, D. Williams, P. Hughes, and M. Sullivan (2018). Watura Jurnti: a 42000–45000-year long occupation sequence from the north-eastern Pilbara. *Archaeology in Oceania*, 53: 137–49.

Martens, T., and T. Craig (2015). A report of the salvage of 46 Aboriginal archaeological sites and nine other heritage places in the North Treacheries and Eyre East project areas (s18_034_NYI / 25-10612), Christmas

Creek project area, Chichester Range, Pilbara. February 2015. Fremantle: Archaeaus Pty Ltd.

Marwick, B. (2009). Change or decay? An interpretation of late Holocene archaeological evidence from the Hamersley Plateau, Western Australia. *Archaeology in Oceania*, 44: 16–22.

Marwick, B. (2005). Element concentrations and magnetic susceptibility of anthrosols: indicators of prehistoric human occupation in the inland Pilbara, Western Australia. *Journal of Archaeological Science*, 32(9): 1357–68. http://doi.org/10.1016/j.jas.2005.03.009.

Marwick, B. (2002). Milly's Cave: evidence for human occupation of the inland Pilbara during the Last Glacial Maximum. In *Barriers, borders, boundaries: proceedings of the 2001 Australian Archaeological Association annual conference*. S. Ulm, C. Westcott, J. Reid, A. Ross, I. Lilley, J. Prangnell and L. Kirkwood, eds. 21–33. Tempus 7. Brisbane: Anthropology Museum, University of Queensland.

Marwick B., P. Hiscock, M. Sullivan and P. Hughes (2017). Landform boundary effects on Holocene forager landscape use in arid South Australia, *Journal of Archaeological Science: Reports* 19: 864–74.

Maynard, L. (1980). A Pleistocene date from an occupation deposit in the Pilbara Region, Western Australia. *Australian Archaeology*, 10: 3–8.

McBryde, I. (1987). Goods from another country: exchange networks and the people of the Lake Eyre Basin. In *Australians to 1788*. D. Mulvaney and J. White, eds. 252–73. Sydney: Fairfax, Syme & Weldon.

McBryde, I. (1978). 'Wil-im-ee Moor-ing', or where do axes come from? *Mankind*, 11: 354–82.

McConnell, K., and S. O'Connor (1997). 40,000 year record of food plants in the southern Kimberley ranges, Western Australia. *Australian Archaeology*, 45: 20–31.

McConvell, P. (1996). Backtracking to Babel: the chronology of Pama-Nyungan expansion in Australia. *Archaeology in Oceania*, 31(3): 125–44.

McDonald, E.M. (2007). *Report on an ethnographic survey of Aboriginal sites Priority Areas 1–3 and consultation regarding archaeological sites Priority Area 1 area, Cloud Break Mine, Chichester Ranges, Pilbara, Western Australia*. A report prepared for the Karlka Nyiyaparli Aboriginal Corporation and Fortescue Metals Group Pty Ltd.

McDonald, E.M., and B. Coldrick (in press). Is it from the Dreaming, or is it rubbish? The significance and meaning of stone artefacts and their sources to Aboriginal people in the Pilbara region of Western Australia'. In *Cultures of stone*. G. Cooney, B. Gilhooly, N. Kelly, and S. Mallía-Guest, eds. Leiden: Sidestone Press.

McDonald, J. (2015). I must go down to the seas again: or, what happens when the sea comes to you? Murujuga rock art as an environmental indicator for Australia's north-west. *Quaternary International*, 385: 124–35. http://doi.org/10.1016/j.quaint.2014.10.056.

McDonald, J. (2005). Archaeological evidence in the De Rose Hill native title claim. *Australian Aboriginal Studies*, 2005/1: 30–44.

McDonald, J., and M. Berry (2017). Murujuga, northwestern Australia: when arid hunter-gatherers became coastal foragers. *The Journal of Island and Coastal Archaeology*, 12(1): 24–43.

McDonald, J., W. Reynen, K. Ditchfield, J. Dortch, B. Stephenson, T. Whitley, I. Ward and P. Veth (2018). Murujuga rockshelter: first evidence for Pleistocene occupation on the Burrup Peninsula. *Quaternary Science Reviews*, 193: 266–87.

McDonald, J., W. Reynen, F. Petchey, K. Ditchfield, C. Byrne, D. Vannieuwenhuyse, M. Leopold and P. Veth (2018). Karnatukul (Serpent's Glen): a new chronology for the oldest site in Australia's Western

Desert. *PLoS One*, 13(9): e0202511. https://doi.org/10.1371/journal.pone.0202511 pmid:30231025.

McDonald, J., and P. Veth (2013a). Rock art in arid landscapes: Pilbara and Western Desert petroglyphs. *Australian Archaeology*, 77: 66–81.

McDonald, J., and P. Veth (2013b). The archaeology of memory: the recursive relationship of Martu rock art and place. *Anthropological Forum*, 23. 367–86.

McDonald, J., and P.M. Veth (2012). The social dynamics of aggregation and dispersal in the Western Desert. In A companion to rock art J. McDonald and P. Veth, eds, 90-102. Chichester, West Sussex, UK: Wiley-Blackwell.

McDonald, J., and P. Veth (2009). Dampier Archipelago petroglyphs: archaeology, scientific values and National Heritage Listing. *Archaeology in Oceania*, 44 (Supplement): 49–69.

McDonald, J., and P. Veth (2008a). Rock art and social identity: a comparison of Holocene graphic systems in arid and fertile environments. In *Archaeology of Oceania: Australia and the Pacific Islands*. I. Lilley, ed. 96–115. Oxford: Blackwell Publishing Ltd.

McDonald, J., and P. Veth (2008b). Rock-art of the Western Desert and Pilbara: pigment dates provide new perspectives on the role of art in the Australian arid zone. *Australian Aboriginal Studies*, 2008/2: 4–21.

McGowan, H., S. Marx, P. Moss, and A. Hammond (2012). Evidence of ENSO mega-drought triggered collapse of prehistory Aboriginal society in northwest Australia. *Geophysical Research Letters*, 39: L22702. http://doi.org/10.1029/2012GL053916.

McGrath, P.F. (2016). Future acts, future heritage? The extraordinary scale and unknown impacts of development-related Indigenous heritage management on native title lands. In *The right to protect sites: Indigenous heritage management in the era of native title*. P.F. McGrath, ed. 49–76. Canberra: Australian Institute of Aboriginal & Torres Strait Islander Studies.

McGrath, P.F., and E. Lee (2016). The fate of Indigenous place-based heritage in the era of native title. In *The right to protect sites: Indigenous heritage management in the era of native title*. P.F. McGrath, ed. 1–25. Canberra: Australian Institute of Aboriginal & Torres Strait Islander Studies.

McHarg, K., and T. Craig (2010). Report of an Indigenous archaeological assessment of the Fortescue Metals Group's Windich South and access road, Chichester Range. Fremantle: Archae-aus Pty Ltd.

McHarg, K., and K. Edwards (2010). Report of an Indigenous archaeological assessment of the Fortescue Metals Group's Christmas Creek access road and waste dump. Fremantle: Archae-aus Pty Ltd.

McKenzie, N., S. van Leeuwen, and A. Pinder (2009). Introduction to the Pilbara Biodiversity Survey, 2002–2007. *Records of the Western Australian Museum*, Supplement 78, 3–89.

McNiven, I. (2008). Inclusions, exclusions and transitions: Torres Strait Islander constructed landscapes over the past 4000 years, northeast Australia. *The Holocene*, 18: 449–62.

Memmott, P. (2002). Sociospatial structures of Australian Aboriginal settlements. *Australian Aboriginal Studies*, 2002/1: 67–86.

Morphy, H. (1995). Landscape and the reproduction of the ancestral past. In *The anthropology of landscape: perspectives on place and space*. E. Hirsch and M. O'Hanlon, eds. 184–209. Oxford: Clarendon Press.

Morse, K. (2009). Emerging from the abyss – archaeology in the Pilbara region of Western Australia. *Archaeology in Oceania*, 44 (Supplement): 1–5.

Morse, K., R. Cameron, and W. Reynen (2014). A tale of three caves: new dates for Pleistocene occupation in the inland Pilbara. *Australian Archaeology*, 79: 167–78.

Mulvaney, J., and J. Kamminga (1999). *Prehistory of Australia*. Sydney: Allen & Unwin.

Mulvaney, K. (2015). *Murujuga Marni: rock art of the macropod hunters and mollusc harvesters*. Crawley: University of Western Australia Press.

Mulvaney, K. (2010). Murujuga Marni. Dampier petroglyphs: shadows in the landscape, echoes across time. PhD thesis, University of New England, Armadale, NSW.

Mulvaney, K. (2009). Dating the Dreaming: extinct fauna in the petroglyphs of the Pilbara region, Western Australia. *Archaeology in Oceania*, 44 (Supplement): 40–48.

Native Welfare Department (1968). Native Welfare Department 625/1968, *Preservation of Aboriginal sites – survey of North West Division*. State Records Office of Western Australia ACC1724.

Nelson, M.C. (1991). The study of technological organization. *Archaeological Method and Theory*, 3: 57–100.

Newcomer, M.H., and C. Karlin (1987). Flint chips from Pincevent. In *The human uses of flint and chert*. G. de Sieveking and M.H. Newcomer, eds. 33–36. Cambridge: Cambridge University Press.

New South Wales Dept of Environment, Climate Change and Water (2010). *Cultural landscapes: a practical guide for park management, NSW*. Sydney: Department of Environment, Climate Change and Water

Nicholson, A., and S. Cane (1991). Desert camps: analysis of Australian Aboriginal proto-historic campsites. In *Ethnoarchaeological approaches to mobile campsites: hunter-gatherer and pastoralist case studies*. C.S. Gamble and W.A. Boismier, eds. 263–354. Ann Arbor, Michigan: International Monographs in Prehistory.

Nyiyaparli Community, C. Bird, and E. McDonald (2015). *Kakutungutanta to Warrie Outcamp: 40,000 years in Nyiyaparli country*. Fremantle: Archae-aus Pty Ltd.

O'Connell, J.F. (1987). Alyawara site structure and its archaeological implications. *American Antiquity*, 50(1): 74–108.

O'Donnell, A.J., E.R. Cook, J.G. Palmer, C.S.M. Turney, G.F.M. Page, and P.F. Grierson (2015). Tree rings show recent high summer–autumn precipitation in northwest Australia is unprecedented within the last two centuries. *PloS One*, 10(6), e0128533. http://doi.org/10.1371/journal.pone.0128533.

O'Connell, J. F., and K. Hawkes, (1984). Food choice and foraging sites among the Alyawara. *Journal of Anthropological Research*, 40(4): 504–535.

Oetelaar, G.A., and D. Meyer (2006). Movement and Native American landscapes: a comparative approach. *Plains Anthropologist*, 51, 355–74

O'Grady, G.N. (1966). Proto-Ngayarda phonology. *Oceanic Linguistics*, 5(2): 71–130.

O'Grady, G.N., and M. Laughren (1997). Palyku is a Ngayarta language. *Australian Journal of Linguistics*, 17: 129–54.

Olive, N. (1997). *Karijini Mirlimirli: Aboriginal histories from the Pilbara*. Fremantle: Fremantle Arts Centre Press.

Palmer, K. (1977). Myth, ritual and rock art. *Archaeology and Physical Anthropology in Oceania*, 12: 38–50.

Pardoe, C. (2003). The Menindee Lakes: a regional survey. *Archaeology in Oceania*, 57: 42–53.

Parker, D.J. (2011). The complexity of lithic simplicity: computer simulation of lithic assemblage formation in Western New South Wales, Australia. MA thesis, Anthropology, University of Auckland, Auckland, New Zealand.

Pellant, C. (2000). *Rocks and minerals*. London: Dorling Kindersley.

Pepper M., P. Doughty and J.S. Keogh (2013). Geodiversity and endemism in the iconic Australian Pilbara region: a review of landscape evolution and biotic response in an ancient refugium. *Journal of Biogeography*, 40(7): 1225–39.

Peterson, N. (1983). Rights, residence and process in Australian territorial organisation. In *Aborigines, land and land rights*. N. Peterson and M. Langton, eds. 134–45. Canberra: Australian Institute of Aboriginal Studies.

Phillipps, R.S. (2012). Documenting socio-economic variability in the Egyptian Neolithic through stone artefact analysis. PhD thesis, University of Auckland, Auckland.

Phillipps, R.S., and S.J. Holdaway (2015). Estimating core number in assemblages: core movement and mobility during the Holocene of the Fayum, Egypt. *Journal of Archaeological Method and Theory*, 70(3): 513–26. http://doi.org/10.1007/s10816-015-9250-2

Pickering, M. (2003). *Modelling hunter-gatherer settlement patterns: an Australian case study*. Oxford: BAR International Series 1103.

Pitman, H.T. (2010). Pointless spinifex: an investigation of Indigenous use of spinifex throughout Australia. BA (Hons) thesis, Archaeology, Flinders University, Adelaide.

Porraz, G. (2009). Middle Palaeolithic mobile toolkits in short-term human occupations: two case studies. *Eurasian Prehistory*, 6: 33–55.

Radcliffe-Brown, A.R. (1931). *The social organization of Australian tribes*. Melbourne: Macmillan.

Rapley, S., and K. Edwards (2010). Preliminary advice of an Indigenous archaeological assessment of survey request areas PAL 50 and PAL 51 within the Cloudbreak Mining Area and survey requests NYI 099, NYI 101 and NYI 106 within the Christmas Creek Mining Area, April, Stage One. Fremantle: Archae-aus Pty Ltd.

Rapley, S., K. McHarg, and K. Edwards (2009). Report of an Indigenous archaeological assessment of the Fortescue Metals Group's proposed Eyre Pit East and North Treacheries Pit, Christmas Creek, Chichester Range, Pilbara. Fremantle: Archae-aus Pty Ltd.

Reeves, J.M., T.T. Barrows, T.J. Cohen, A.S. Kiem, H.C. Bostock, K.E. Fitzsimmons et al. (2013). Climate variability over the last 35,000 years recorded in marine and terrestrial archives in the Australian region: An OZ-INTIMATE compilation. *Quaternary Science Reviews*, 74: 21–34. http://doi.org/10.1016/j.quascirev.2013.01.001.

Reeves, J.M., H.C. Bostock, L.K. Ayliffe, T.T. Barrows, P. De Deckker, L.S. Devriendt et al. (2013). Palaeoenvironmental change in tropical Australasia over the last 30,000 years – a synthesis by the OZ-INTIMATE group. *Quaternary Science Reviews*, 74: 97–114. http://doi.org/10.1016/j.quascirev.2012.11.027.

Reeves J.M., A.R. Chivas, A. García, S. Holt, M.J.J. Couapel, B.G. Jones et al. (2008) The sedimentary record of palaeoenvironments and sea-level change in the Gulf of Carpentaria, Australia, through the last glacial cycle *Quaternary International*, 183: 3–22.

Reynen, W., D. Vannieuwenhuyse, K. Morse, C. Monks and J. Balme (2018). What happened after the Last Glacial Maximum? Transitions in site use on an inland island in north-western Australia. *Archaeology in Oceania*, 53: 150–62.

Rhoads, J.W., (1992). Significant sites and non-site archaeology: a case study from south-east Australia. *World Archaeology*, 24(2): 198–217.

Rick, J.W., (1987). Dates as data: an examination of the Peruvian pre-ceramic record. *American Antiquity*, 52: 55–73.

Ridges, M. (2006). Scale and its effects on understanding regional behavioural systems: an Australian case study. In *Confronting scale in archaeology*. G. Lock and B.L. Molyneaux, eds. 145–61. Boston, MA: Springer.

Riede, F. (2012). Theory for the a-theoretical: niche construction theory and its implications for environmental archaeology. In *N-TAG TEN. Proceedings of the 10th Nordic TAG conference at Stiklestad, Norway 2009*. R. Berge, M.E. Jasinski and K. Sogannes, eds. 87–98. Oxford: Archaeopress, BAR International Series S2399.

Robins, R.P. (1998). Patterns in the landscape: A case study in nonsite archaeology from Southwest Queensland. *Memoirs of the Queensland Museum, Cultural Heritage Series*, 1: 23–56.

Rose, D.B. (1996). *Nourishing terrains: Australian Aboriginal views of landscape and wilderness*. Canberra: Australian Heritage Commission.

Rossignol, J., and L. Wandsnider eds. (1992). *Space, time and archaeological landscapes*. New York: Plenum Press.

Rouillard, A., P.F. Greenwood, K. Grice, G. Skrzypek, S. Dogramaci, C. Turney, and P.F. Grierson (2016). Interpreting vegetation change in tropical arid ecosystems from sediment molecular fossils and their stable isotope compositions: a baseline study from the Pilbara region of northwest Australia. *Palaeogeography, Palaeoclimatology, Palaeoecology*, 459: 495–507. http://doi.org/10.1016/j.palaeo.2016.07.023.

Rouillard, A., G. Skrzypek, S. Dogramaci, C. Turney, and P.F. Grierson (2015). Impacts of high inter-annual variability of rainfall on a century of extreme hydrologic regime of northwest Australia. *Hydrology and Earth System Sciences*, 19(4): 2057–78. http://doi.org/10.5194/hess-19-2057-2015.

Rouillard, A., G. Skrzypek, C.S.M. Turney, S. Dogramaci, Q. Hua, A. Zawadzki et al. (2016). Evidence for extreme floods in arid subtropical northwest Australia during the Little Ice Age chronozone (CE 1400–1850). *Quaternary Science Reviews*, 144: 107–22. http://doi.org/10.1016/j.quascirev.2016.05.004.

Ryan, I., and K. Morse (2009). Towards a late Holocene archaeology of the inland Pilbara. *Archaeology in Oceania*, 44 (Supplement): 6–15.

Schlanger, S.H. (1992). Recognizing persistent places in Anasazi settlement systems. In *Space, time and archaeological landscapes*. J. Rossignol and L. Wandsnider, eds. 91–112. New York: Plenum Press.

Shiner, J. (2009). Persistent places: an approach to the interpretation of assemblage variation in deflated surface stone artefacts distributions from western New South Wales, Australia. In *New directions in archaeological science*. A. Fairbairn, S. O'Connor, and B. Marwick, eds. 25–41. Terra Australis 28. Canberra: Australian National University E Press.

Shiner, J. (2008). *Place as occupational histories: an investigation of the deflated archaeological surface record of Pine Point and Langwell Stations, western New South Wales, Australia*. BAR International Series 1763. Oxford: Archaeopress.

Shott, M.J. (2010). Size dependence in assemblage measures: essentialism, materialism, and 'SHE' analysis in archaeology. *American Antiquity*, 75(4): 886–906. http://doi.org/10.7183/0002-7316.75.4.886.

Shott, M.J. (2008). Lower Paleolithic industries, time, and the meaning of assemblage variation. In *Time in archaeology: time perspectivism revisited*. S. Holdaway and L. Wandsnider, eds. 46–60. Salt Lake City: University of Utah Press.

Shott, M.J. (1996). An exegesis of the curation concept. *Journal of Anthropological Research*, 52(3): 259–80.

Shulmeister, J. and B.G. Lees (1995). Pollen evidence from tropical Australia for the onset of an ENSO-dominated climate at c. 4000 BP. *The Holocene*, 5 (1):10–8.

Simonson, B.M., S.W. Hassler, and K.A. Schubel (1993). Lithology and proposed revisions in stratigraphic nomenclature of the Wittenoom Formation (Dolomite) and overlying formations, Hamersley Group,

Western Australia. *Geological Survey Report*, 34: 65–80.

Sinclair, L. (2015a). A report of the salvage of 21 Aboriginal archaeological sites and three other heritage places in the Christmas Creek access and waste section 18, Christmas Creek project area (S18_036_NYI / 25-14646), Chichester Range, Pilbara. Fremantle: Archae-aus Pty Ltd.

Sinclair, L. (2015b). A report on the salvage of 56 Aboriginal sites and 16 other heritage places within FMG's Cathedrals Pit s18 Area. Fremantle: Archae-aus Pty Ltd.

Sinclair, L., and N. Wright (2012). *Report of an Indigenous archaeological assessment of 19 Sites within Fortescue Metals Group's Christmas Creek Mining and Infrastructure Phase 22 project area*. Fremantle: Archae-aus Pty Ltd.

Skrzypek, G., S. Dogramaci, and P. Grierson (2013). Geochemical and hydrological processes controlling groundwater salinity of a large inland wetland of northwestern Australia. *Chemical Geology*, 357: 164–77.

Skrzypek, G., S. Dogramaci, A. Rouillard, and P.F. Grierson (2016). Groundwater seepage controls salinity in a hydrologically terminal basin of semi-arid northwest Australia. *Journal of Hydrology*, 542: 627–36. http://doi.org/10.1016/j.jhydrol.2016.09.033

Slack, M.J., M. Fillios, and R. Fullagar (2009). Aboriginal settlement during the LGM at Brockman, Pilbara region, Western Australia. *Archaeology in Oceania*, 44 (Supplement): 32–39.

Slack, M.J., K. Connell, A. Davis, L.A. Gliganic, W.B. Law and M. Meyer (2017). Post-Last Glacial Maximum settlement of the West Angelas region in the inland Hamersley Plateau. *Australian Archaeology*, 83: 127–42.

Slack, M.J., W.B. Law and L.A. Gliganic (2018). Pleistocene settlement of the eastern Hamersley Plateau: a regional study of 22 rock-shelter sites. *Archaeology in Oceania*, 55: 191–204.

Smith, A.B. (2002). *Under a bilari tree I born: the story of Alice Bilari Smith*. Fremantle: Fremantle Arts Centre Press.

Smith, M.A. (2013). *The archaeology of Australia's deserts*. Cambridge: Cambridge University Press.

Smith, M.A. (2005). Desert archaeology, linguistic stratigraphy and the spread of the Western Desert language. In *Desert peoples: archaeological perspectives*. P. Veth, M.A. Smith, and P. Hiscock, eds. 222–42. Cambridge: Cambridge University Press.

Smith, M.A. (1986). The antiquity of seedgrinding in arid Australia. *Archaeology in Oceania*, 21(1): 29–39.

Smith, M.A., and J. Ross (2008). What happened at 1500–1000 cal. BP in Central Australia? Timing, impact and archaeological signatures. *The Holocene*, 18(3): 379–88. http://doi.org/10.1177/0959683607087928.

Smith, M.A., and N.D. Sharp (1993) Pleistocene sites in Australia, New Guinea, and Island Melanesia: geographic and temporal structure of the archaeological record. In *Sahul in Review*. M.A. Smith, M. Spriggs, and B. Fankhauser, eds, 37–59. Canberra: Department of Prehistory, Research School of Pacific Studies, Australian National University.

Smith, M.A., A.N. Williams, C.S.M. Turney, and M.L. Cupper (2008). Human–environment interactions in Australian drylands: exploratory time-series analysis of archaeological records. *The Holocene*, 18(3): 389–401. http://doi.org/10.1177/0959683607087929.

Stanner, W.E.H. (2011). The Dreaming. In *The Dreaming and other essays*. W.E.H. Stanner, ed. 47–57. ProQuest ebook.

Stanner, W.E.H. (1965). Aboriginal territorial organisation: estate, range, domain and regime. *Oceania*, 36: 1–26.

Sterelny, K. (2011). From hominins to humans: how *sapiens* became behaviourally modern. *Philosophical Transactions of the*

Royal Society of London. Series B, Biological Sciences, 366 (1566): 809–22.

Stern, N. (2015). The archaeology of the Willandra: its empirical structure and narrative potential. In *Long history, deep time: deepening histories of place*. A. McGrath and M.A. Jebb, eds. 221–40. Canberra: ANU Press.

Stern, N. (2008). Time averaging and the structure of Late Pleistocene archaeological deposits in South West Tasmania. In *Time in archaeology: time perspectivism revisited*. S. Holdaway and L. Wandsnider, eds. 134–48. Salt Lake City: University of Utah Press.

Stern, N. (1993). The structure of the Lower Pleistocene archaeological record: a case study from the Koobi Fora Formation, with comments. *Current Anthropology*, 34(3), 201–25.

Stevens, R. (2016). Native title and the Aboriginal Heritage Act (WA): an awkward relationship. *Journal of the Australian Association of Consulting Archaeologists*, 4 (Supplement): 29–39.

Sullivan, M., P. Hiscock and P. Hughes (2014). Three scales: GIS, GPS and digital site and data recording technology in archaeological salvage at Olympic Dam in arid South Australia. *Journal of the Anthropological Society of South Australia*, 38: 85–107.

Sutton, N., G. Summerhayes, and A. Ford (2015). Regional interaction networks in southern Papua New Guinea during the late Holocene: evidence from the chemical characterisation of chert artefacts. *Proceedings of the Prehistoric Society*, 81: 343–59. http://doi.org/10.1017/ppr.2015.14.

Taçon, P.S.C. (1994). Socialising landscapes: the long-term implications of signs, symbols and marks on the land. *Archaeology in Oceania*, 29: 117–29.

Thackway, R., and I.D. Cresswell (1995). *An interim biogeographic regionalisation for Australia: a framework for establishing the national system of reserves*. Canberra: Australian Nature Conservation Agency.

Thomas, D.H. (1975). Non-site sampling in archaeology: up the creek without a site? In *Sampling in archaeology*. J. Mueller, ed. 61–81. Tucson: University of Arizona Press.

Thorne, A., and A. Trendall (2001). Geology of the Fortescue Group, Pilbara Craton, Western Australia. *Bulletin of Geological Survey of Western Australia*, 144. Perth: Geological Survey of Western Australia.

Tilley, C., and K. Cameron-Daum (2017). *An anthropology of landscape: the extraordinary in the ordinary*. London: UCL Press.

Tindale, N.B. (1974). *Aboriginal tribes of Australia: their terrain, environmental controls, distribution, limits, and proper names*. Berkeley: University of California Press.

Tonkinson, R. (1978). *The Mardudjara Aborigines: living the dream in Australia's desert*. New York: Holt, Rinehart & Winston.

Tonkinson, R. (1974). *The Jigalong mob: Aboriginal victors of the desert crusade*. Menlo Park: Cummings Publishing Company.

Torrence, R. (2002). Cultural landscapes on Garua Island, Papua New Guinea. *Antiquity*, 76: 766–76.

Torrence, R. (1983). Time budgeting and hunter-gatherer technology. In *Hunter-gatherer economy in prehistory: a European perspective*. G. Bailey, ed. 11–22. Cambridge: Cambridge University Press.

Ulm, S., G. Mate, C. Dalley, and S. Nichols (2013). A working profile: the changing face of professional archaeology in Australia. *Australian Archaeology*, 76: 34–43.

van der Kaars, S. (1991). Palynology of eastern Indonesia marine piston-cores: a Late Quaternary vegetational and climatic record of Australasia, *Palaeogeography, Palaeoclimatology, Palaeoecology*, 85: 239–302.

van der Kaars, S., and P. De Deckker (2002). A Late Quaternary pollen record from deep sea core Fr10/95, GC17 offshore Cape Range Peninsula, northwestern Western Australia. *Review of Palaeobotany and Palynology*, 120: 17–39.

van der Kaars, S., P. De Deckker, and F. Gingele (2006). A 100,000-year record of annual and seasonal rainfall and temperature for northwestern Australia based on a pollen record obtained offshore. *Journal of Quaternary Science*, 21(8): 879–89.

Van Vreeswyk, A.M.E., A.L. Payne, K.A. Leighton, and P. Hennig (2004). An inventory and condition survey of the Pilbara region, Western Australia. *Technical Bulletin* 92. Perth: Department of Agriculture, Western Australia.

Veitch, B., F. Hook, and E. Bradshaw (2005). A note on radiocarbon dates from the Paraburdoo, Mount Brockman and Yandicoogina areas of the Hamersley Plateau, Pilbara, Western Australia. *Australian Archaeology*, 60, 58–61.

Veth, P.M. (2006). Social dynamism in the archaeology of the Western Desert. In *The social archaeology of Indigenous societies*. B. David, B. Barker and I. McNiven, eds. 242–53. Canberra: Aboriginal Studies Press.

Veth, P.M. (2005a). Between the desert and the sea: archaeologies of the Western Desert and Pilbara regions, Australia. In *23 degrees south: archaeology and environmental history of the southern deserts*. M. Smith and P. Hesse, eds. 132–41. Canberra: National Museum of Australia.

Veth, P.M. (2005b). Cycles of aridity and human mobility: risk minimisation among the Late Pleistocene foragers of the Western Desert, Australia. In *Desert peoples: archaeological perspectives*. P. Veth, M. Smith and P. Hiscock, eds. 100–15. Malden MA: Blackwell Publishing.

Veth, P.M. (2000). Origins of the Western Desert language: convergence in linguistic and archaeological space and time model. *Archaeology in Oceania*, 35(1): 11–19.

Veth, P.M. (1996). Current archaeological evidence from the Little and Great Sandy Deserts. In *Archaeology of Northern Australia*. P. Veth and P. Hiscock, eds. 50–65.

Tempus 4. St Lucia: Anthropology Museum, University of Queensland.

Veth, P.M. (1995). Aridity and settlement in North-west Australia. *Antiquity*, 69: 733–46.

Veth, P.M. (1993). *Islands in the interior: the dynamics of prehistoric adaptations within the arid zone of Australia*. Ann Arbor, Michigan: International Monographs in Prehistory.

Veth, P.M. (1989), Islands in the interior: a model for the colonisation of arid zone, *Archaeology in Oceania*, 24: 81–92.

Veth, P.M. (1987), Martujarra prehistory: variation in arid zone adaptations. *Australian Archaeology*, 25: 102–11.

Veth, P.M., K. Aplin, L. Wallis, T. Manne, T. Pulsford, E. White, and A. Chappell (2007). *The archaeology of the Montebello Islands: Late Quaternary foragers on an arid coastline*. Oxford: Archaeopress.

Veth, P.M., K. Ditchfield, and F. Hook (2014). Maritime deserts of the Australian northwest. *Australian Archaeology*, 79, 156–166.

Veth, P.M., P. Hiscock, and A. Williams (2011). Are tulas and ENSO linked in Australia? *Australian Archaeology*, 72: 7–14.

Veth, P.M., J. McDonald, and B. White (2008). Dating of Bush Turkey Rockshelter 3 in the Calvert Ranges establishes early Holocene occupation of Little Sandy Desert, Western Australia. *Australian Archaeology*, 66: 33–44.

Veth, P.M., and B. O'Brien (1986). Middens on the Abydos Plain, northwest Australia. *Australian Archaeology*, 22: 45–49.

Veth, P.M., M. Smith, J. Bowler, K. Fitzsimmons, A. Williams, and P. Hiscock (2009). Excavations at Parnkupirti, Lake Gregory, Great Sandy Desert: OSL ages for occupation before the Last Glacial Maximum. *Australian Archaeology*, 69: 1–10.

Veth, P.M., N. Stern, J. McDonald, J. Balme, and I. Davidson (2011). The role of information exchange in the colonization of Sahul. In *Information and its role in hunter-gatherer bands*. R. Whallon, W.A. Lovis and

R.K. Hitchcock, eds. 203–20. Los Angeles: Cotsen Institute of Archaeology Press.

Veth, P. M., and F.J. Walsh, (1988). The concept of "staple" plant foods in the Western desert region of Western Australia. *Australian Aboriginal Studies*, 1988(2): 19–25.

Veth, P.M., I. Ward, T. Manne, S. Ulm, K. Ditchfield, J. Dortch et al. (2017). Early human occupation of a maritime desert, Barrow Island, North-West Australia. *Quaternary Science Reviews*, 168: 19–29.

Vinnicombe, P. (2002). Petroglyphs of the Dampier Archipelago: background to development and descriptive analysis. *Rock Art Research*, 19: 1–28.

Vita-Finzi, C., and E. Higgs (1970). Prehistoric economy in the Mount Carmel area of Palestine: site catchment analysis. *Proceedings of the Prehistoric Society*, 36: 1–37.

Walker, M.J.C., M. Berkelhammer, S. Bjorck, L.C. Cwynar et al. (2012) Formal subdivision of the Holocene Series/Epoch: a discussion paper by Working Group for INTIMATE (Integration of ice-core, marine and terrestrial records) and the Subcommittee on Quaternary Stratigraphy (International Commissionon Stratigraphy). *Journal of Quaternary Science*, 27(7): 649–59.

Wallis, L.A. (2001). Environmental history of northwest Australia based on phytolith analysis at Carpenter's Gap 1. *Quaternary International*, 83–85: 103–17.

Wallis, L.A., and J. Matthews (2016). Built structures in rockshelters of the Pilbara, Western Australia. *Records of the Western Australian Museum*, 31: 1–26.

Walsh, F.J. (2008). To hunt and to hold: Martu Aboriginal people's uses and knowledge of their country, with implications for co-management in Karlamilyi (Rudall River) National Park and the Great Sandy Desert, Western Australia. PhD thesis, University of Western Australia.

Wangka Maya Pilbara Aboriginal Language Centre (2012). *Nyiyaparli dictionary*. South Hedland: Wangka Maya Pilbara Aboriginal Language Centre.

Ward, G.K. (1983). Archaeology and legislation in Australia. In *Australian field archaeology: a guide to techniques*. G. Connah, ed. 18–42. Canberra: Australian Institute of Aboriginal Studies.

Ward, I., P. Veth, L. Prossor, T. Denham, K. Ditchfield, T. Manne, P. Kendrick, C. Byrne, F. Hook and U. Troitzsch (2017). 50,000 years of archaeological site stratigraphy and micromorphology in Boodie Cave, Barrow Island, Western Australia. *Journal of Archaeological Science: Reports*, 15: 344–69.

Webb, C. (1993). The lithification of a sandy environment. *Archaeology in Oceania*, 28: 105–11.

Whallon, R. (2006). Social networks and information: non-'utilitarian' mobility among hunter-gatherers. *Journal of Anthropological Archaeology*, 25(2): 259–70. http://doi.org/10.1016/j.jaa.2005.11.004.

Whallon, R. and W.A. Lovis (2016). Hunter-gatherer landscape perception and landscape 'marking' The multidimensional construction of meaning. In *Marking the land: hunter-gatherer creation of meaning in their environment*. W.A. Lovis and R. Whallon, eds. 276–85. New York: Routledge.

White, P. (2011). Changing perspectives in Australian archaeology, part I. Regional archaeology in Australia. *Technical Reports of the Australian Museum*, Online, 23(1): 3–5. http://doi.org/10.3853/j.1835-4211.23.2011.1566.

Williams, A.N. (2013). A new population curve for prehistoric Australia. *Proceedings of the Royal Society*, 280: 20130486. http://dx.doi.org/10.1098/rspb.2013.0486.

Williams, A.N. (2012). The use of summed radiocarbon probability distributions in archaeology: a review of methods. *Journal of Archaeological Science*, 39(3): 578–89.

Williams, A.N., C.M. Santoro, M.A. Smith, and C. Latorre (2008). The impact of ENSO in the Atacama Desert and Australian arid zone: exploratory time-series analysis of archaeological records. *Rivista de Antropologia Chilena*, 40: 245–59.

Williams, A.N., S. Ulm, M.A. Smith, and J. Reid (2014). AustArch: a database of 14C and non-14C ages from archaeological sites in Australia – composition, compilation and review (data paper). *Internet Archaeology*, 36. http://dx.doi.org/10.11141/ia.36.6.

Williams, A.N., S. Ulm, A.R. Cook, M.C. Langley, and M. Collard (2013). Human refugia in Australia during the Last Glacial Maximum and Terminal Pleistocene: A geospatial analysis of the 25–12ka Australian archaeological record. *Journal of Archaeological Science*, 40: 4612–25. http://doi.org/10.1016/j.jas.2013.06.015.

Williams, A.N., S. Ulm, I.D. Goodwin, and M. Smith (2010). Hunter-gatherer response to late Holocene climatic variability in northern and central Australia. *Journal of Quaternary Science*, 25(6): 831–38. http://doi.org/10.1002/jqs.1416.

Williams, A.N., S. Ulm, C.S.M. Turney, D. Rohde, and G. White (2015). Holocene demographic changes and the emergence of complex societies in prehistoric Australia. *Plos One*, 10, e0128661. http://doi.org/10.1371/journal.pone.0128661.

Williams, A.N., P. Veth, W. Steffen, S. Ulm, C.S.M. Turney, J.M. Reeves, et al. (2015). A continental narrative: human settlement patterns and Australian climate change over the last 35,000 years. *Quaternary Science Reviews*, 123: 91–112. http://doi.org/10.1016/j.quascirev.2015.06.018

Williams, M. (2018). Report on the geomorphology and quaternary geology of HD07-3A-PAD13 rockshelter, Pilbara, Western Australia. In *Rockshelter excavations in the East Hamersley Range, Pilbara region, Western Australia*. D.N. Cropper and W.B. Law, eds. 429–33. Oxford: Archaeopress.

Williams, M., E. Cook, S. van der Kaars, T. Barrows, J. Shulmeister, and P. Kershaw (2009). Glacial and deglacial climatic patterns in Australia and surrounding regions from 35,000 to 10,000 years ago reconstructed from terrestrial and near shore proxy data. *Quaternary Science Reviews*, 28: 2398–419.

Windle, J., and J. Rolfe (2003). Valuing Aboriginal cultural heritage in central Queensland. *Australian Archaeology*, 56: 35–41.

Wragg-Sykes, R.M. (2012). Creating country: Late Middle Palaeolithic landscape enculturation. In *Unravelling the Palaeolithic: ten years of research at the Centre for the Archaeology of Human Origins* (CAHO, University of Southampton). K. Ruebens, I. Romanowska and R. Bynoe, eds. 73–83. Oxford: BAR International Series 2400.

Wright, B. (1979). Aboriginal sites and their protection. In *Aborigines of the West: their past and their present*. R.M. Berndt and C.H. Berndt, eds. 367–83. Nedlands: University of Western Australia Press.

Wright, B.J. (1968). *Rock art of the Pilbara region, north-west Australia*. Canberra: Australian Institute of Aboriginal Studies.

Wright, N., and T. Craig (2011). Report of an Indigenous archaeological assessment of the Fortescue Metals Group's Christmas Creek Mining and Infrastructure area. Fremantle: Archae-aus Pty Ltd.

Wright, N., and H. Tierney (2012). A report of an Indigenous archaeological assessment of 22 sites within Fortescue Metals Group's Christmas Creek Mining and Infrastructure Phase 23 Project Area. Fremantle: Archae-aus Pty Ltd.

Wright, W.J. (1997). Tropical-extratropical cloudbands and Australian rainfall: I. climatology. *International Journal of Climatology*, 17: 807–29.

Wyrwoll K-H., and G.H. Miller (2001). Initiation of the Australian summer monsoon

14,000 years ago. *Quaternary International*, 83–85: 119–28.

Wyrwoll, K-H., G.W. Kendrick and J.A. Long (1993). The geomorphology and Late Cenozoic geomorphological evolution of the Cape Range–Exmouth Gulf region, *Records of the Western Australian Museum* (Supplement 45): 1–23.

Yabaroo. (1899). *Aborigines of north-west Australia: a vocabulary, etc*. Perth: J.W. Barnard.

Young, L., and A. Vitenbergs (2007). *Lola Young: medicine woman and teacher*. Fremantle: Fremantle Arts Centre Press.

Zeanah, D.W., B.F. Codding, R.B. Bird, and D.W. Bird, (2017). Mosaics of fire and water: the co-emergence of anthropogenic landscapes and intensive seed exploitation in the Australian arid zone. *Australian Archaeology*, 83(1–2): 2–19. https://doi.org/10.1080/03122417.2017.1359876

INDEX

14 Mile Pool 62, 73, 106, 202

Aboriginal Affairs, Department of (DAA) 5, 10, 52
Aboriginal Cultural Material Committee 10, 14
Aboriginal Heritage Act 1972 (WA) 9–12, 52, 93, 170
Aboriginal people
  as Traditional Owners 2, 5, 52, 77, 180, 231
  Garawa 231
  Guruma 1, 90–91
  Martu 1, 37, 77–78, 280
  Nyiyaparli 1, 52, 77–82, 90, 180, 250, 279–280, 290
  perspectives on heritage 12, 14, 52, 230, 288
  Warlpiri 231
Abydos Plain 22, 198
analytical scales 45, 101
animals 83, 284
antiquity 4, 6, 27
Archae-aus 2, 18, 37–39, 52, 95–96, 98, 256
archaeological sites
  as constructs 12, 46, 163, 229, 268
  as palimpsests 8, 47, 48, 160, 162, 227, 38
  site types
    quarry 34, 48, 53, 60, 117, 174–176, 181, 183, 234, 238, 286, 288
    reduction area 8, 37–40, 53, 93–95, 102–107, 120, 130, 133–136, 148, 183, 205–208, 218–222, 238, 251, 257, 270
    rockshelter 2, 6–8, 24–26, 31, 46–48, 52–54, 104, 169–226, 233, 285
    surface artefact scatter 4, 8, 11, 36–37, 46–49, 53–54, 93–105, 132, 159, 174, 181, 210, 229, 235, 238–240, 251–252, 277
archaeology
  academic 4, 5
  compliance 2, 5, 13, 16, 18, 27–29, 35–36, 47, 93, 97, 163, 186, 194, 229–232, 286
  consulting 1–5, 9–10, 15–17, 170, 186, 238, 251
  landscape 13, 81, 104–109, 119, 198, 202, 216, 225–227, 229–234, 247, 266, 268, 280–281, 287–288
  published 4, 24, 27, 77, 198
Arnhem Land 21
artefact types
  adze 34, 155–157, 222–224, 286
  backed artefact 33–34, 155, 222
  macroblades 33, 34, 203, 222
AustArch database 28
Australian Small Tool Tradition 33

background scatter 8, 46, 53, 93, 99, 106, 160, 287
Barrow Island 4, 21
Barton, H. 49
basal dates 28, 29, 187, 205
Bastion Shelter 31, 226
Binford, L. 42–44, 38
blades 34, 101, 138, 155, 222–223, 286, 289
bones 7
bone tools 7, 90
Brown, S.H. 185, 226
burrens 34, 222

cache 174–176, 179–180, 185, 225, 246, 254, 285–286
campsites 12, 79, 50, 80, 91, 174, 231–232, 280, 286, 38
Carnarvon 2
charcoal 7–8, 29–30, 186–187, 194
Chichester Range 16, 22, 52, 56–65, 75, 96, 170, 186, 198, 202, 238, 286, 289
Christmas Creek 2, 15–18, 65, 82, 94–98, 102–105, 120, 124, 139, 155, 162, 169, 184–185, 195, 199, 202, 224, 252–256, 276–281, 284–288
Cloudbreak mine 2, 15–16, 18, 52, 65, 82, 97, 103
Coffee Table Shelter 226
Coldrick, B. 52, 230, 280, 288
community of practice 52, 230
Cook Pool waterhole (Jitumpulpa) 63
country, concept of 2, 12, 15, 46, 50–52, 78–81, 230–231, 276, 279, 284, 288–290
Crawford, I. 83
cultural landscape 12–13, 51, 278, 283–284, 288

data collection 52, 73, 95, 104, 130, 186, 207, 229
  and presentation 28, 48, 122, 170
demographic change 27, 32
depth-age curve 31, 33
deserts 2, 32, 41, 233. *See also* Western Desert
Dibble, H.I. 44, 126, 130
discard rate 26, 31, 42–44, 101, 124, 162, 168, 38, 195–198, 207
Djadjiling 24, 29, 34, 198
Douglass, M.J. 45, 126–127, 132
Dreaming, The. *See* Kukutpa
drought 55, 74, 76, 202

El Niño Southern Oscillation (ENSO) 26, 76, 202
Emu Bore 63
environmental change 27, 73, 199
  Last Glacial Maximum 6, 9, 22–25, 32, 35, 74, 91, 198
  mid-Holocene period 26, 73, 76, 202, 256
environmental compliance 97
ethnography 12, 22, 34, 47, 85–87, 84–86, 174, 187, 225, 38
exchange of objects 34, 42, 82

Fanning, P. 50, 132
fieldwork 15, 52, 120, 266
fish traps 72, 90, 233, 287
flood 62–64, 74–77, 81, 168, , 202–203, 278
food sources 80, 82–83, 91, 233, 247, 286, 288
Fortescue Marsh (Martuyitha) 16, 22, 55, 61–62, 65, 72–82, 83–85, 103–106, 132, 148, 202, 250, 256, 276–278, 290
Fortescue Metals Group 2, 55
Fortescue River 61–62, 65, 75, 76–77, 90, 290
Fortescue Valley 56
funding 6, 35

Gascoyne 2, 32
Goman Pool (Nguwarna) 63
Goodiadarrie Hills 56
Gould, R.A. 37, 285
Great Sandy Desert 2, 37
grey literature 1, 28, 36, 48
grinding material 28, 33, 39, 90, 102–103, 158, 174, 247, 254, 269, 285–287
  millstone 35, 90, 159–161, 174, 239, 242, 254
  muller 35, 174, 186, 239, 254

Hamersley Plateau 29
Hamersley Range 4, 6, 22, 27, 31, 61, 78, 202, 279
heritage 1, 9–13, 50, 53, 230, 288–290
  legislation 1, 9–11, 229–230. *See also* Aboriginal Heritage Act 1972 (WA)
Holdaway, S. 45, 50, 127, 132
Holocene 9, 21–22, 25–31, 76, 196–197,

199, 202, 256
Hope Downs 24, 29, 33–35, 195
human occupation 9, 21, 91, 119–120, 162, 169, 186–187, 195–203, 220–221, 232–233, 255
  12,000 years ago to present 26–34
  30,000 years ago and beyond 256, 279
  hunter-gatherer groups 12, 37, 41–43, 51, 230, 234, 283–284

Indian Ocean 2, 56, 73
Ingold, T. 51, 230, 234, 284
initiation 79, 82, 289
iron ore 55, 59
isolated artefact. *See* background scatter

Jeerinah Formation 59
Jigalong 77, 279
journey/journeying/traveling/wayfaring 51–52, 78, 230, 234, 247, 269, 276, 284, 288
Jundaru 24, 33, 35, 198

Kakutungutanta Creek 198–199, 202, 221, 225, 249–251, 254–256, 279
Kalumburu 83
kangaroo 72, 90, 180
Kimberley 83, 202
kinship 80–81
Kuhn, S.I. 44–46
Kukutpa 52, 230, 280, 284, 290

landscape-scale analysis 50, 95, 103–108, 126, 224, 229, 234, 247, 268, 281
Lands, Planning and Heritage, Department of 10
land use 7, 9, 23–25, 37, 41–45, 102, 164, 202, 230, 276
languages 78–80
  Ngayardic linguistic group 78
  Pama-Nyungan 28
  Wati 28, 32
lithic artefact production. *See* stone artefacts
Little Sandy Desert 2, 37, 61, 78

Madinna Formation 59
Madjedbebe (formerly Malakunanja II) 21
Mankarlyirrkurra 79, 82
Marandu Creek 256, 267–270, 276
Marillana A 25, 33, 198
Marra Mamba Formation 59, 238
Martu country 37, 77–78, 280
Martuyitha. *See* Fortescue Marsh (Martuyitha)
McDonald, E.M. 32, 52, 203, 230, 280, 288
Mesa J 25, 35
millstones. *See* grinding material
Milly's Cave 25
Minimum Analytical Nodule Analysis (MANA) 94
mining activity 3, 18, 55, 77, 170, 235, 280
Mirlimpirrinha 64
mobility 23, 37–45, 49, 101–103, 108, 119, 124, 132–134, 155–157, 205–210, 220, 230–233, 281. *See also* hunter-gatherer groups
Moojarri Well 64
Moorimoordinina Native Well (Karntama) 62
Mulgundun Native Well 63
Mulvaney, K.J. 185, 226
Murujuga 4

Native Title Act 1994 10
Newman 78
Newman Orebody XXIX 24, 29, 33, 185
Newman Rockshelter 24, 29, 33, 185
New South Wales 44, 126, 285
'non-site' archaeology 46, 95
North West Cape 73
North West Shelf 9, 73
Nyiyaparli country 52, 77–83, 90, 101, 180, 250, 279–280, 290

Oakover Creek 78
off-site archaeology. *See* 'non-site' archaeology
Optically Stimulated Luminescence (OSL) 7

Packsaddle area 27, 32, 185, 226
palaeo-environment 72–73, 202
persistent place 162, 221, 233–234, 247, 255, 276–280, 284–287, 289
place. *See* country, concept of
Pleistocene 4, 21, 25–30, 35, 73–74, 197–198, 203, 279
population expansion 26, 28, 31, 199, 202
Principal Components Analysis (PCA) 106, 108
provisioning. *See* storage

quarries 34, 48, 54, 95, 117–118, 120, 174, 183, 238, 247, 286, 38

radiocarbon dating 27–31, 186–199
rainfall 2, 26, 56–58, 65
recording standards 10–11, 14–15, 47, 95, 103, 165
reduction indicators 8, 37–40, 49, 103, 108, 130, 133, 139, 140, 148, 183, 218–221
reduction sequence 37, 43, 45, 120, 140, 205, 208, 221–222
regional diversity 15, 93, 160, 205, 234, 242, 276
repository 5
rock art 5, 26, 42, 284
rockshelters 2, 6–8, 22–25, 29, 46–48, 52, 95, 104–105, 233, 234, 251–255, 276, 279, 285
  associations 181–183
  characteristics 170–173
  chronology 186–195
  diagnostic artefacts 221–223
  excavated assemblages 203–205
  in a landscape 225–227
  mobility indicators 205–210
  patterns of use in time and space 198–200
  raw material diversity 210–217
  reduction intensity 218
  sieve fractions and small flakes 219–221
  site occupation histories 195–198
  stone features in 179–180

surface assemblages in 174–179
Rouillard, A. 62–63, 76
Roy Hill Station 56
Rudall River 36, 101
Ryan, I. 36, 102

Sahul 3
Sandy Creek 63
sea levels 9, 22–23, 26, 75
sedentism 41. *See also* mobility
sedimentation 27, 32, 47, 56, 72
seed grinding 28, 33, 82, 90
Shannon index (H) 106
SHE analysis 119
sieve 7
significance assessment 10, 14–16, 29, 36, 46, 77, 165, 232, 290
significant sites 79, 250, 280, 289
Simpson Desert 49
sites
  definition/recording 10–11, 36, 80, 93–95, 155, 160, 162, 235, 38, 246
  occupation of 3–4, 9, 21–34, 49, 91, 119, 120, 231, 235, 255, 279
Skrzypek, G. 56, 64
songlines 78, 230, 279–280
spatial patterning 7–8, 13, 105, 38–39, 120, 121, 131, 162
stone features 48, 234, 238, 246–247, 251
  arrangement 4, 32, 46, 179, 181, 287
  cairns 179, 180
  niche 174, 177, 179–180, 285, 287
storage. *See* cache
stratigraphic resolution 8, 25, 47
surface archaeology
  core reduction 37, 40, 285
  cortex type 40, 44, 252, 260–261, 285
  flake size 25, 40, 44–45, 103, 107–109, 127, 133, 242–245
  retouched artefacts 155–157, 239, 252

taskscape 51, 247, 254, 269, 276, 278, 283, 287, 289
technological organisation 37, 41–46, 49, 101–102
test pits 7–8, 29, 48–49, 170–171, 187, 194

time averaging 48–49
t-tests 138

van der Kaars, S. 73
vegetation 22–24, 63–72, 97–100, 238,
    255, 256, 269
  acacia 74, 82–84, 98
  eucalypts 22, 66, 74, 83, 90, 97–98,
    101, 162, 238, 249, 252, 256
  mulga 65–66, 72, 75, 82, 90, 91,
    97–101, 162, 238, 249, 252,
    256–258, 269, 276
  spinifex 83, 90–91, 97, 99, 238, 249
Veth, P. 36–39, 49, 101–102, 232, 280

Warrie Outcamp 63
water permanency 37–38, 61–65,
    74–76, 81, 232–233, 247, 254,
    278, 280
Watura Jurnti 24, 26, 31
weather patterns 75
Western Australian Museum 5
Western Desert 27–28, 32–34, 232, 280
Wittenoom 56, 57
World Heritage Committee 13

yams 82
Yandicoogina 33–34
Yanyuwa country 286
Yurlu Kankala 24, 198

www.ingramcontent.com/pod-product-compliance
Lightning Source LLC
Chambersburg PA
CBHW080421230426
43662CB00015B/2178